KÖNIGLICHE FAMILIE LEHRER

Higasa Akai

16

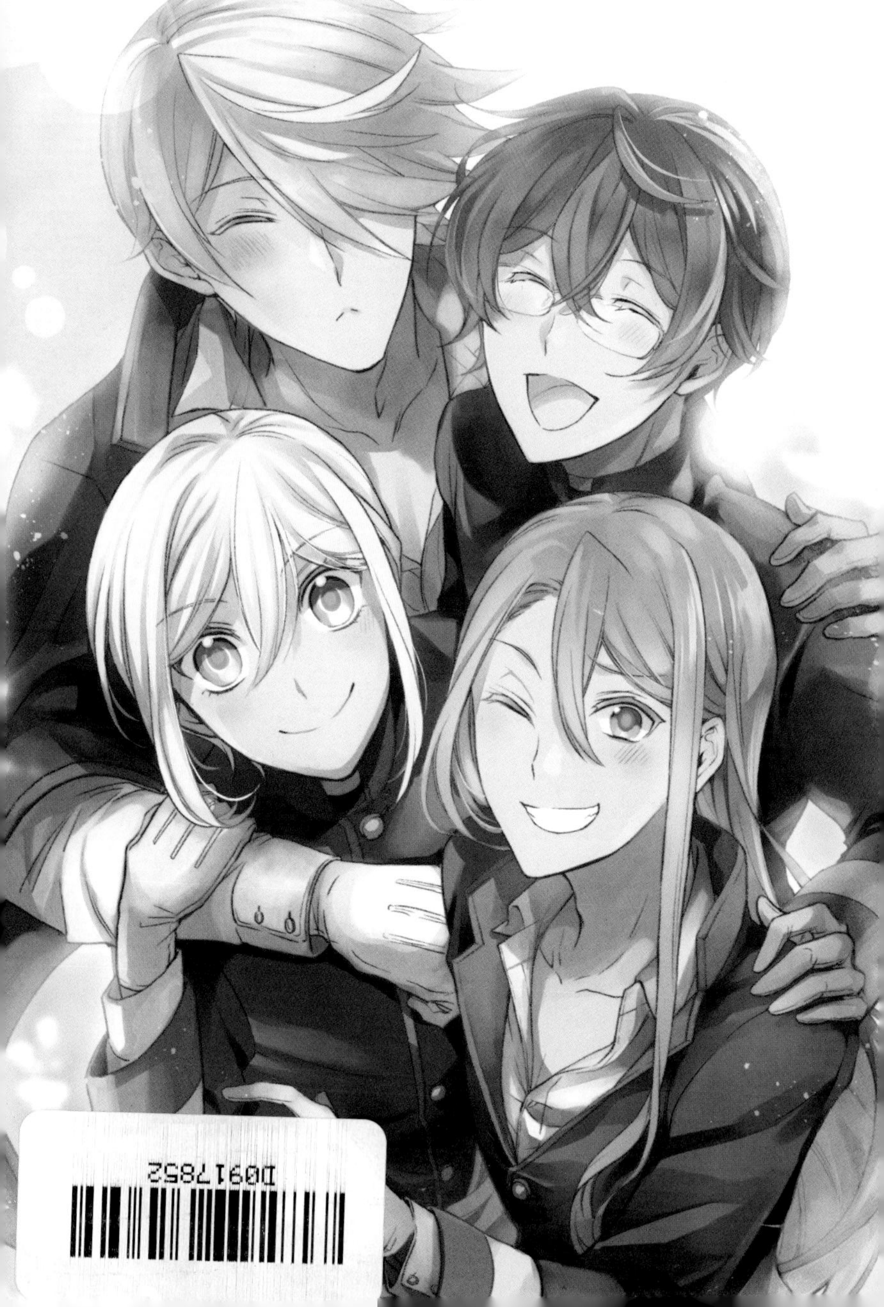

CONTENTS

KÖNIGLICHE FAMILIE LEHREN

Chapter 91

The Angry Blow

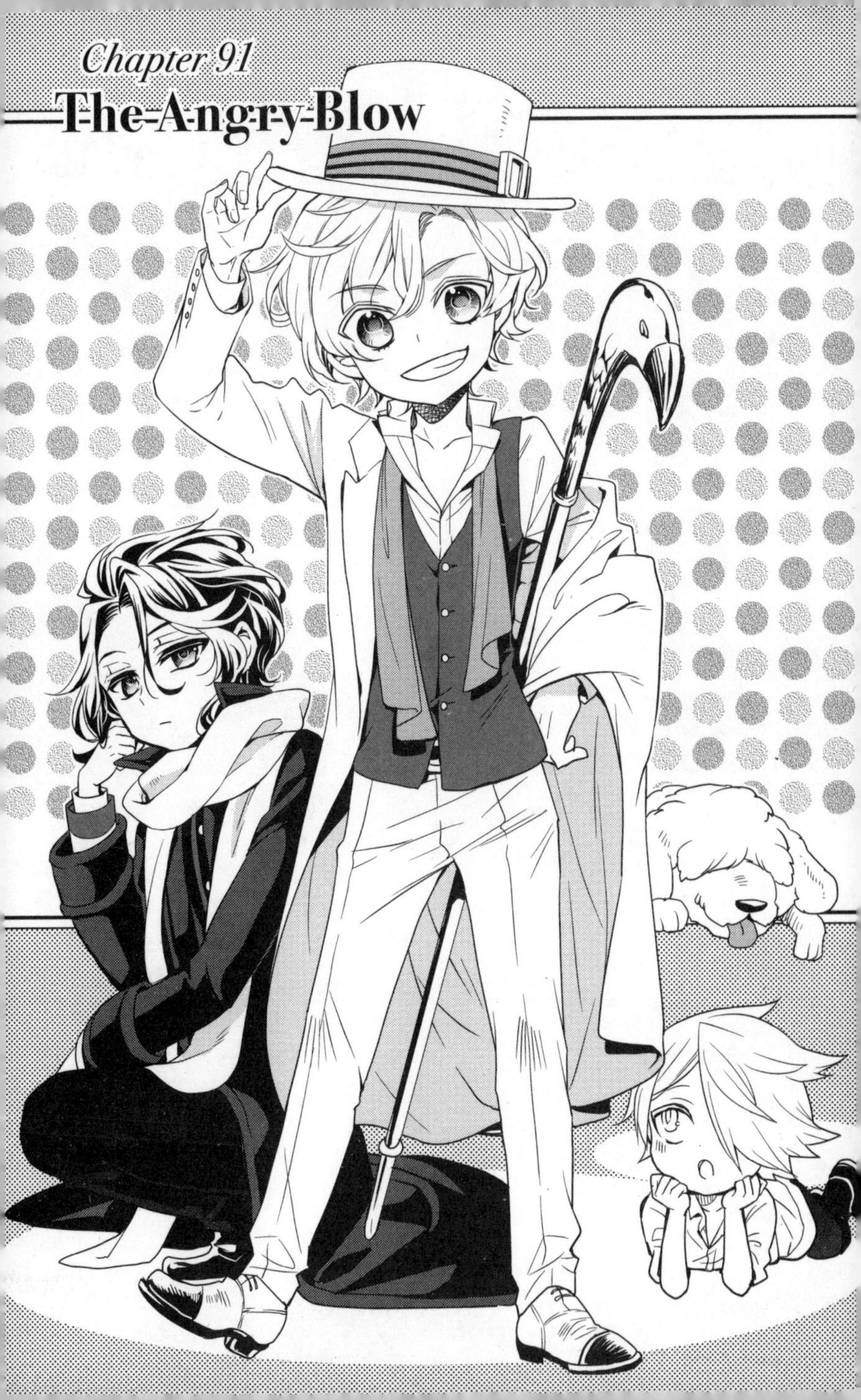

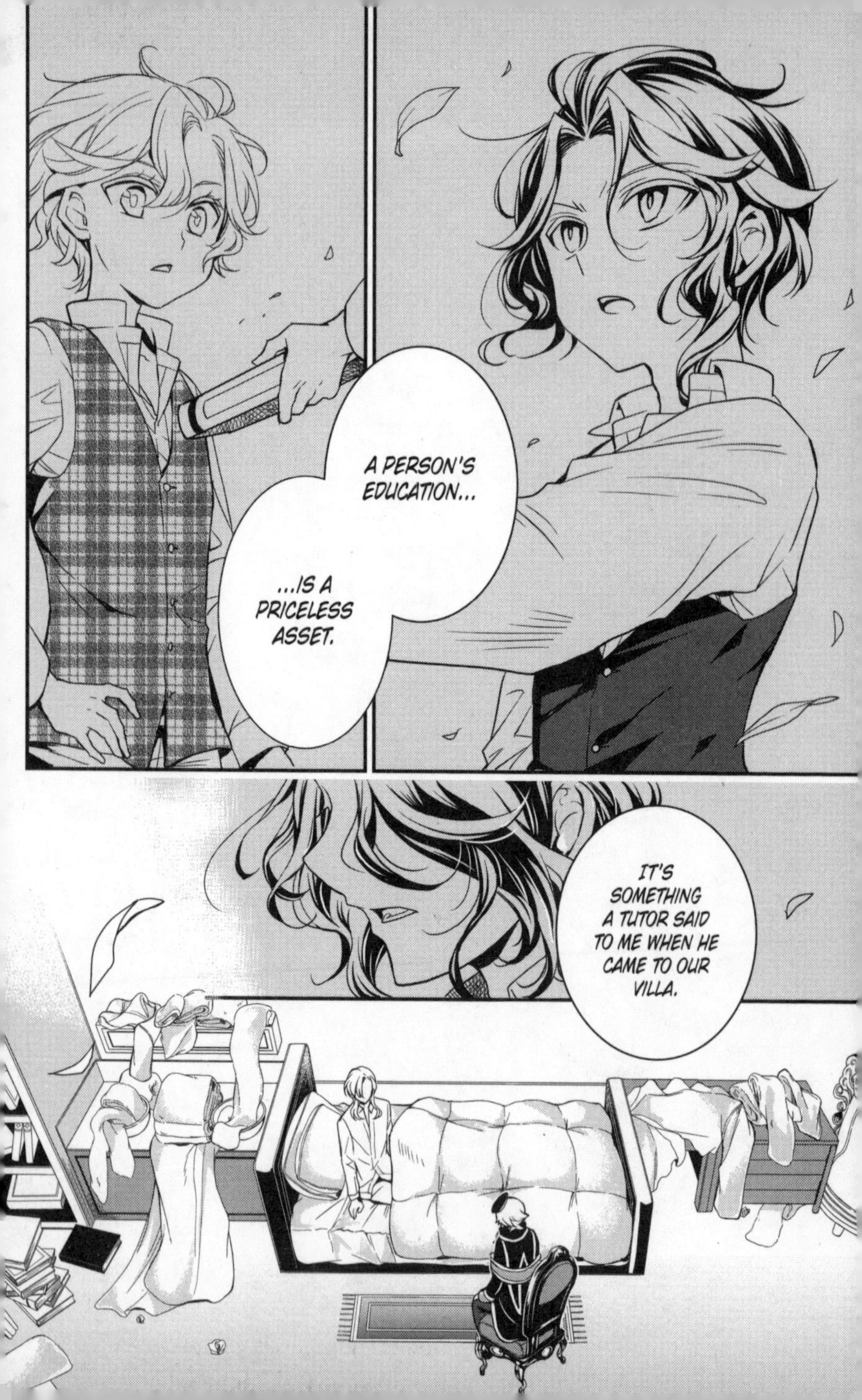
A PERSON'S EDUCATION...
...IS A PRICELESS ASSET.
IT'S SOMETHING A TUTOR SAID TO ME WHEN HE CAME TO OUR VILLA.

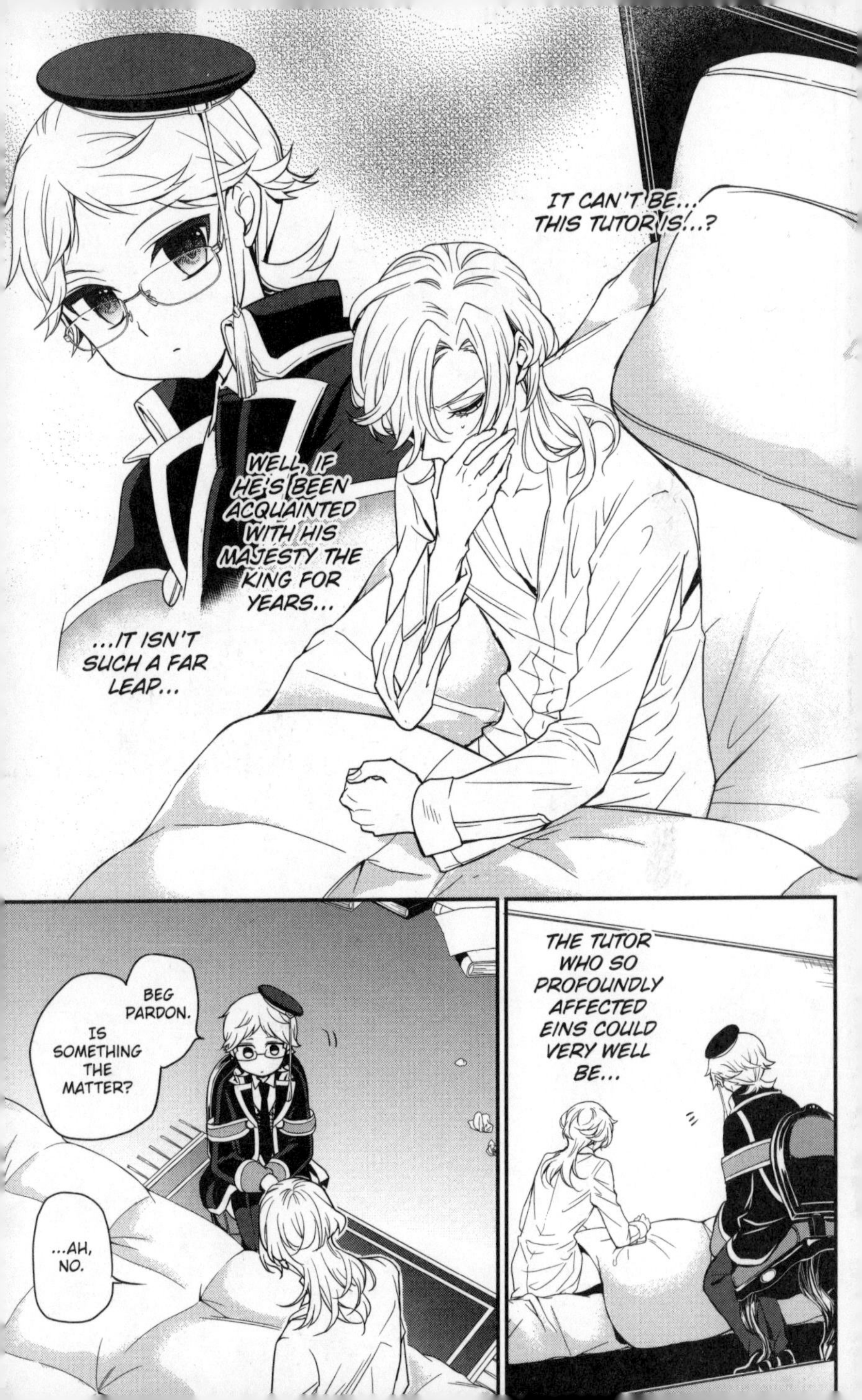
IT CAN'T BE... THIS TUTOR IS...?
WELL, IF HE'S BEEN ACQUAINTED WITH HIS MAJESTY THE KING FOR YEARS...
...IT ISN'T SUCH A FAR LEAP...
THE TUTOR WHO SO PROFOUNDLY AFFECTED EINS COULD VERY WELL BE...
BEG PARDON. IS SOMETHING THE MATTER?
...AH, NO.

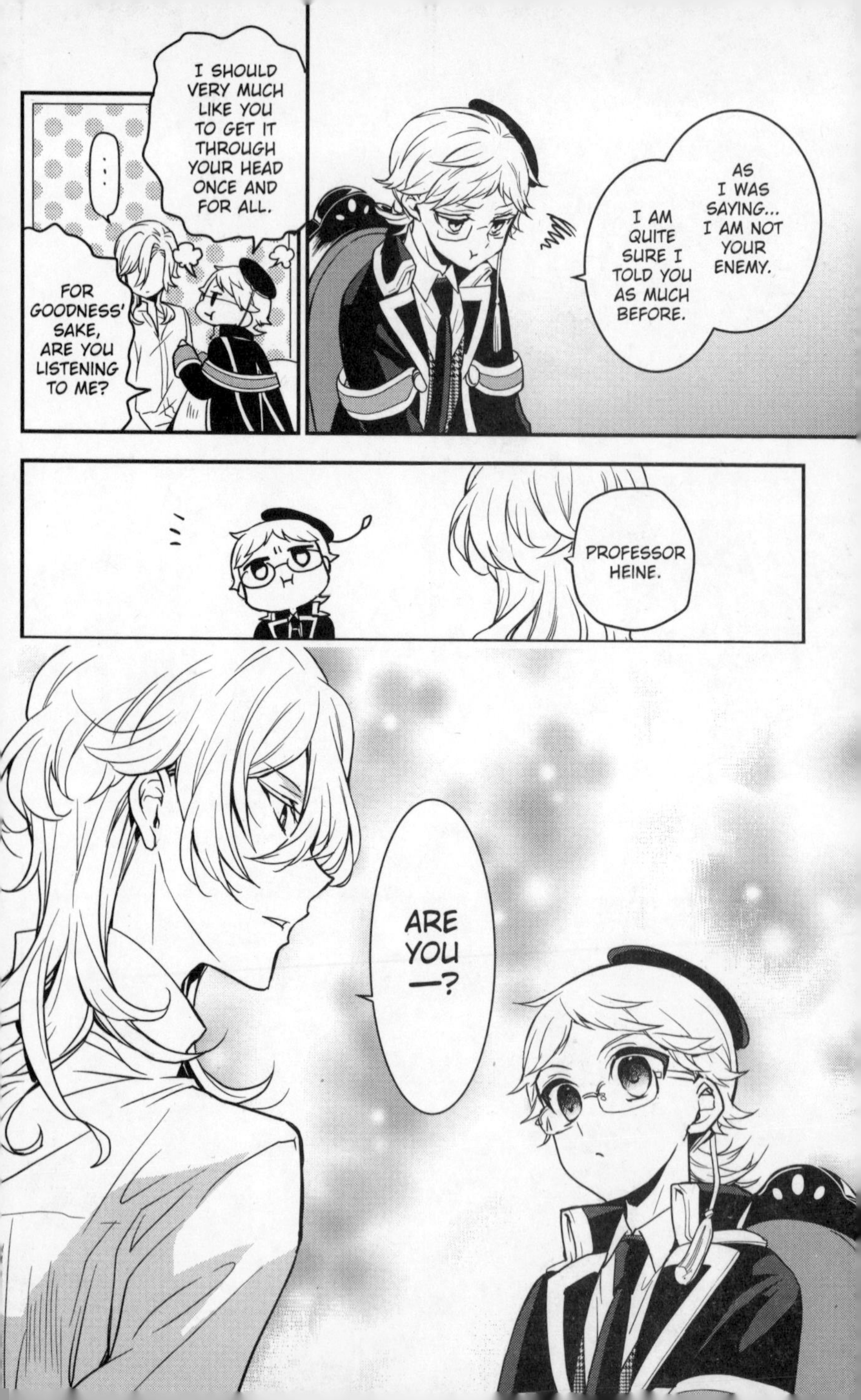
AS I WAS SAYING... I AM NOT YOUR ENEMY.
I AM QUITE SURE I TOLD YOU AS MUCH BEFORE.
I SHOULD VERY MUCH LIKE YOU TO GET IT THROUGH YOUR HEAD ONCE AND FOR ALL.
...
FOR GOODNESS' SAKE, ARE YOU LISTENING TO ME?
PROFESSOR HEINE.
ARE YOU—?

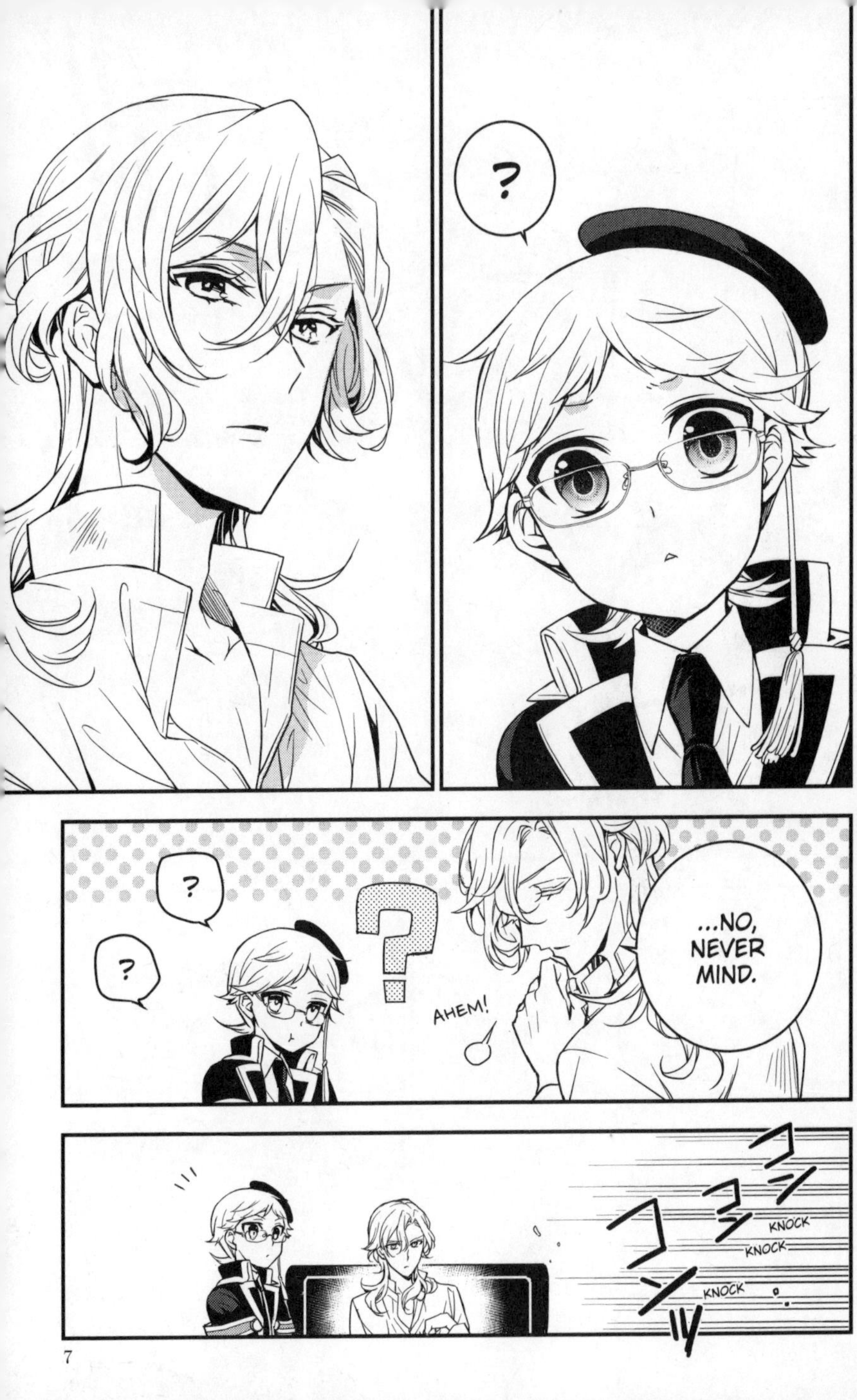
?
...NO, NEVER MIND.
AHEM!
?
?
?
KNOCK
KNOCK
KNOCK

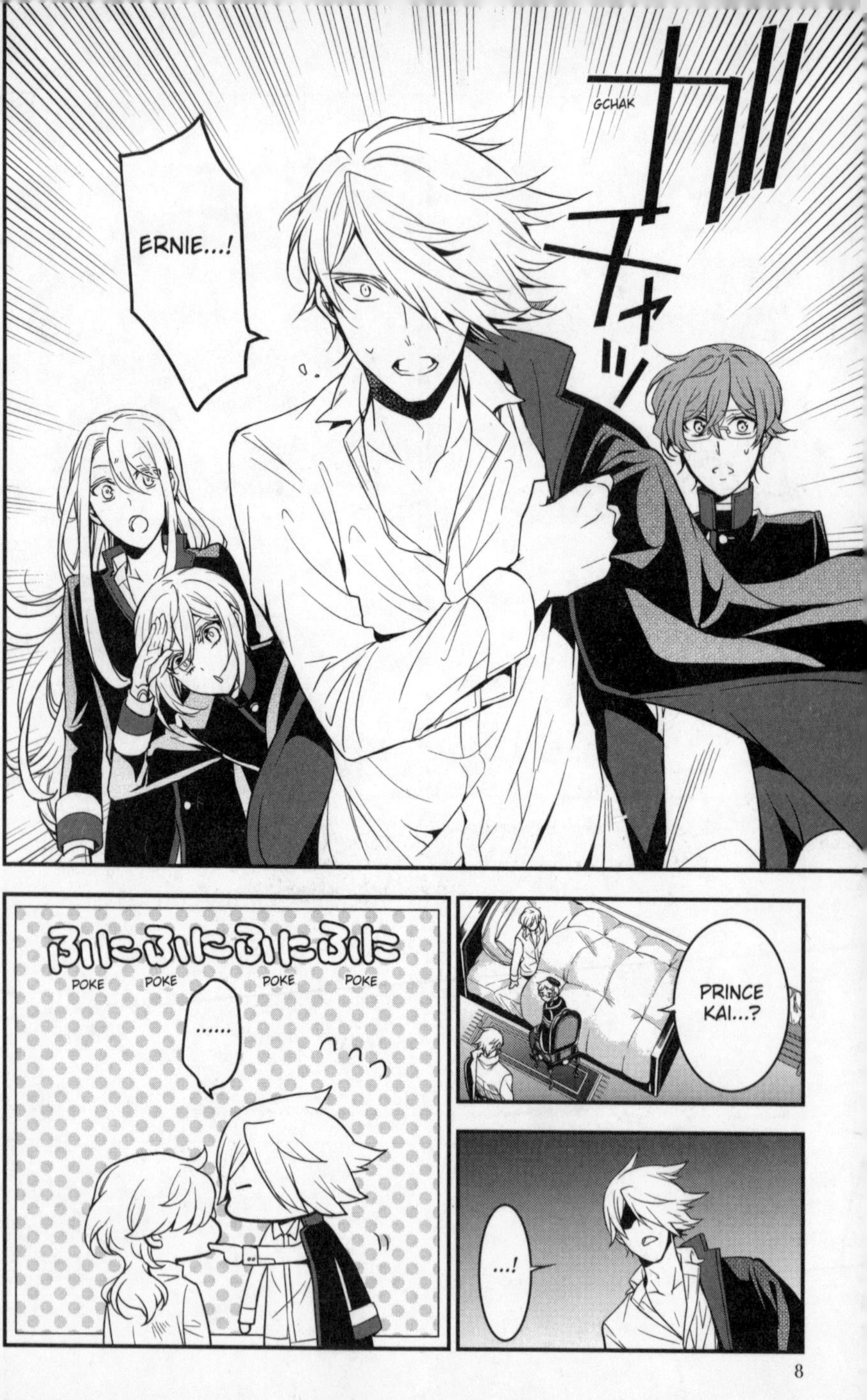
ガチャッ
GCHAK
ERNIE...!
PRINCE KAI...?
...!
ふにふにふにふに
POKE POKE POKE POKE
......

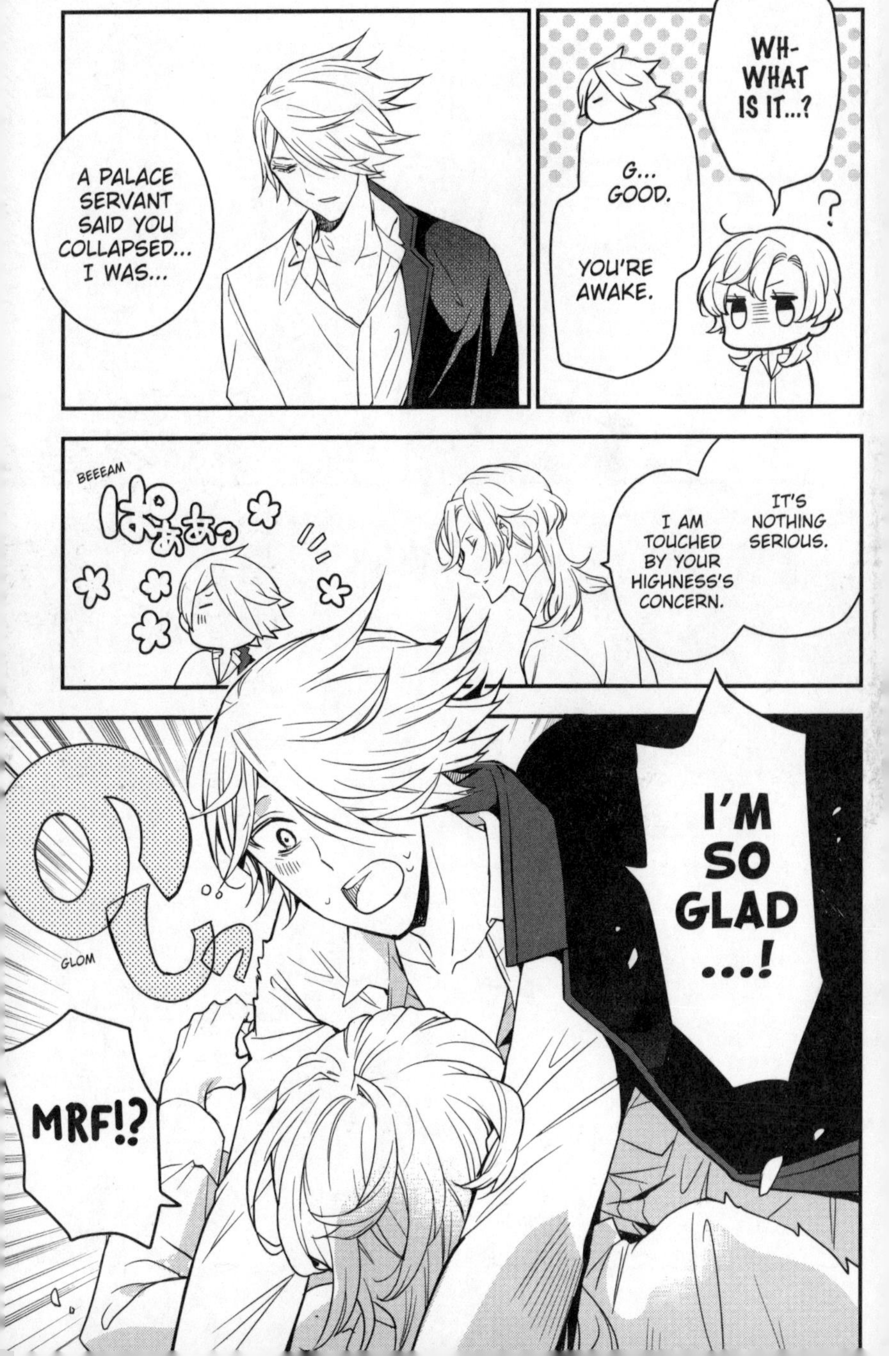
WH-WHAT IS IT...?
G... GOOD.
YOU'RE AWAKE.
A PALACE SERVANT SAID YOU COLLAPSED... I WAS...
IT'S NOTHING SERIOUS.
I AM TOUCHED BY YOUR HIGHNESS'S CONCERN.
BEEEAM
ぱあぁっ
I'M SO GLAD...!
GLOM
MRF!?

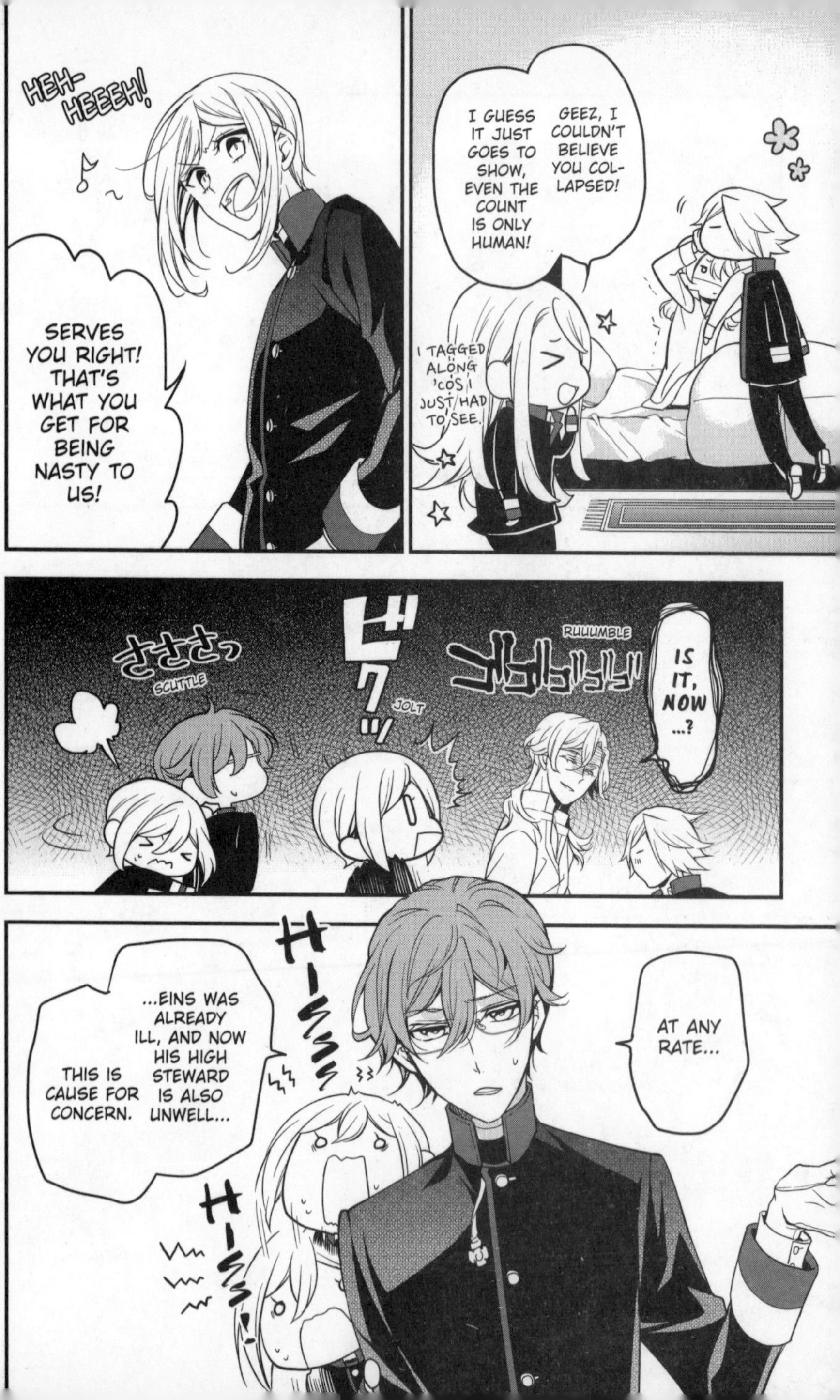
GEEZ, I COULDN'T BELIEVE YOU COL-LAPSED!
I GUESS IT JUST GOES TO SHOW, EVEN THE COUNT IS ONLY HUMAN!
I TAGGED ALONG 'COS I JUST HAD TO SEE.
HEH-HEEEEH!
SERVES YOU RIGHT! THAT'S WHAT YOU GET FOR BEING NASTY TO US!
IS IT, NOW ...?
RUUUMBLE
ビクッ
JOLT
さささっ
SCUTTLE
AT ANY RATE...
...EINS WAS ALREADY ILL, AND NOW HIS HIGH STEWARD IS ALSO UNWELL...
THIS IS CAUSE FOR CONCERN.

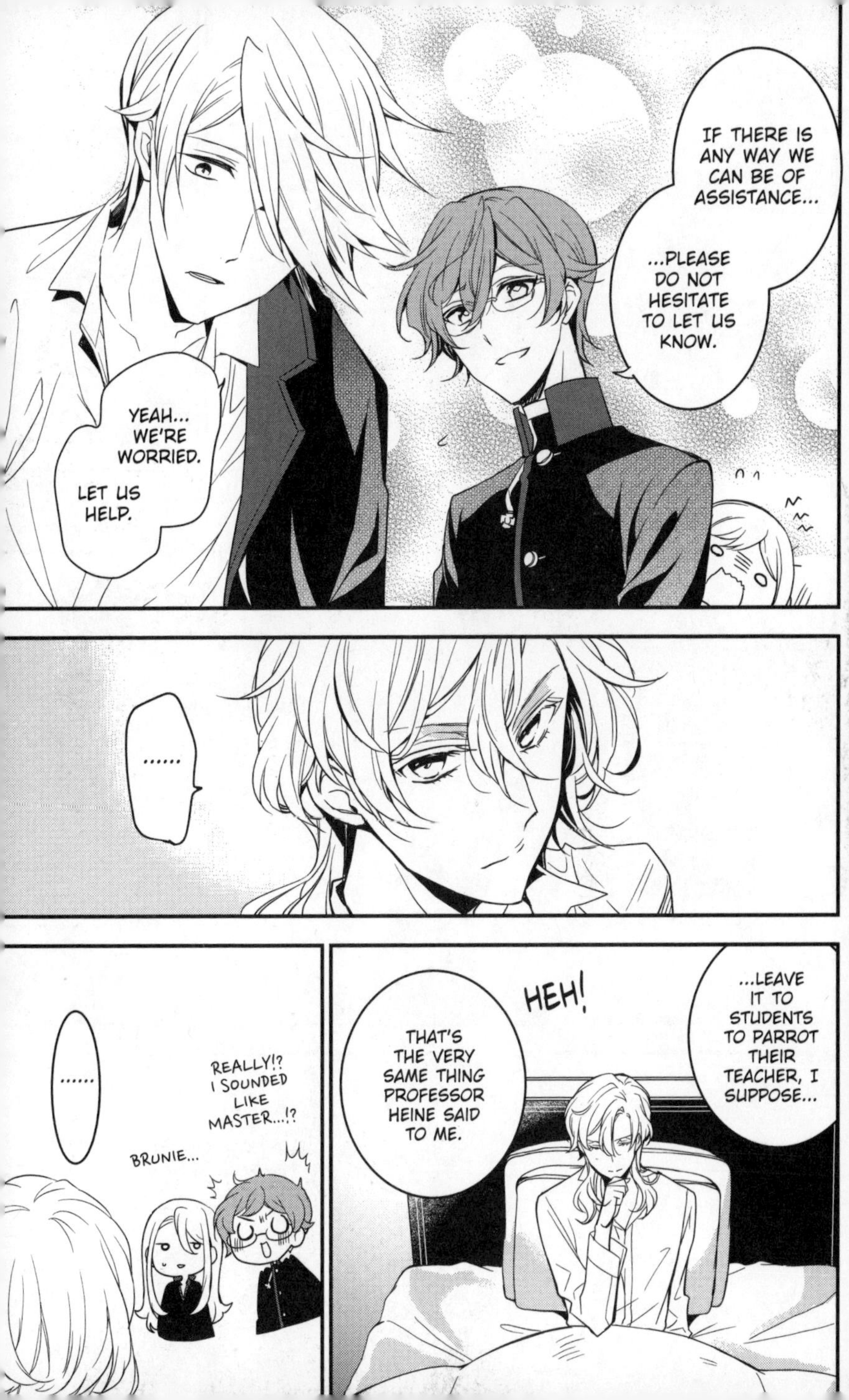
IF THERE IS ANY WAY WE CAN BE OF ASSISTANCE...
...PLEASE DO NOT HESITATE TO LET US KNOW.
YEAH... WE'RE WORRIED.
LET US HELP.
......
...LEAVE IT TO STUDENTS TO PARROT THEIR TEACHER, I SUPPOSE...
HEH!
THAT'S THE VERY SAME THING PROFESSOR HEINE SAID TO ME.
......
REALLY!? I SOUNDED LIKE MASTER...!?
BRUNIE...

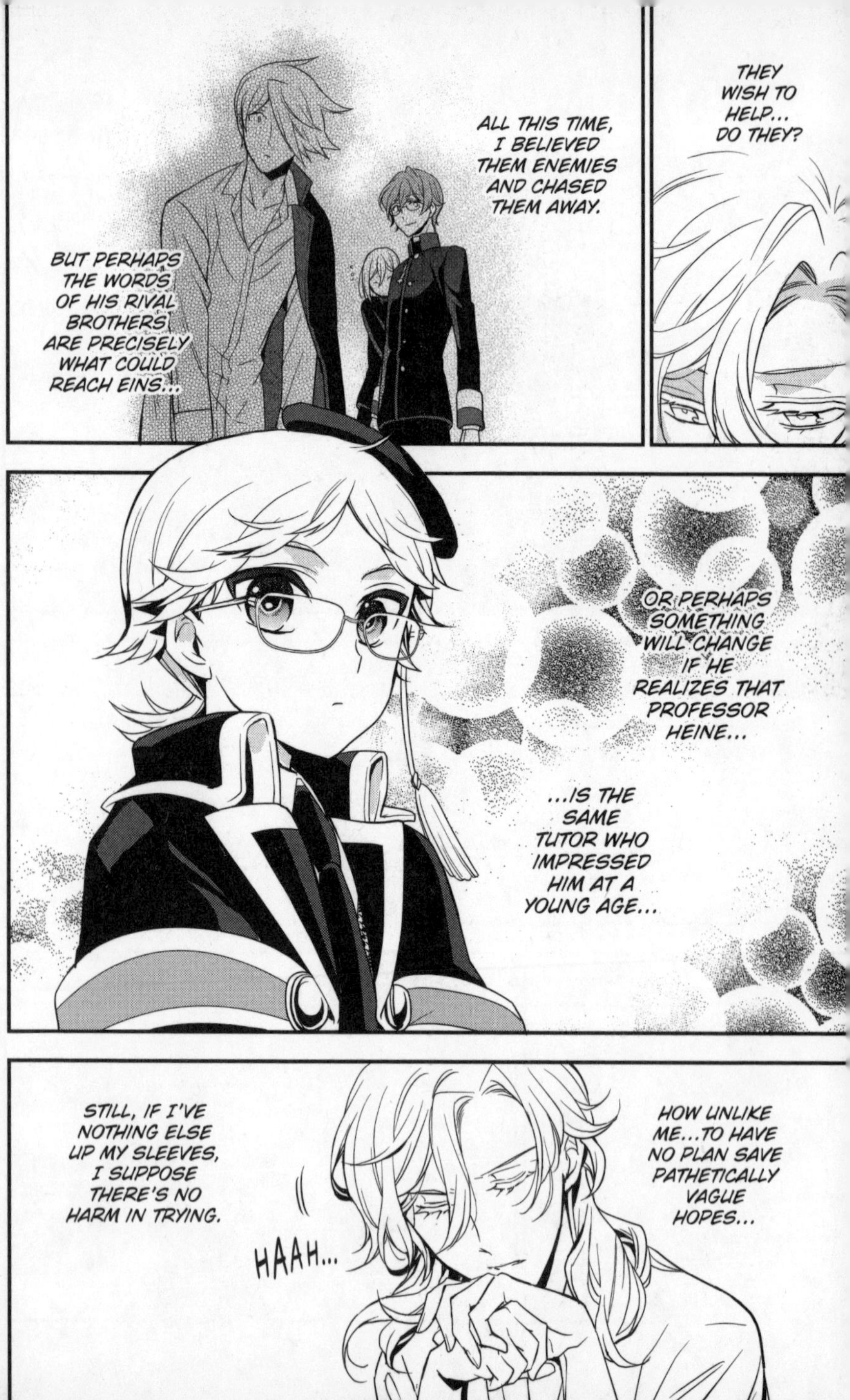
THEY WISH TO HELP... DO THEY?
ALL THIS TIME, I BELIEVED THEM ENEMIES AND CHASED THEM AWAY.
BUT PERHAPS THE WORDS OF HIS RIVAL BROTHERS ARE PRECISELY WHAT COULD REACH EINS...
OR PERHAPS SOMETHING WILL CHANGE IF HE REALIZES THAT PROFESSOR HEINE...
...IS THE SAME TUTOR WHO IMPRESSED HIM AT A YOUNG AGE...
HOW UNLIKE ME...TO HAVE NO PLAN SAVE PATHETICALLY VAGUE HOPES...
HAAH...
STILL, IF I'VE NOTHING ELSE UP MY SLEEVES, I SUPPOSE THERE'S NO HARM IN TRYING.

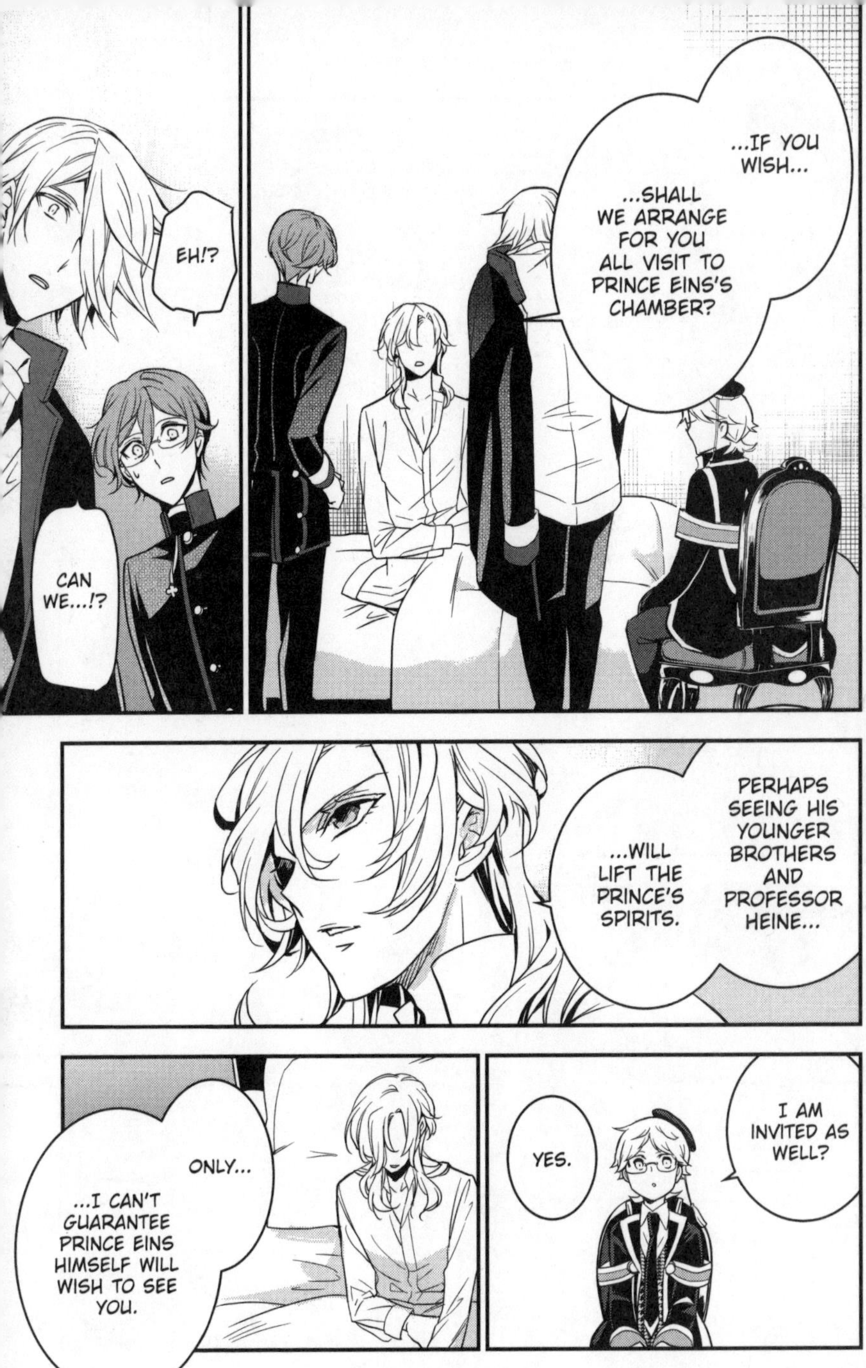
...IF YOU WISH...
...SHALL WE ARRANGE FOR YOU ALL VISIT TO PRINCE EINS'S CHAMBER?
EH!?
CAN WE...!?
PERHAPS SEEING HIS YOUNGER BROTHERS AND PROFESSOR HEINE...
...WILL LIFT THE PRINCE'S SPIRITS.
I AM INVITED AS WELL?
YES.
ONLY...
...I CAN'T GUARANTEE PRINCE EINS HIMSELF WILL WISH TO SEE YOU.

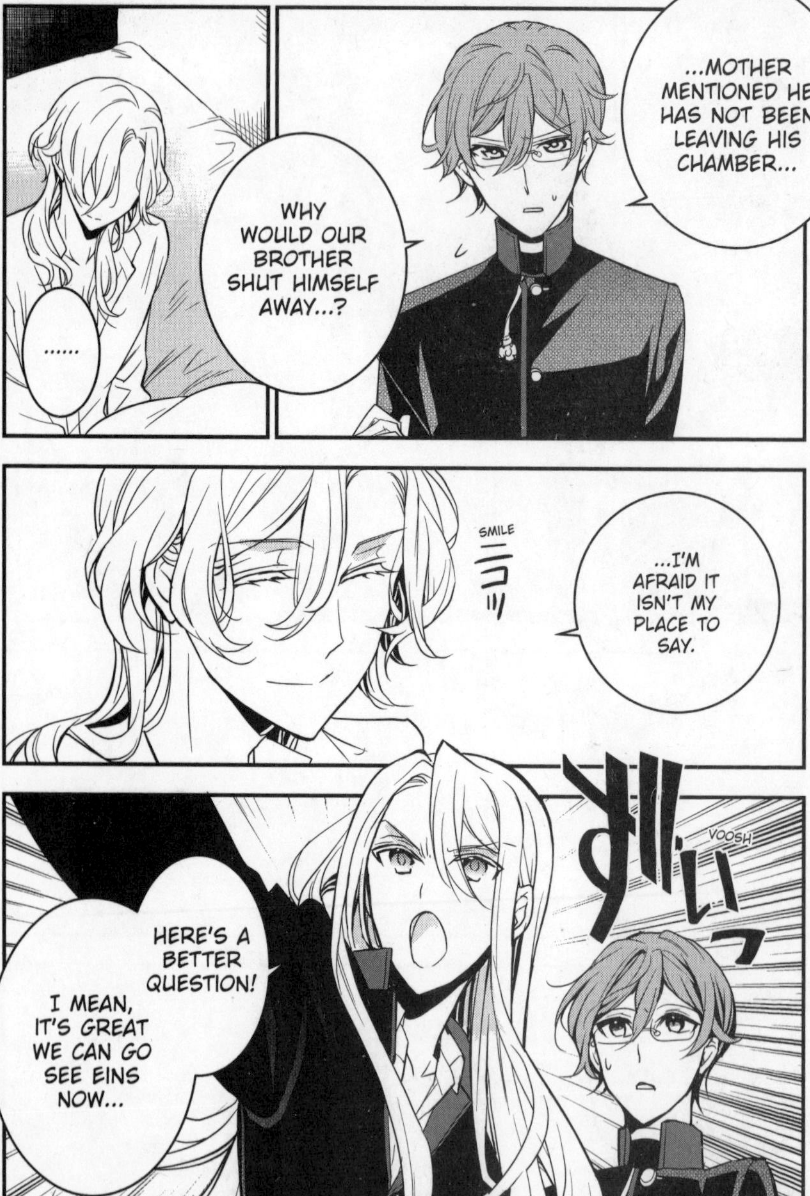
...MOTHER MENTIONED HE HAS NOT BEEN LEAVING HIS CHAMBER...
WHY WOULD OUR BROTHER SHUT HIMSELF AWAY...?
......
SMILE
...I'M AFRAID IT ISN'T MY PLACE TO SAY.
VOOSH
HERE'S A BETTER QUESTION!
I MEAN, IT'S GREAT WE CAN GO SEE EINS NOW...

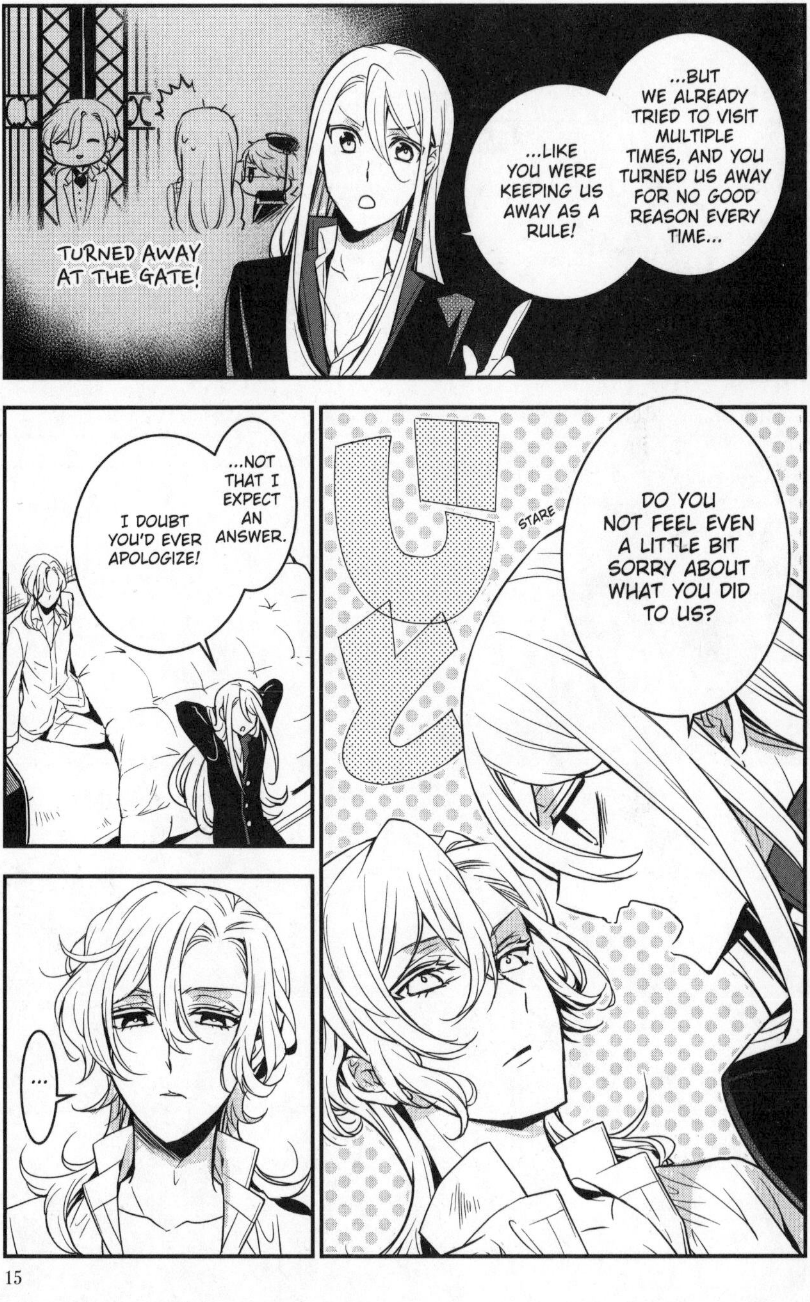
...BUT WE ALREADY TRIED TO VISIT MULTIPLE TIMES, AND YOU TURNED US AWAY FOR NO GOOD REASON EVERY TIME...
...LIKE YOU WERE KEEPING US AWAY AS A RULE!
TURNED AWAY AT THE GATE!
DO YOU NOT FEEL EVEN A LITTLE BIT SORRY ABOUT WHAT YOU DID TO US?
STARE
...NOT THAT I EXPECT AN ANSWER.
I DOUBT YOU'D EVER APOLOGIZE!
...

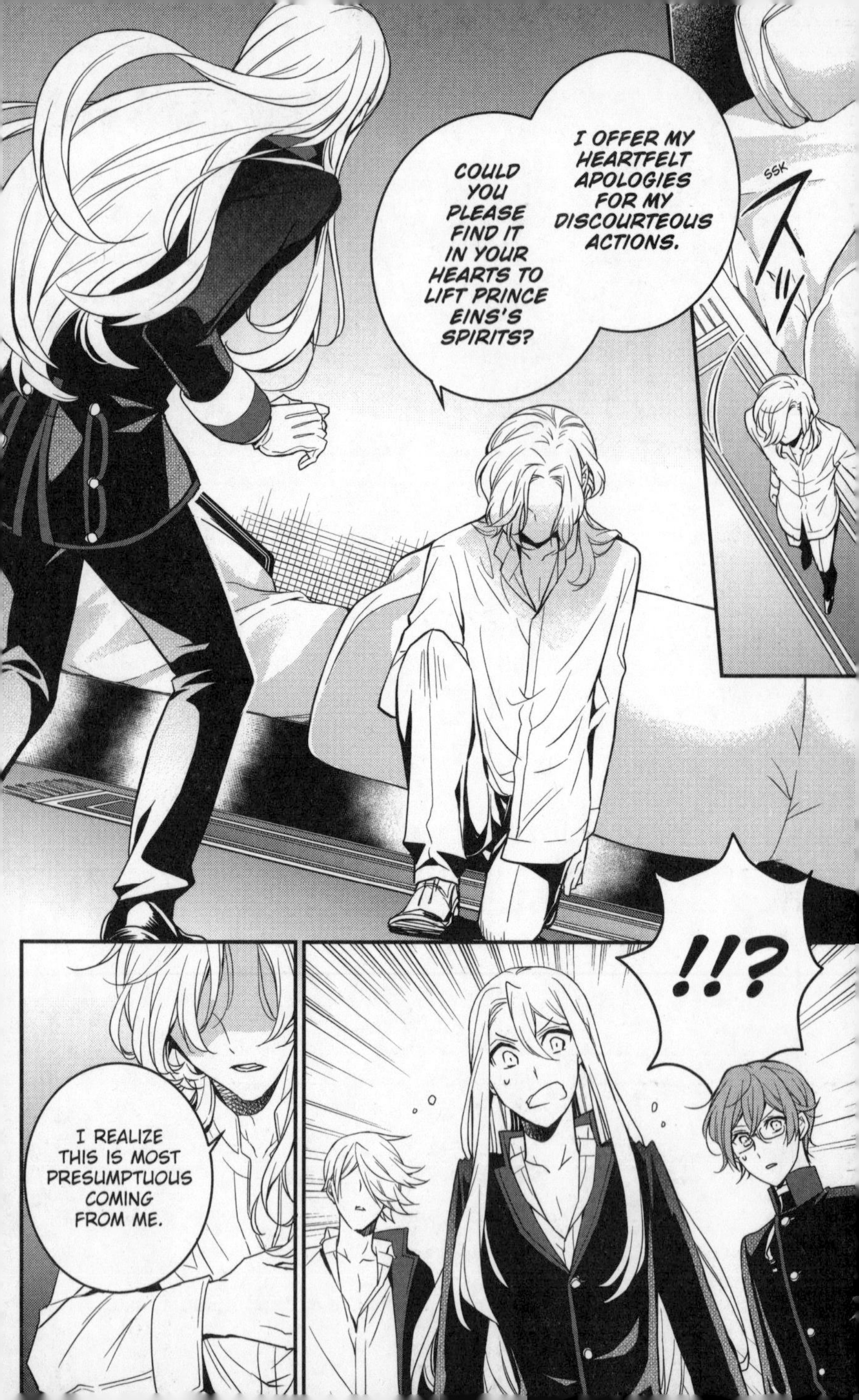
SSK
I OFFER MY HEARTFELT APOLOGIES FOR MY DISCOURTEOUS ACTIONS.
COULD YOU PLEASE FIND IT IN YOUR HEARTS TO LIFT PRINCE EINS'S SPIRITS?
!!?
I REALIZE THIS IS MOST PRESUMPTUOUS COMING FROM ME.

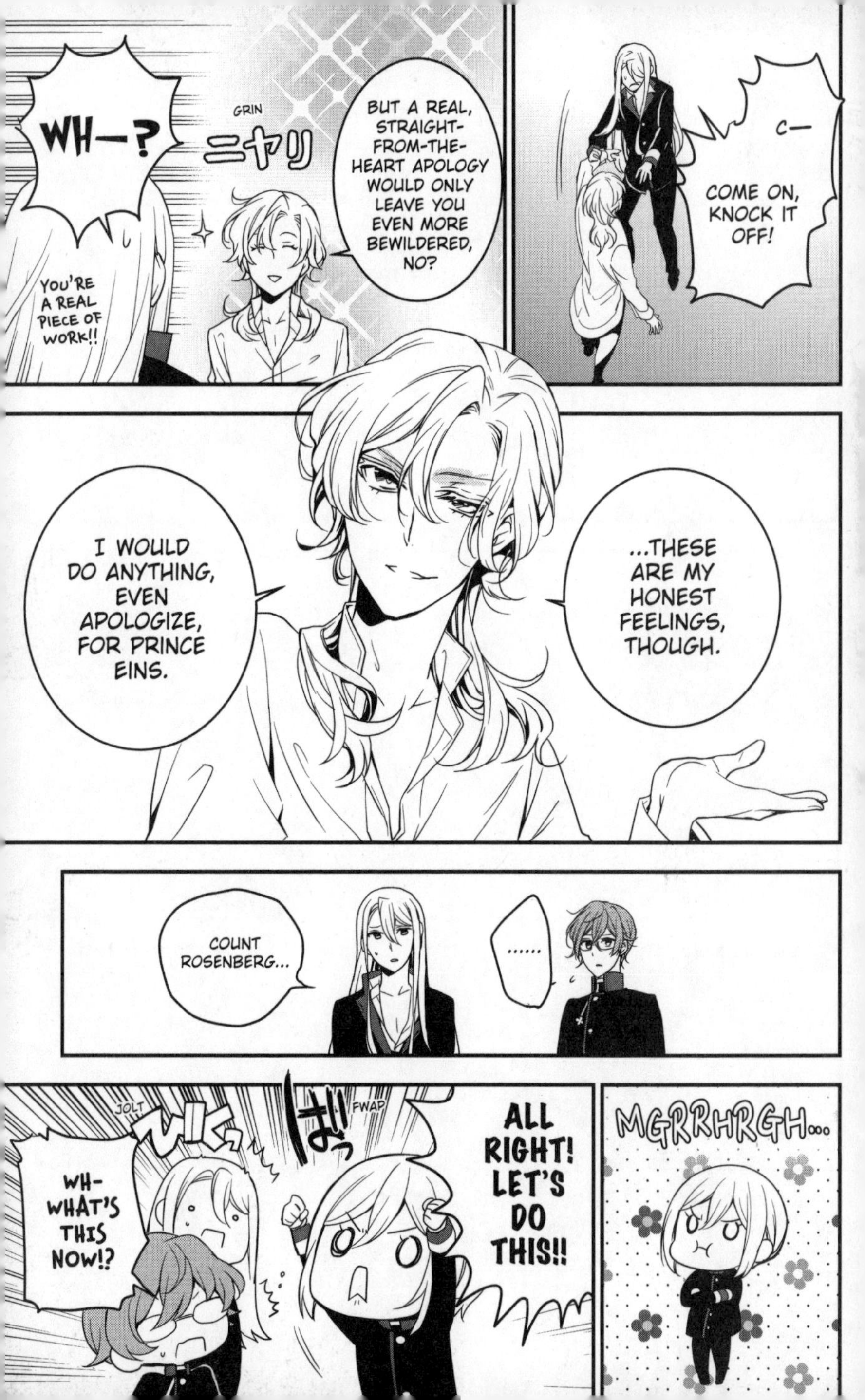
C—
COME ON, KNOCK IT OFF!
BUT A REAL, STRAIGHT-FROM-THE-HEART APOLOGY WOULD ONLY LEAVE YOU EVEN MORE BEWILDERED, NO?
GRIN
ニヤリ
WH—?
YOU'RE A REAL PIECE OF WORK!!
...THESE ARE MY HONEST FEELINGS, THOUGH.
I WOULD DO ANYTHING, EVEN APOLOGIZE, FOR PRINCE EINS.
......
COUNT ROSENBERG...
MGRRHRGH...
ALL RIGHT! LET'S DO THIS!!
FWAP
ぱっ
JOLT
びくっ
WH-WHAT'S THIS NOW!?

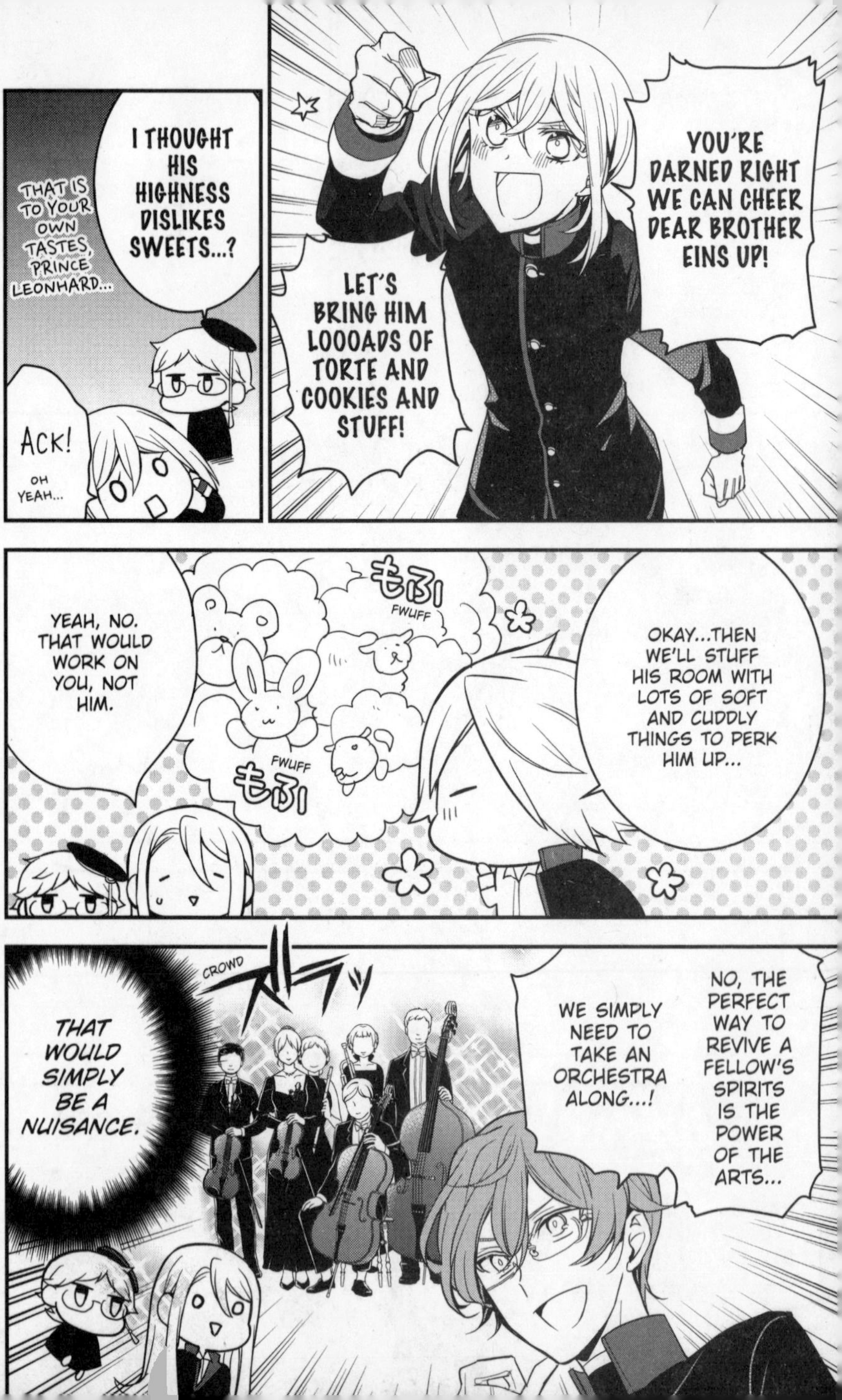
YOU'RE DARNED RIGHT WE CAN CHEER DEAR BROTHER EINS UP!
LET'S BRING HIM LOOOADS OF TORTE AND COOKIES AND STUFF!
I THOUGHT HIS HIGHNESS DISLIKES SWEETS...?
THAT IS TO YOUR OWN TASTES, PRINCE LEONHARD...
ACK!
OH YEAH...
OKAY...THEN WE'LL STUFF HIS ROOM WITH LOTS OF SOFT AND CUDDLY THINGS TO PERK HIM UP...
もふ
FWUFF
もふ
FWUFF
YEAH, NO. THAT WOULD WORK ON YOU, NOT HIM.
NO, THE PERFECT WAY TO REVIVE A FELLOW'S SPIRITS IS THE POWER OF THE ARTS...
WE SIMPLY NEED TO TAKE AN ORCHESTRA ALONG...!
ズラッ
CROWD
THAT WOULD SIMPLY BE A NUISANCE.

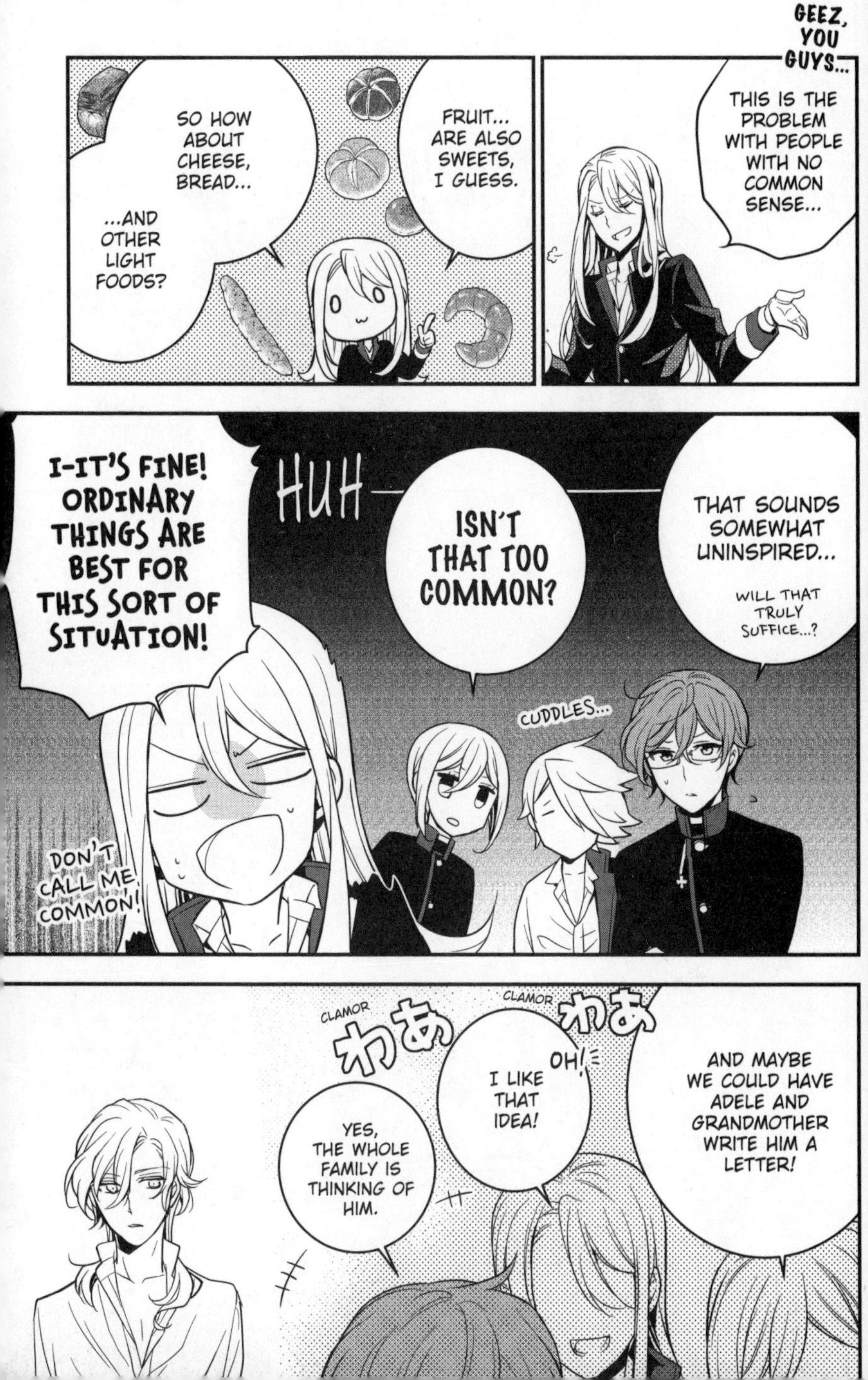
GEEZ, YOU GUYS...
THIS IS THE PROBLEM WITH PEOPLE WITH NO COMMON SENSE...
FRUIT... ARE ALSO SWEETS, I GUESS.
SO HOW ABOUT CHEESE, BREAD...
...AND OTHER LIGHT FOODS?
THAT SOUNDS SOMEWHAT UNINSPIRED...
WILL THAT TRULY SUFFICE...?
HUH
ISN'T THAT TOO COMMON?
CUDDLES...
I-IT'S FINE! ORDINARY THINGS ARE BEST FOR THIS SORT OF SITUATION!
DON'T CALL ME COMMON!
CLAMOR
わあ
AND MAYBE WE COULD HAVE ADELE AND GRANDMOTHER WRITE HIM A LETTER!
OH!
I LIKE THAT IDEA!
YES, THE WHOLE FAMILY IS THINKING OF HIM.
CLAMOR
わあ

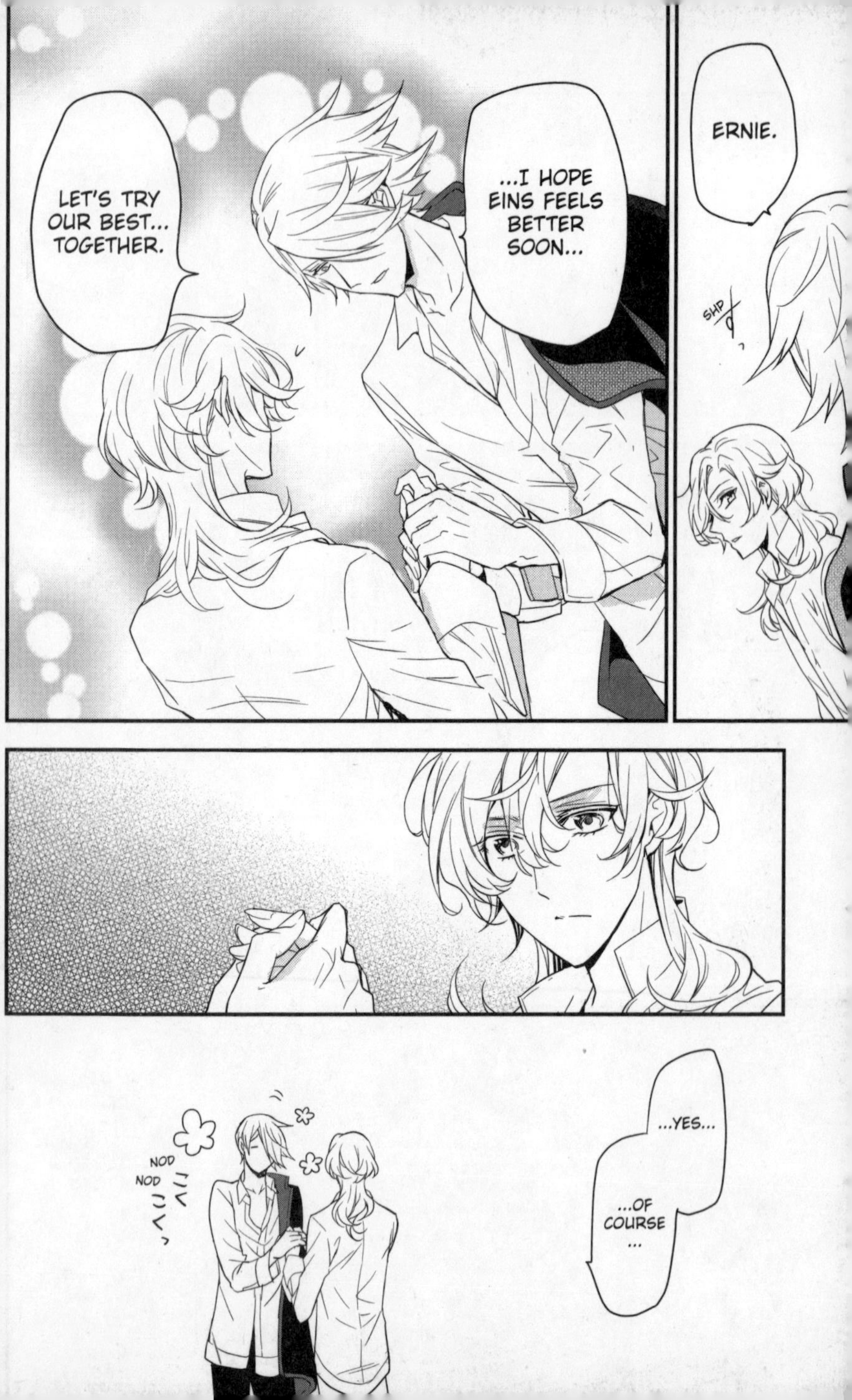
ERNIE.
SHP
...I HOPE EINS FEELS BETTER SOON...
LET'S TRY OUR BEST... TOGETHER.
...YES...
...OF COURSE ...
NOD NOD
こく こく

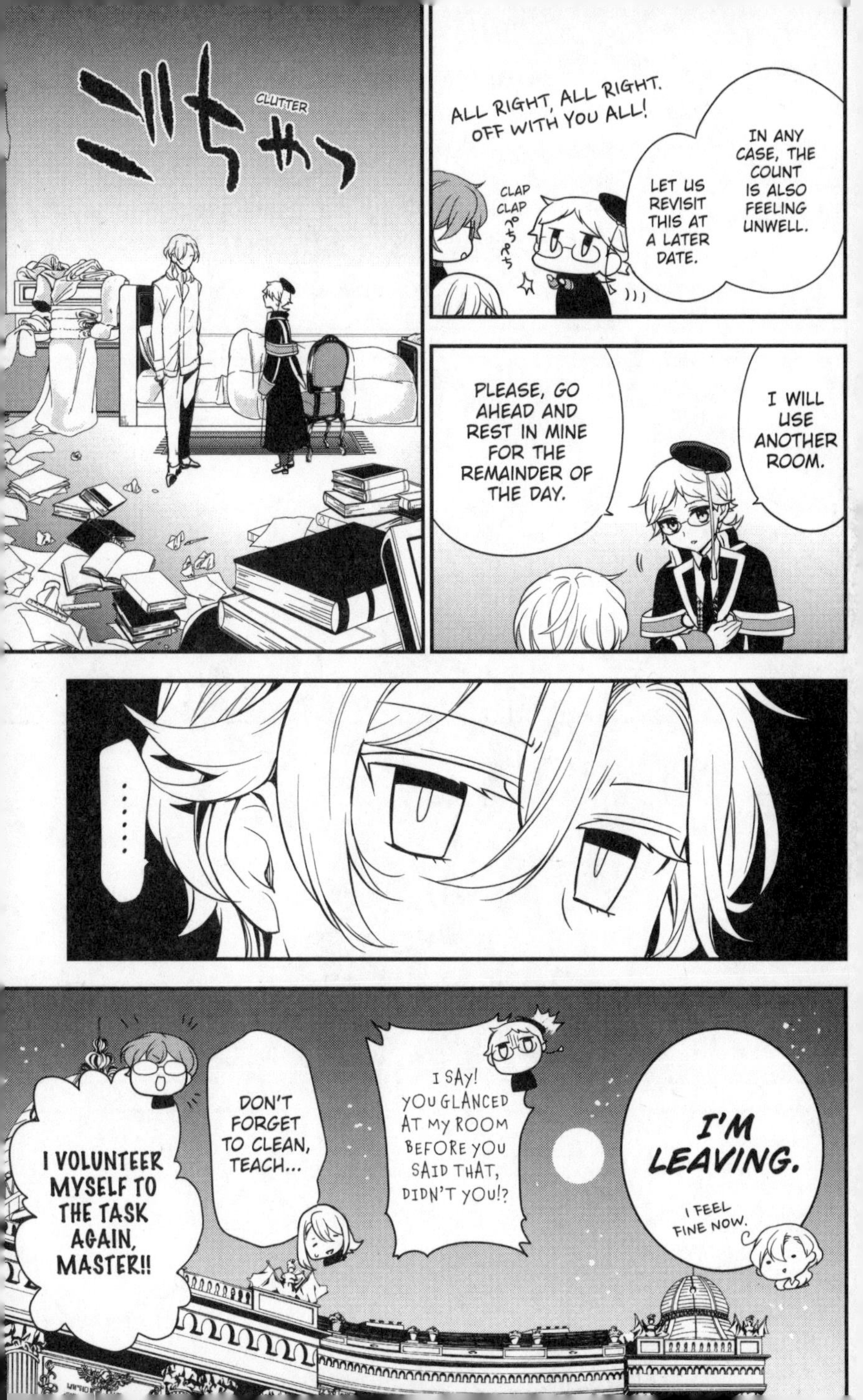
IN ANY CASE, THE COUNT IS ALSO FEELING UNWELL.
LET US REVISIT THIS AT A LATER DATE.
ALL RIGHT, ALL RIGHT. OFF WITH YOU ALL!
CLAP CLAP
ぺちぺち
I WILL USE ANOTHER ROOM.
PLEASE, GO AHEAD AND REST IN MINE FOR THE REMAINDER OF THE DAY.
ごちゃっ
CLUTTER
……
I'M LEAVING.
I FEEL FINE NOW.
I SAY! YOU GLANCED AT MY ROOM BEFORE YOU SAID THAT, DIDN'T YOU!?
DON'T FORGET TO CLEAN, TEACH…
I VOLUNTEER MYSELF TO THE TASK AGAIN, MASTER!!

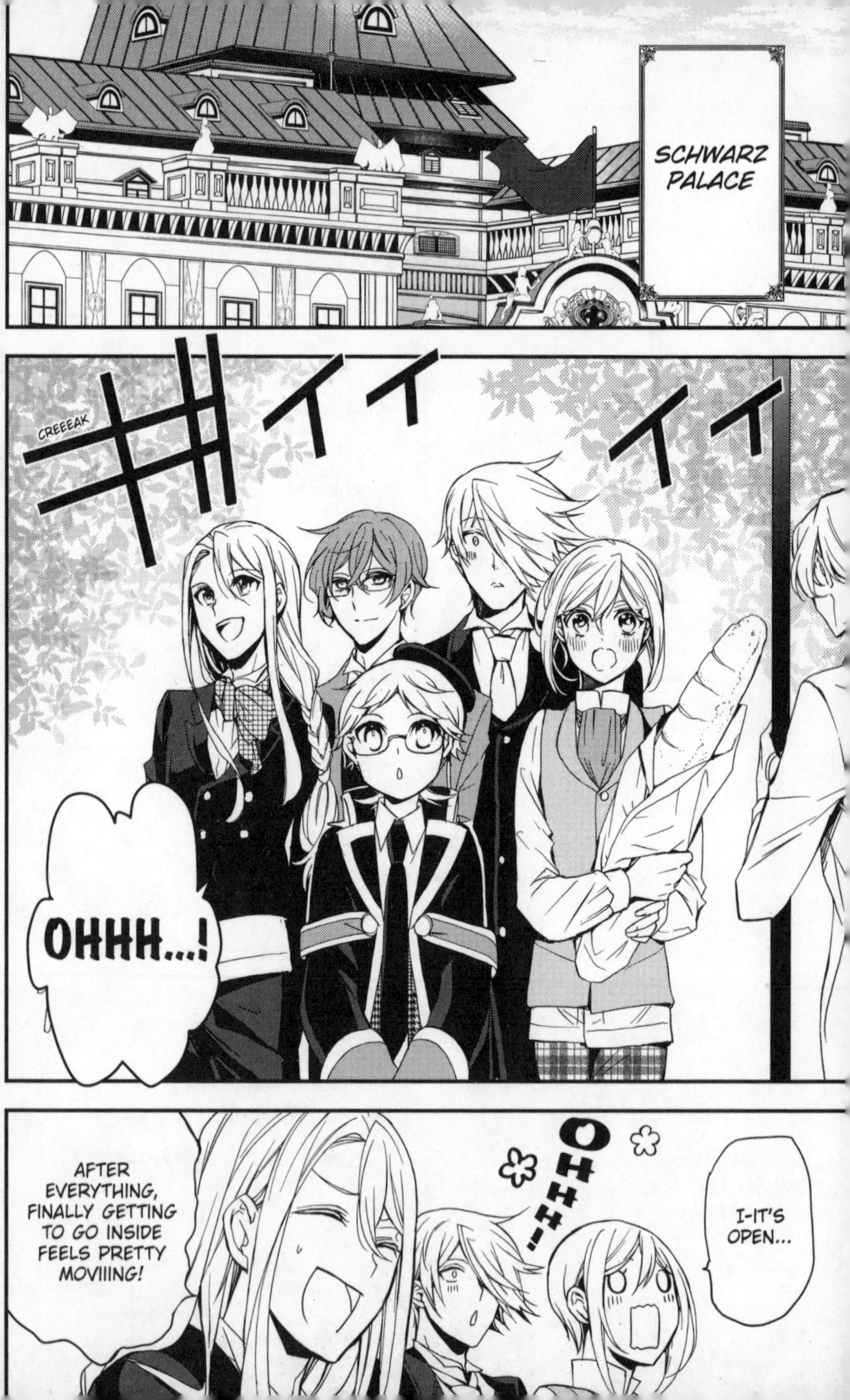
SCHWARZ PALACE
ギイイ
CREEEAK
OHHH...!
I-IT'S OPEN...
OHHHH!
AFTER EVERYTHING, FINALLY GETTING TO GO INSIDE FEELS PRETTY MOVIIING!

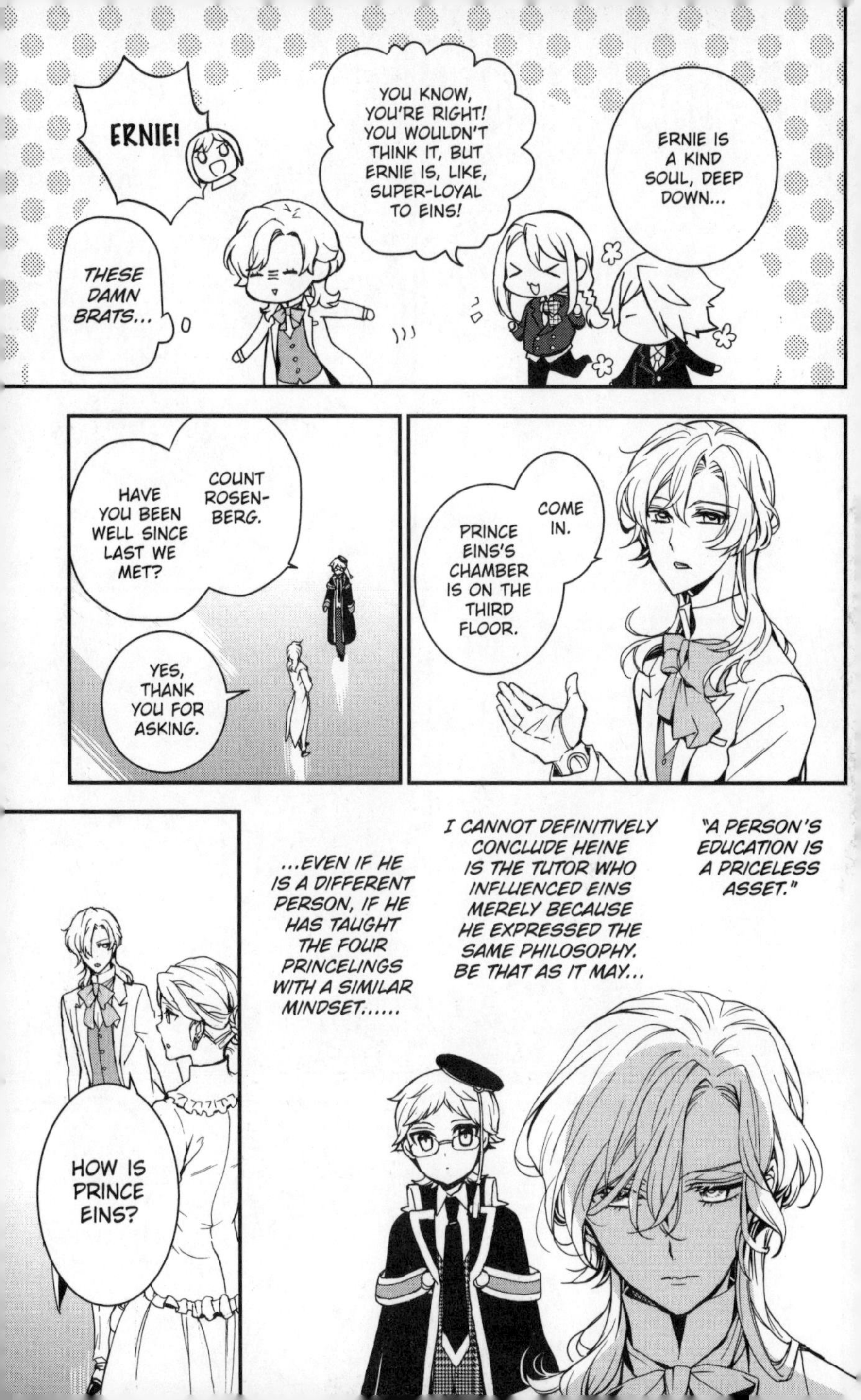
ERNIE IS A KIND SOUL, DEEP DOWN...
YOU KNOW, YOU'RE RIGHT! YOU WOULDN'T THINK IT, BUT ERNIE IS, LIKE, SUPER-LOYAL TO EINS!
ERNIE!
THESE DAMN BRATS...
COME IN.
PRINCE EINS'S CHAMBER IS ON THE THIRD FLOOR.
COUNT ROSEN-BERG.
HAVE YOU BEEN WELL SINCE LAST WE MET?
YES, THANK YOU FOR ASKING.
"A PERSON'S EDUCATION IS A PRICELESS ASSET."
I CANNOT DEFINITIVELY CONCLUDE HEINE IS THE TUTOR WHO INFLUENCED EINS MERELY BECAUSE HE EXPRESSED THE SAME PHILOSOPHY. BE THAT AS IT MAY...
...EVEN IF HE IS A DIFFERENT PERSON, IF HE HAS TAUGHT THE FOUR PRINCELINGS WITH A SIMILAR MINDSET......
HOW IS PRINCE EINS?

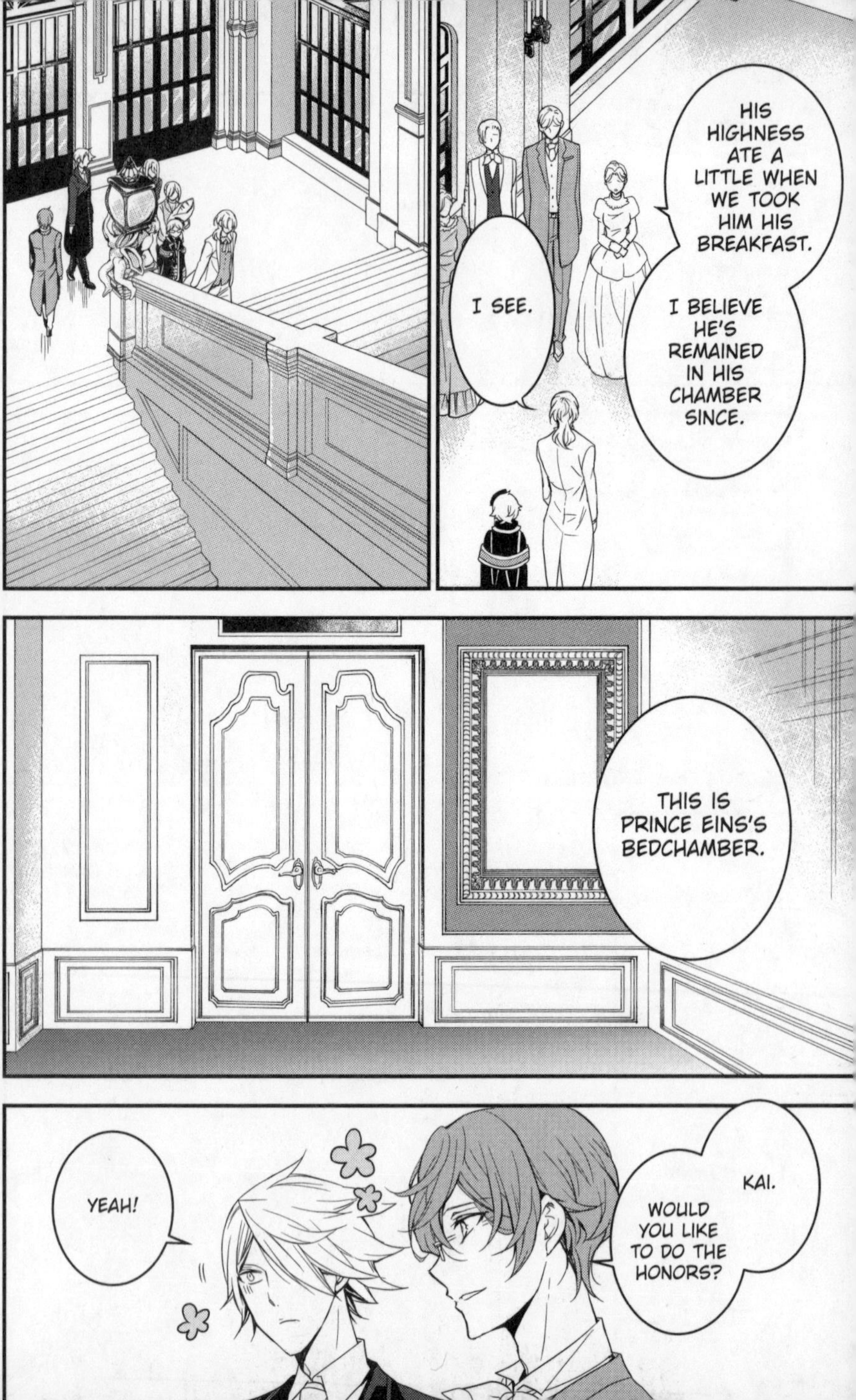
HIS HIGHNESS ATE A LITTLE WHEN WE TOOK HIM HIS BREAKFAST.
I BELIEVE HE'S REMAINED IN HIS CHAMBER SINCE.
I SEE.
THIS IS PRINCE EINS'S BEDCHAMBER.
KAI.
WOULD YOU LIKE TO DO THE HONORS?
YEAH!

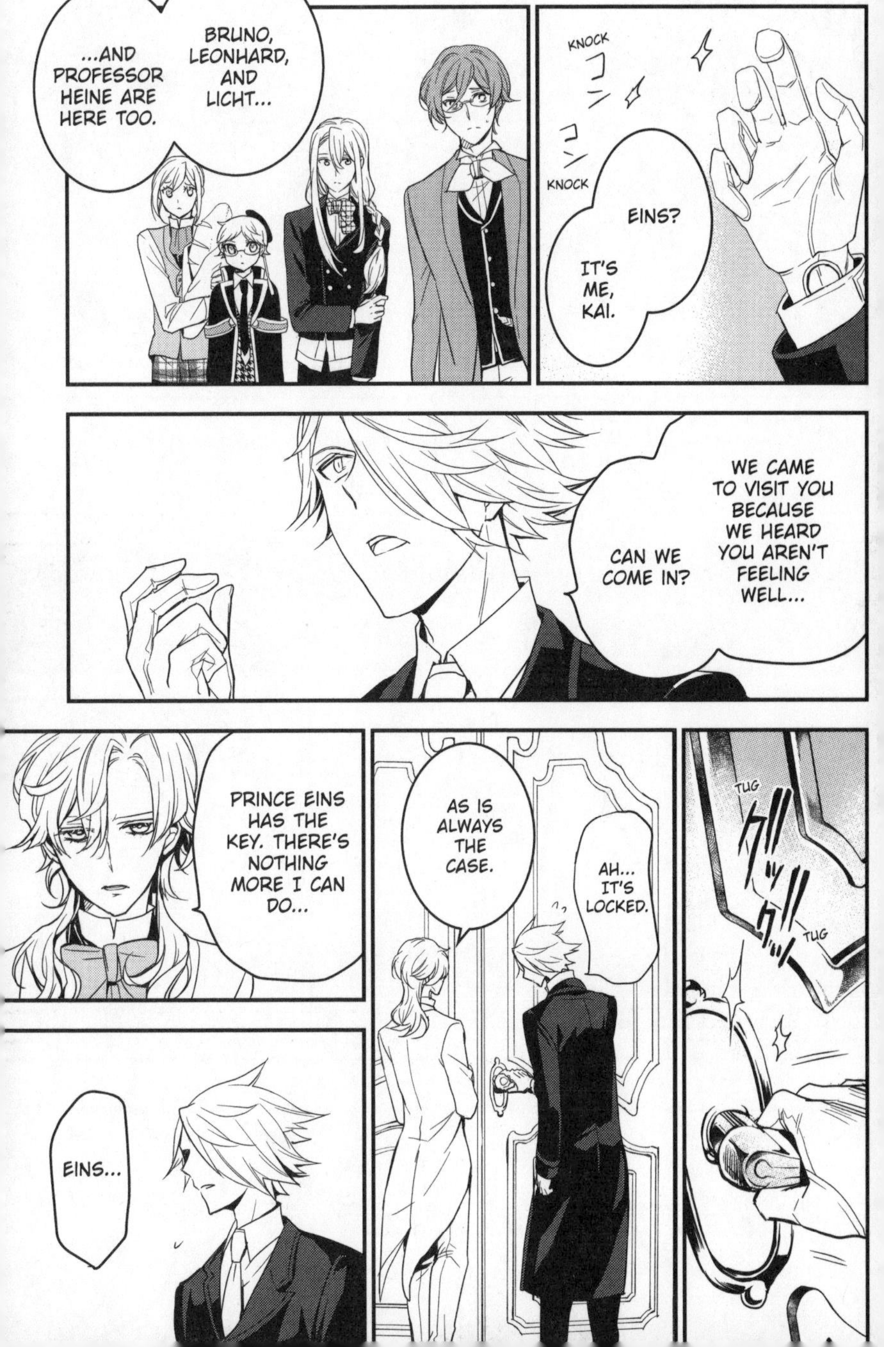
KNOCK
KNOCK
EINS?
IT'S ME, KAI.
BRUNO, LEONHARD, AND LICHT...
...AND PROFESSOR HEINE ARE HERE TOO.
WE CAME TO VISIT YOU BECAUSE WE HEARD YOU AREN'T FEELING WELL...
CAN WE COME IN?
TUG
TUG
AH... IT'S LOCKED.
AS IS ALWAYS THE CASE.
PRINCE EINS HAS THE KEY. THERE'S NOTHING MORE I CAN DO...
EINS...

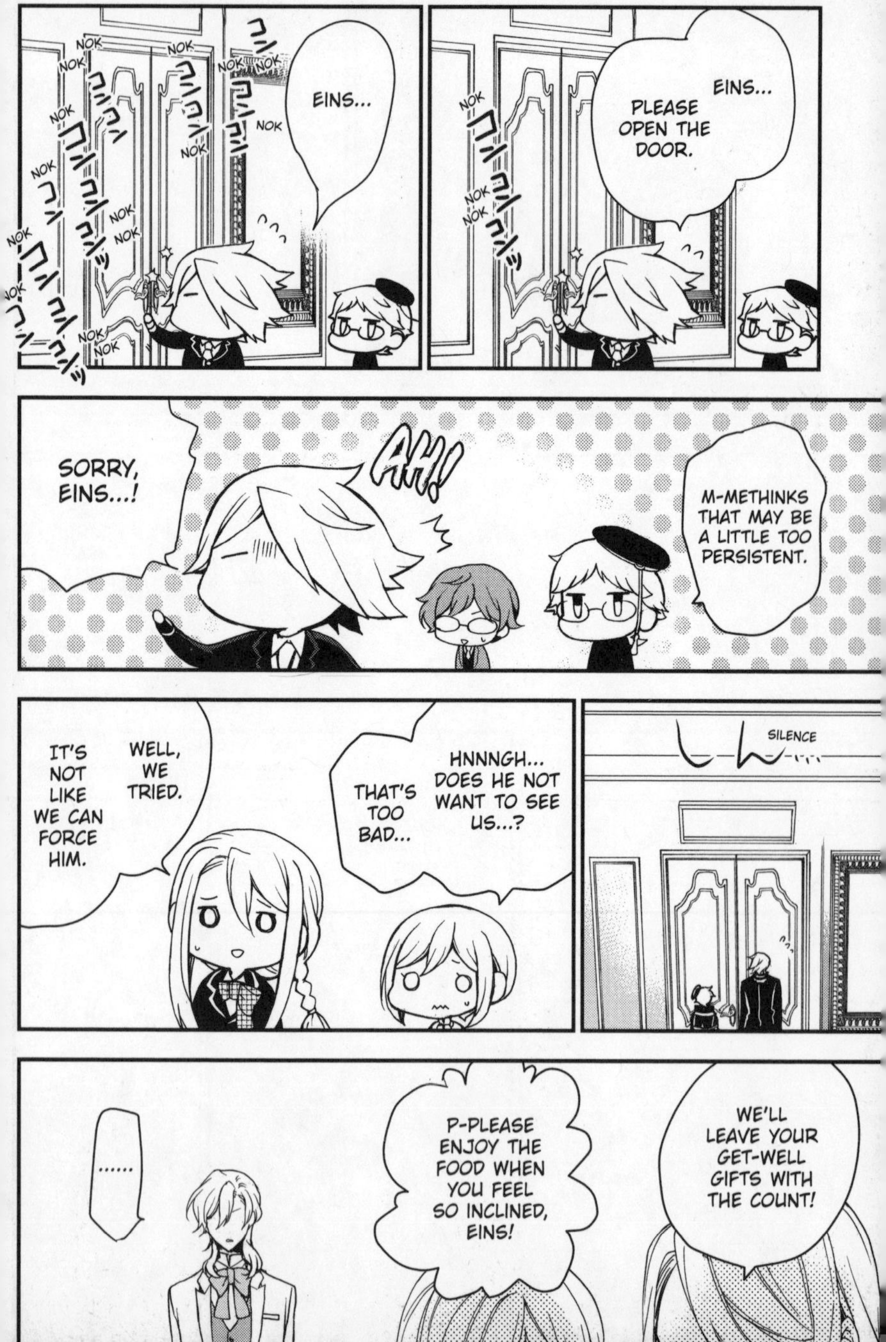
NOK
EINS...
PLEASE OPEN THE DOOR.
NOK NOK
NOK NOK NOK NOK NOK NOK NOK NOK NOK NOK NOK NOK NOK NOK
EINS...
M-METHINKS THAT MAY BE A LITTLE TOO PERSISTENT.
AH!
SORRY, EINS...!
SILENCE
HNNNGH... DOES HE NOT WANT TO SEE US...?
THAT'S TOO BAD...
WELL, WE TRIED.
IT'S NOT LIKE WE CAN FORCE HIM.
WE'LL LEAVE YOUR GET-WELL GIFTS WITH THE COUNT!
P-PLEASE ENJOY THE FOOD WHEN YOU FEEL SO INCLINED, EINS!
......

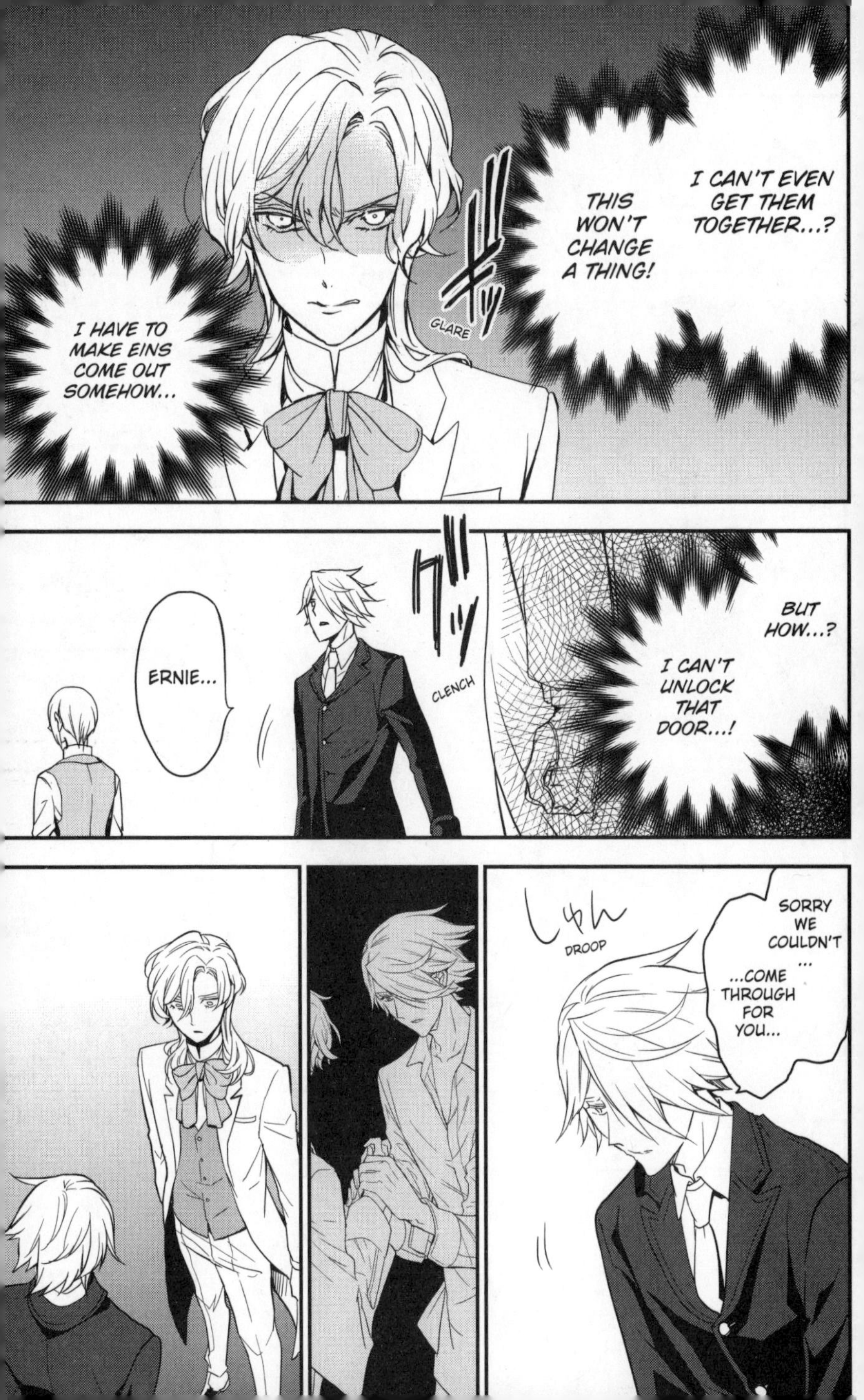
I CAN'T EVEN GET THEM TOGETHER...?
THIS WON'T CHANGE A THING!
ギッ
GLARE
I HAVE TO MAKE EINS COME OUT SOMEHOW...
BUT HOW...?
I CAN'T UNLOCK THAT DOOR...!
グッ
CLENCH
ERNIE...
SORRY WE COULDN'T ...
...COME THROUGH FOR YOU...
しゅん
DROOP

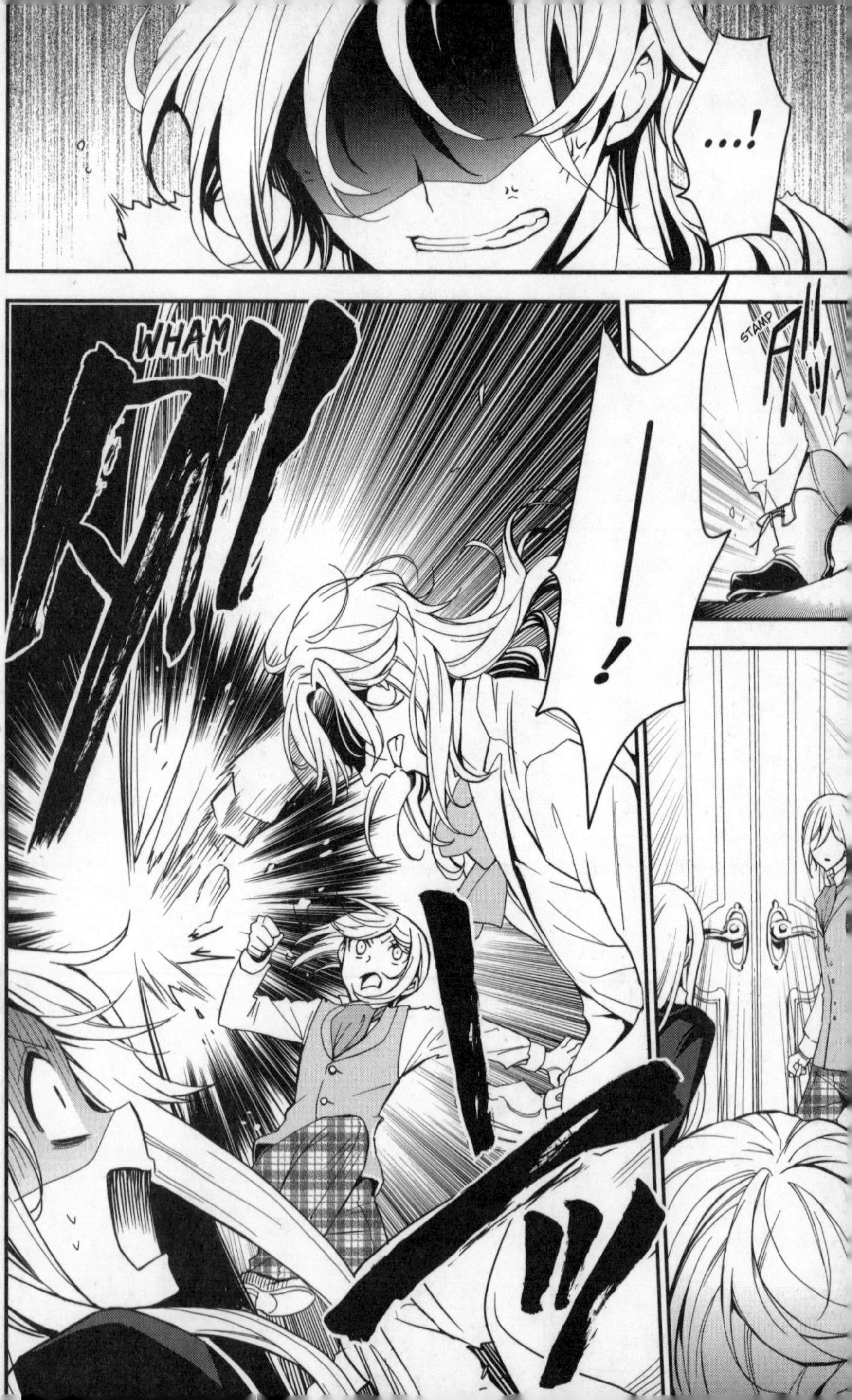
...!
STAMP
!!
WHAM

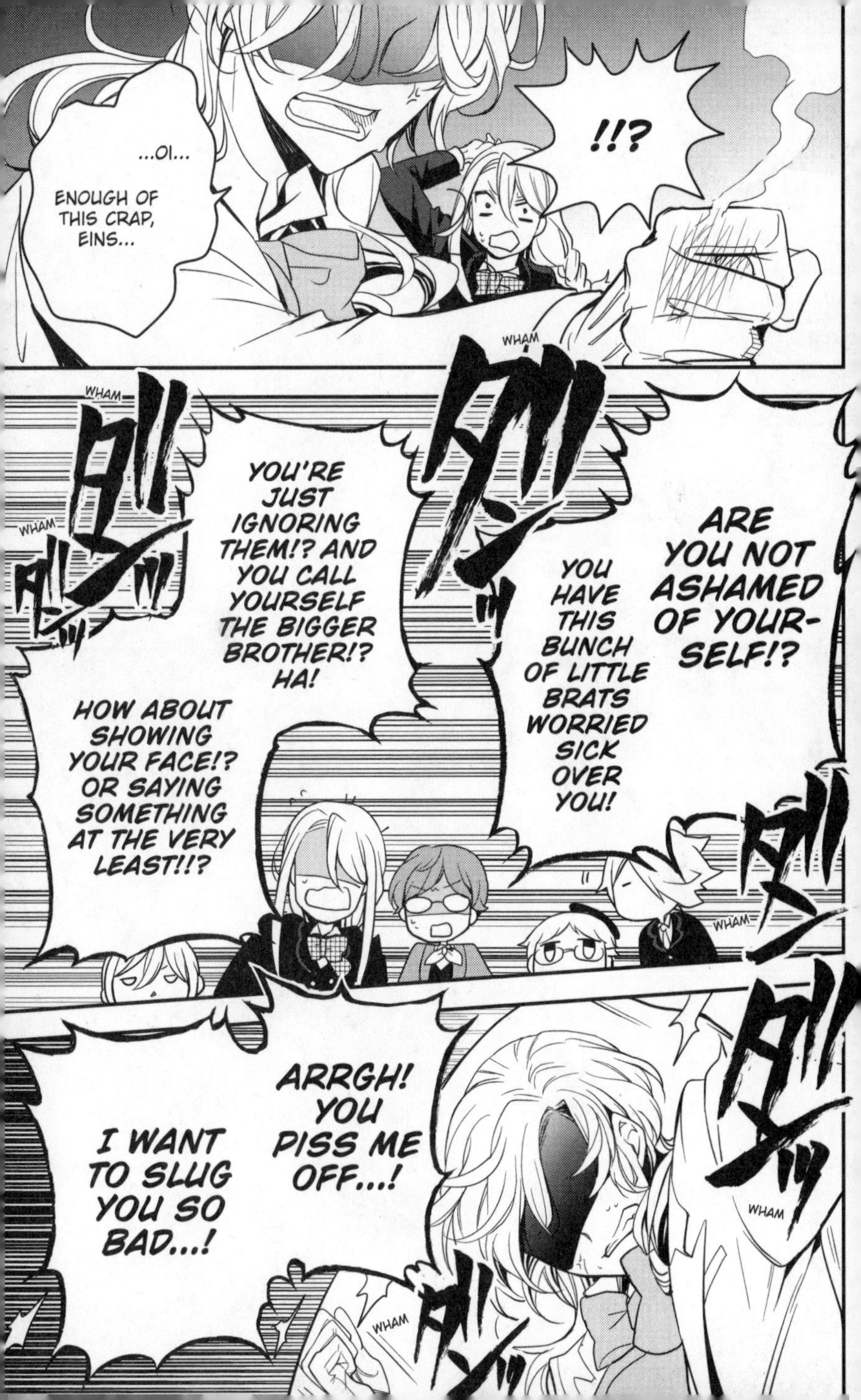
!!?
...OI...
ENOUGH OF THIS CRAP, EINS...
WHAM
WHAM
WHAM
ARE YOU NOT ASHAMED OF YOURSELF!?
YOU HAVE THIS BUNCH OF LITTLE BRATS WORRIED SICK OVER YOU!
YOU'RE JUST IGNORING THEM!? AND YOU CALL YOURSELF THE BIGGER BROTHER!? HA!
HOW ABOUT SHOWING YOUR FACE!? OR SAYING SOMETHING AT THE VERY LEAST!!?
WHAM
WHAM
ARRGH! YOU PISS ME OFF...!
I WANT TO SLUG YOU SO BAD...!
WHAM

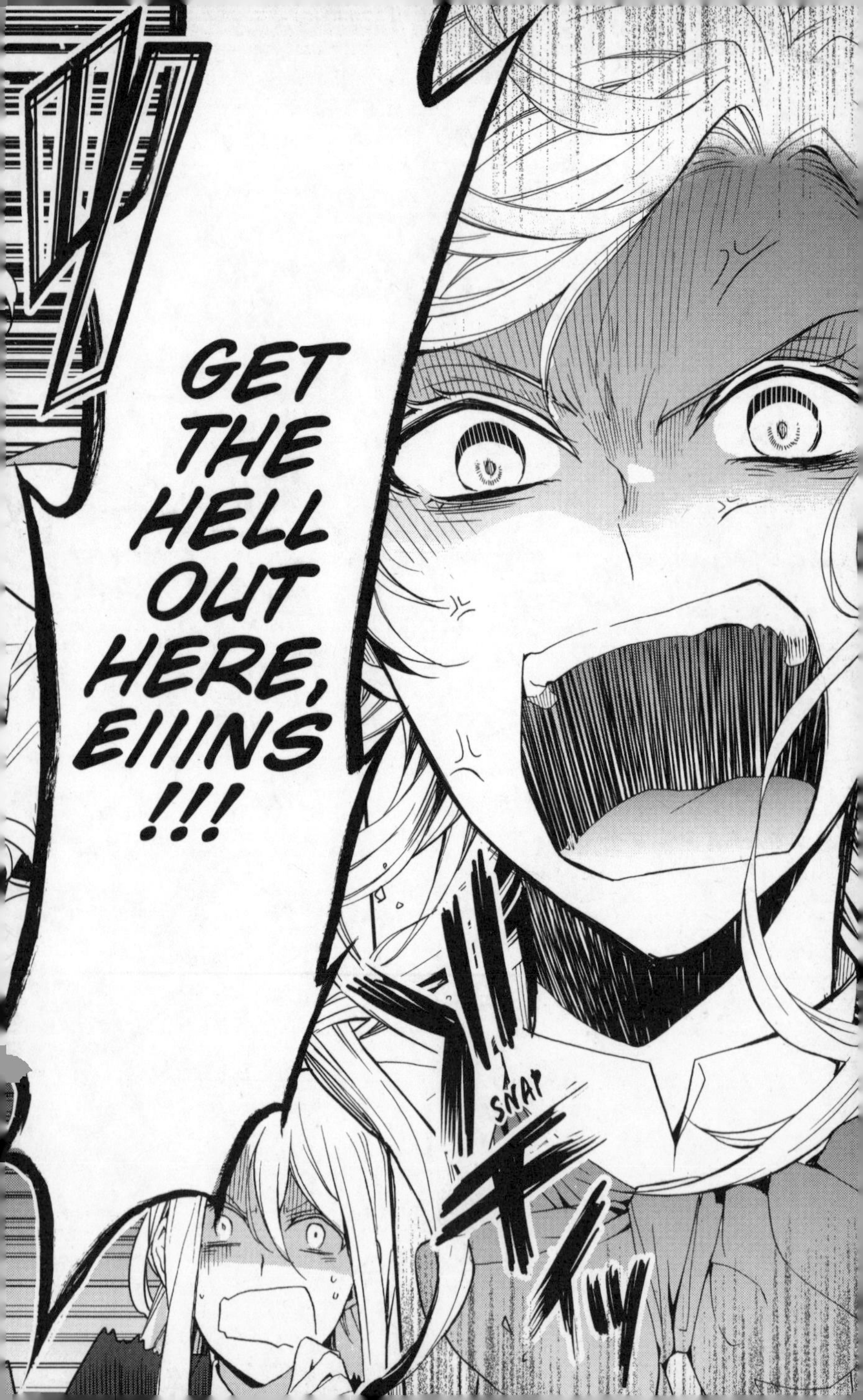
GET THE HELL OUT HERE, EIIINS!!!
SNAP

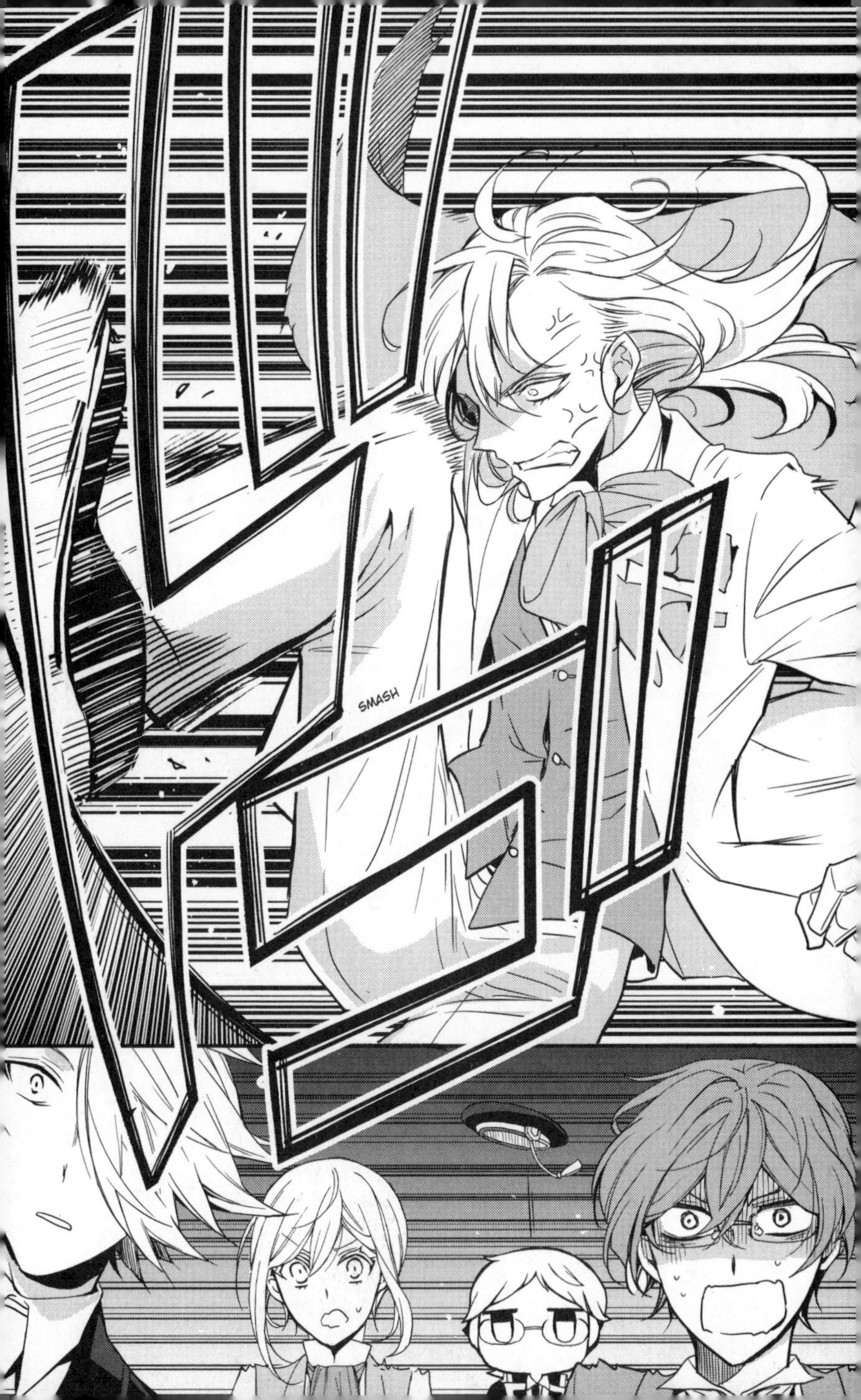
SMASH

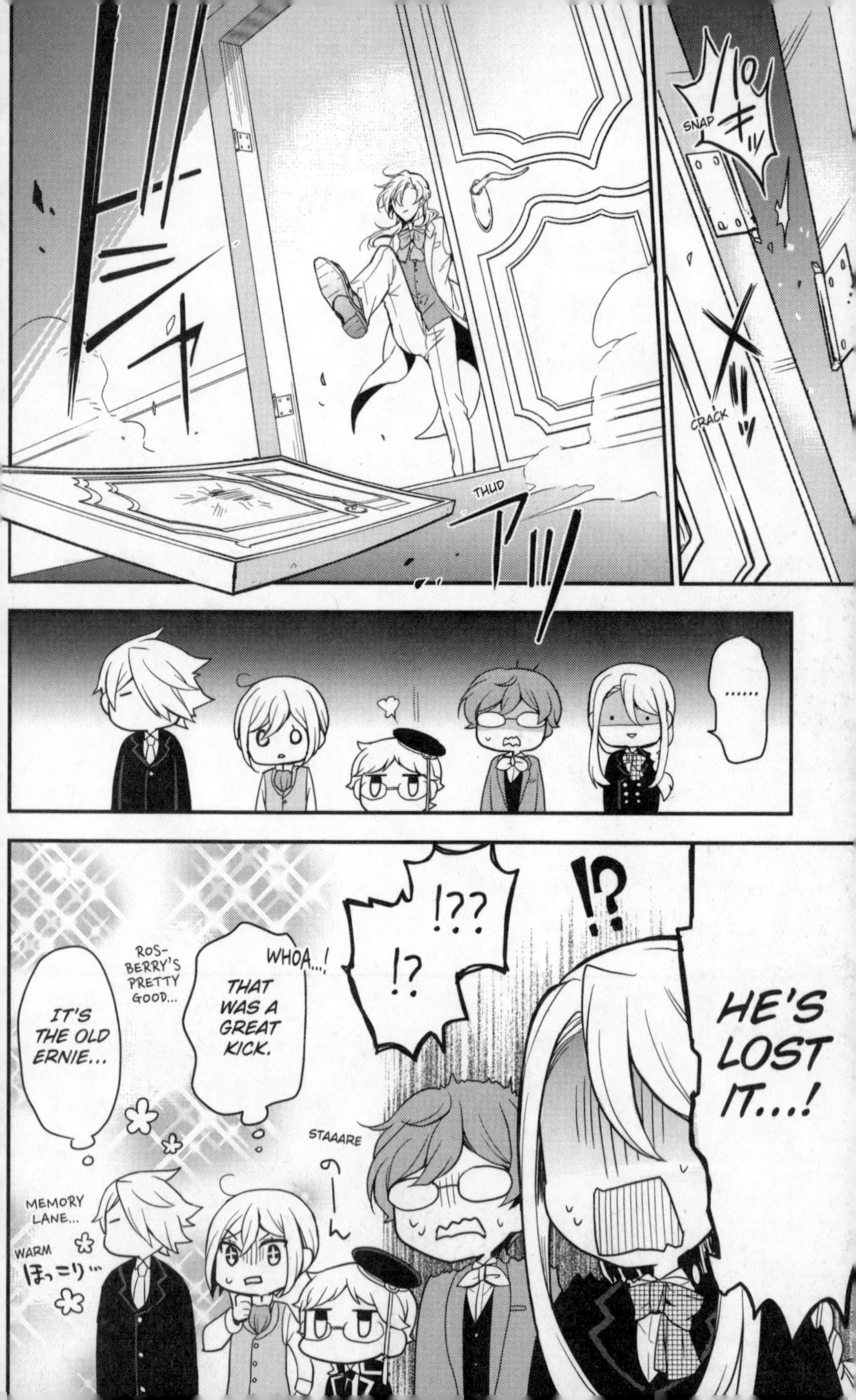

SNAP
CRACK
THUD
......
!?
HE'S LOST IT...!
!??
!?
WHOA...!
THAT WAS A GREAT KICK.
ROS-BERRY'S PRETTY GOOD...
STAAARE
のーん
IT'S THE OLD ERNIE...
MEMORY LANE...
WARM
ほっこり

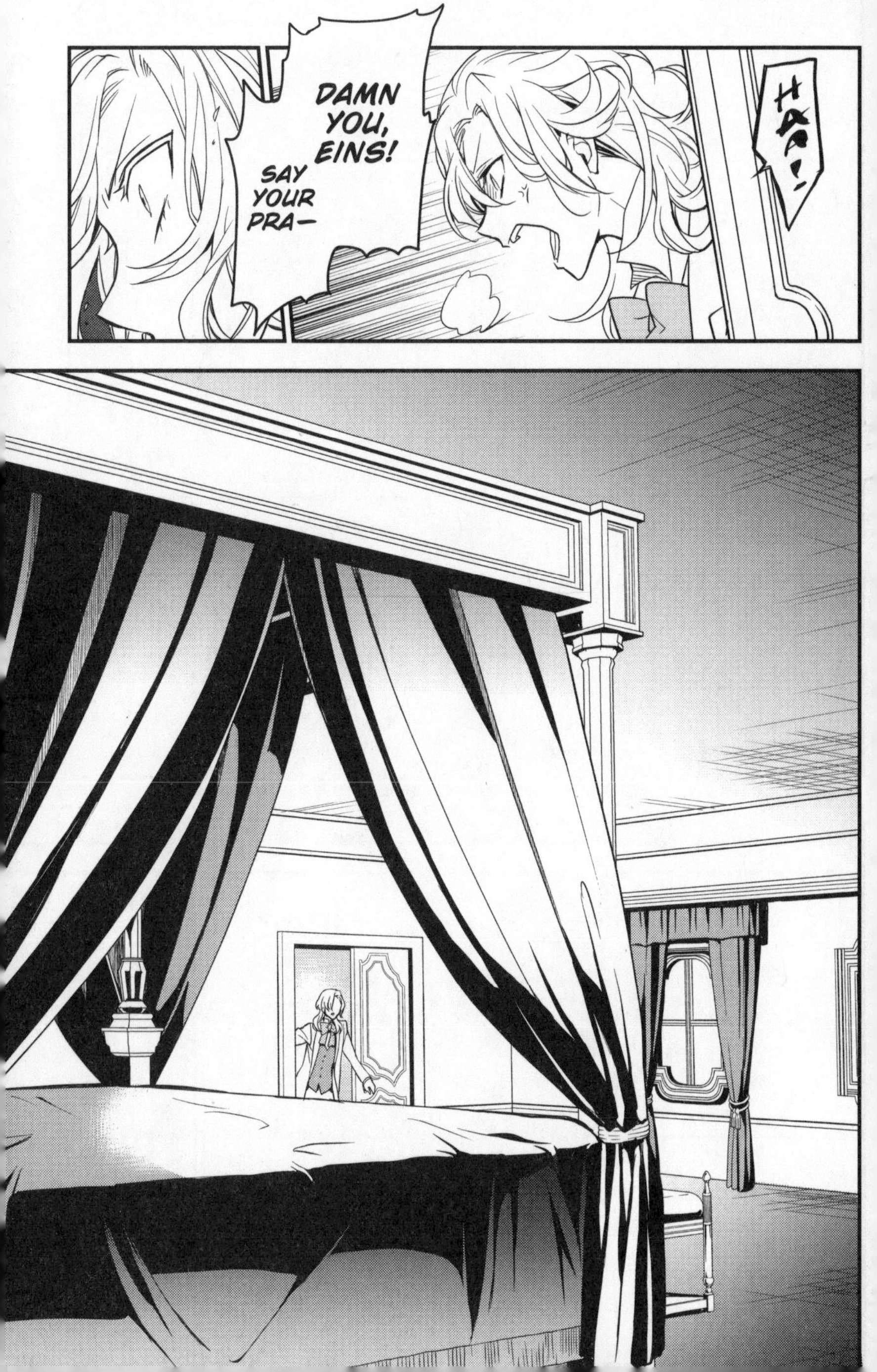
HAA!
DAMN YOU, EINS!
SAY YOUR PRA—

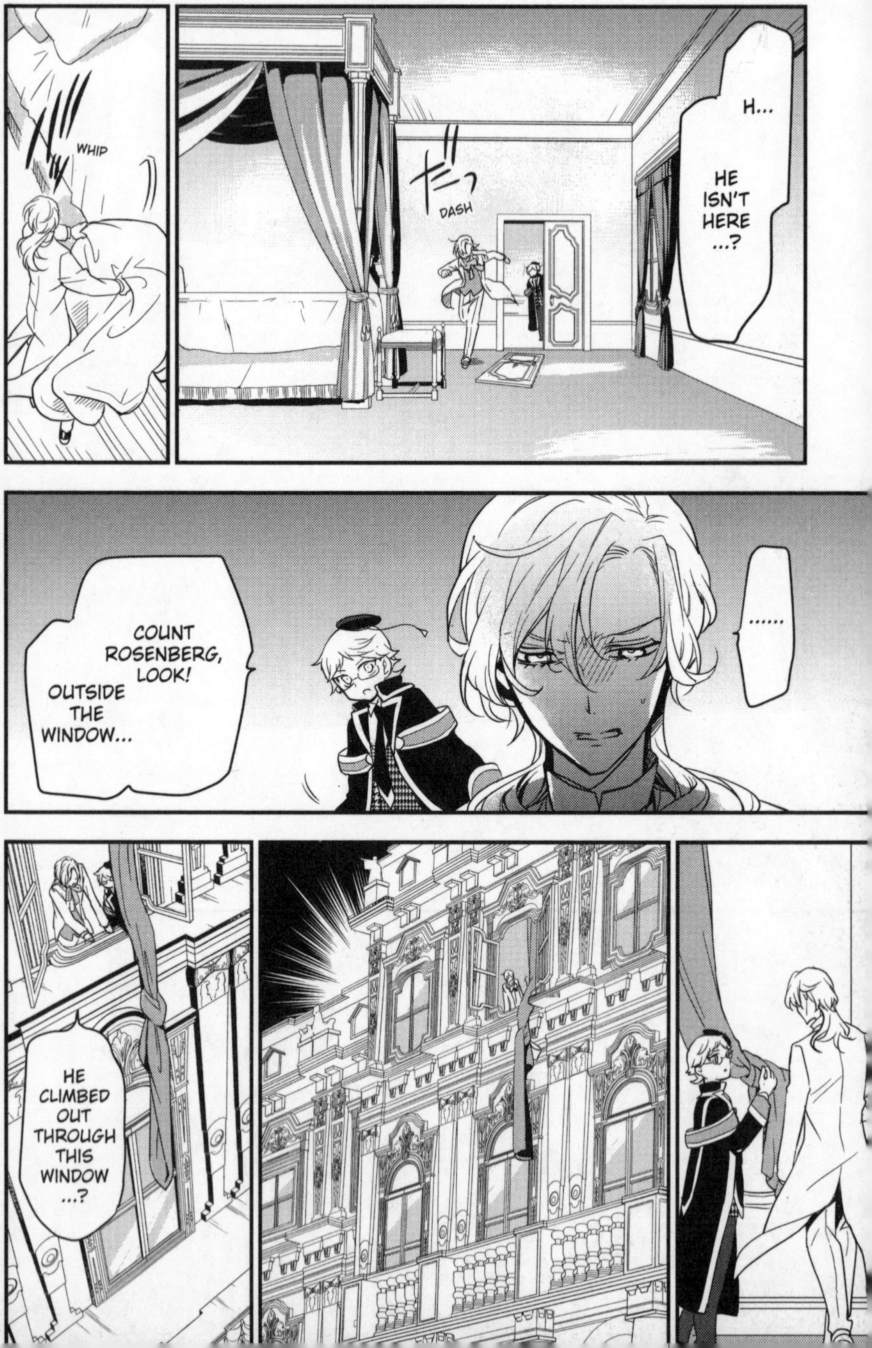
H...
HE ISN'T HERE ...?
DASH
WHIP
......
COUNT ROSENBERG, LOOK!
OUTSIDE THE WINDOW...
HE CLIMBED OUT THROUGH THIS WINDOW ...?

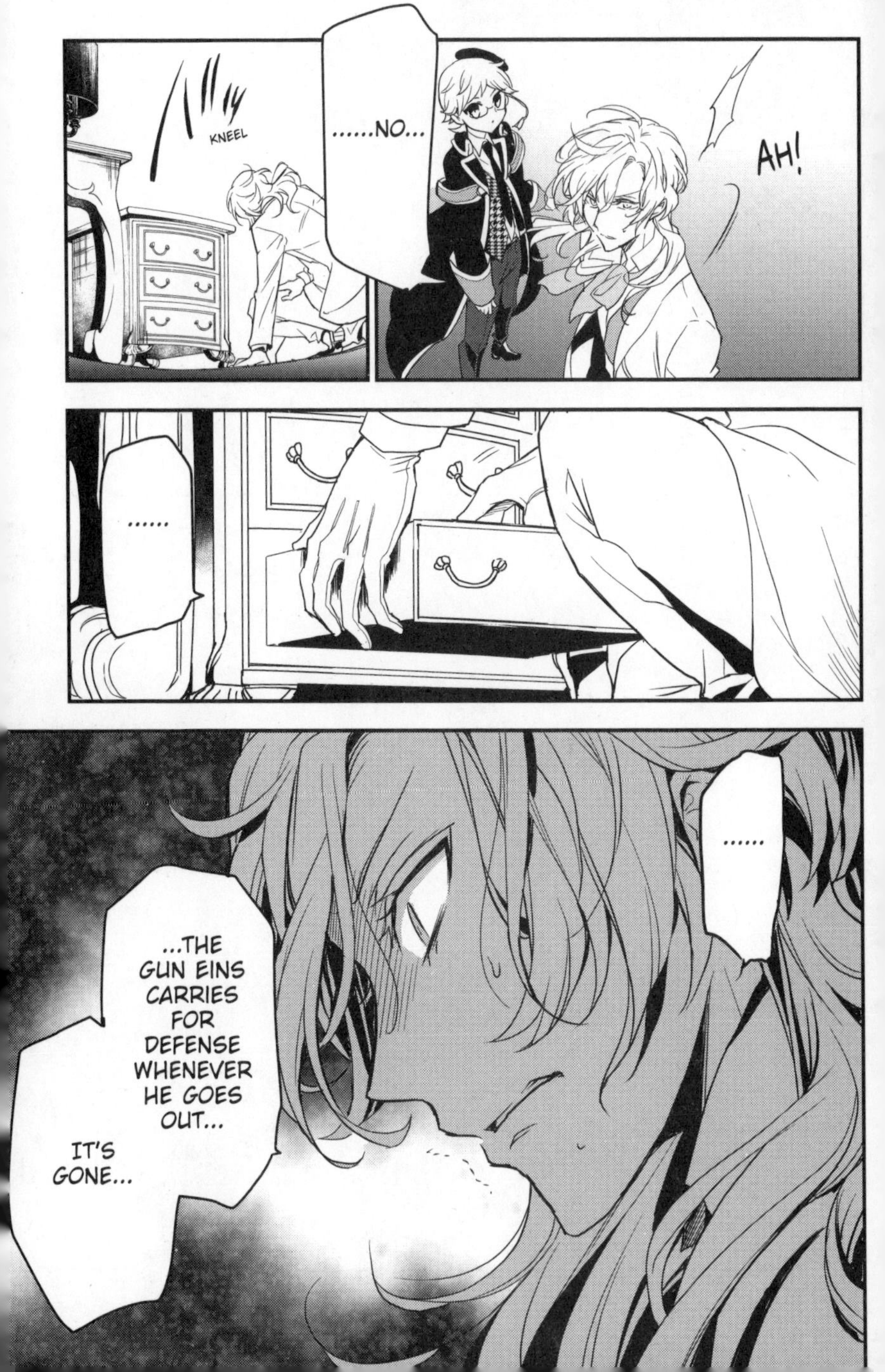
AH!
......NO...
KNEEL
......
......
...THE GUN EINS CARRIES FOR DEFENSE WHENEVER HE GOES OUT...
IT'S GONE...

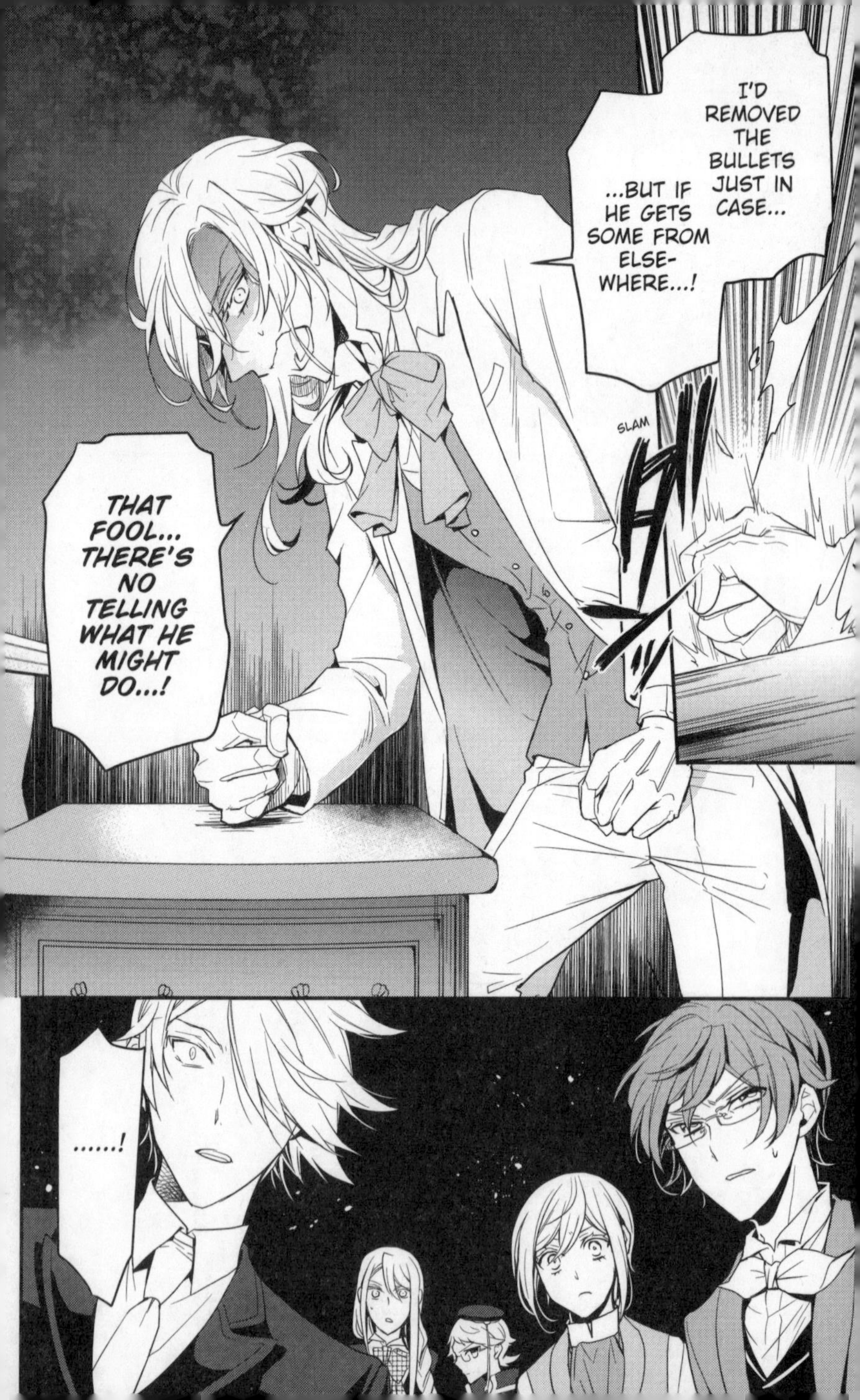
I'D REMOVED THE BULLETS JUST IN CASE...
...BUT IF HE GETS SOME FROM ELSE-WHERE...!
SLAM
THAT FOOL... THERE'S NO TELLING WHAT HE MIGHT DO...!
......!

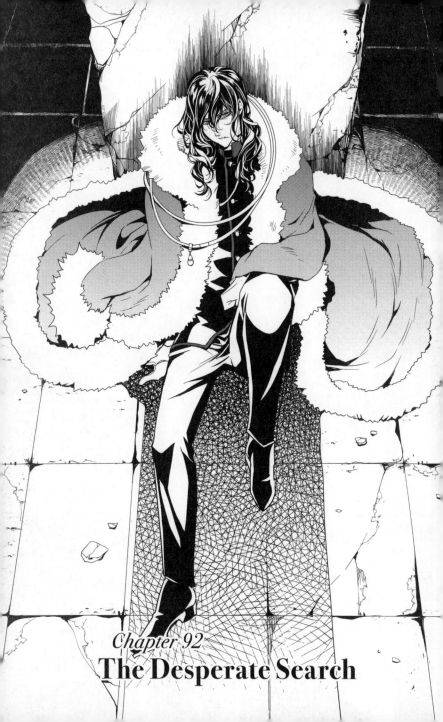

Chapter 92
The Desperate Search

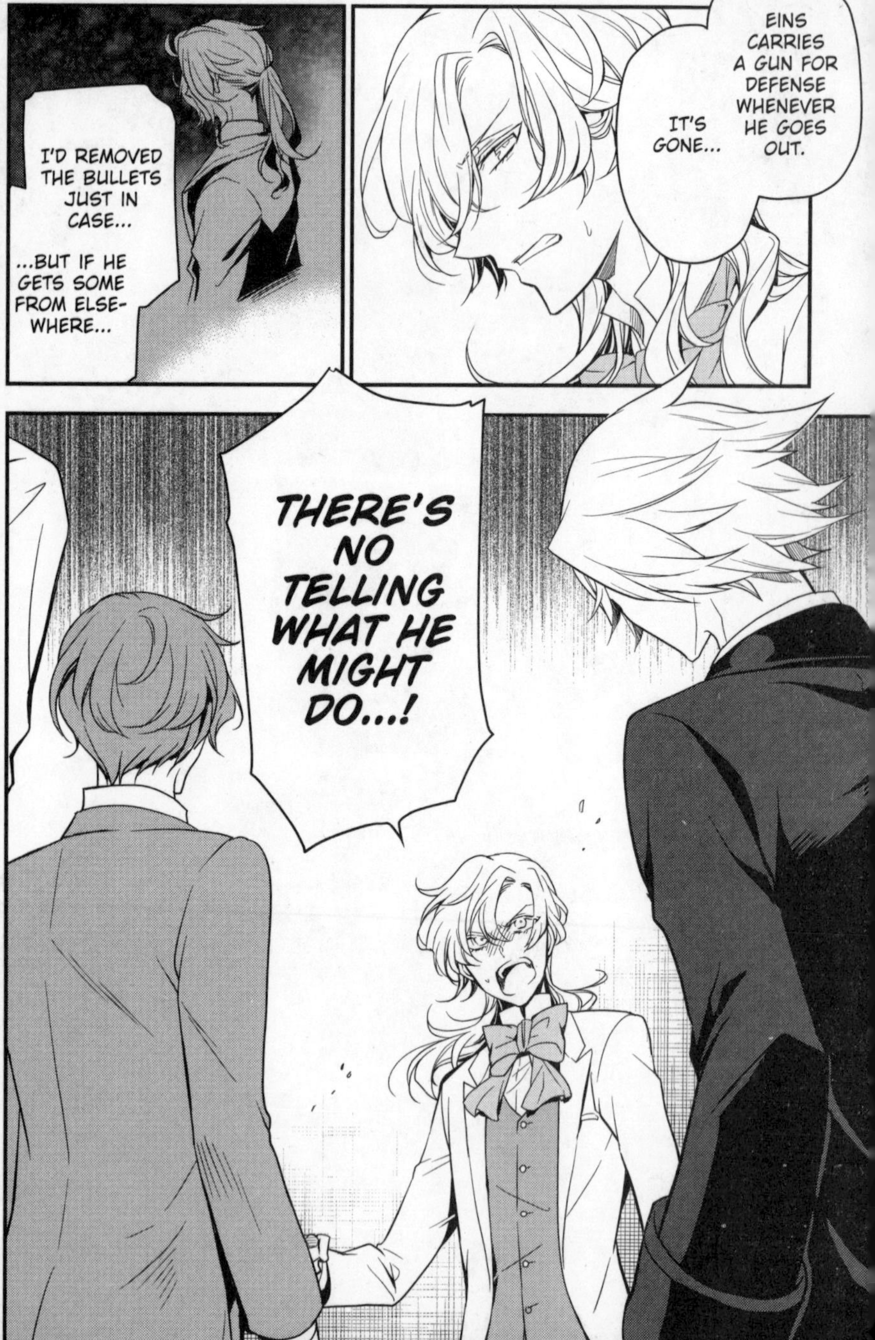
EINS CARRIES A GUN FOR DEFENSE WHENEVER HE GOES OUT.
IT'S GONE...
I'D REMOVED THE BULLETS JUST IN CASE...
...BUT IF HE GETS SOME FROM ELSE-WHERE...
THERE'S NO TELLING WHAT HE MIGHT DO...!

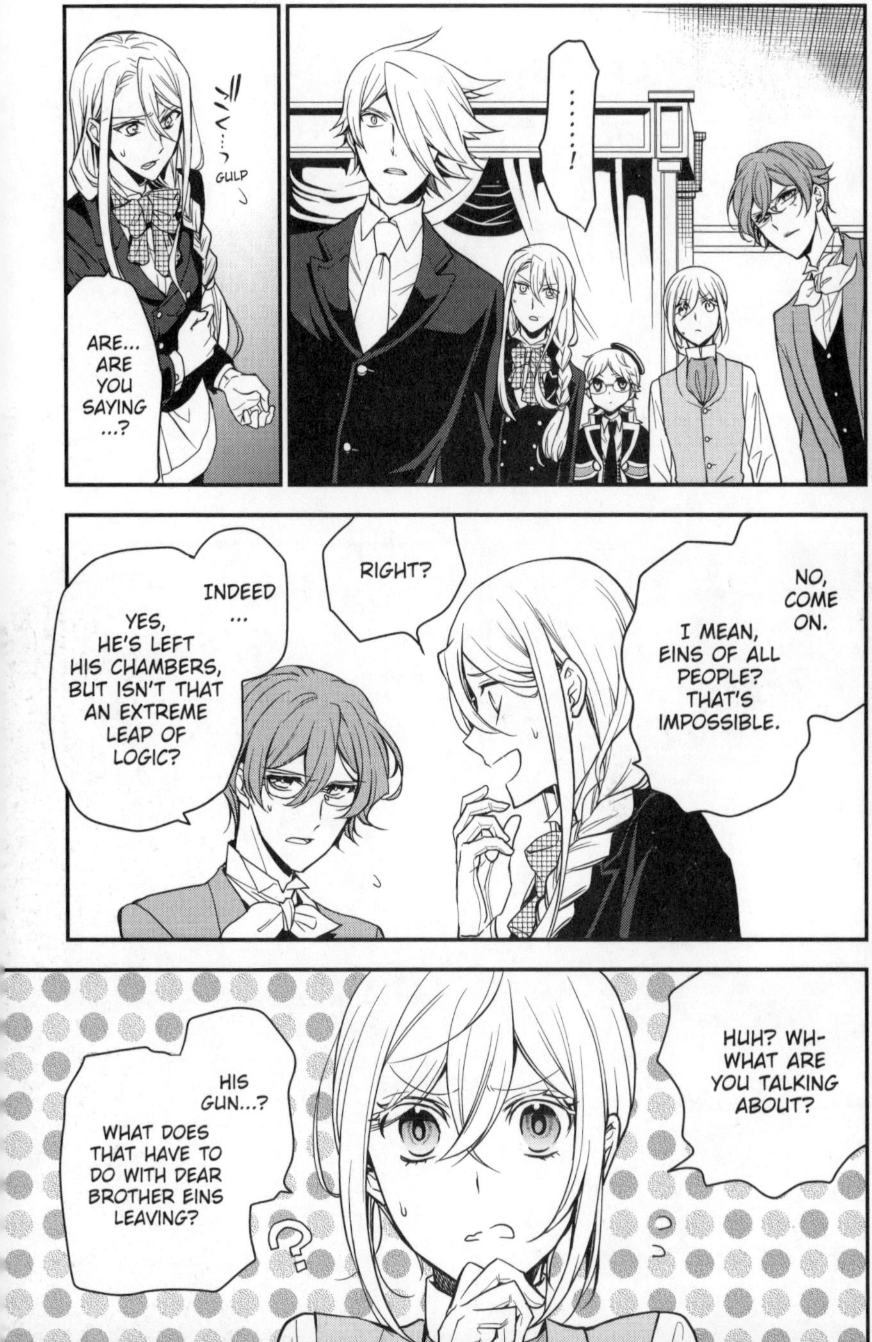
......!
GULP
ARE... ARE YOU SAYING ...?
NO, COME ON.
I MEAN, EINS OF ALL PEOPLE? THAT'S IMPOSSIBLE.
RIGHT?
INDEED ...
YES, HE'S LEFT HIS CHAMBERS, BUT ISN'T THAT AN EXTREME LEAP OF LOGIC?
HUH? WH-WHAT ARE YOU TALKING ABOUT?
HIS GUN...?
WHAT DOES THAT HAVE TO DO WITH DEAR BROTHER EINS LEAVING?

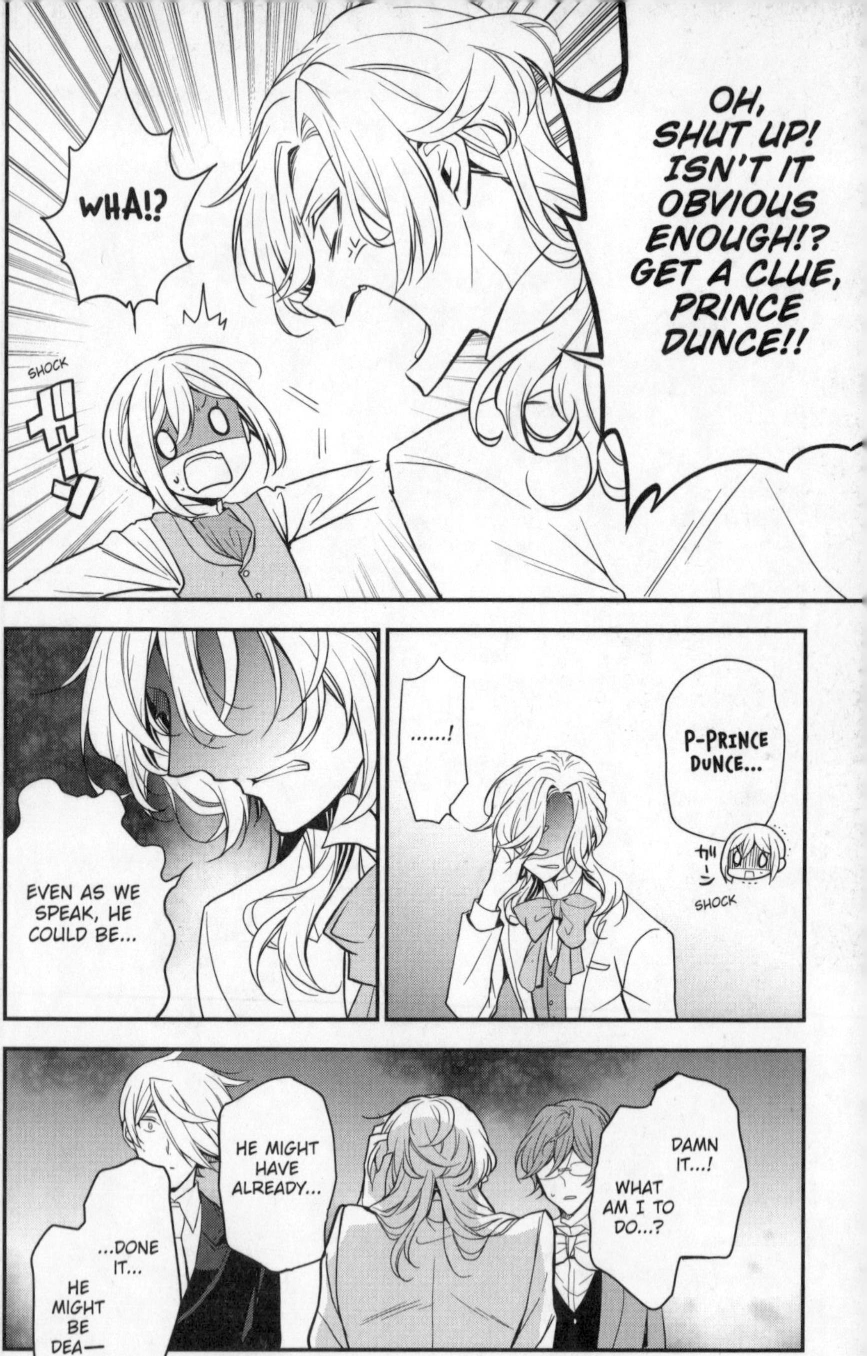
OH, SHUT UP! ISN'T IT OBVIOUS ENOUGH!? GET A CLUE, PRINCE DUNCE!!
WHA!?
SHOCK
P-PRINCE DUNCE...
SHOCK
......!
EVEN AS WE SPEAK, HE COULD BE...
DAMN IT...!
WHAT AM I TO DO...?
HE MIGHT HAVE ALREADY...
...DONE IT...
HE MIGHT BE DEA—

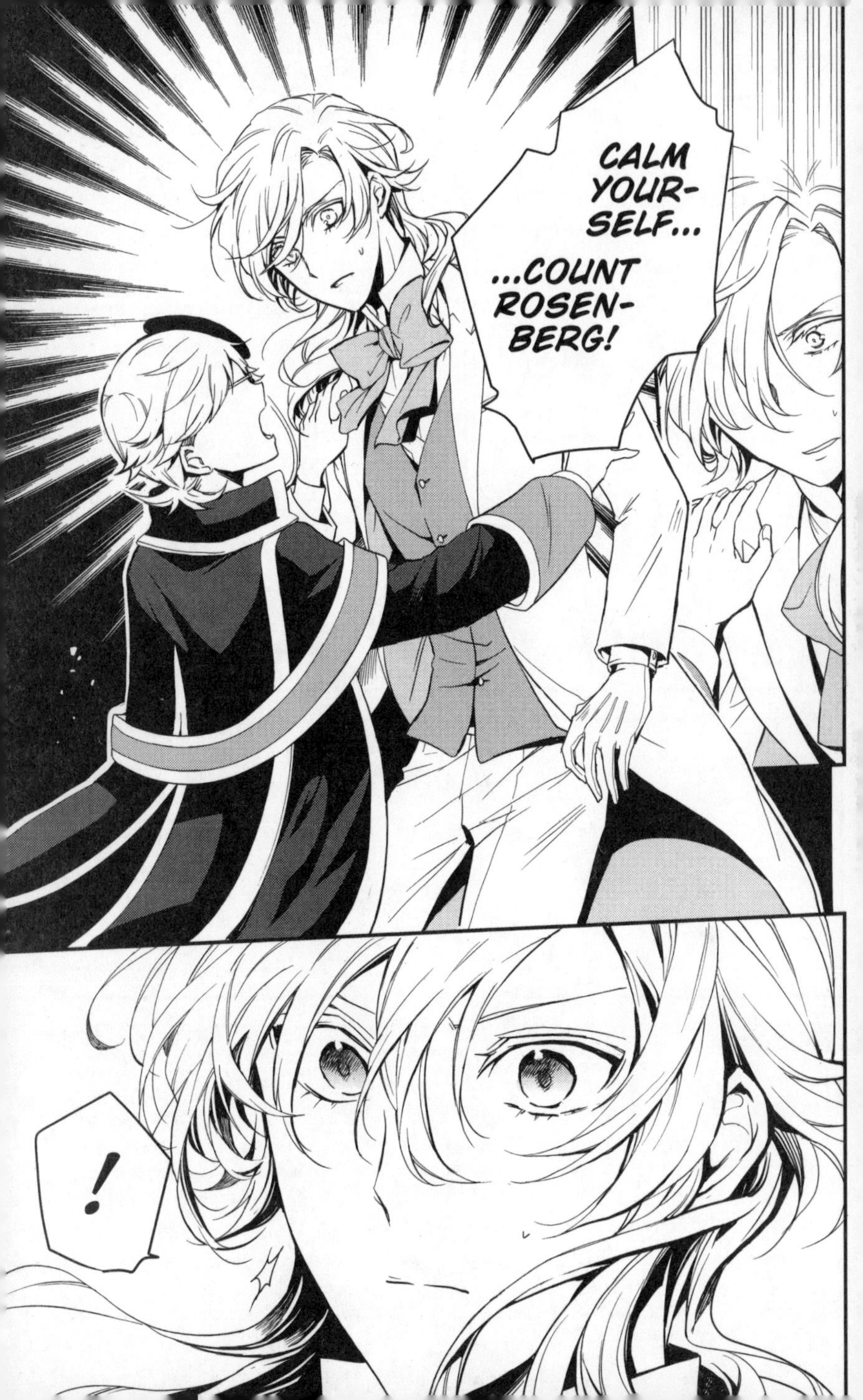
CALM YOUR-SELF...
...COUNT ROSEN-BERG!
!

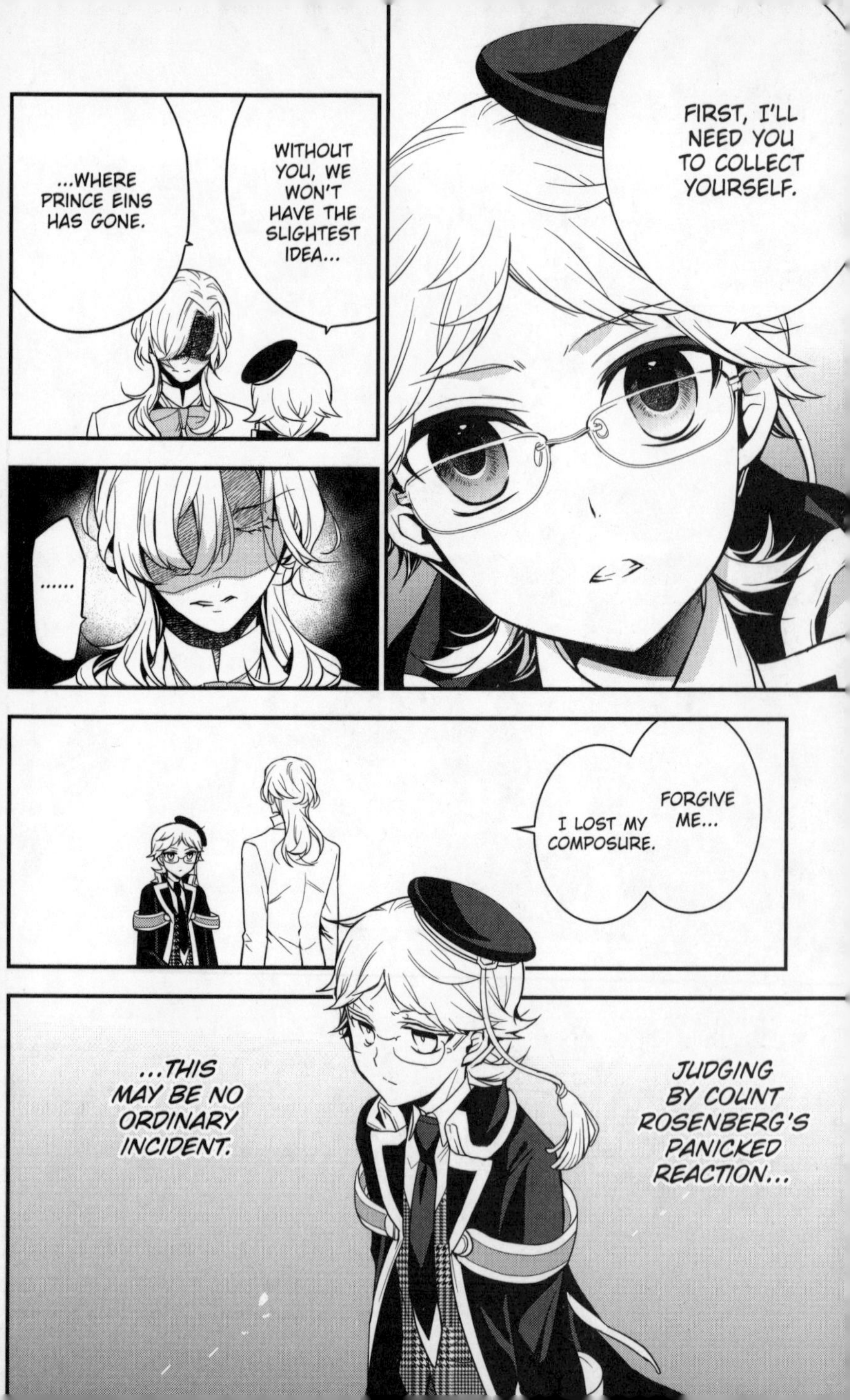
FIRST, I'LL NEED YOU TO COLLECT YOURSELF.
WITHOUT YOU, WE WON'T HAVE THE SLIGHTEST IDEA...
...WHERE PRINCE EINS HAS GONE.
......
FORGIVE ME...
I LOST MY COMPOSURE.
JUDGING BY COUNT ROSENBERG'S PANICKED REACTION...
...THIS MAY BE NO ORDINARY INCIDENT.

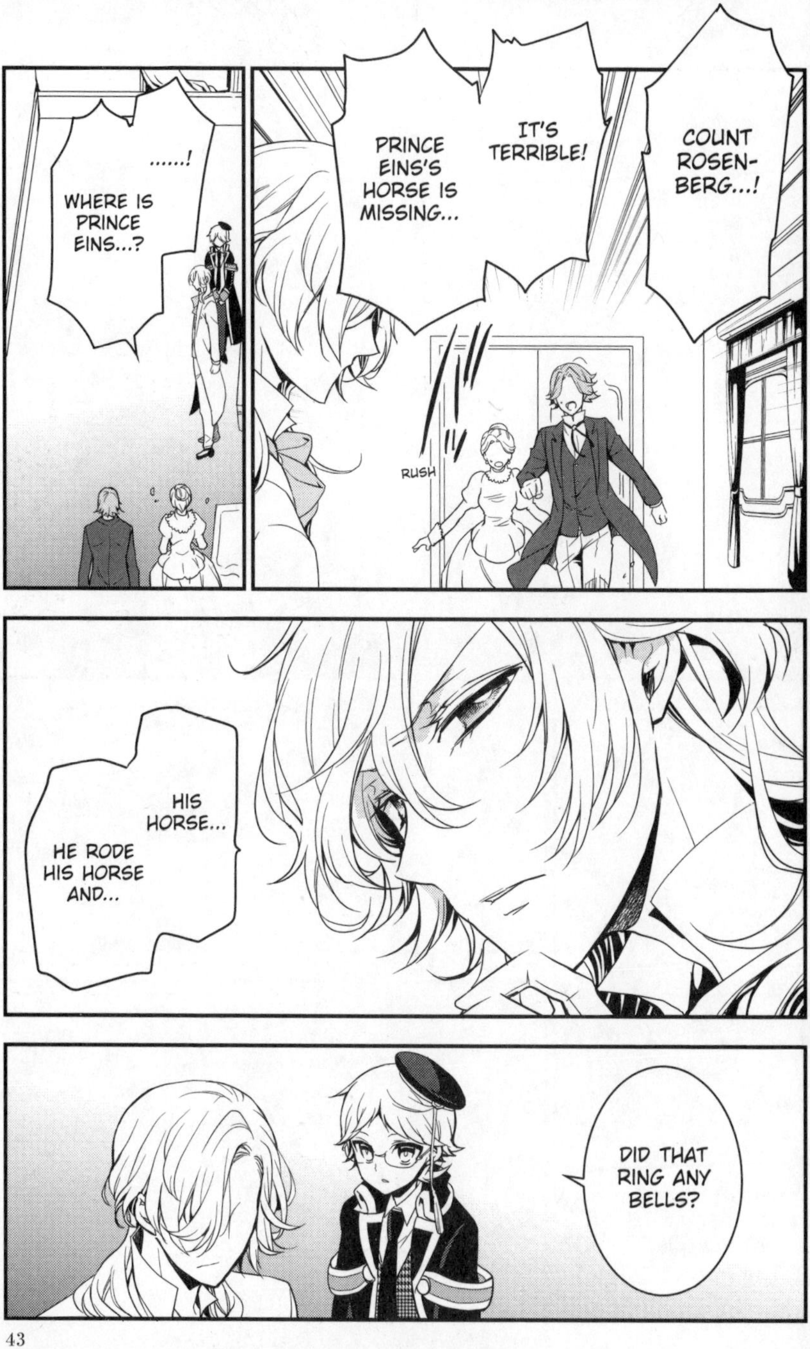
COUNT ROSEN-BERG...!
IT'S TERRIBLE!
PRINCE EINS'S HORSE IS MISSING...
RUSH
......!
WHERE IS PRINCE EINS...?
HIS HORSE...
HE RODE HIS HORSE AND...
DID THAT RING ANY BELLS?

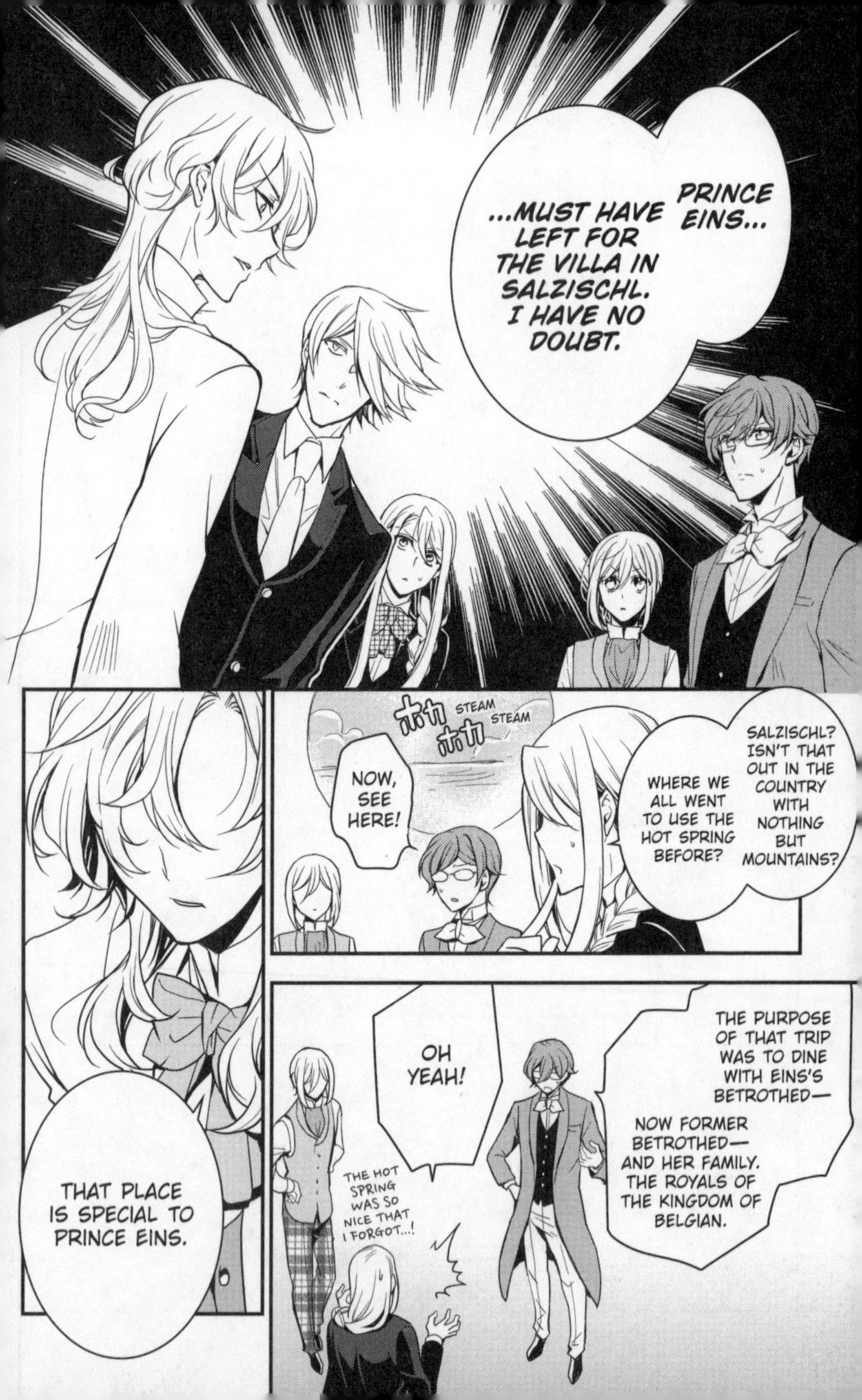
PRINCE EINS...
...MUST HAVE LEFT FOR THE VILLA IN SALZISCHL. I HAVE NO DOUBT.
SALZISCHL? ISN'T THAT OUT IN THE COUNTRY WITH NOTHING BUT MOUNTAINS?
WHERE WE ALL WENT TO USE THE HOT SPRING BEFORE?
STEAM STEAM
NOW, SEE HERE!
THE PURPOSE OF THAT TRIP WAS TO DINE WITH EINS'S BETROTHED—
NOW FORMER BETROTHED— AND HER FAMILY. THE ROYALS OF THE KINGDOM OF BELGIAN.
OH YEAH!
THE HOT SPRING WAS SO NICE THAT I FORGOT...!
THAT PLACE IS SPECIAL TO PRINCE EINS.

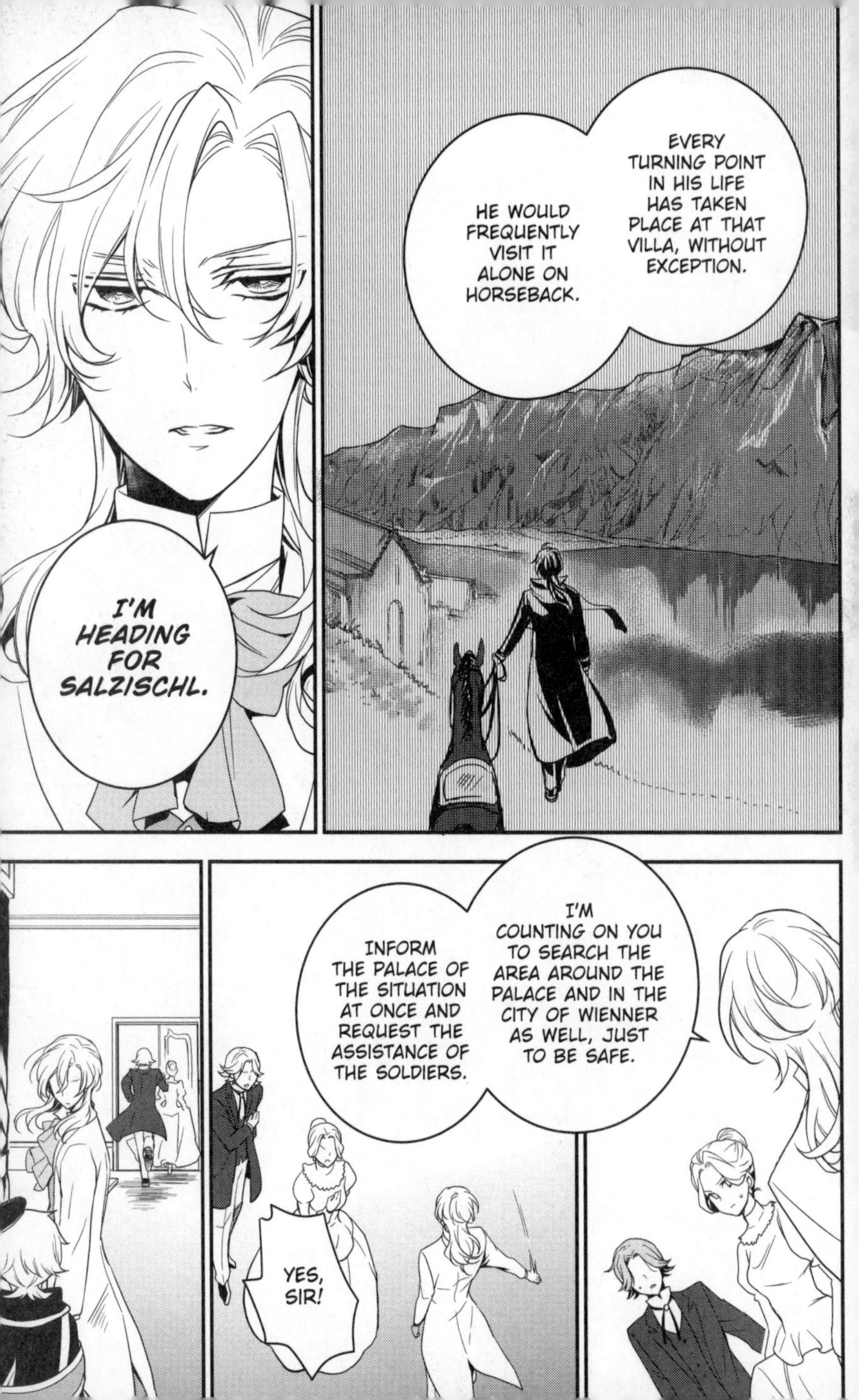
EVERY TURNING POINT IN HIS LIFE HAS TAKEN PLACE AT THAT VILLA, WITHOUT EXCEPTION.
HE WOULD FREQUENTLY VISIT IT ALONE ON HORSEBACK.
I'M HEADING FOR SALZISCHL.
I'M COUNTING ON YOU TO SEARCH THE AREA AROUND THE PALACE AND IN THE CITY OF WIENNER AS WELL, JUST TO BE SAFE.
INFORM THE PALACE OF THE SITUATION AT ONCE AND REQUEST THE ASSISTANCE OF THE SOLDIERS.
YES, SIR!

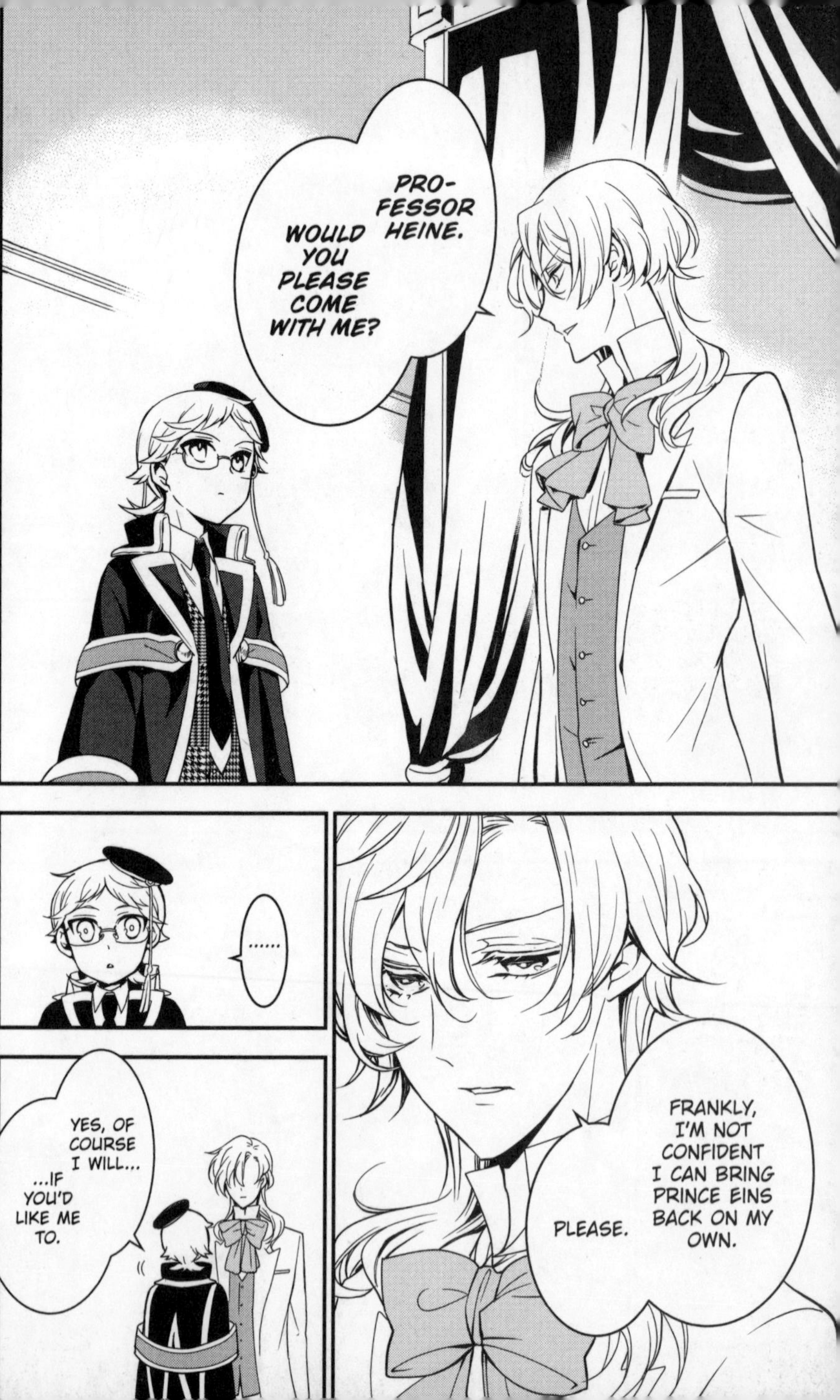
PRO-FESSOR HEINE.
WOULD YOU PLEASE COME WITH ME?
FRANKLY, I'M NOT CONFIDENT I CAN BRING PRINCE EINS BACK ON MY OWN.
PLEASE.
......
YES, OF COURSE I WILL...
...IF YOU'D LIKE ME TO.

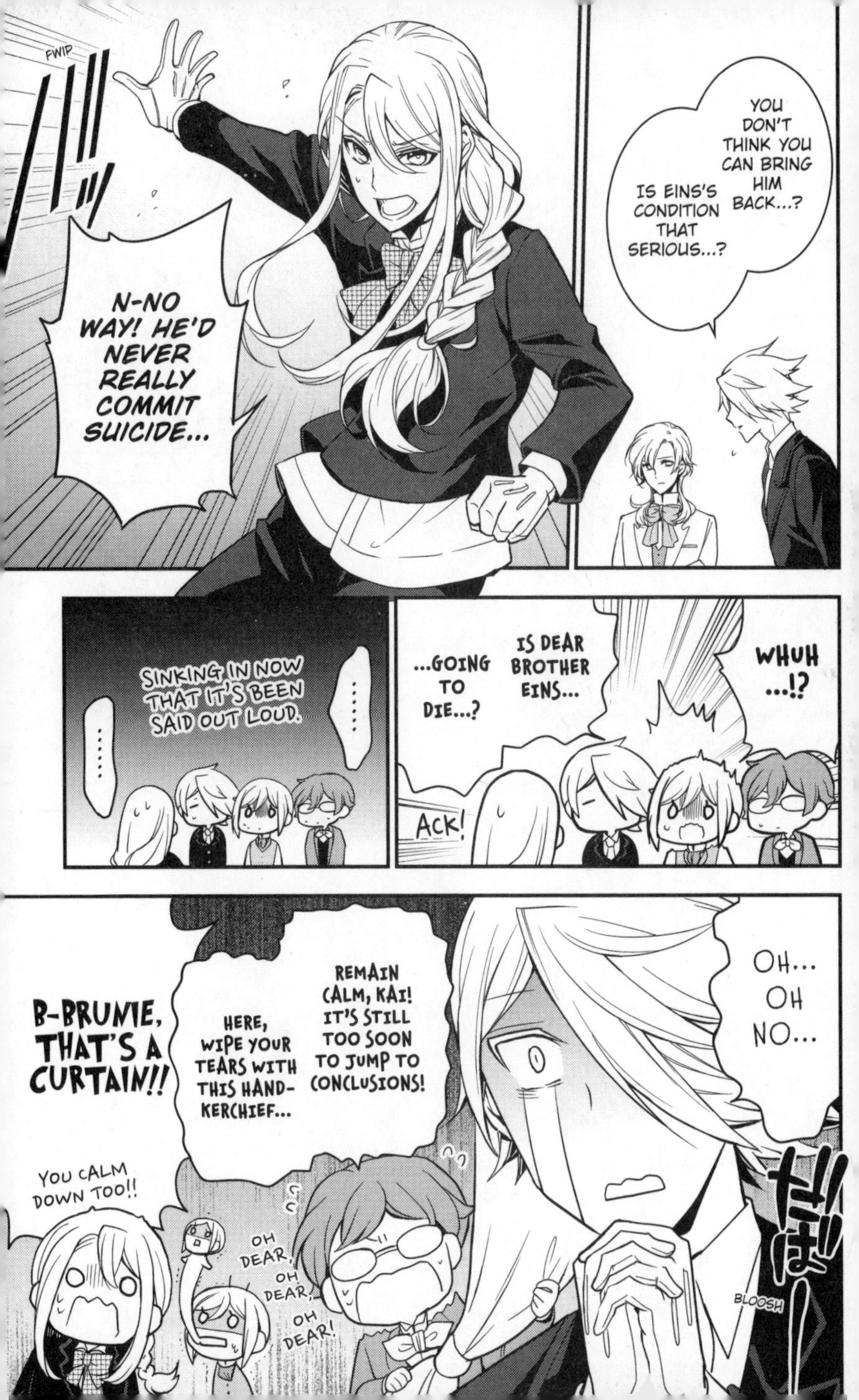

YOU DON'T THINK YOU CAN BRING HIM BACK...?
IS EINS'S CONDITION THAT SERIOUS...?
FWIP
N-NO WAY! HE'D NEVER REALLY COMMIT SUICIDE...
WHUH ...!?
IS DEAR BROTHER EINS...
...GOING TO DIE...?
ACK!
......
SINKING IN NOW THAT IT'S BEEN SAID OUT LOUD.
......
OH... OH NO...
BLOOSH
REMAIN CALM, KAI! IT'S STILL TOO SOON TO JUMP TO CONCLUSIONS!
HERE, WIPE YOUR TEARS WITH THIS HAND-KERCHIEF...
B-BRUNIE, THAT'S A CURTAIN!!
YOU CALM DOWN TOO!!
OH DEAR, OH DEAR, OH DEAR!

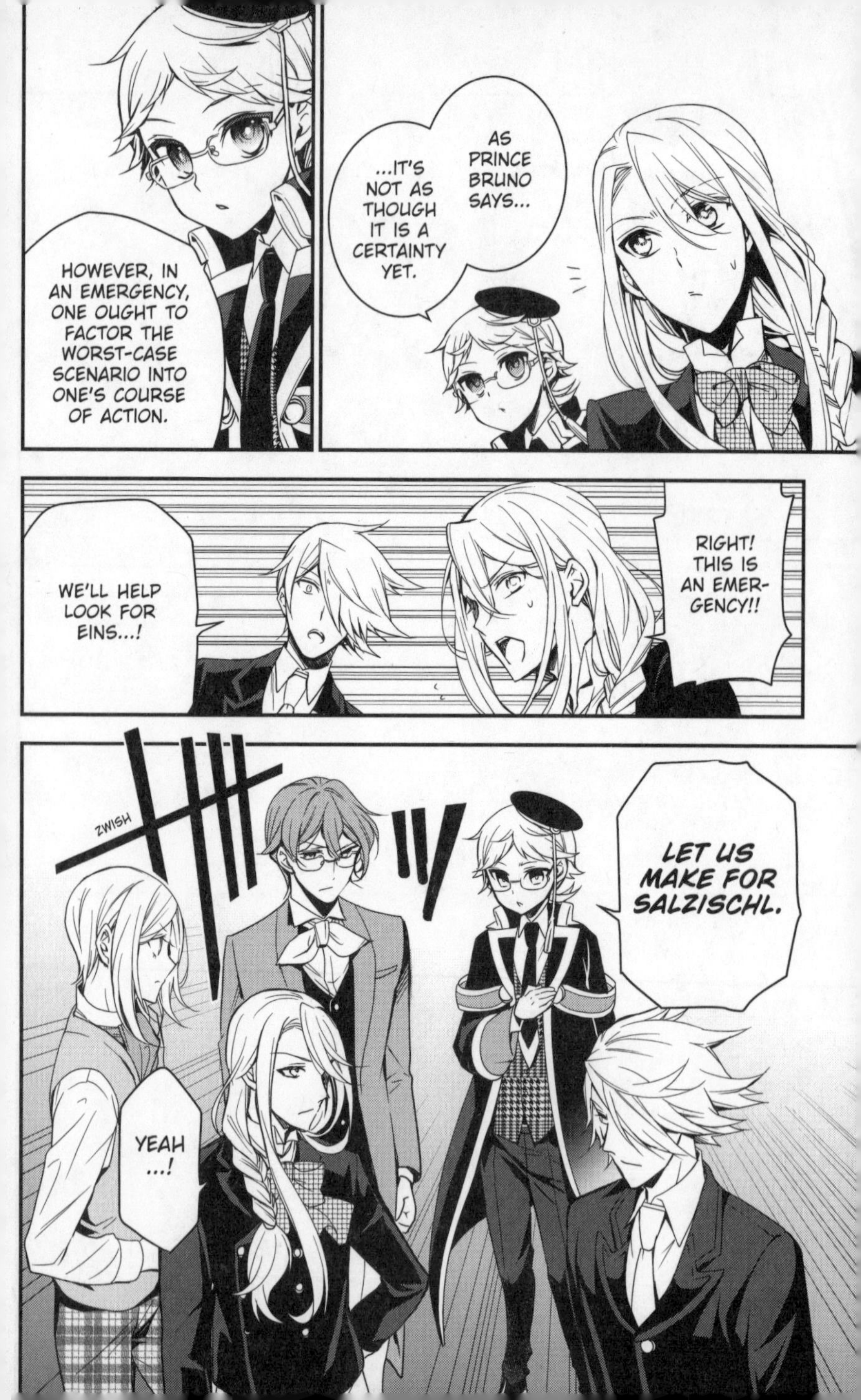
AS PRINCE BRUNO SAYS...
...IT'S NOT AS THOUGH IT IS A CERTAINTY YET.
HOWEVER, IN AN EMERGENCY, ONE OUGHT TO FACTOR THE WORST-CASE SCENARIO INTO ONE'S COURSE OF ACTION.
RIGHT! THIS IS AN EMER-GENCY!!
WE'LL HELP LOOK FOR EINS...!
LET US MAKE FOR SALZISCHL.
ZWISH
YEAH ...!

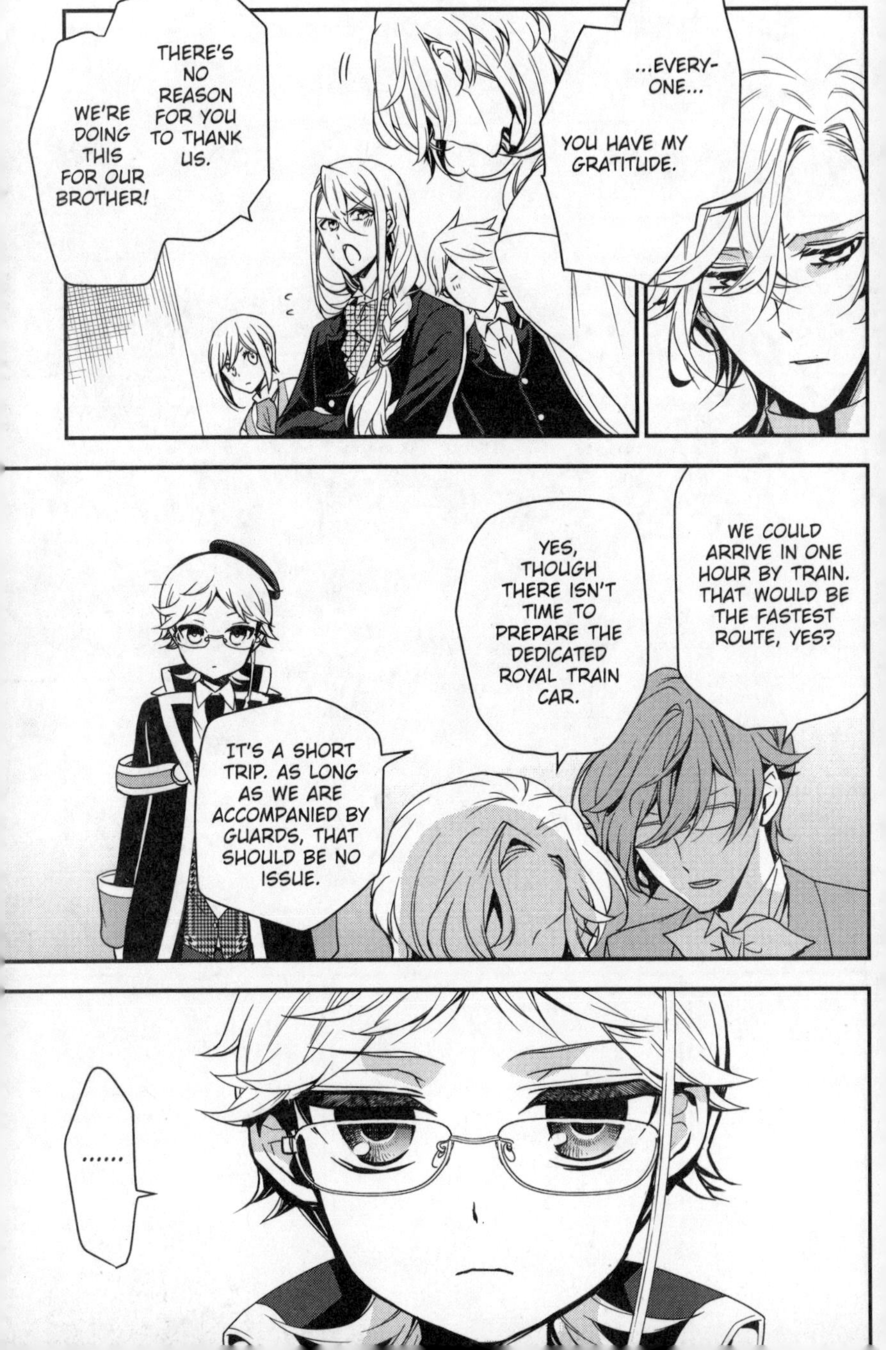
...EVERY-ONE...
YOU HAVE MY GRATITUDE.
THERE'S NO REASON FOR YOU TO THANK US.
WE'RE DOING THIS FOR OUR BROTHER!
WE COULD ARRIVE IN ONE HOUR BY TRAIN. THAT WOULD BE THE FASTEST ROUTE, YES?
YES, THOUGH THERE ISN'T TIME TO PREPARE THE DEDICATED ROYAL TRAIN CAR.
IT'S A SHORT TRIP. AS LONG AS WE ARE ACCOMPANIED BY GUARDS, THAT SHOULD BE NO ISSUE.
......

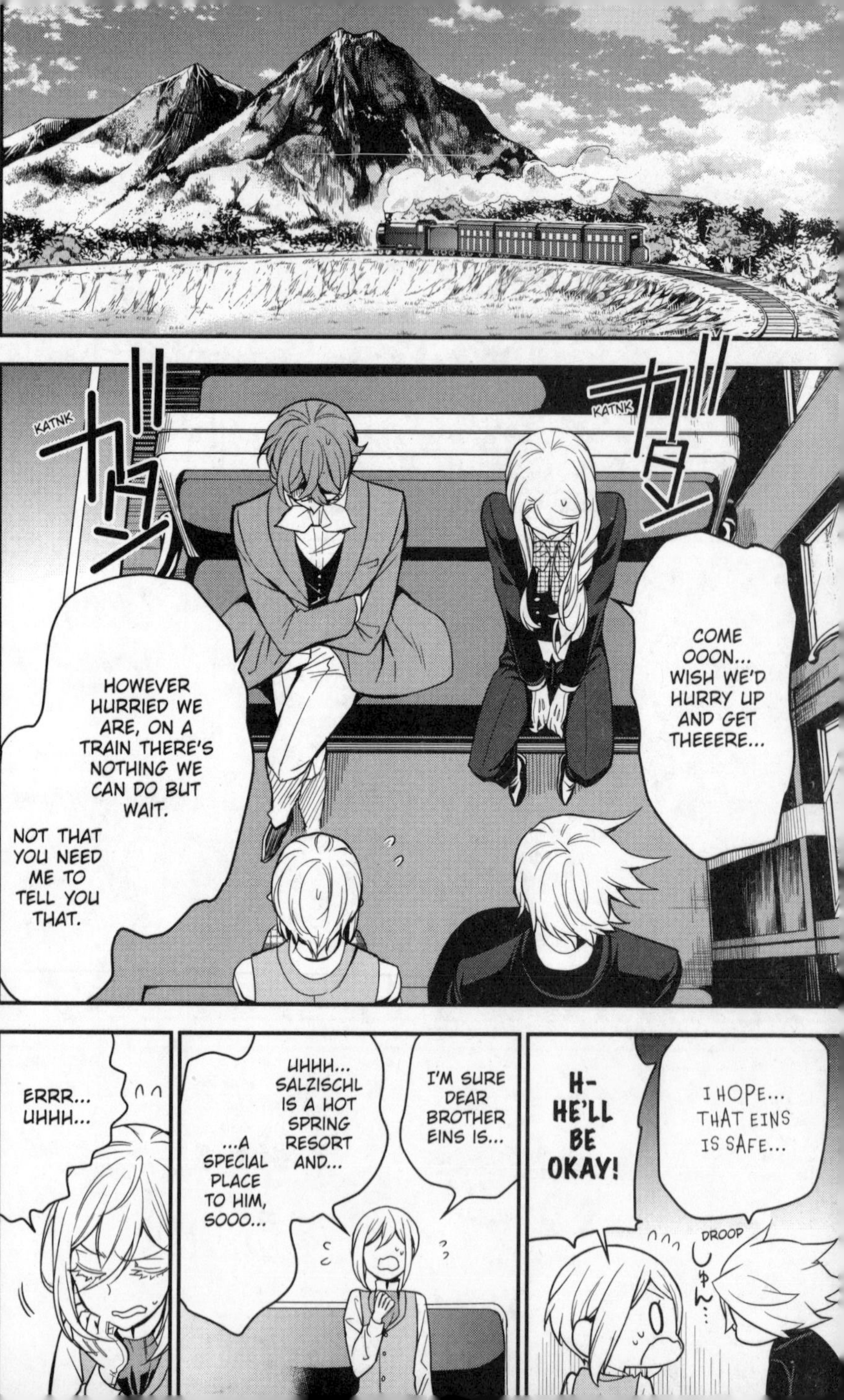
KATNK
KATNK
COME OOON... WISH WE'D HURRY UP AND GET THEEERE...
HOWEVER HURRIED WE ARE, ON A TRAIN THERE'S NOTHING WE CAN DO BUT WAIT.
NOT THAT YOU NEED ME TO TELL YOU THAT.
I HOPE... THAT EINS IS SAFE...
H- HE'LL BE OKAY!
DROOP
I'M SURE DEAR BROTHER EINS IS...
UHHH... SALZISCHL IS A HOT SPRING RESORT AND...
...A SPECIAL PLACE TO HIM, SOOO...
ERRR... UHHH...

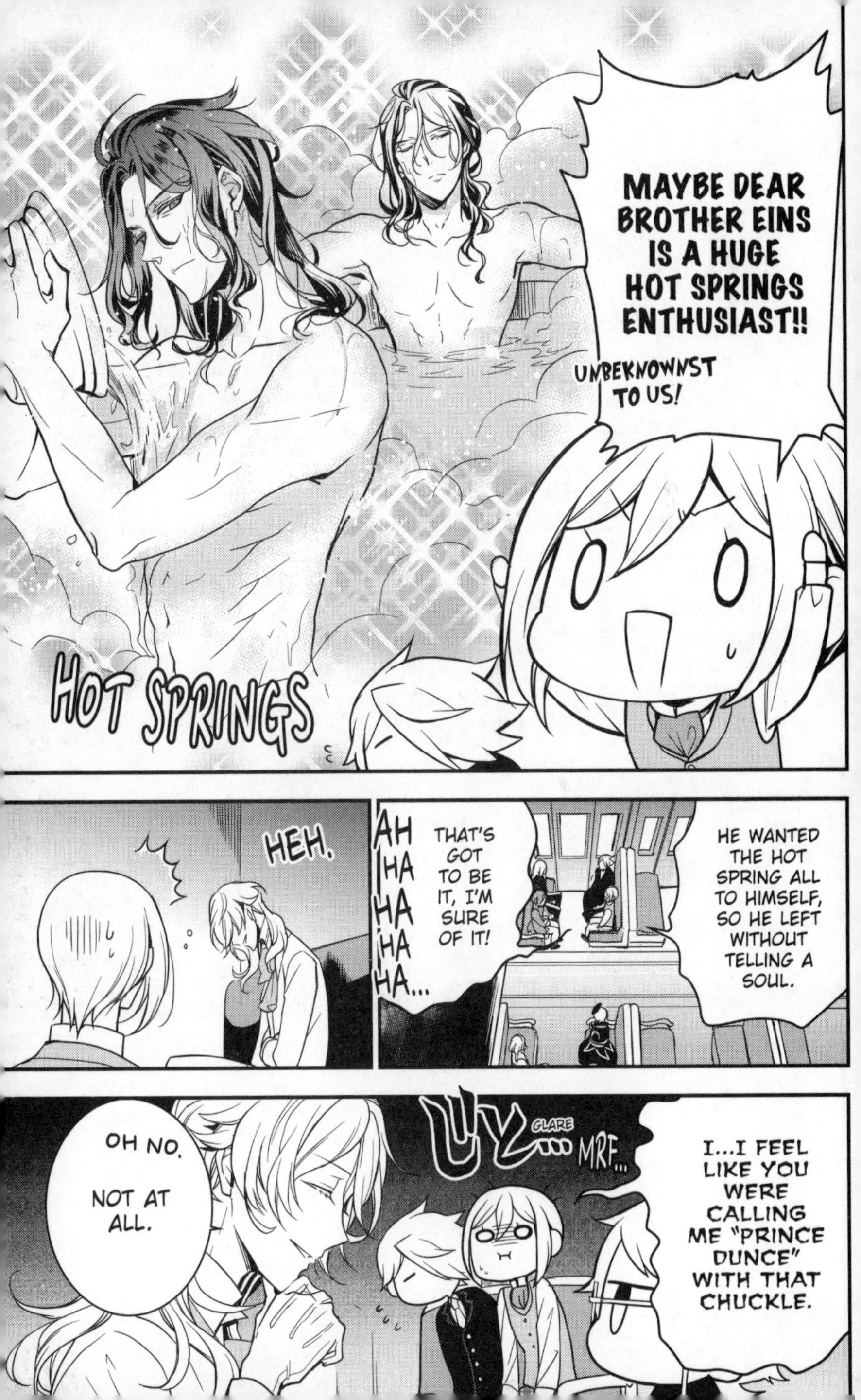
MAYBE DEAR BROTHER EINS IS A HUGE HOT SPRINGS ENTHUSIAST!!
UNBEKNOWNST TO US!
HOT SPRINGS
HE WANTED THE HOT SPRING ALL TO HIMSELF, SO HE LEFT WITHOUT TELLING A SOUL.
THAT'S GOT TO BE IT, I'M SURE OF IT!
AH HA HA HA HA...
HEH.
I...I FEEL LIKE YOU WERE CALLING ME "PRINCE DUNCE" WITH THAT CHUCKLE.
MRF...
GLARE
OH NO.
NOT AT ALL.

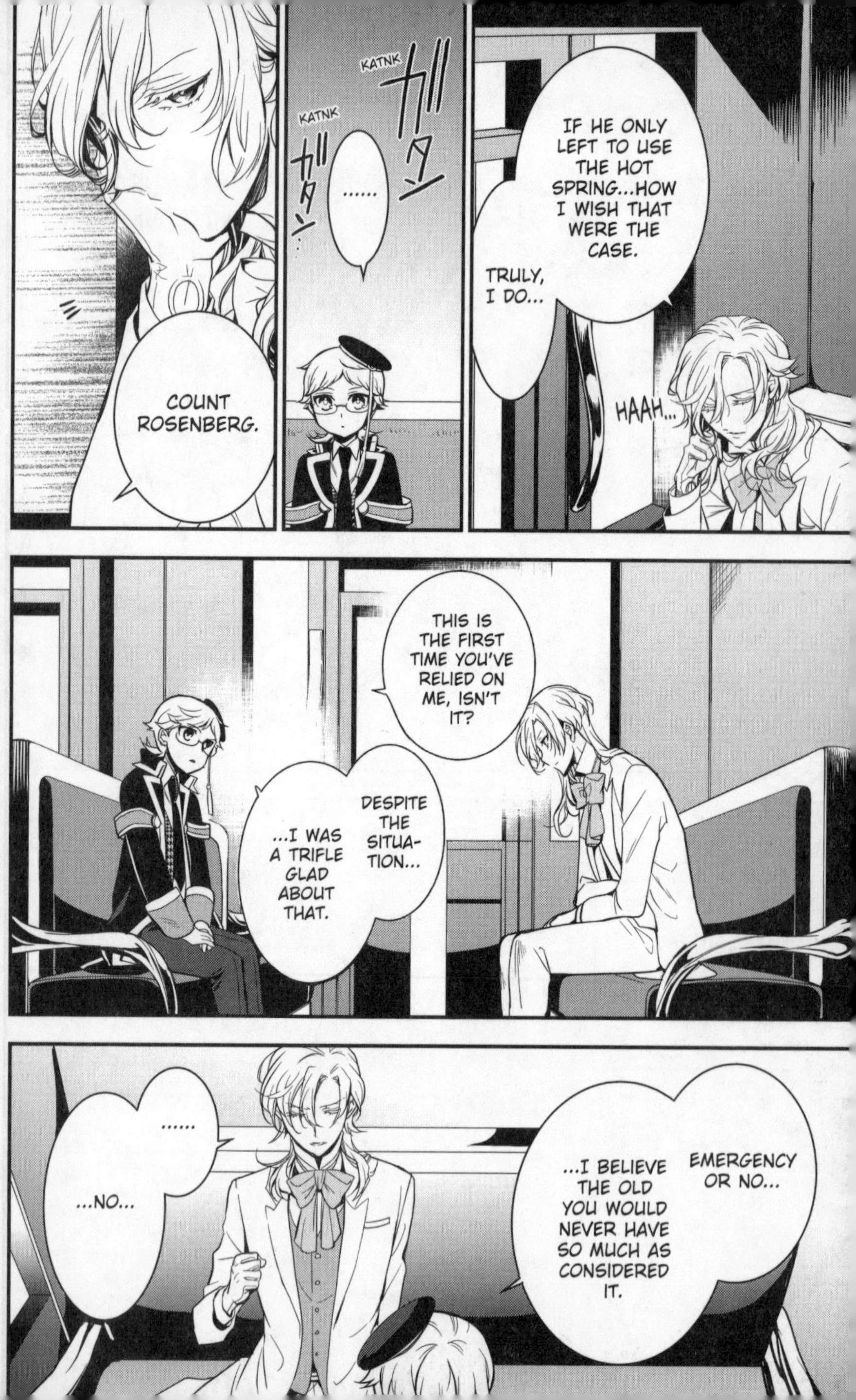
IF HE ONLY LEFT TO USE THE HOT SPRING...HOW I WISH THAT WERE THE CASE.
TRULY, I DO...
HAAH...
KATNK
KATNK
......
COUNT ROSENBERG.
THIS IS THE FIRST TIME YOU'VE RELIED ON ME, ISN'T IT?
DESPITE THE SITUA-TION...
...I WAS A TRIFLE GLAD ABOUT THAT.
EMERGENCY OR NO...
...I BELIEVE THE OLD YOU WOULD NEVER HAVE SO MUCH AS CONSIDERED IT.
......
...NO...

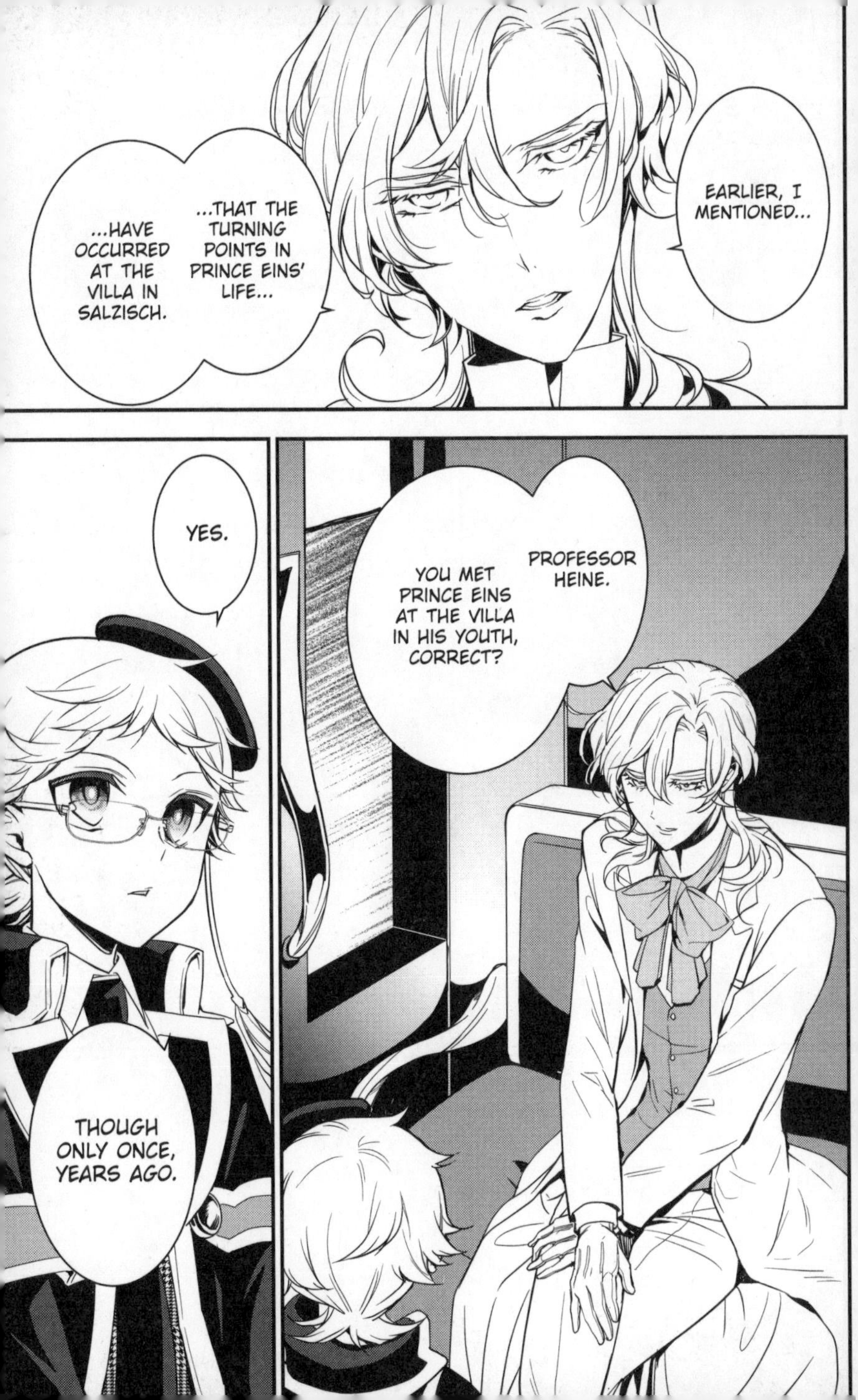
EARLIER, I MENTIONED...
...THAT THE TURNING POINTS IN PRINCE EINS' LIFE...
...HAVE OCCURRED AT THE VILLA IN SALZISCH.
PROFESSOR HEINE.
YOU MET PRINCE EINS AT THE VILLA IN HIS YOUTH, CORRECT?
YES.
THOUGH ONLY ONCE, YEARS AGO.

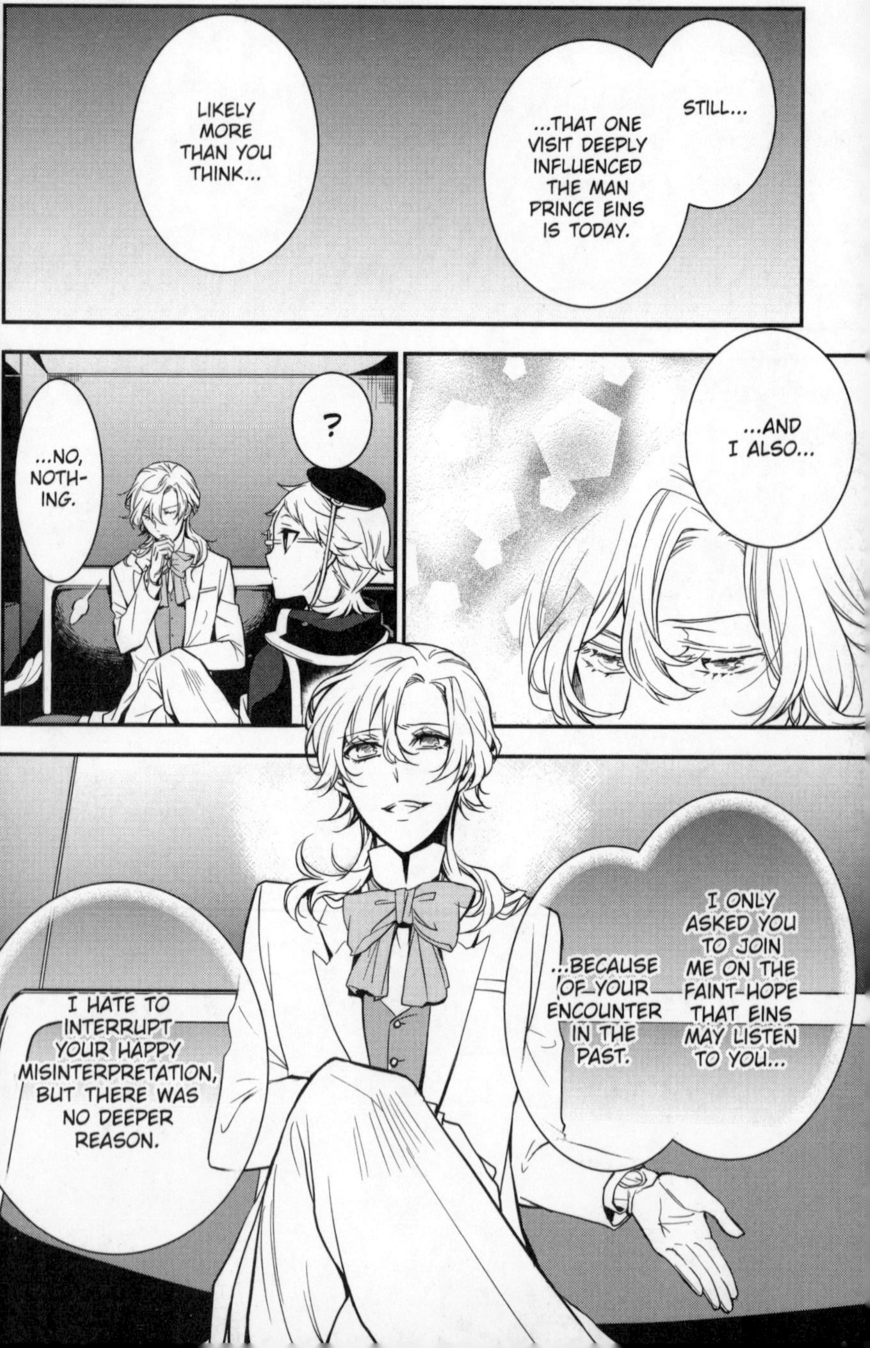
STILL...
...THAT ONE VISIT DEEPLY INFLUENCED THE MAN PRINCE EINS IS TODAY.
LIKELY MORE THAN YOU THINK...
...AND I ALSO...
?
...NO, NOTHING.
I ONLY ASKED YOU TO JOIN ME ON THE FAINT HOPE THAT EINS MAY LISTEN TO YOU...
...BECAUSE OF YOUR ENCOUNTER IN THE PAST.
I HATE TO INTERRUPT YOUR HAPPY MISINTERPRETATION, BUT THERE WAS NO DEEPER REASON.

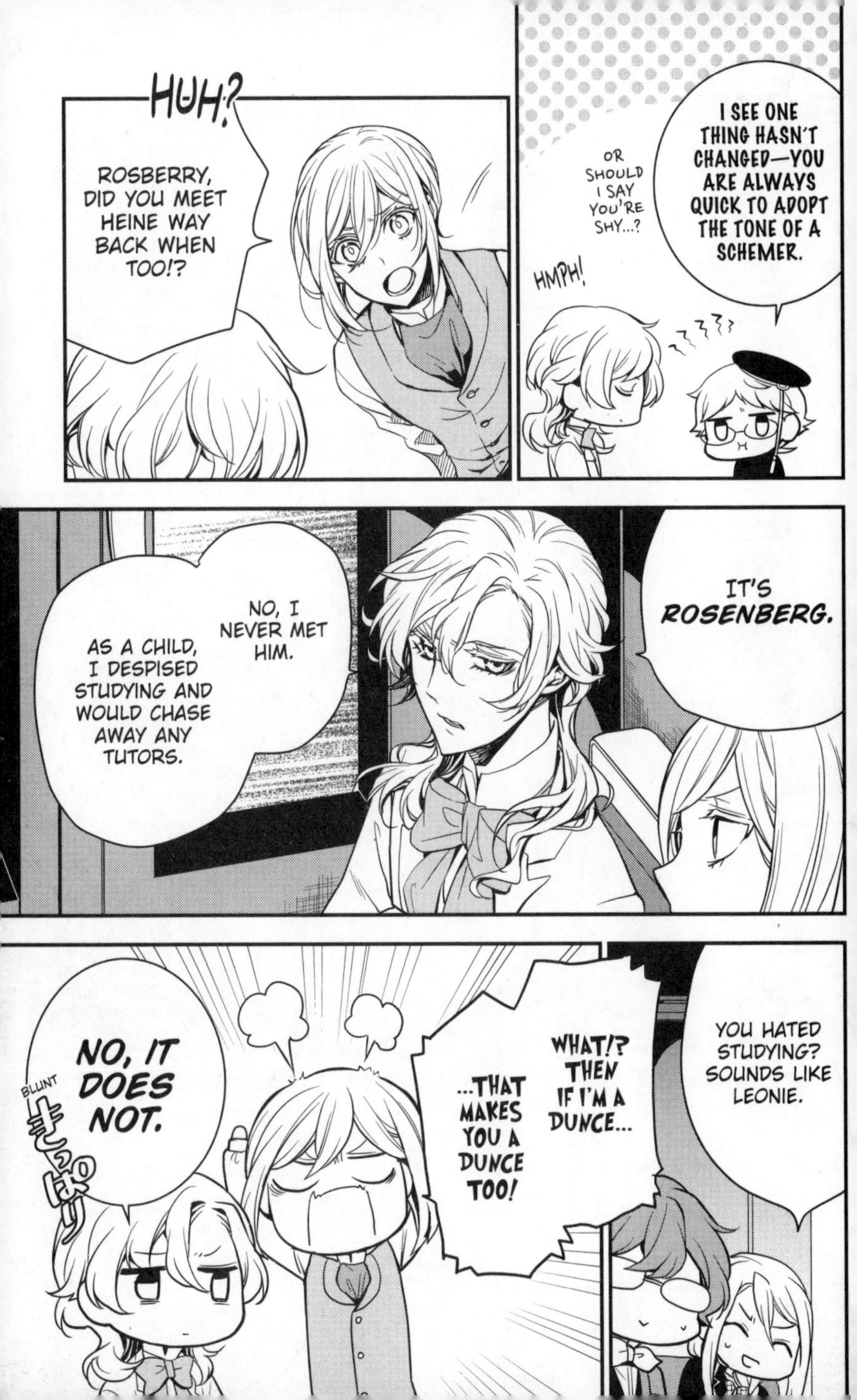
I SEE ONE THING HASN'T CHANGED—YOU ARE ALWAYS QUICK TO ADOPT THE TONE OF A SCHEMER.
OR SHOULD I SAY YOU'RE SHY...?
HMPH!
HUH!?
ROSBERRY, DID YOU MEET HEINE WAY BACK WHEN TOO!?
IT'S ROSENBERG.
NO, I NEVER MET HIM.
AS A CHILD, I DESPISED STUDYING AND WOULD CHASE AWAY ANY TUTORS.
YOU HATED STUDYING? SOUNDS LIKE LEONIE.
WHAT!? THEN IF I'M A DUNCE...
...THAT MAKES YOU A DUNCE TOO!
NO, IT DOES NOT.
BLUNT
きっぱり

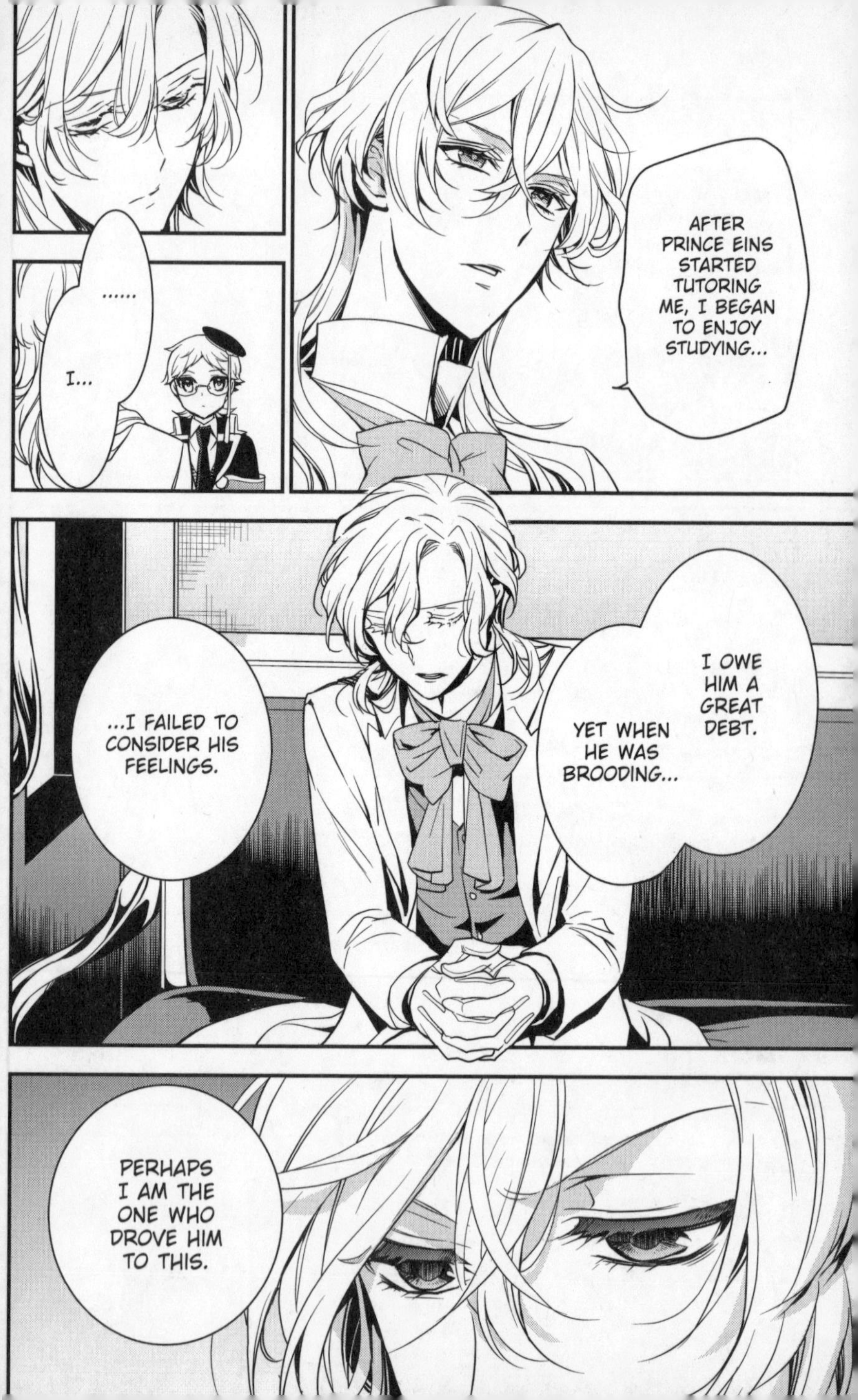

AFTER PRINCE EINS STARTED TUTORING ME, I BEGAN TO ENJOY STUDYING...
...... I...
I OWE HIM A GREAT DEBT.
YET WHEN HE WAS BROODING...
...I FAILED TO CONSIDER HIS FEELINGS.
PERHAPS I AM THE ONE WHO DROVE HIM TO THIS.

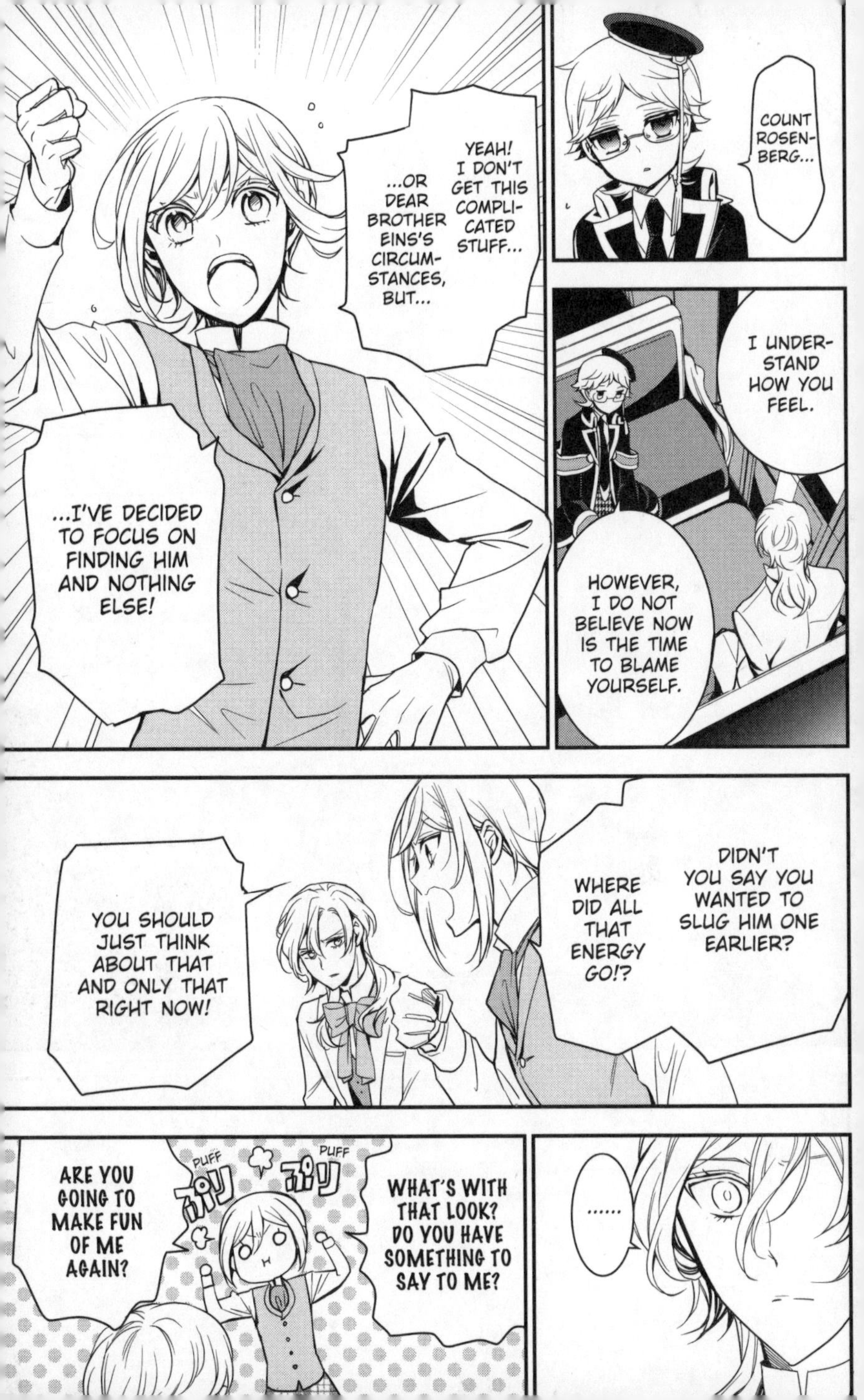
COUNT ROSENBERG...
I UNDERSTAND HOW YOU FEEL.
HOWEVER, I DO NOT BELIEVE NOW IS THE TIME TO BLAME YOURSELF.
YEAH! I DON'T GET THIS COMPLICATED STUFF...
...OR DEAR BROTHER EINS'S CIRCUMSTANCES, BUT...
...I'VE DECIDED TO FOCUS ON FINDING HIM AND NOTHING ELSE!
DIDN'T YOU SAY YOU WANTED TO SLUG HIM ONE EARLIER?
WHERE DID ALL THAT ENERGY GO!?
YOU SHOULD JUST THINK ABOUT THAT AND ONLY THAT RIGHT NOW!
......
WHAT'S WITH THAT LOOK? DO YOU HAVE SOMETHING TO SAY TO ME?
PUFF
PUFF
ARE YOU GOING TO MAKE FUN OF ME AGAIN?

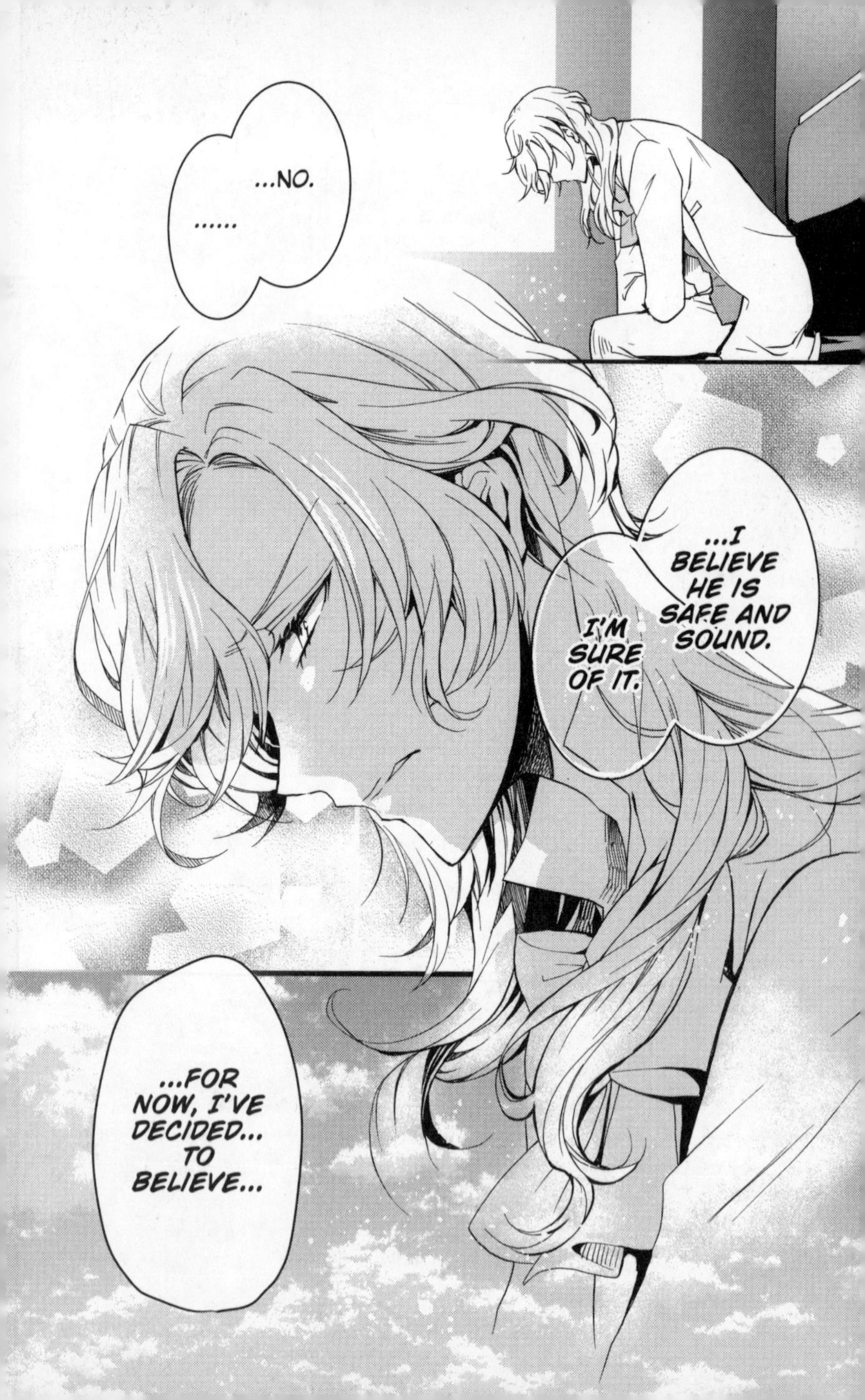
...NO.
......
...I BELIEVE HE IS SAFE AND SOUND.
I'M SURE OF IT.
...FOR NOW, I'VE DECIDED... TO BELIEVE...

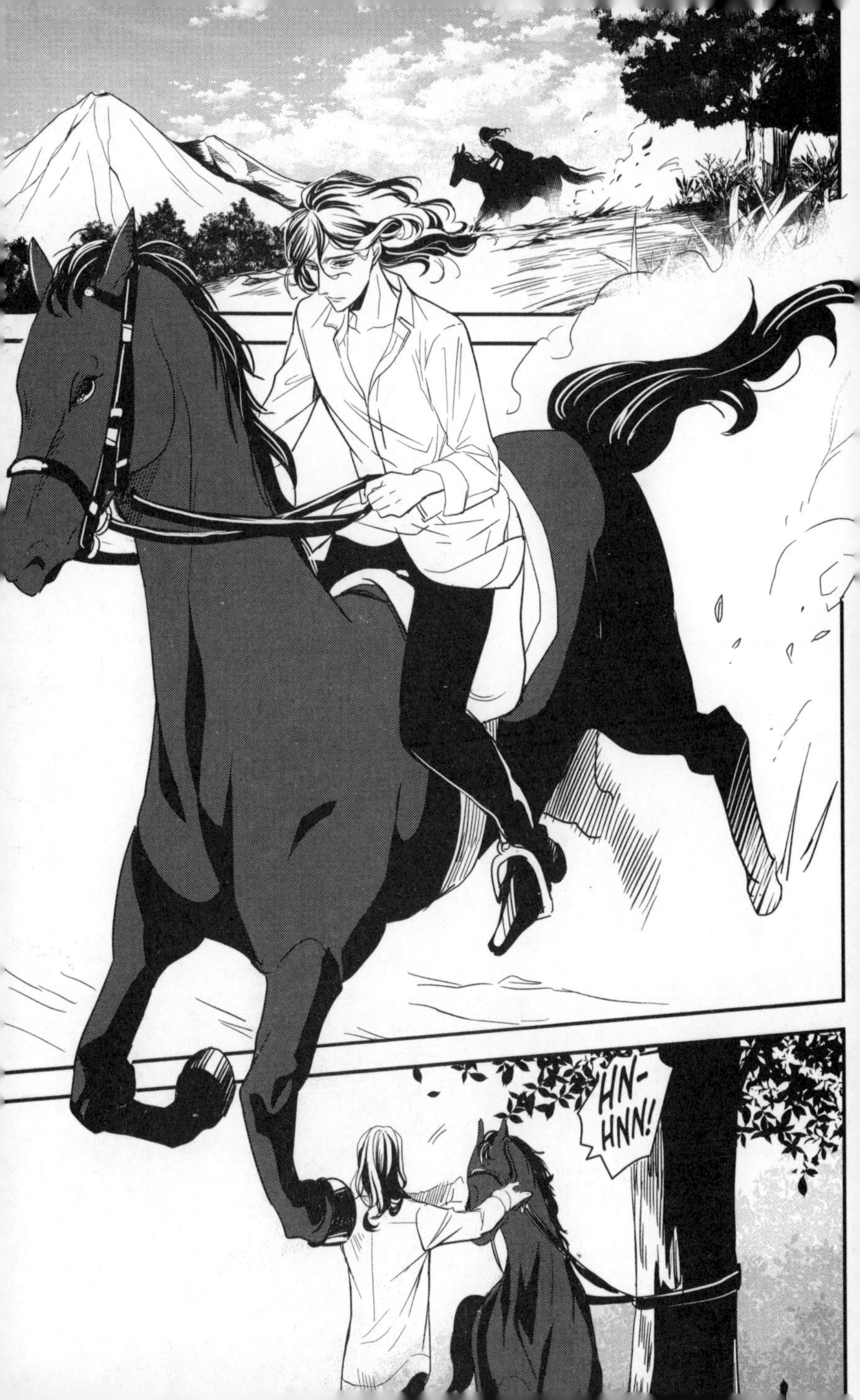
HN-
HNN!

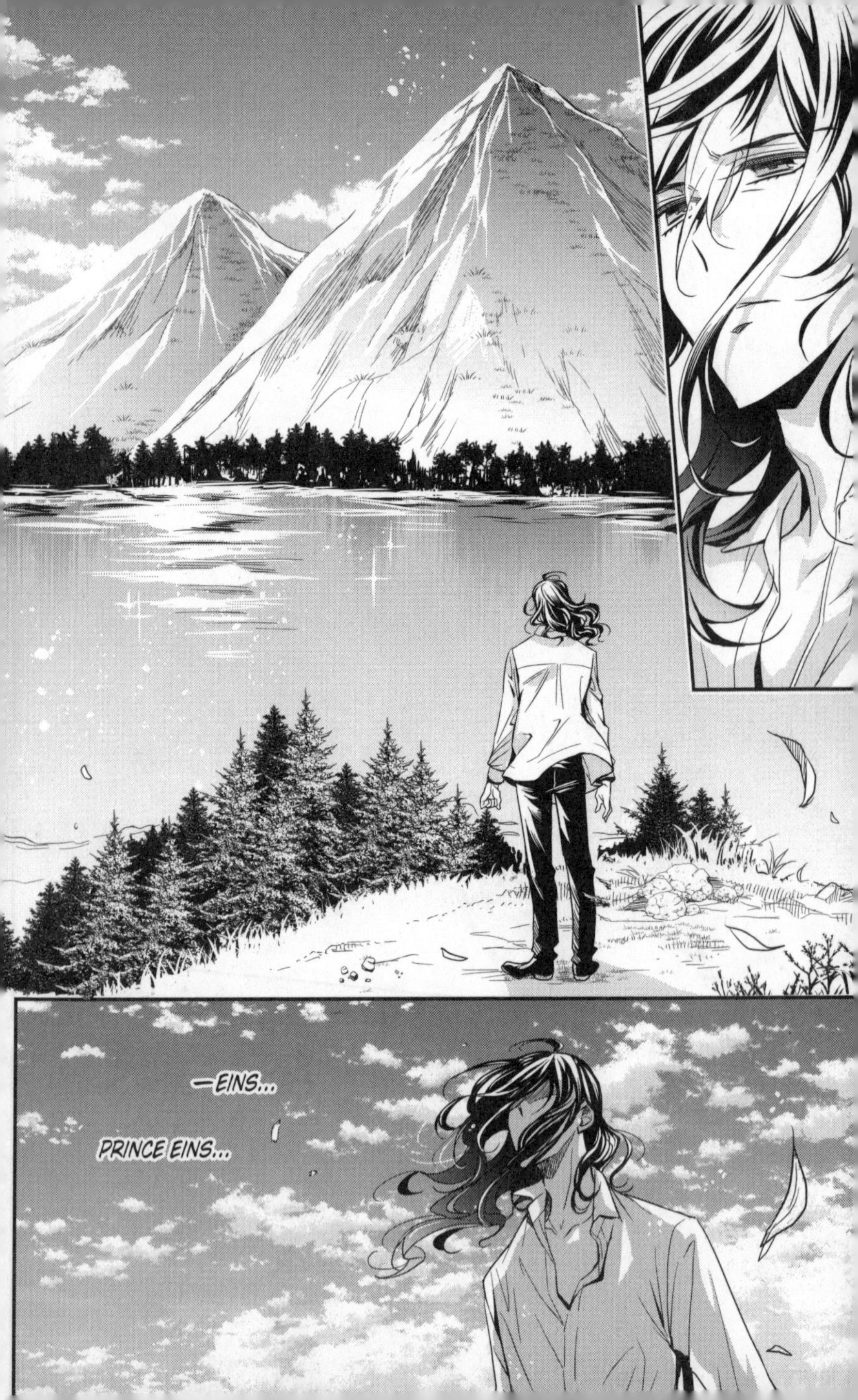
—EINS...
PRINCE EINS...

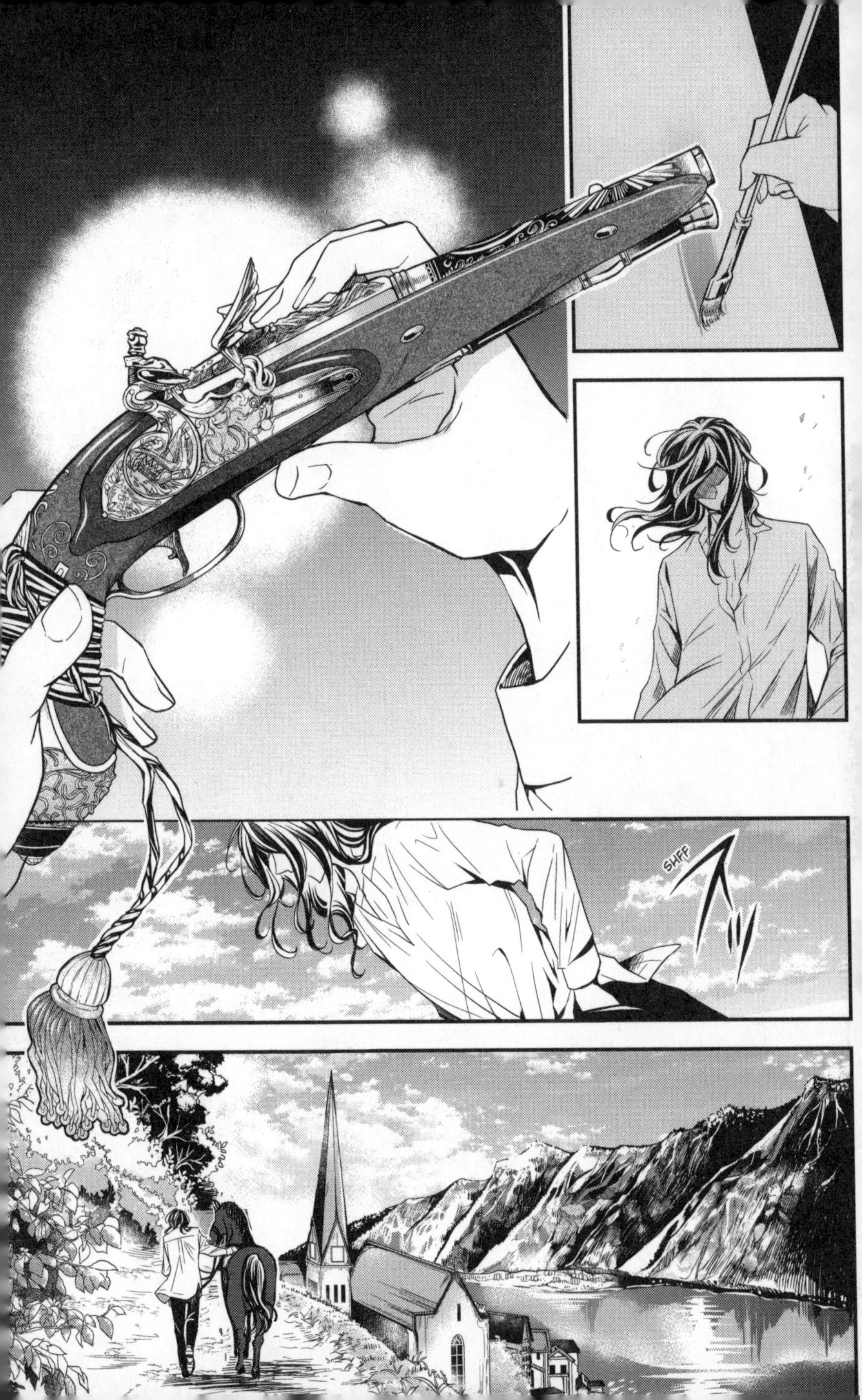
SHFF

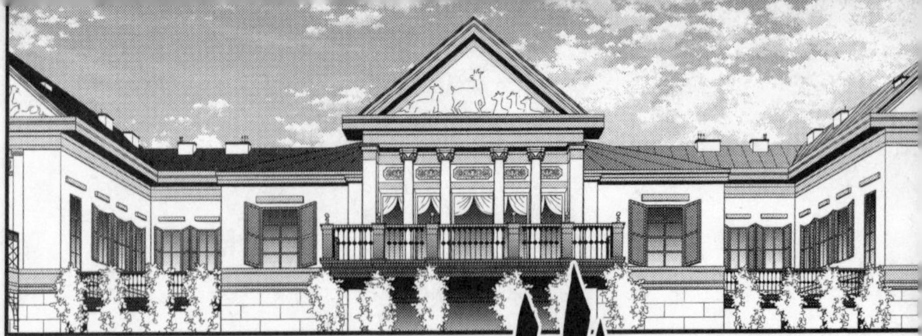

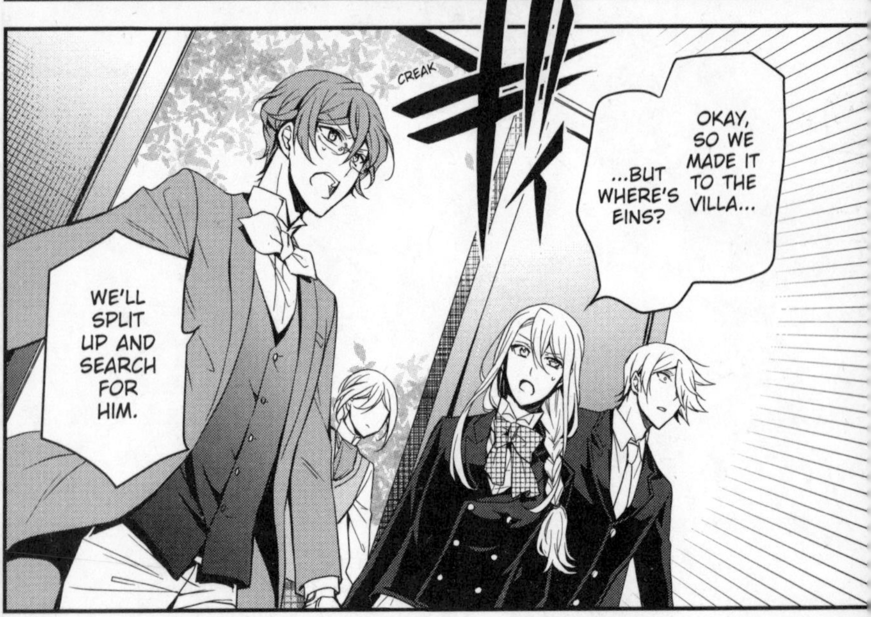
OKAY, SO WE MADE IT TO THE VILLA...
...BUT WHERE'S EINS?
CREAK
WE'LL SPLIT UP AND SEARCH FOR HIM.

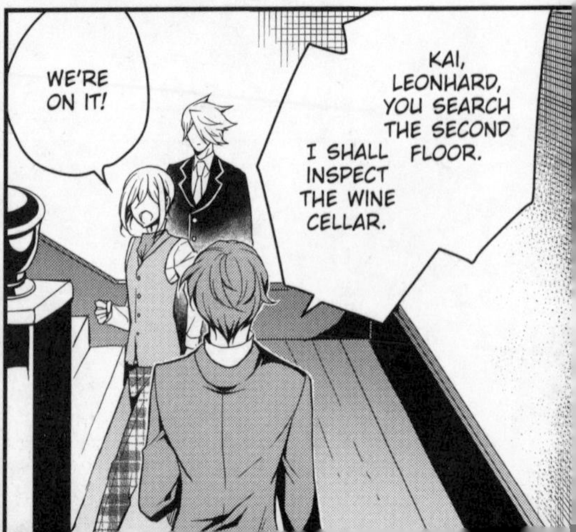
KAI, LEONHARD, YOU SEARCH THE SECOND FLOOR.
I SHALL INSPECT THE WINE CELLAR.
WE'RE ON IT!

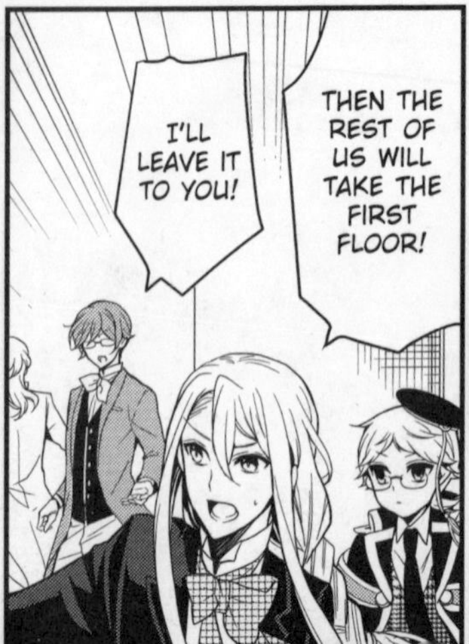
THEN THE REST OF US WILL TAKE THE FIRST FLOOR!
I'LL LEAVE IT TO YOU!

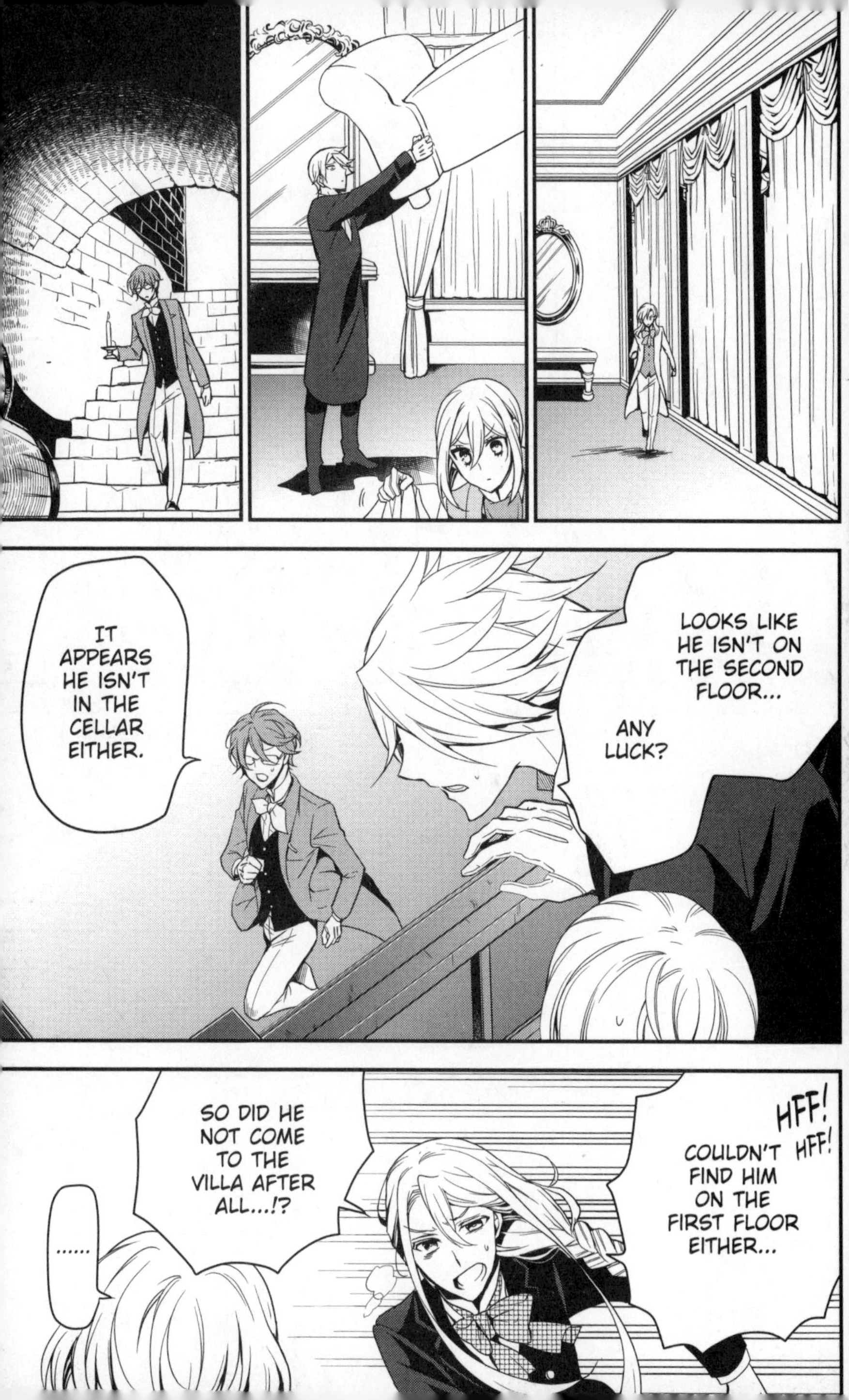
LOOKS LIKE HE ISN'T ON THE SECOND FLOOR...
ANY LUCK?
IT APPEARS HE ISN'T IN THE CELLAR EITHER.
HFF! HFF!
COULDN'T FIND HIM ON THE FIRST FLOOR EITHER...
SO DID HE NOT COME TO THE VILLA AFTER ALL...!?
......

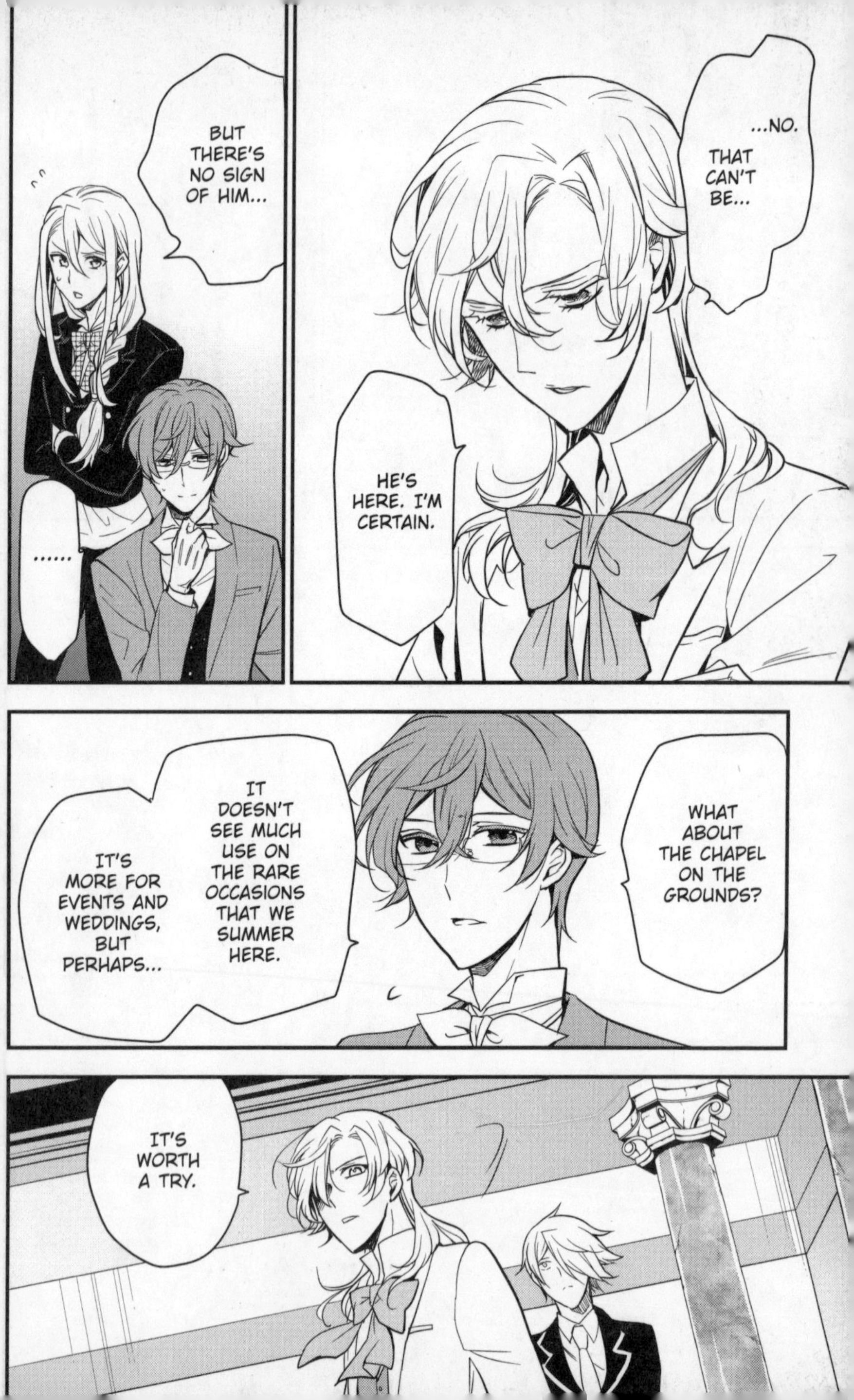
...NO.
THAT CAN'T BE...
HE'S HERE. I'M CERTAIN.
BUT THERE'S NO SIGN OF HIM...
......
WHAT ABOUT THE CHAPEL ON THE GROUNDS?
IT DOESN'T SEE MUCH USE ON THE RARE OCCASIONS THAT WE SUMMER HERE.
IT'S MORE FOR EVENTS AND WEDDINGS, BUT PERHAPS...
IT'S WORTH A TRY.

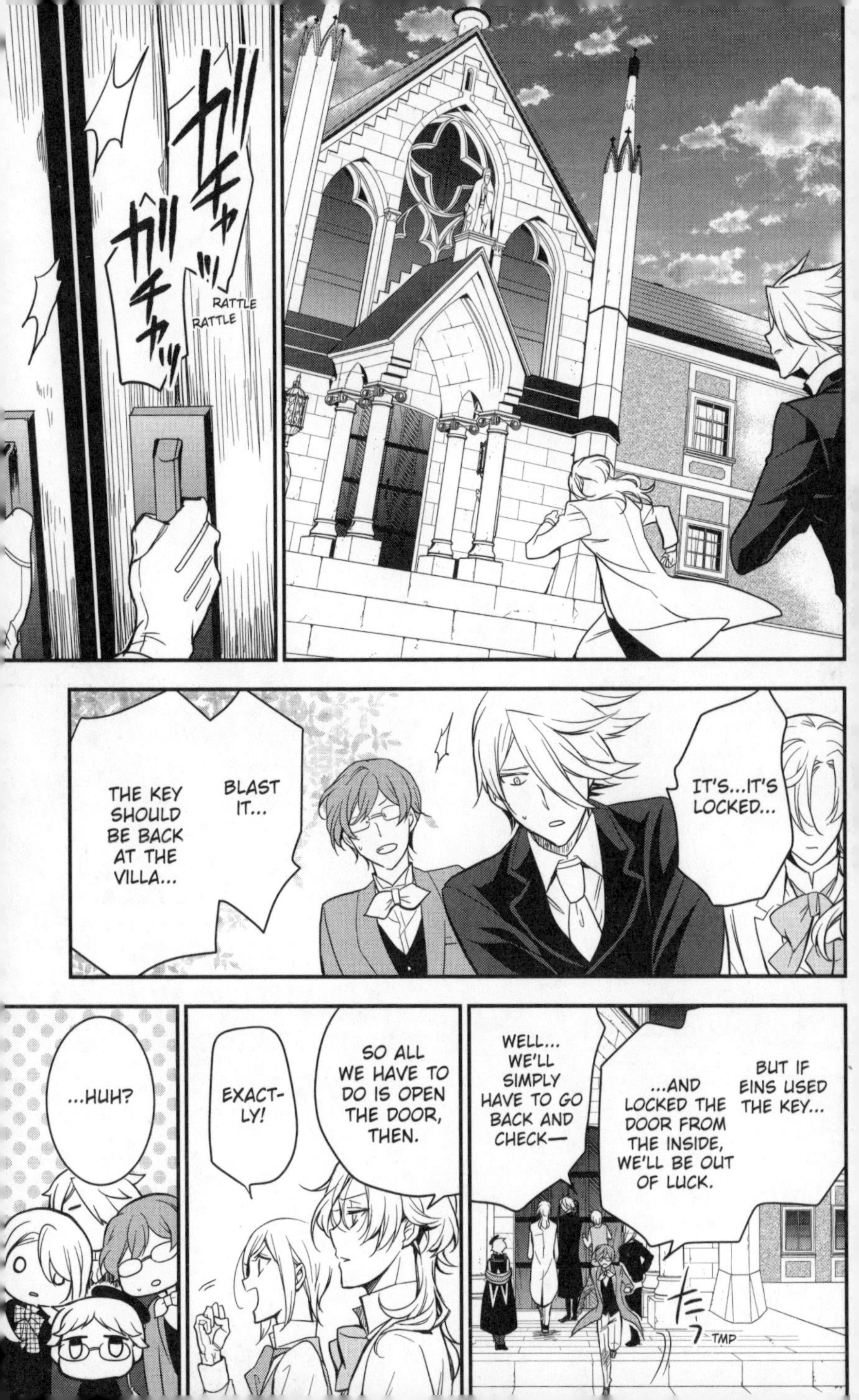
RATTLE
RATTLE
IT'S...IT'S LOCKED...
BLAST IT...
THE KEY SHOULD BE BACK AT THE VILLA...
BUT IF EINS USED THE KEY...
...AND LOCKED THE DOOR FROM THE INSIDE, WE'LL BE OUT OF LUCK.
WELL... WE'LL SIMPLY HAVE TO GO BACK AND CHECK—
TMP
SO ALL WE HAVE TO DO IS OPEN THE DOOR, THEN.
EXACT-LY!
...HUH?

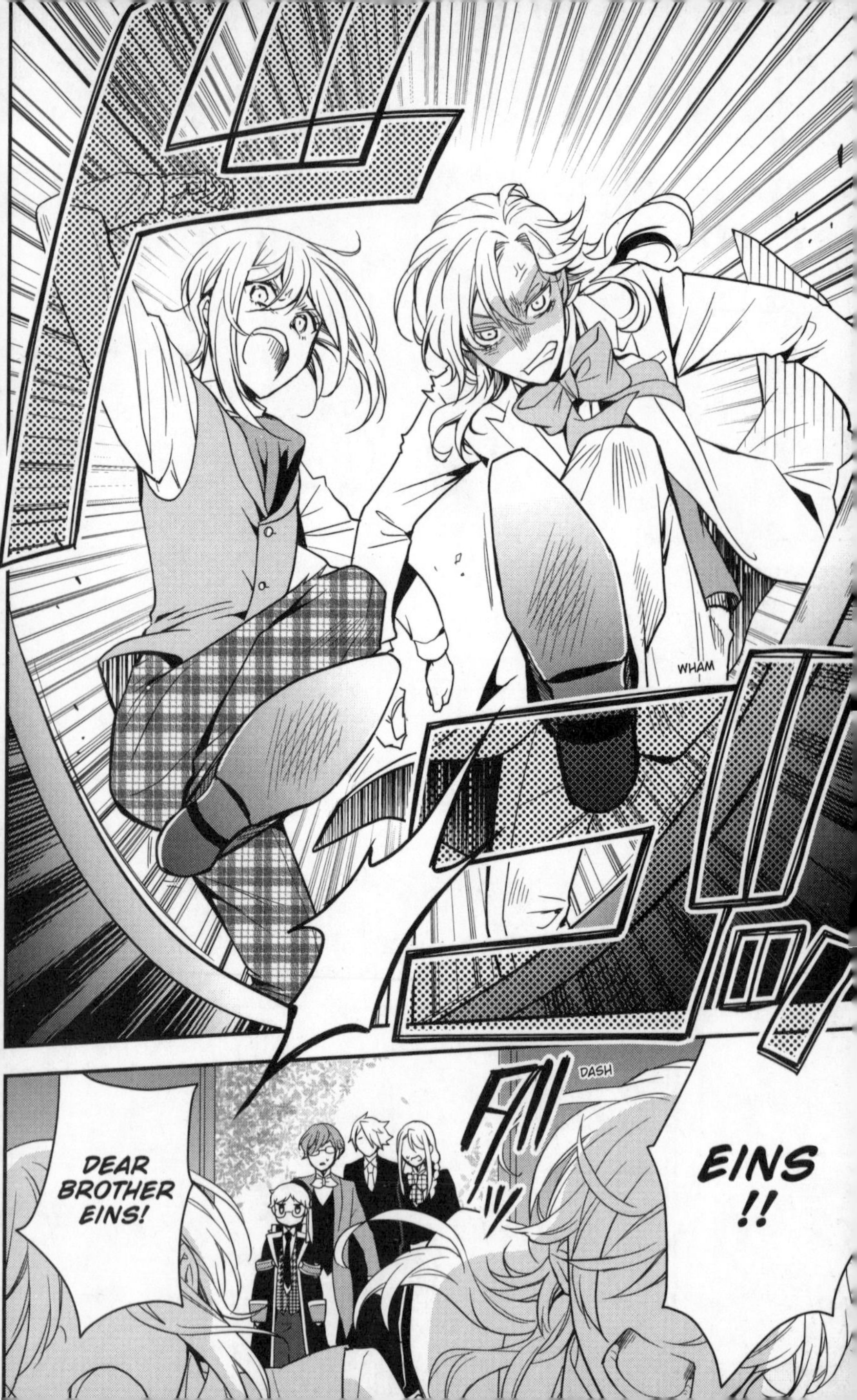
WHAM
DASH
EINS !!
DEAR BROTHER EINS!

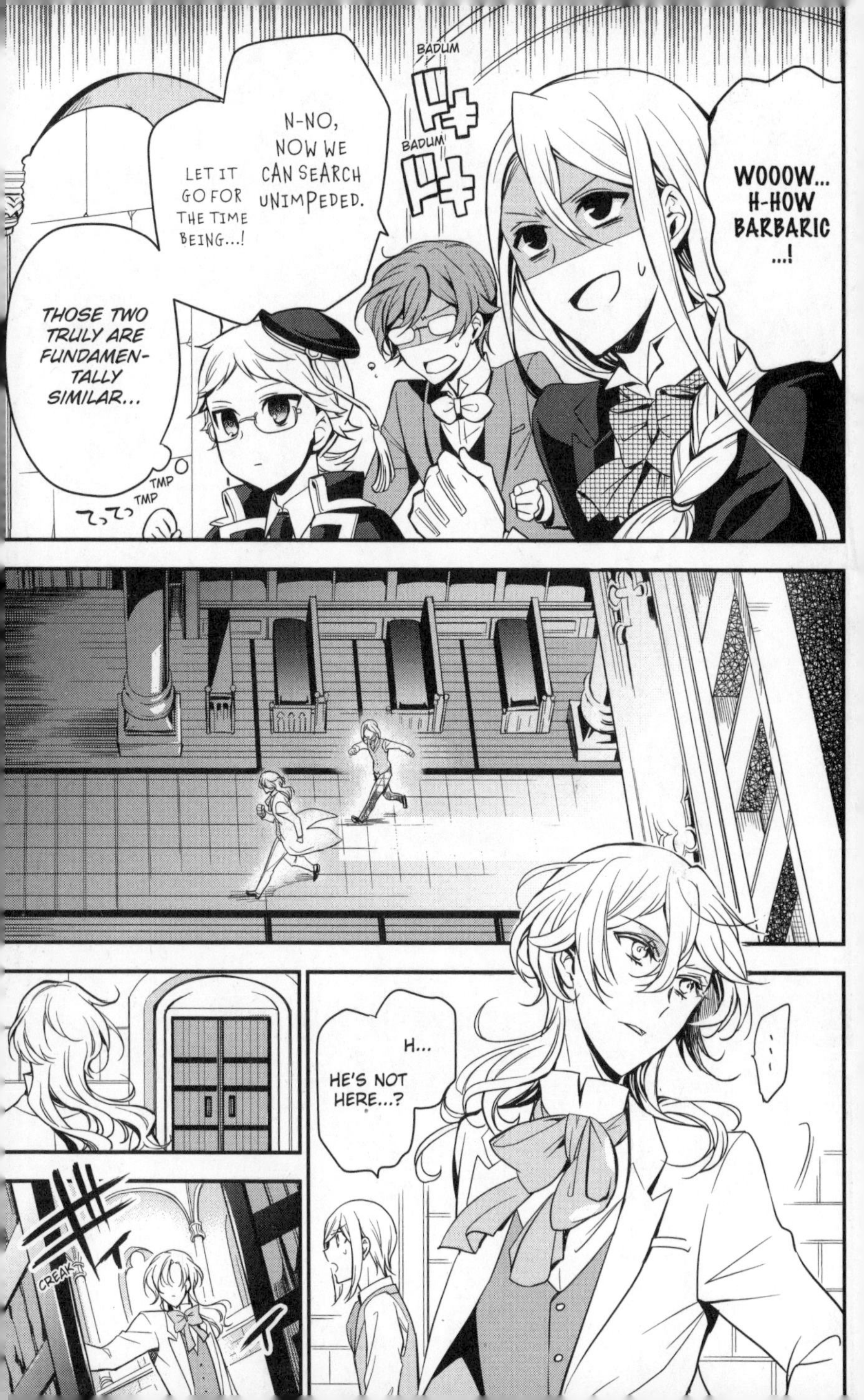
WOOOW... H-HOW BARBARIC ...!
BADUM
ドキ
BADUM
ドキ
N-NO, NOW WE CAN SEARCH UNIMPEDED.
LET IT GO FOR THE TIME BEING...!
THOSE TWO TRULY ARE FUNDAMEN-TALLY SIMILAR...
TMP TMP
てってっ
...
H... HE'S NOT HERE...?
CREAK

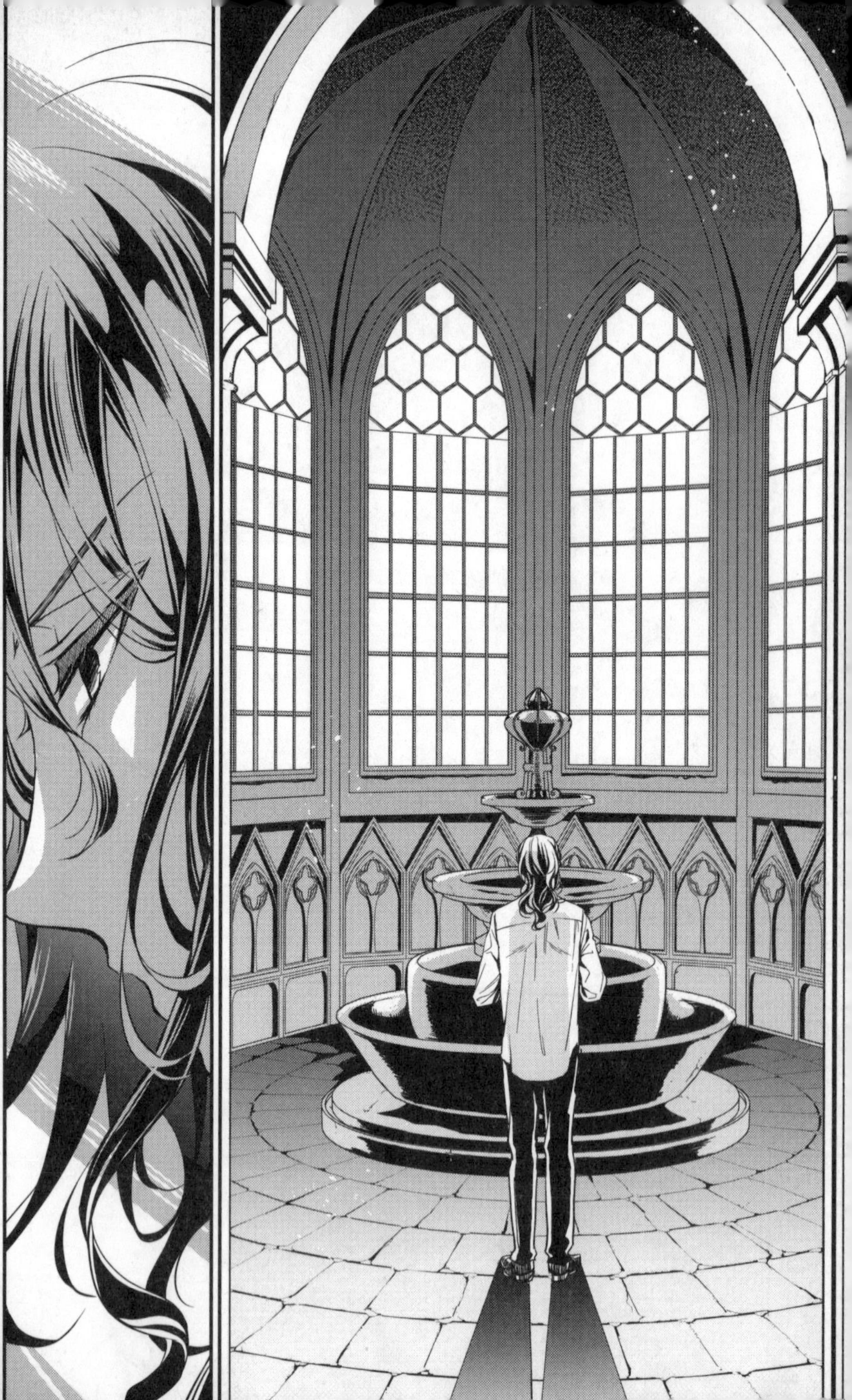

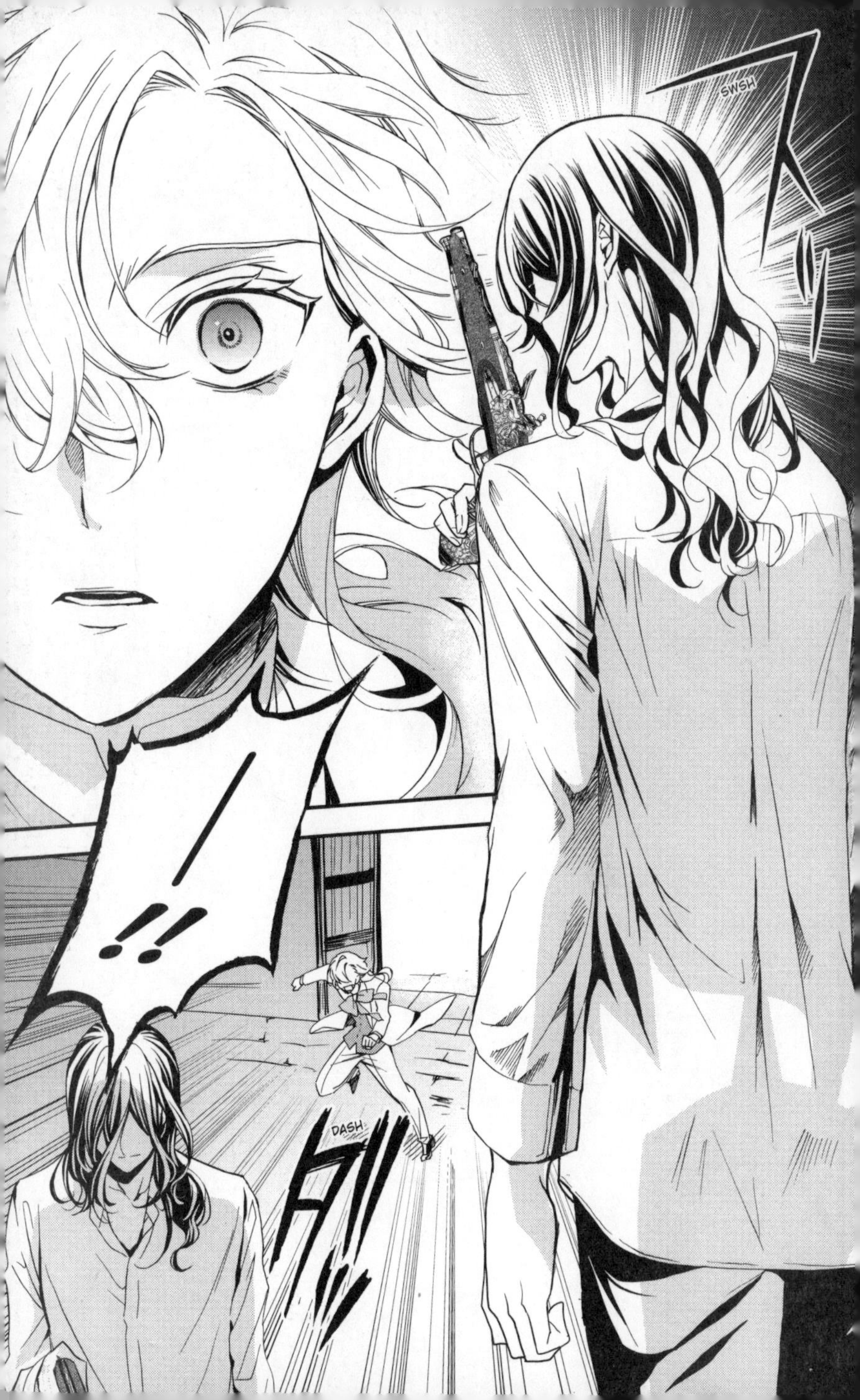
SWSH
—!!
DASH

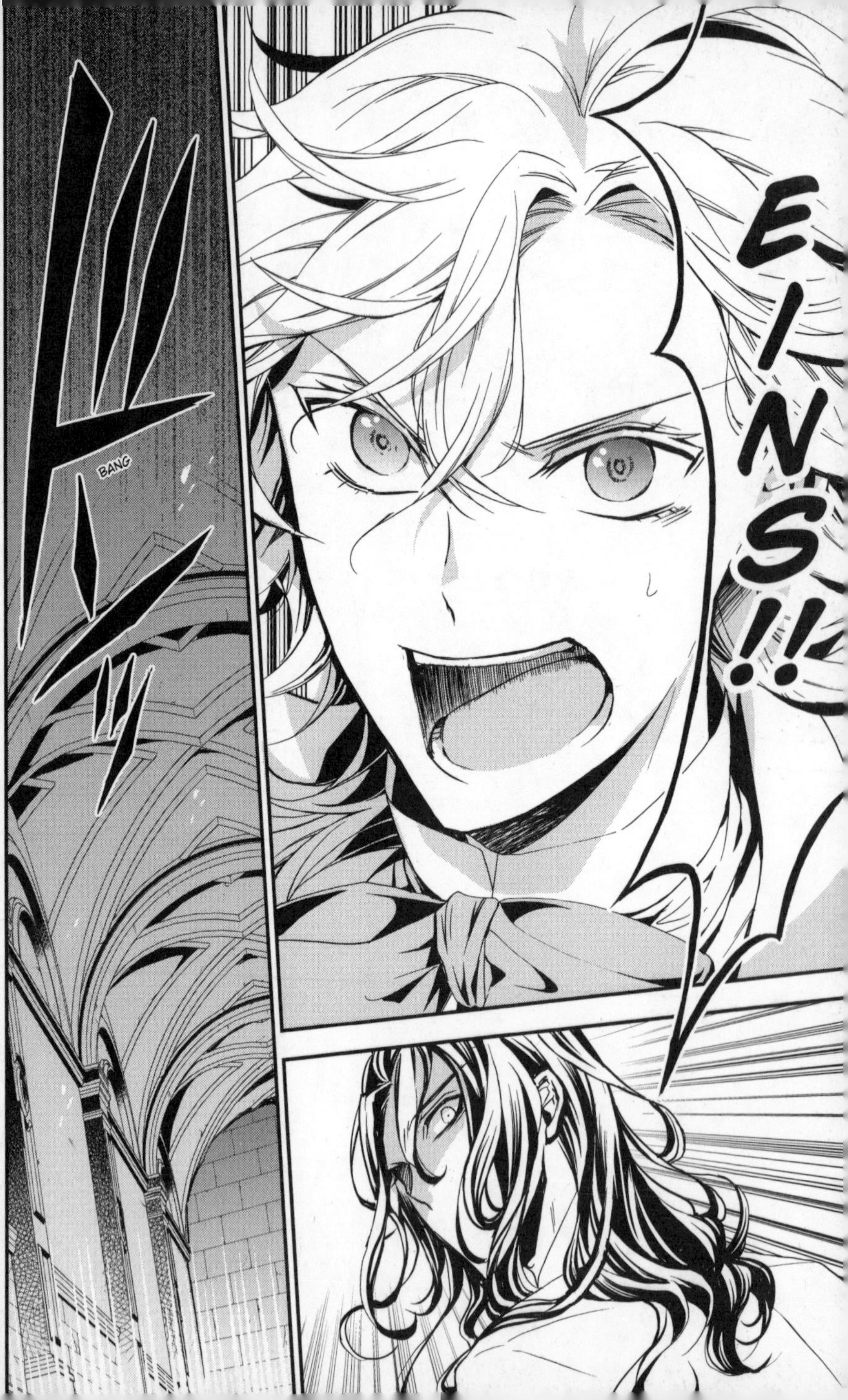
E-I-N-S!!
BANG

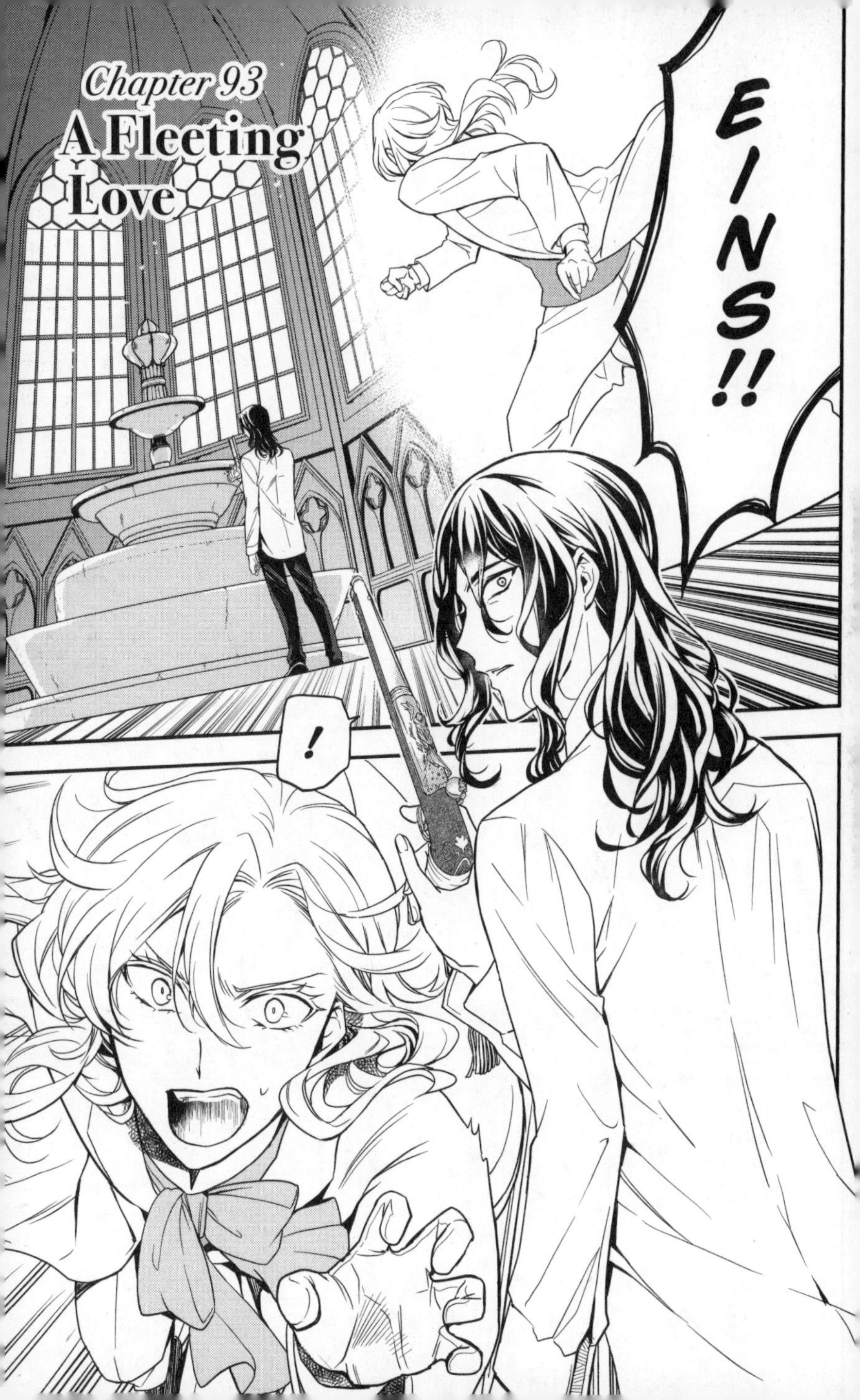
Chapter 93
A Fleeting Love
EINS!!
!

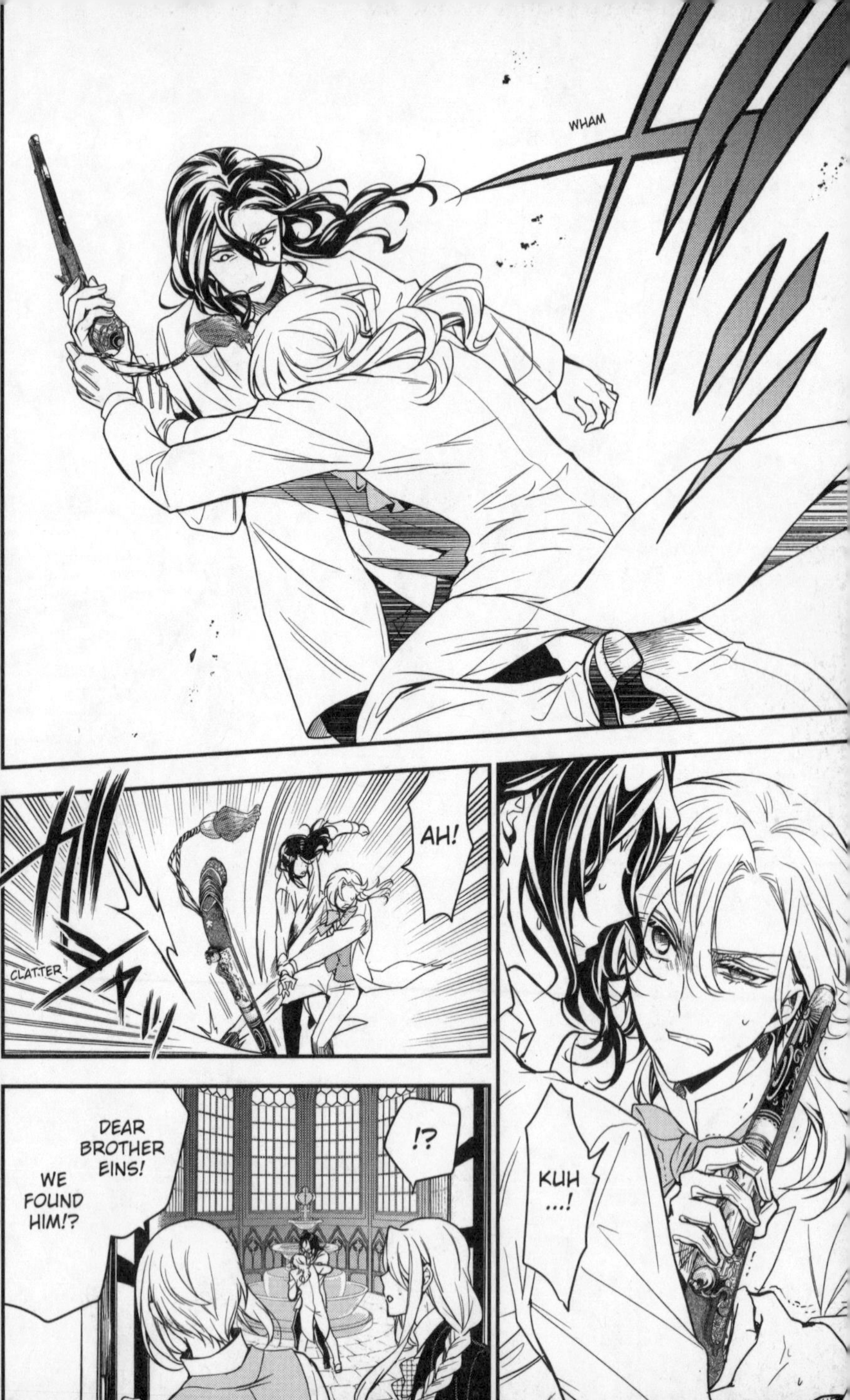
WHAM
KUH ...!
AH!
CLATTER
!?
DEAR BROTHER EINS!
WE FOUND HIM!?

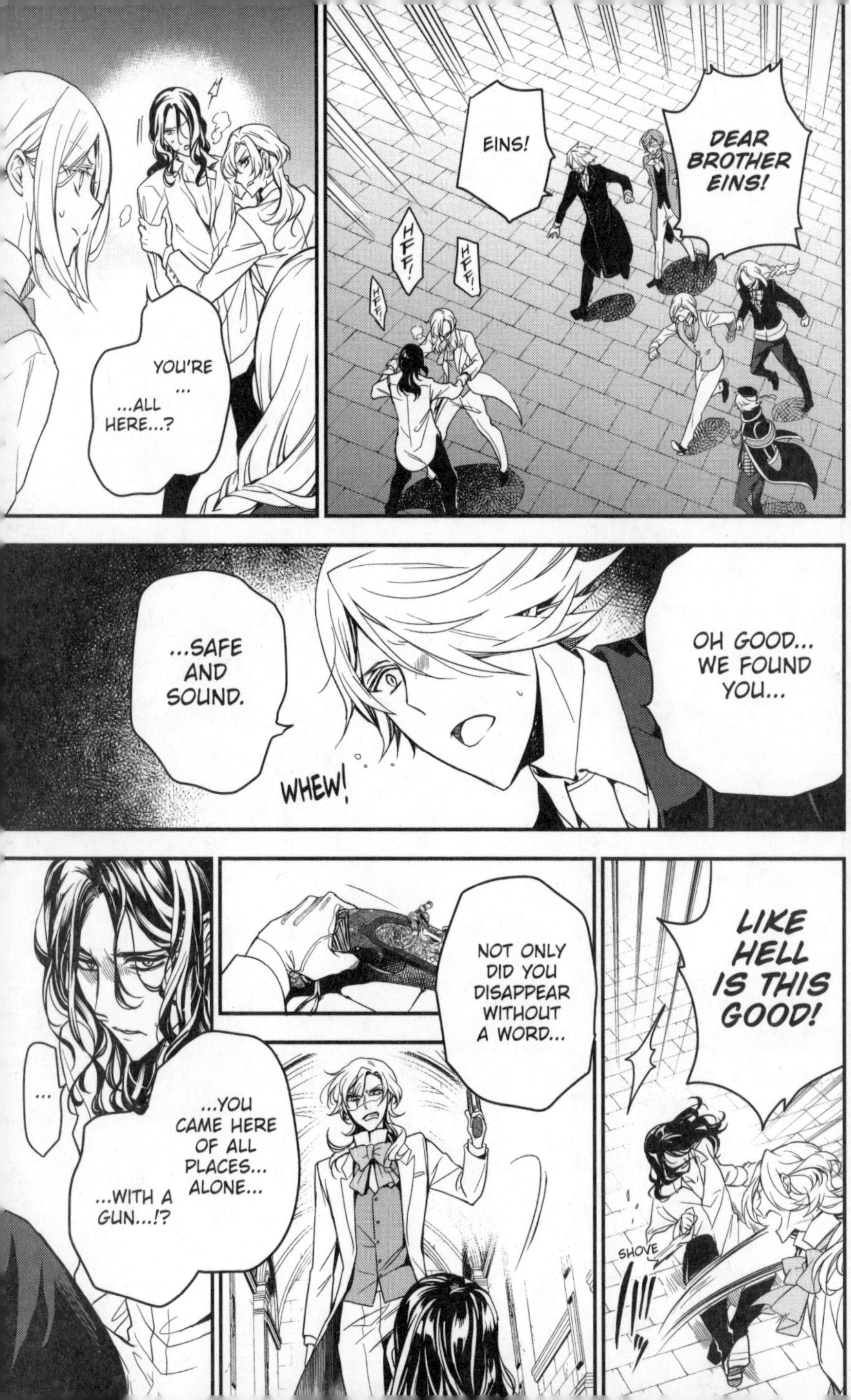
DEAR BROTHER EINS!
EINS!
HFF!
HFF!
HFF!
YOU'RE ...
...ALL HERE...?
OH GOOD... WE FOUND YOU...
WHEW!
...SAFE AND SOUND.
LIKE HELL IS THIS GOOD!
SHOVE
NOT ONLY DID YOU DISAPPEAR WITHOUT A WORD...
...YOU CAME HERE OF ALL PLACES... ALONE...
...WITH A GUN...!?
...

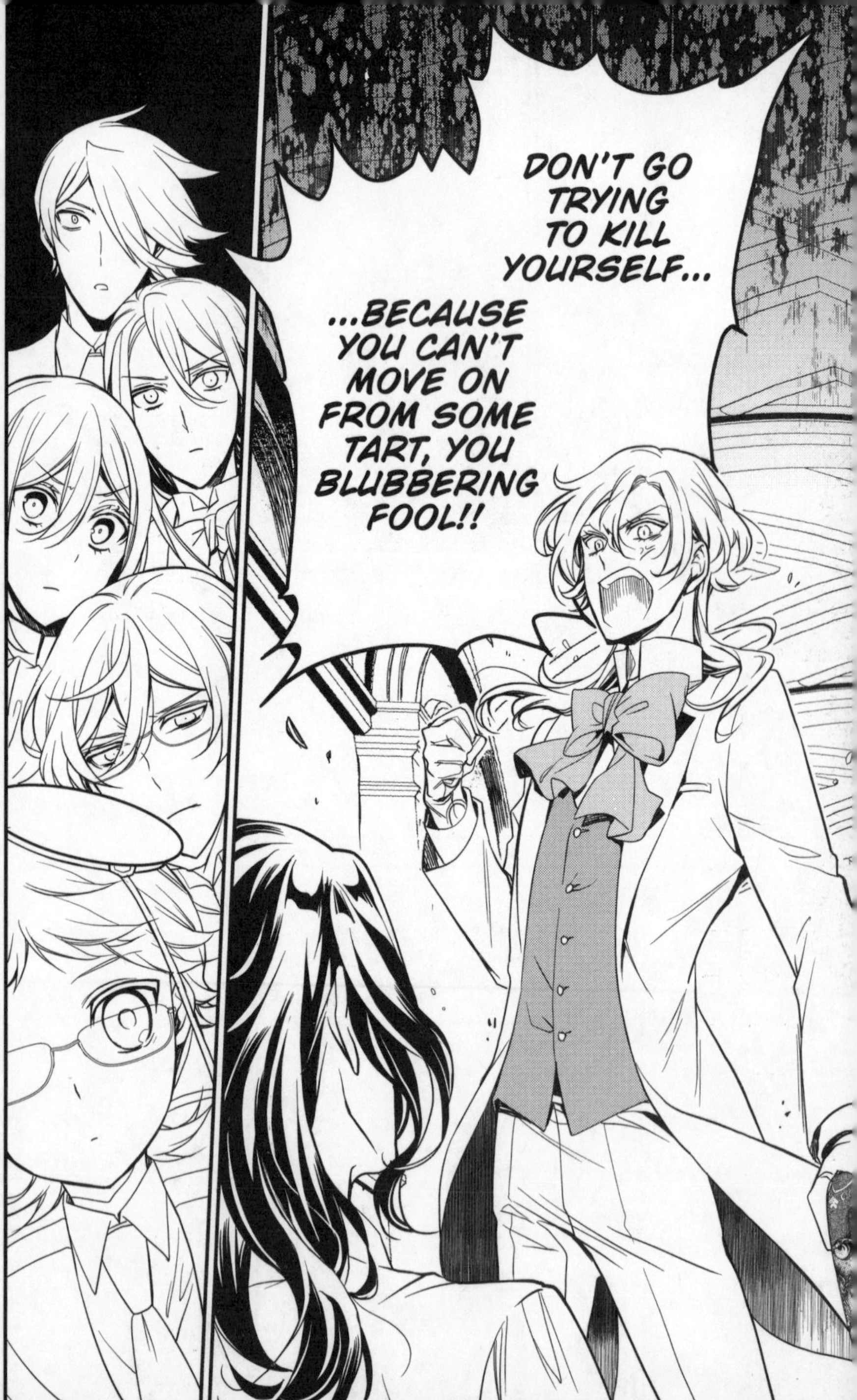
DON'T GO TRYING TO KILL YOURSELF...
...BECAUSE YOU CAN'T MOVE ON FROM SOME TART, YOU BLUBBERING FOOL!!

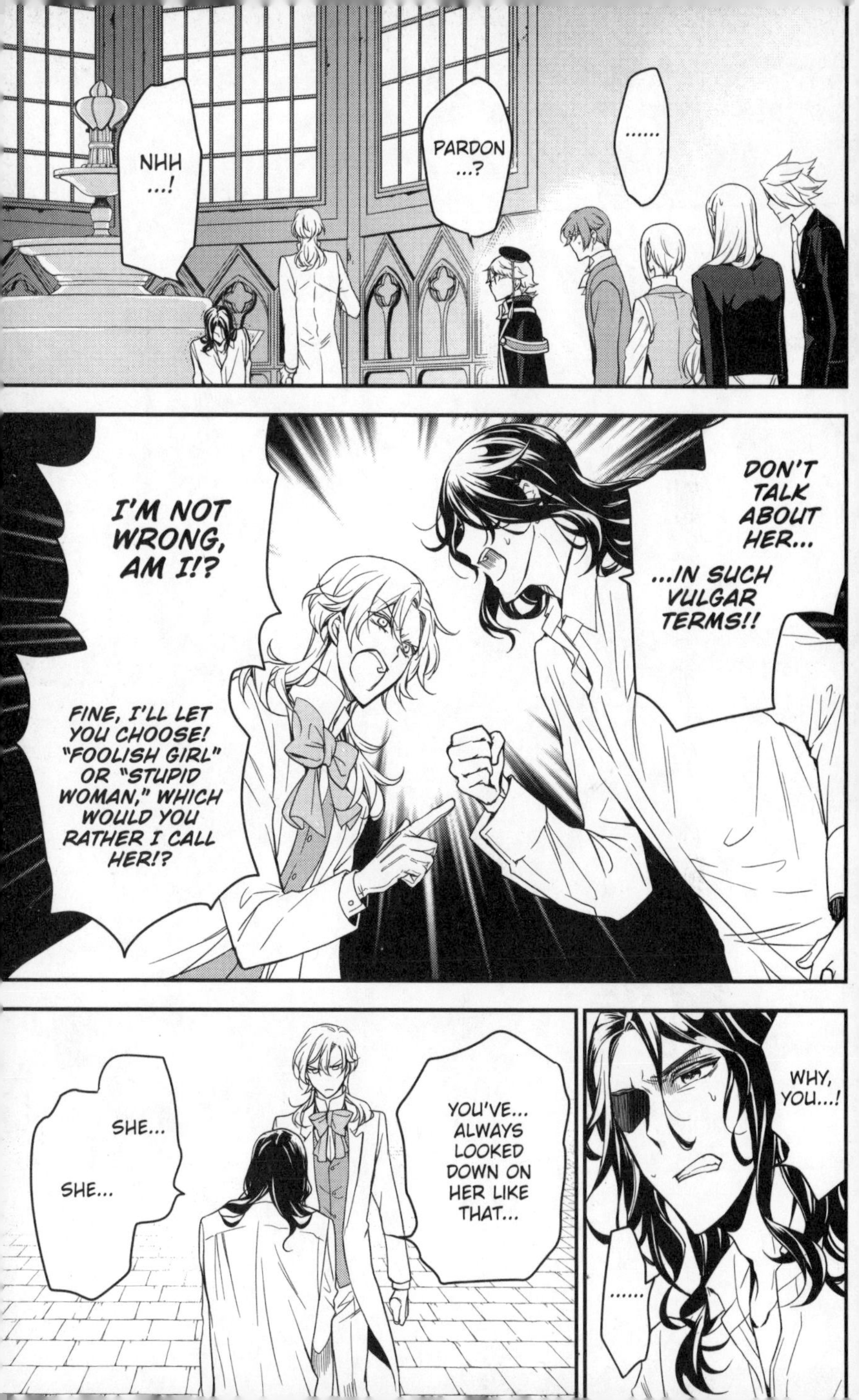
......
PARDON ...?
NHH ...!
DON'T TALK ABOUT HER...
...IN SUCH VULGAR TERMS!!
I'M NOT WRONG, AM I!?
FINE, I'LL LET YOU CHOOSE! "FOOLISH GIRL" OR "STUPID WOMAN," WHICH WOULD YOU RATHER I CALL HER!?
WHY, YOU...!
......
YOU'VE... ALWAYS LOOKED DOWN ON HER LIKE THAT...
SHE...
SHE...

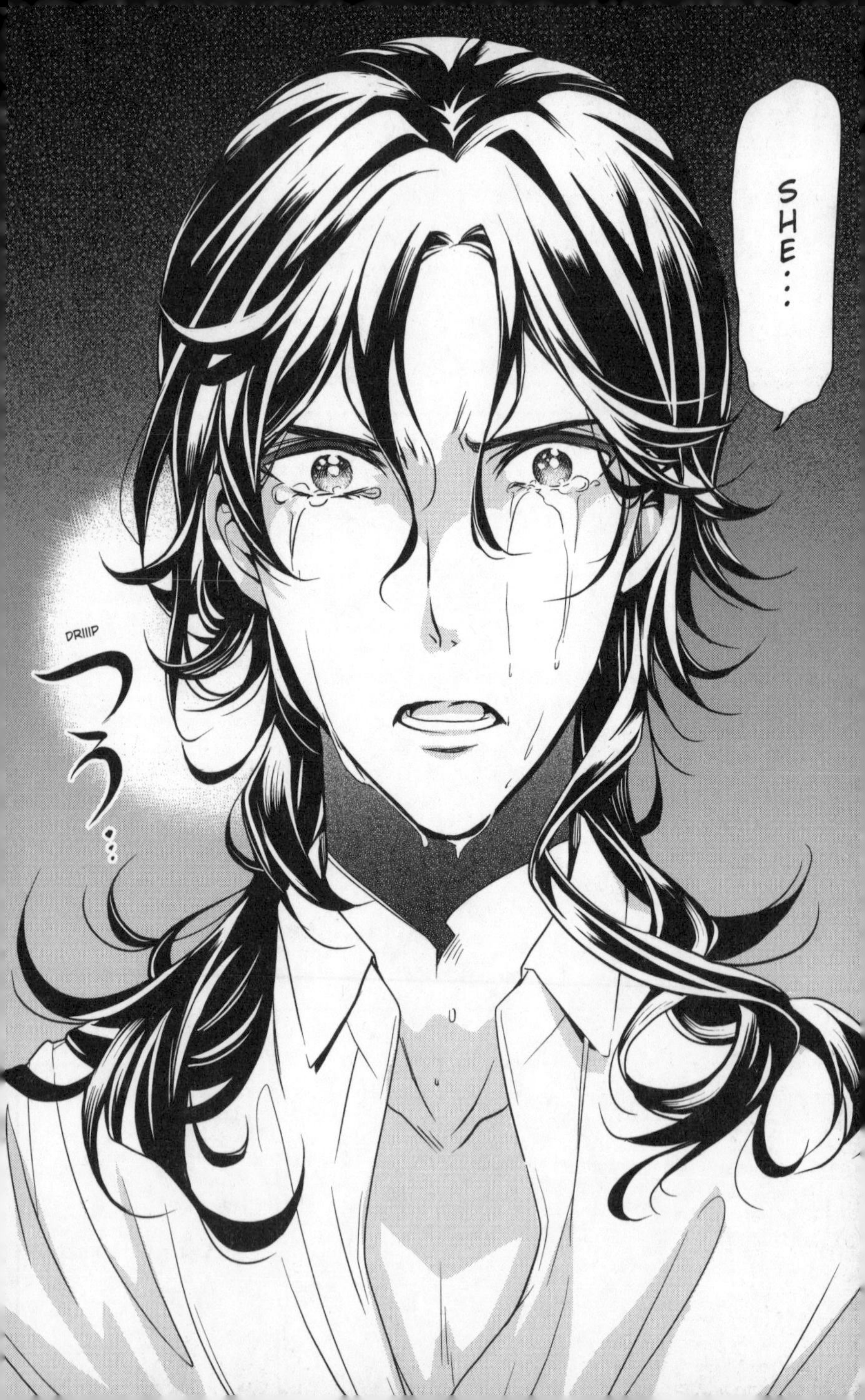
SHE...
DRIIIP
う...

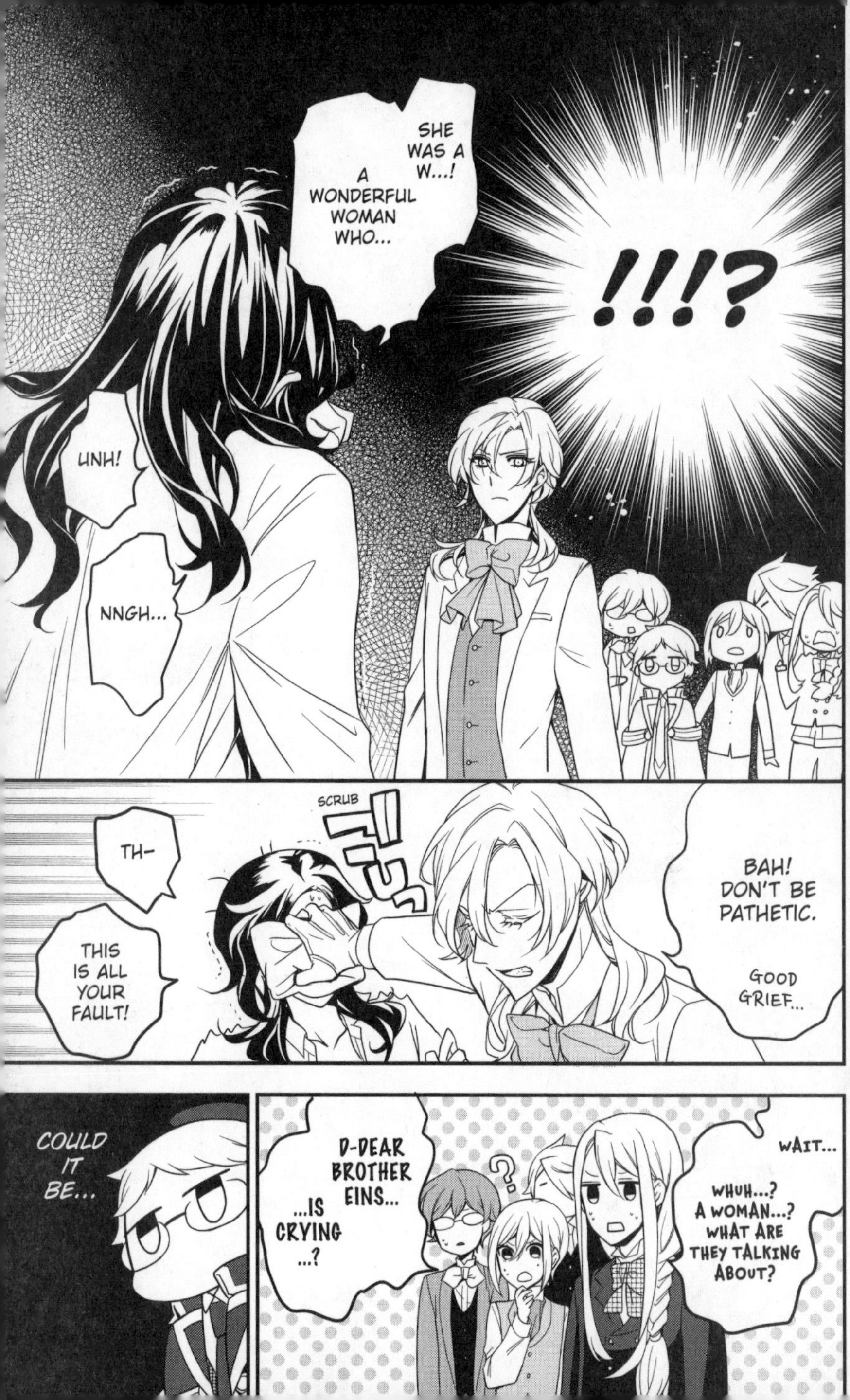
SHE WAS A W...! A WONDERFUL WOMAN WHO...
!!!?
UNH!
NNGH...
BAH! DON'T BE PATHETIC.
GOOD GRIEF...
SCRUB
TH-
THIS IS ALL YOUR FAULT!
WAIT...
WHUH...? A WOMAN...? WHAT ARE THEY TALKING ABOUT?
?
D-DEAR BROTHER EINS... ...IS CRYING ...?
COULD IT BE...

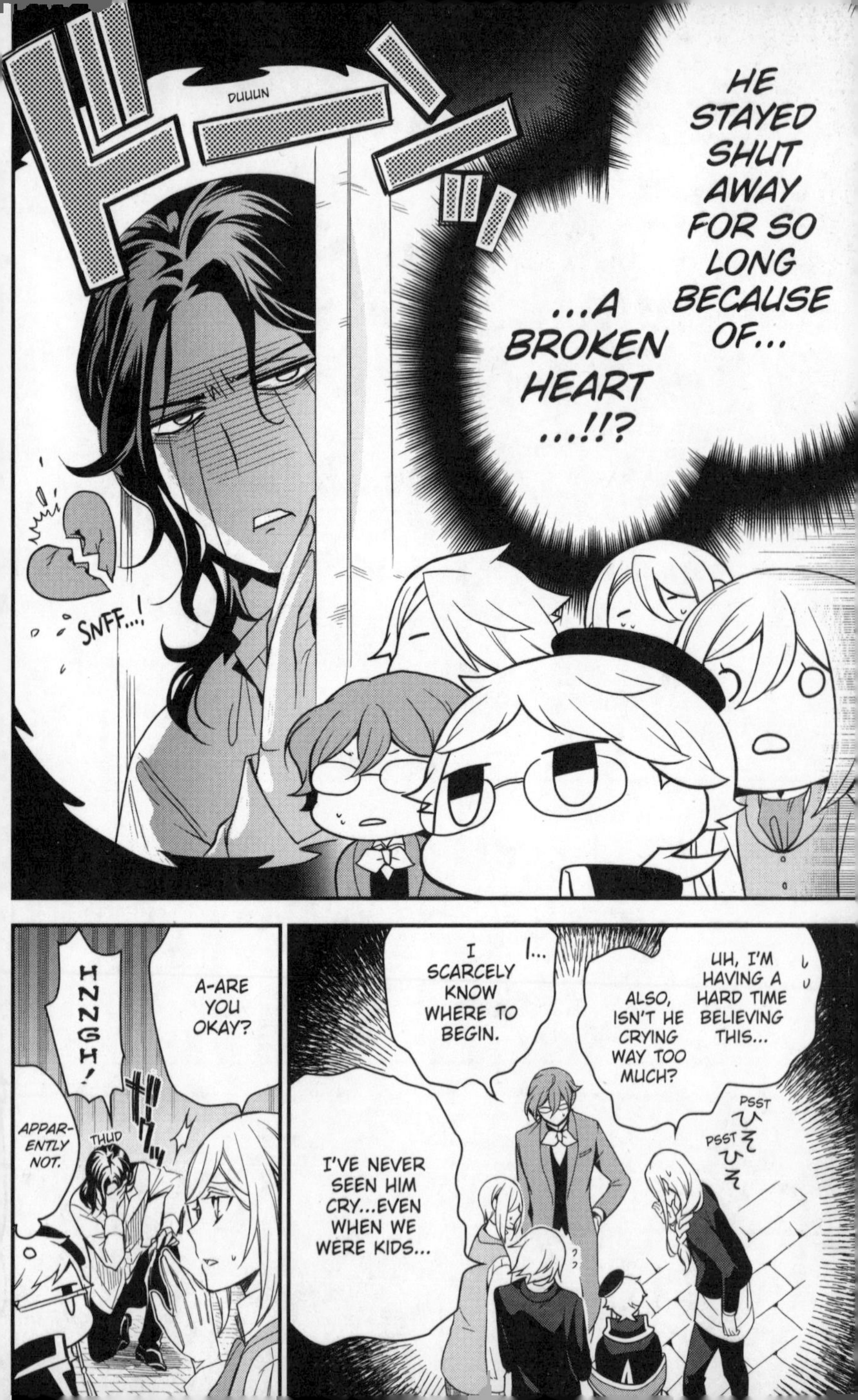
DUUUN
HE STAYED SHUT AWAY FOR SO LONG BECAUSE OF...
...A BROKEN HEART ...!!?
SNFF...!
UH, I'M HAVING A HARD TIME BELIEVING THIS...
ALSO, ISN'T HE CRYING WAY TOO MUCH?
I...
I SCARCELY KNOW WHERE TO BEGIN.
PSST
PSST
I'VE NEVER SEEN HIM CRY...EVEN WHEN WE WERE KIDS...
HNNGH!
A-ARE YOU OKAY?
THUD
APPARENTLY NOT.

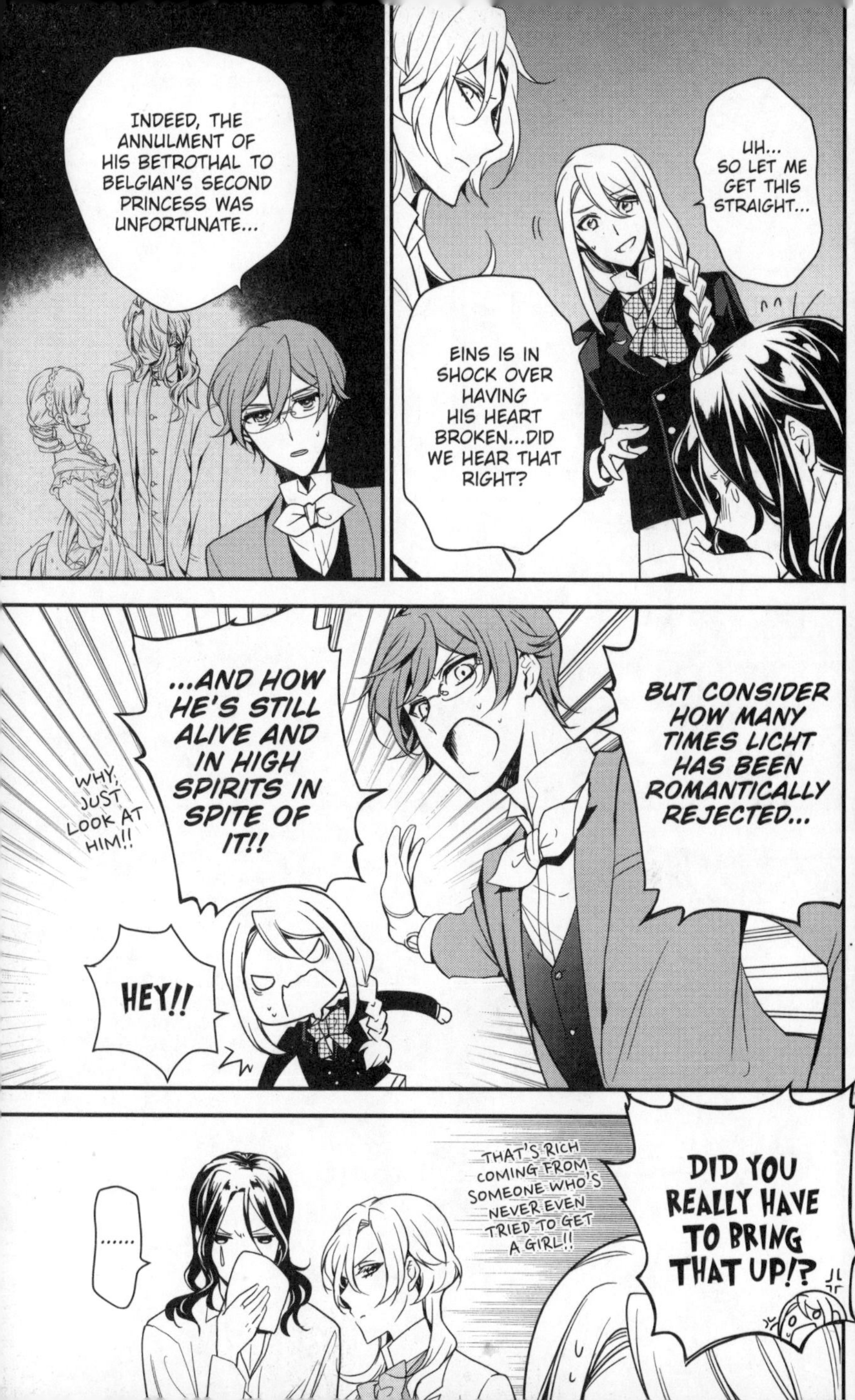
UH... SO LET ME GET THIS STRAIGHT...
EINS IS IN SHOCK OVER HAVING HIS HEART BROKEN...DID WE HEAR THAT RIGHT?
INDEED, THE ANNULMENT OF HIS BETROTHAL TO BELGIAN'S SECOND PRINCESS WAS UNFORTUNATE...
BUT CONSIDER HOW MANY TIMES LICHT HAS BEEN ROMANTICALLY REJECTED...
...AND HOW HE'S STILL ALIVE AND IN HIGH SPIRITS IN SPITE OF IT!!
WHY, JUST LOOK AT HIM!!
HEY!!
DID YOU REALLY HAVE TO BRING THAT UP!?
THAT'S RICH COMING FROM SOMEONE WHO'S NEVER EVEN TRIED TO GET A GIRL!!
......

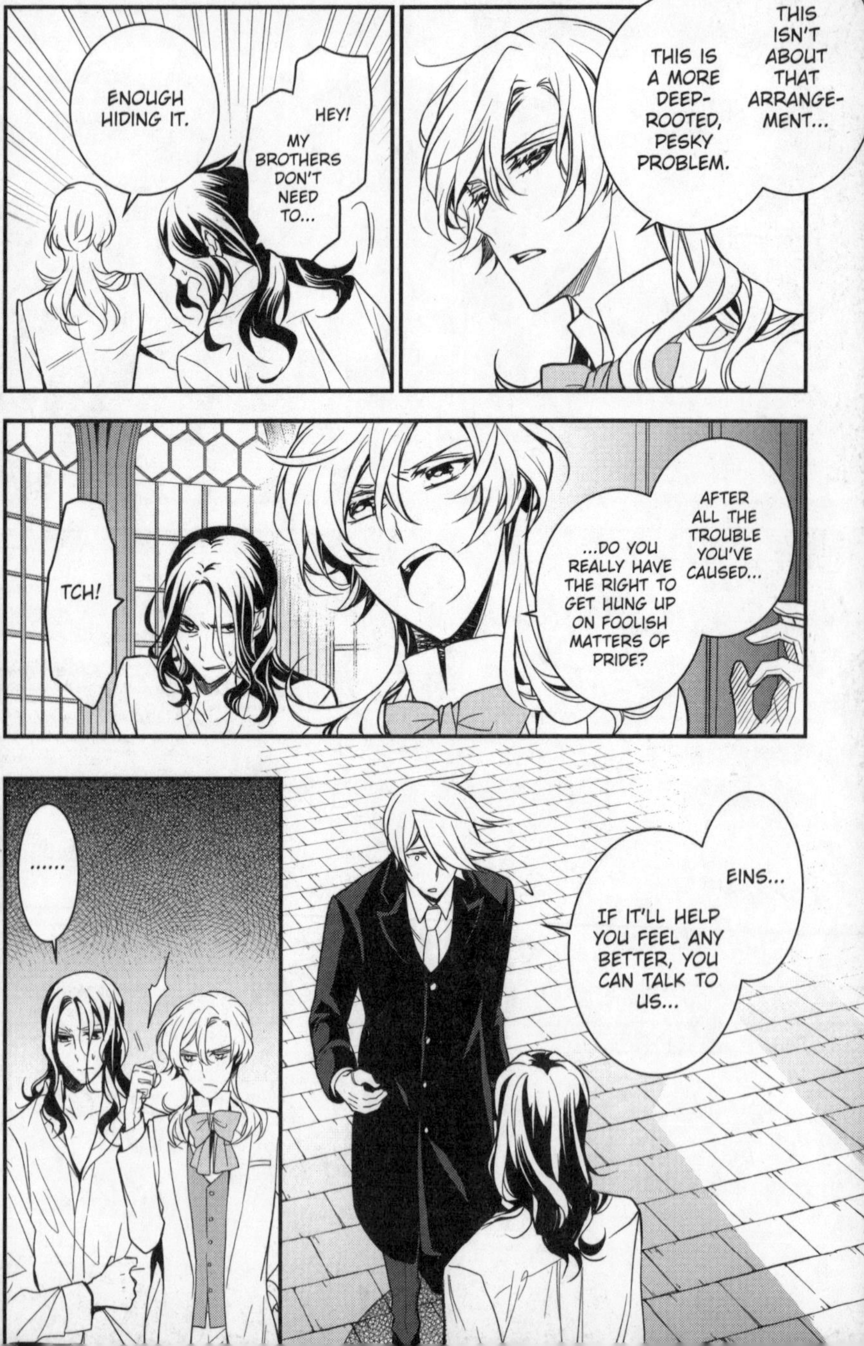
THIS ISN'T ABOUT THAT ARRANGE-MENT...
THIS IS A MORE DEEP-ROOTED, PESKY PROBLEM.
HEY!
MY BROTHERS DON'T NEED TO...
ENOUGH HIDING IT.
AFTER ALL THE TROUBLE YOU'VE CAUSED...
...DO YOU REALLY HAVE THE RIGHT TO GET HUNG UP ON FOOLISH MATTERS OF PRIDE?
TCH!
EINS...
IF IT'LL HELP YOU FEEL ANY BETTER, YOU CAN TALK TO US...
......

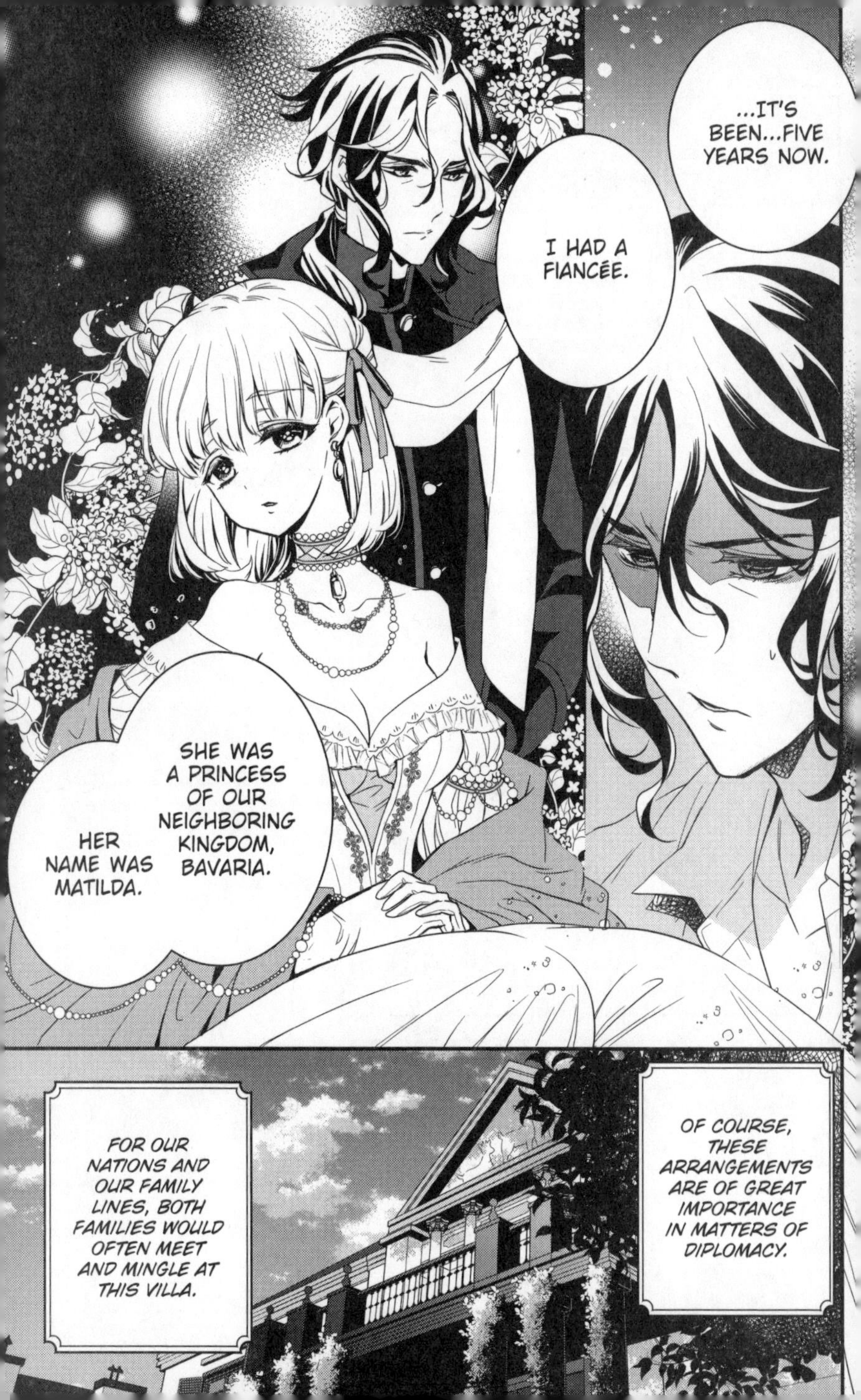
...IT'S BEEN...FIVE YEARS NOW.
I HAD A FIANCÉE.
SHE WAS A PRINCESS OF OUR NEIGHBORING KINGDOM, BAVARIA.
HER NAME WAS MATILDA.
OF COURSE, THESE ARRANGEMENTS ARE OF GREAT IMPORTANCE IN MATTERS OF DIPLOMACY.
FOR OUR NATIONS AND OUR FAMILY LINES, BOTH FAMILIES WOULD OFTEN MEET AND MINGLE AT THIS VILLA.

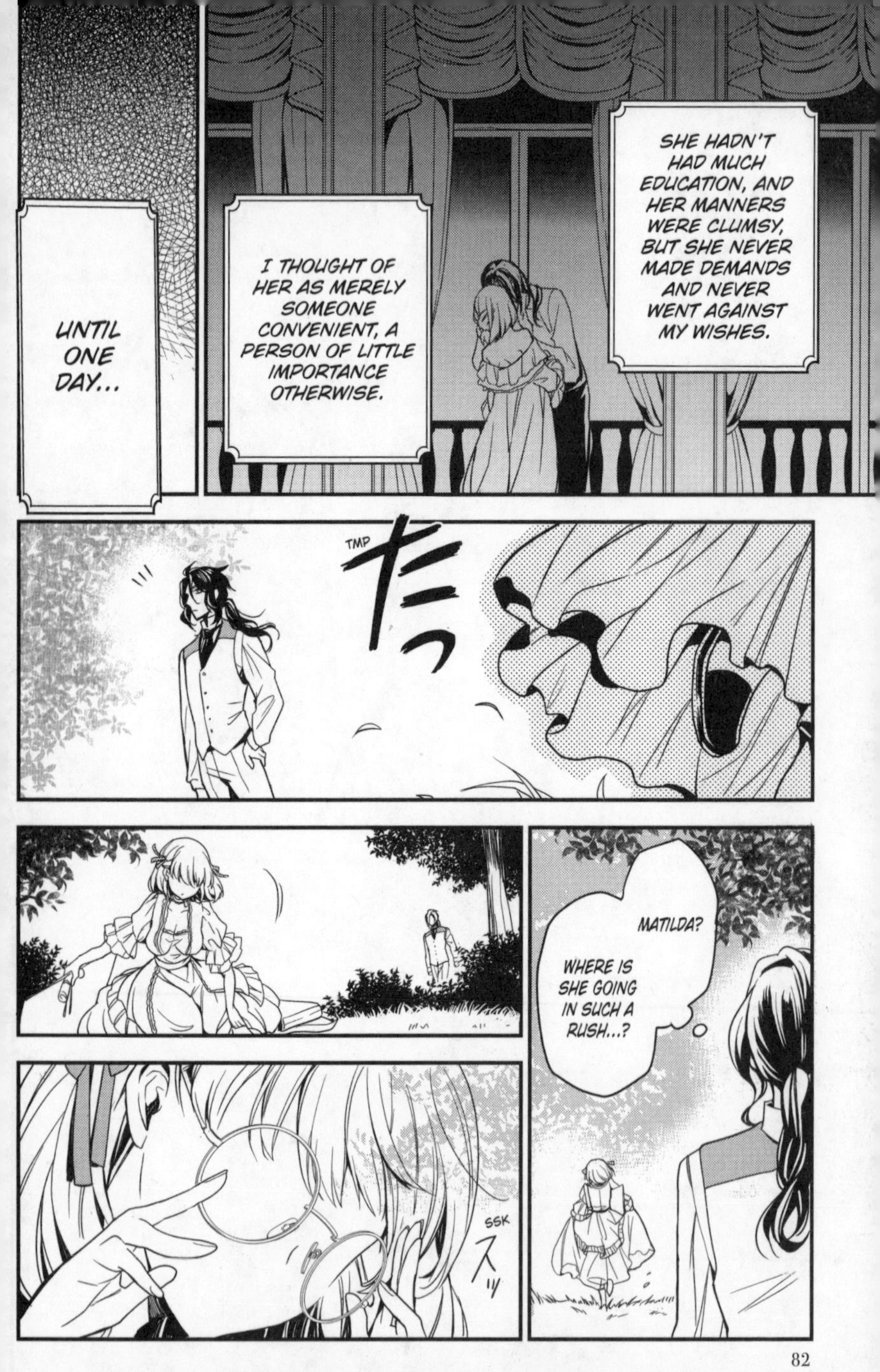
SHE HADN'T HAD MUCH EDUCATION, AND HER MANNERS WERE CLUMSY, BUT SHE NEVER MADE DEMANDS AND NEVER WENT AGAINST MY WISHES.
I THOUGHT OF HER AS MERELY SOMEONE CONVENIENT, A PERSON OF LITTLE IMPORTANCE OTHERWISE.
UNTIL ONE DAY...
TMP
MATILDA?
WHERE IS SHE GOING IN SUCH A RUSH...?
SSK

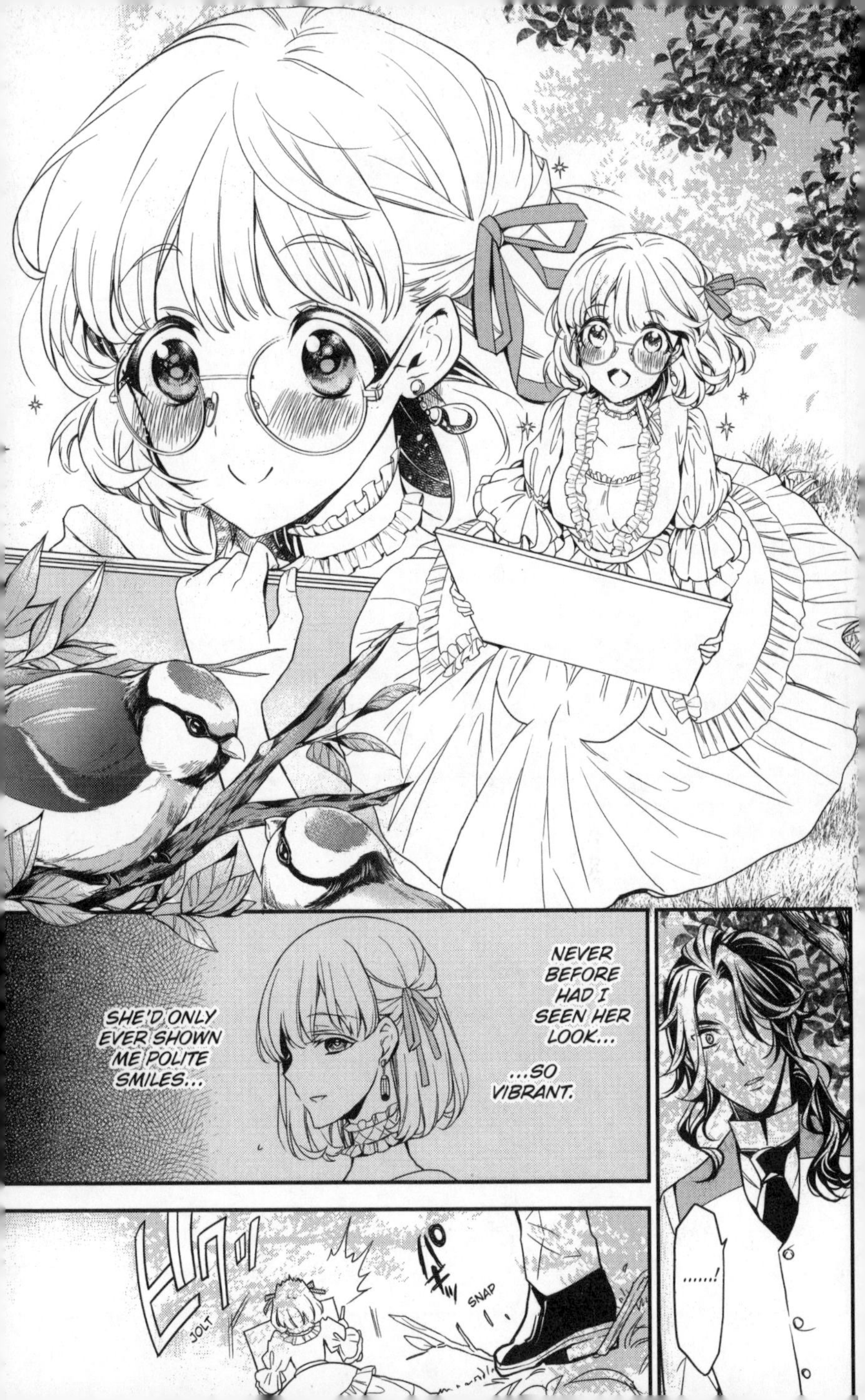
......!
NEVER BEFORE HAD I SEEN HER LOOK...
...SO VIBRANT.
SHE'D ONLY EVER SHOWN ME POLITE SMILES...
SNAP
JOLT

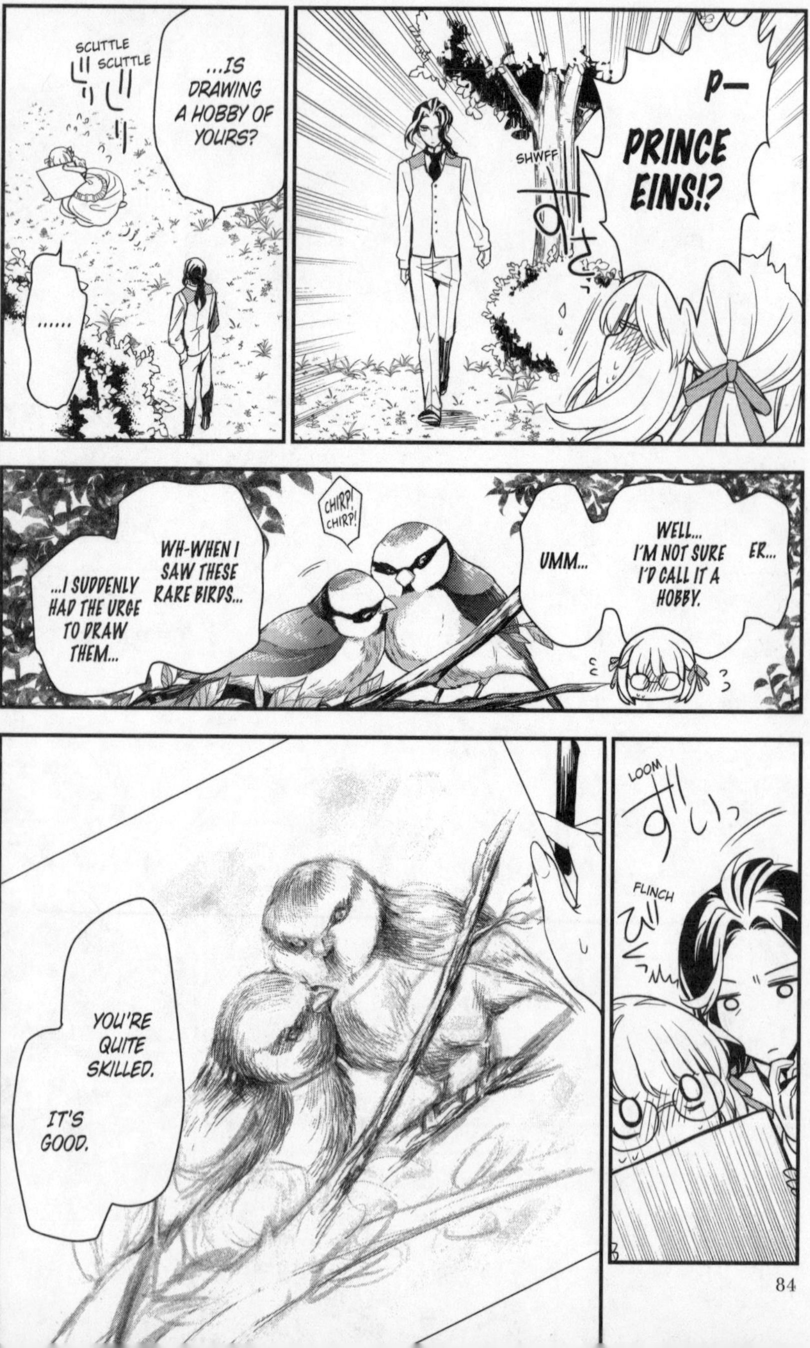
P—
PRINCE EINS!?
SHWFF
SCUTTLE
SCUTTLE
...IS DRAWING A HOBBY OF YOURS?
......
ER...
WELL... I'M NOT SURE I'D CALL IT A HOBBY.
UMM...
CHIRP! CHIRP!
WH-WHEN I SAW THESE RARE BIRDS...
...I SUDDENLY HAD THE URGE TO DRAW THEM...
LOOM
FLINCH
YOU'RE QUITE SKILLED.
IT'S GOOD.

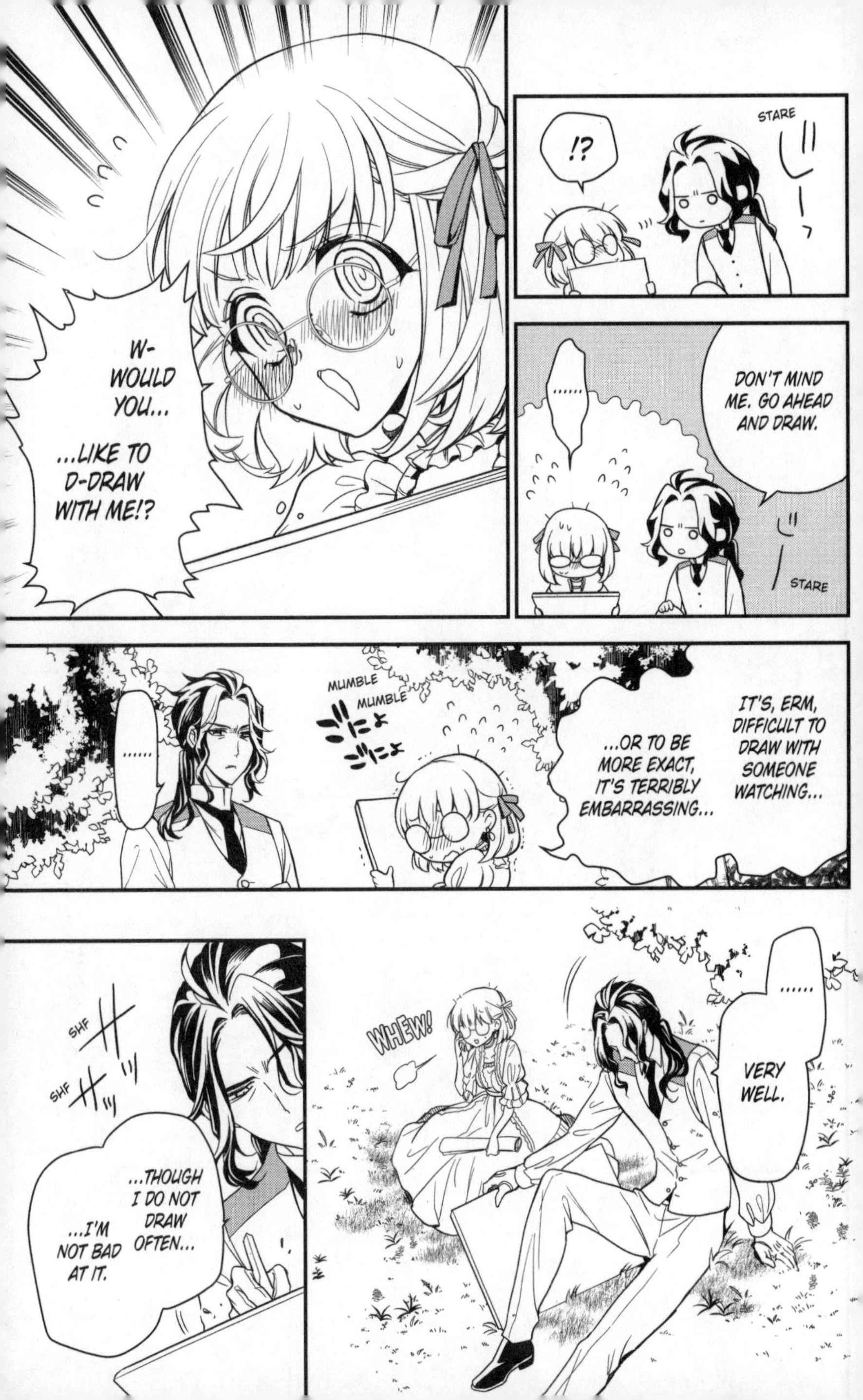
STARE
!?
DON'T MIND ME. GO AHEAD AND DRAW.
......
STARE
W-WOULD YOU...
...LIKE TO D-DRAW WITH ME!?
IT'S, ERM, DIFFICULT TO DRAW WITH SOMEONE WATCHING...
...OR TO BE MORE EXACT, IT'S TERRIBLY EMBARRASSING...
MUMBLE MUMBLE
......
......
VERY WELL.
WHEW!
...THOUGH I DO NOT DRAW OFTEN...
...I'M NOT BAD AT IT.
SHF
SHF

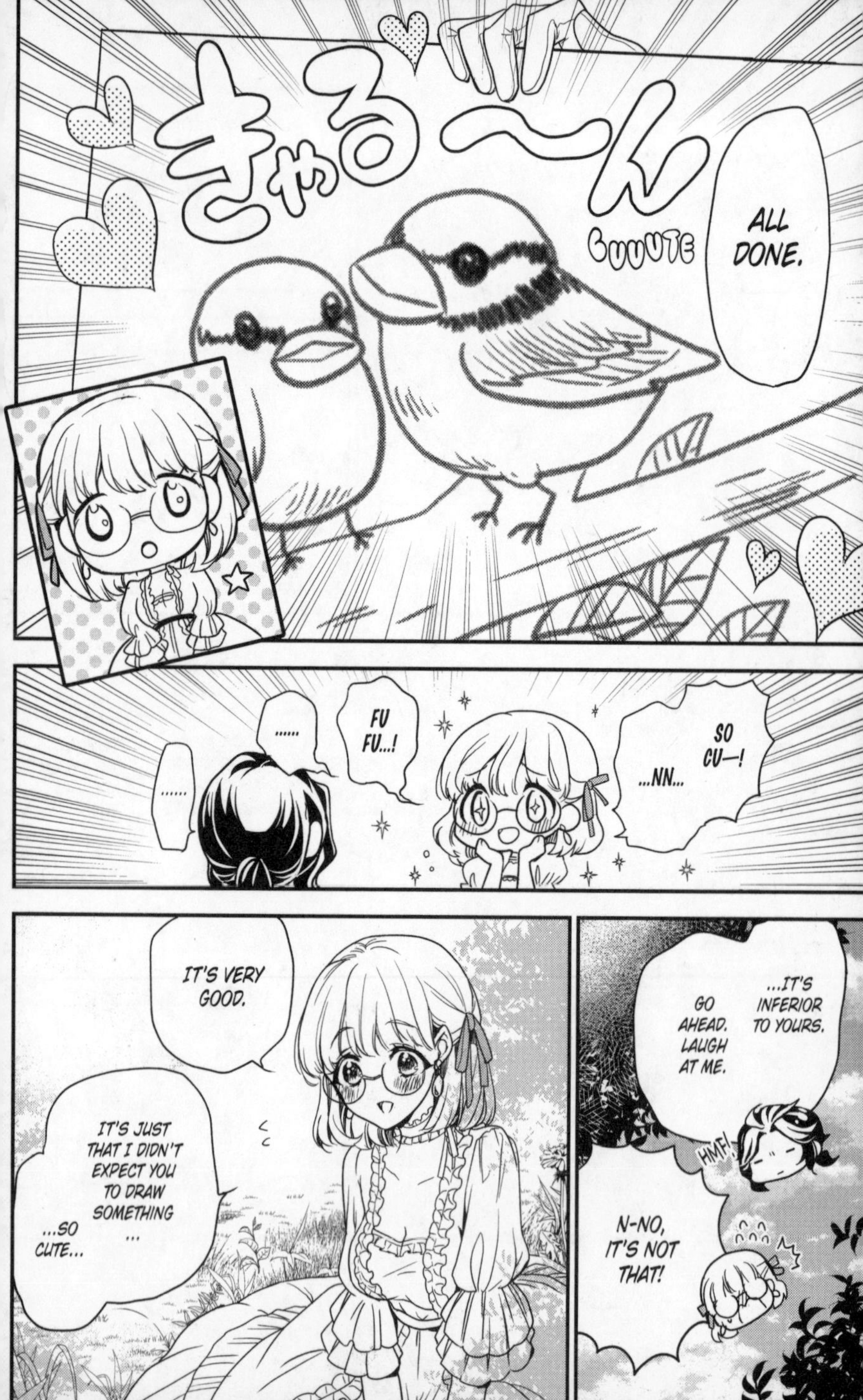
ALL DONE.
きゅる〜ん
CUUUTE
SO CU—!
...NN...
FU FU...!
......
......
...IT'S INFERIOR TO YOURS.
GO AHEAD. LAUGH AT ME.
HMF!
N-NO, IT'S NOT THAT!
IT'S VERY GOOD.
IT'S JUST THAT I DIDN'T EXPECT YOU TO DRAW SOMETHING ...SO CUTE...

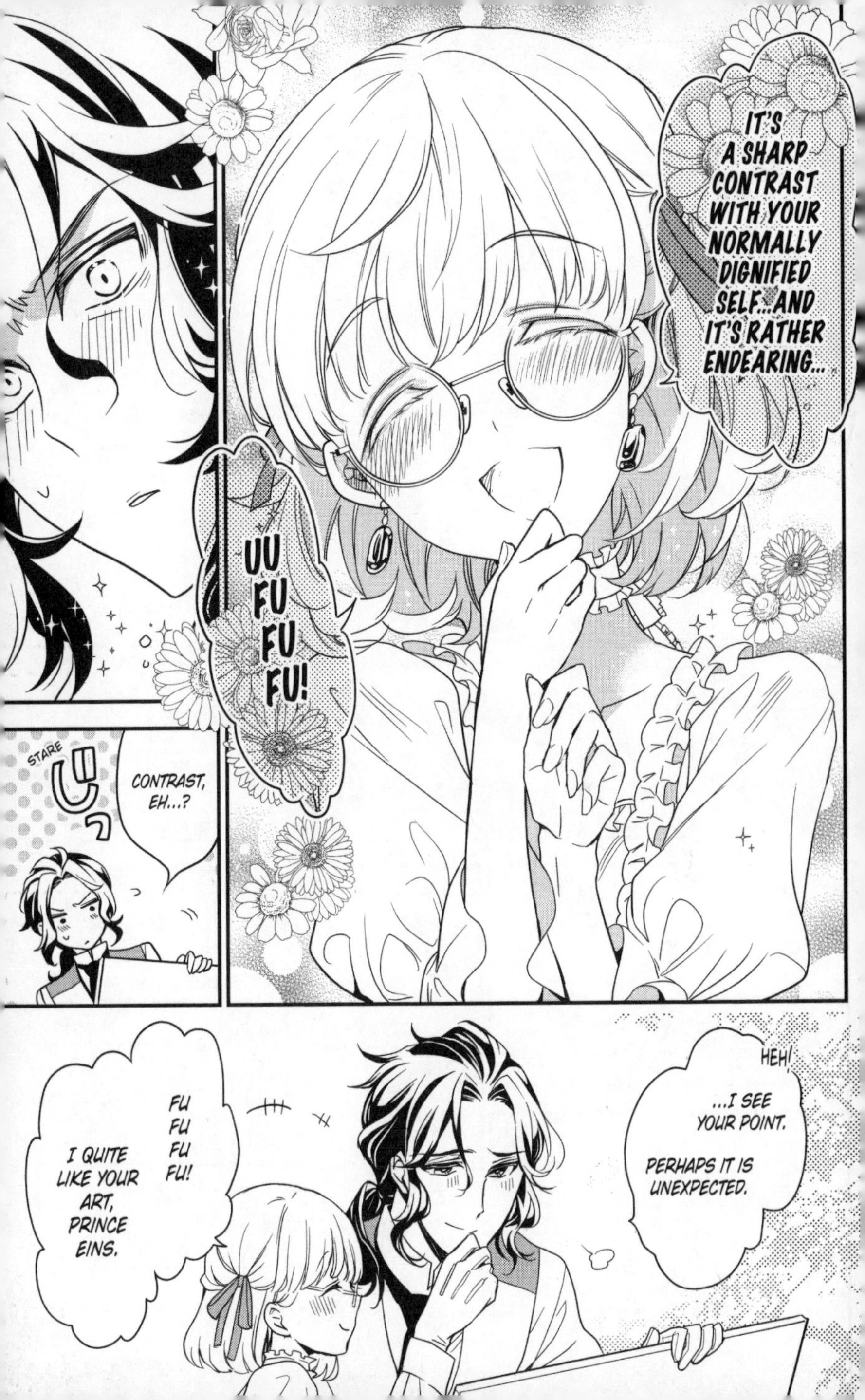
IT'S A SHARP CONTRAST WITH YOUR NORMALLY DIGNIFIED SELF...AND IT'S RATHER ENDEARING...
UUFUFUFU!
STARE
じっ
CONTRAST, EH...?
HEH!
...I SEE YOUR POINT.
PERHAPS IT IS UNEXPECTED.
FU FU FU FU!
I QUITE LIKE YOUR ART, PRINCE EINS.

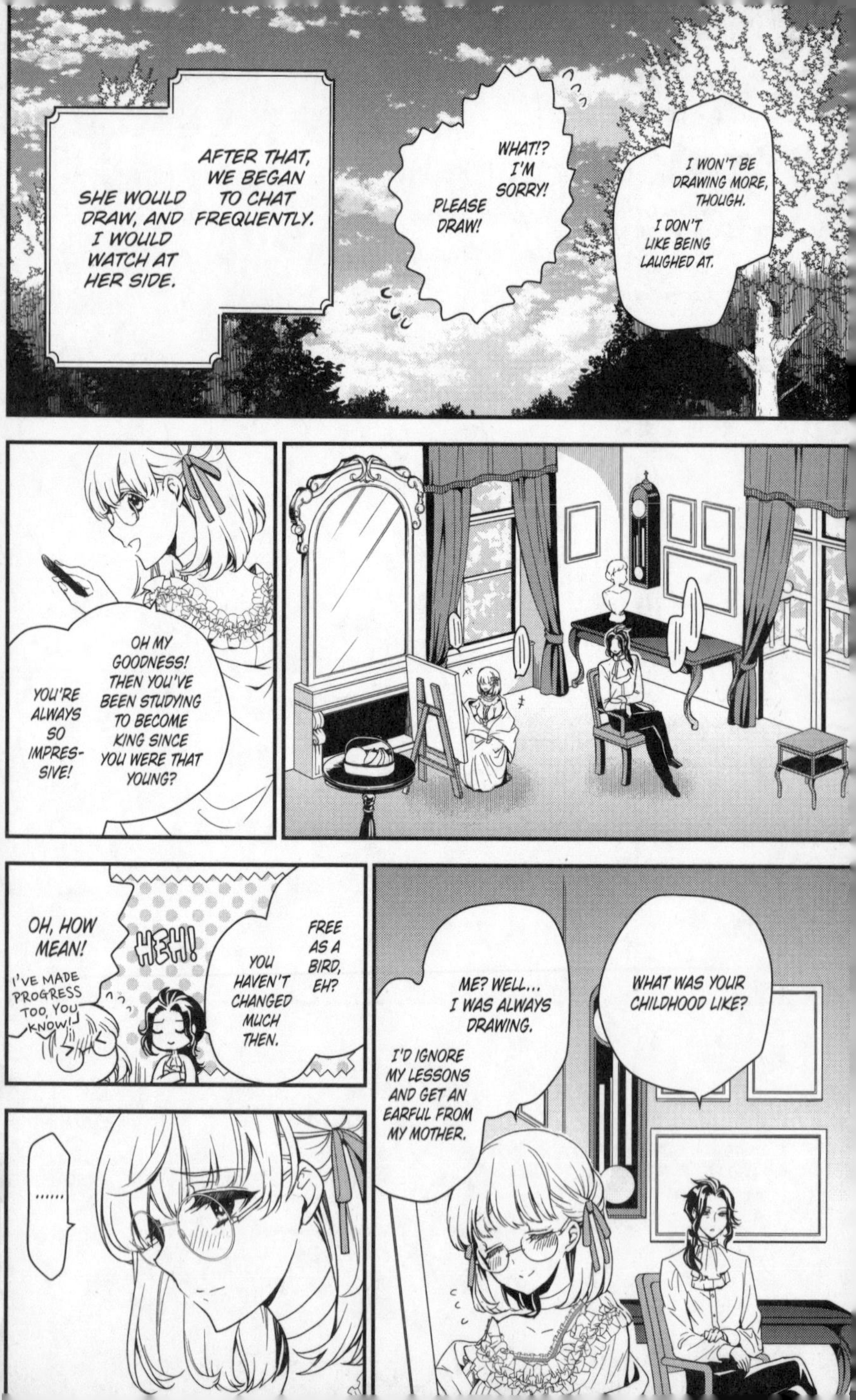
I WON'T BE DRAWING MORE, THOUGH.
I DON'T LIKE BEING LAUGHED AT.
WHAT!? I'M SORRY!
PLEASE DRAW!
AFTER THAT, WE BEGAN TO CHAT FREQUENTLY.
SHE WOULD DRAW, AND I WOULD WATCH AT HER SIDE.
OH MY GOODNESS! THEN YOU'VE BEEN STUDYING TO BECOME KING SINCE YOU WERE THAT YOUNG?
YOU'RE ALWAYS SO IMPRES-SIVE!
WHAT WAS YOUR CHILDHOOD LIKE?
ME? WELL... I WAS ALWAYS DRAWING.
I'D IGNORE MY LESSONS AND GET AN EARFUL FROM MY MOTHER.
FREE AS A BIRD, EH?
YOU HAVEN'T CHANGED MUCH THEN.
HEH!
OH, HOW MEAN!
I'VE MADE PROGRESS TOO, YOU KNOW!
......

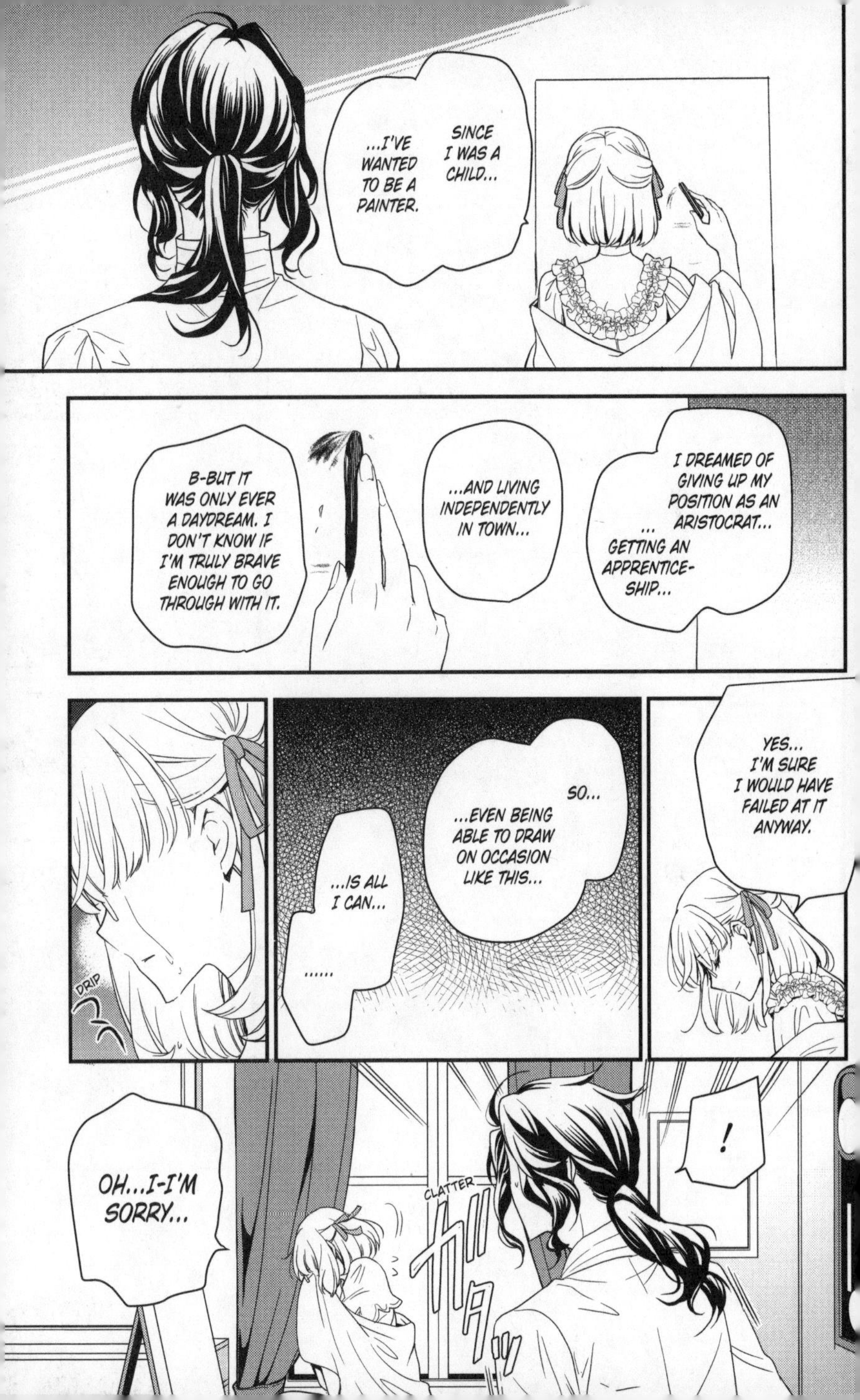
SINCE I WAS A CHILD...
...I'VE WANTED TO BE A PAINTER.
I DREAMED OF GIVING UP MY POSITION AS AN ARISTOCRAT...
...GETTING AN APPRENTICESHIP...
...AND LIVING INDEPENDENTLY IN TOWN...
B-BUT IT WAS ONLY EVER A DAYDREAM. I DON'T KNOW IF I'M TRULY BRAVE ENOUGH TO GO THROUGH WITH IT.
YES... I'M SURE I WOULD HAVE FAILED AT IT ANYWAY.
SO...
...EVEN BEING ABLE TO DRAW ON OCCASION LIKE THIS...
...IS ALL I CAN...
......
DRIP
!
CLATTER
OH...I-I'M SORRY...

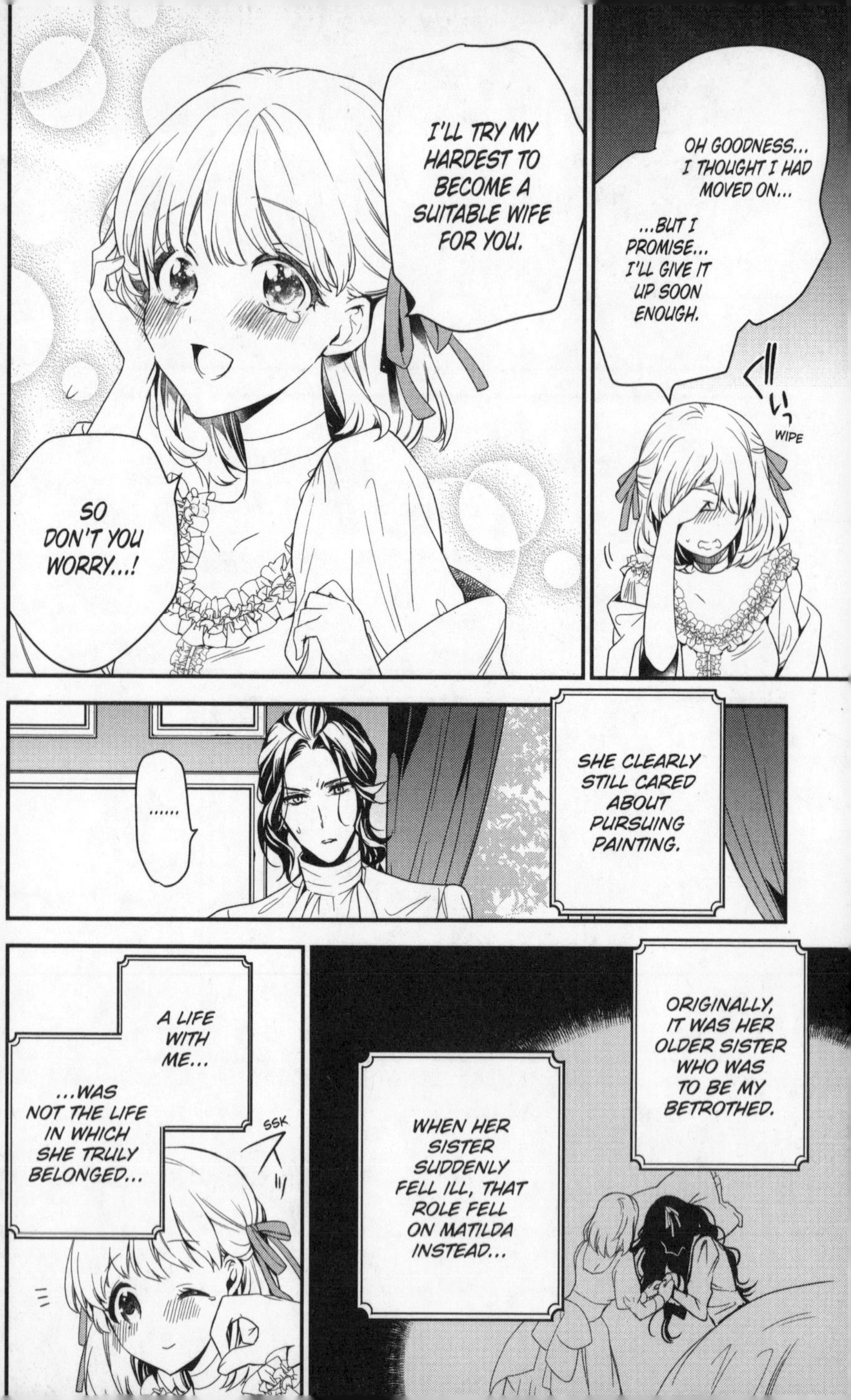
OH GOODNESS... I THOUGHT I HAD MOVED ON...
...BUT I PROMISE... I'LL GIVE IT UP SOON ENOUGH.
WIPE
I'LL TRY MY HARDEST TO BECOME A SUITABLE WIFE FOR YOU.
SO DON'T YOU WORRY...!
SHE CLEARLY STILL CARED ABOUT PURSUING PAINTING.
......
ORIGINALLY, IT WAS HER OLDER SISTER WHO WAS TO BE MY BETROTHED.
WHEN HER SISTER SUDDENLY FELL ILL, THAT ROLE FELL ON MATILDA INSTEAD...
A LIFE WITH ME...
...WAS NOT THE LIFE IN WHICH SHE TRULY BELONGED...
SSK

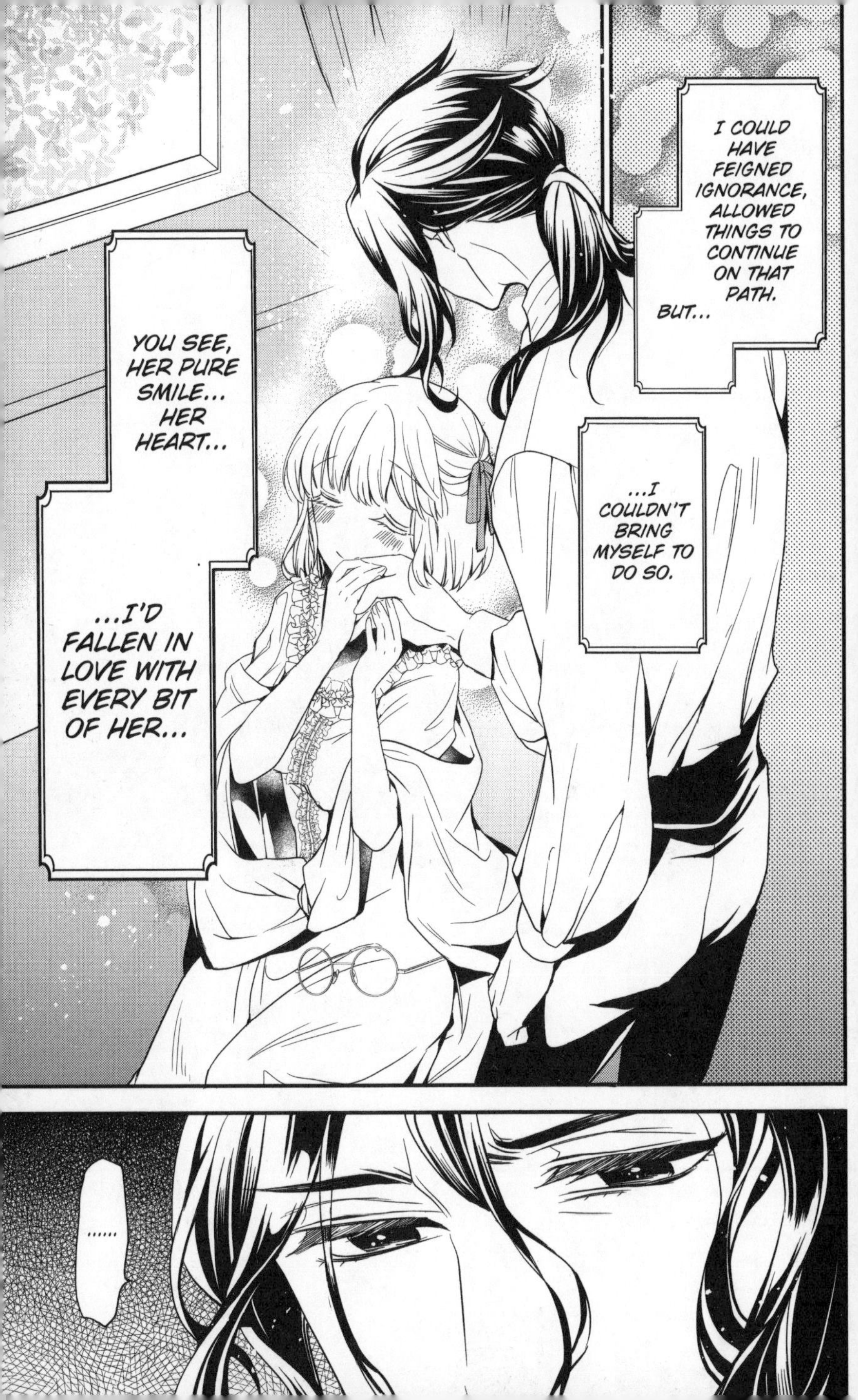
I COULD HAVE FEIGNED IGNORANCE, ALLOWED THINGS TO CONTINUE ON THAT PATH.
BUT...
...I COULDN'T BRING MYSELF TO DO SO.
YOU SEE, HER PURE SMILE... HER HEART...
...I'D FALLEN IN LOVE WITH EVERY BIT OF HER...
......

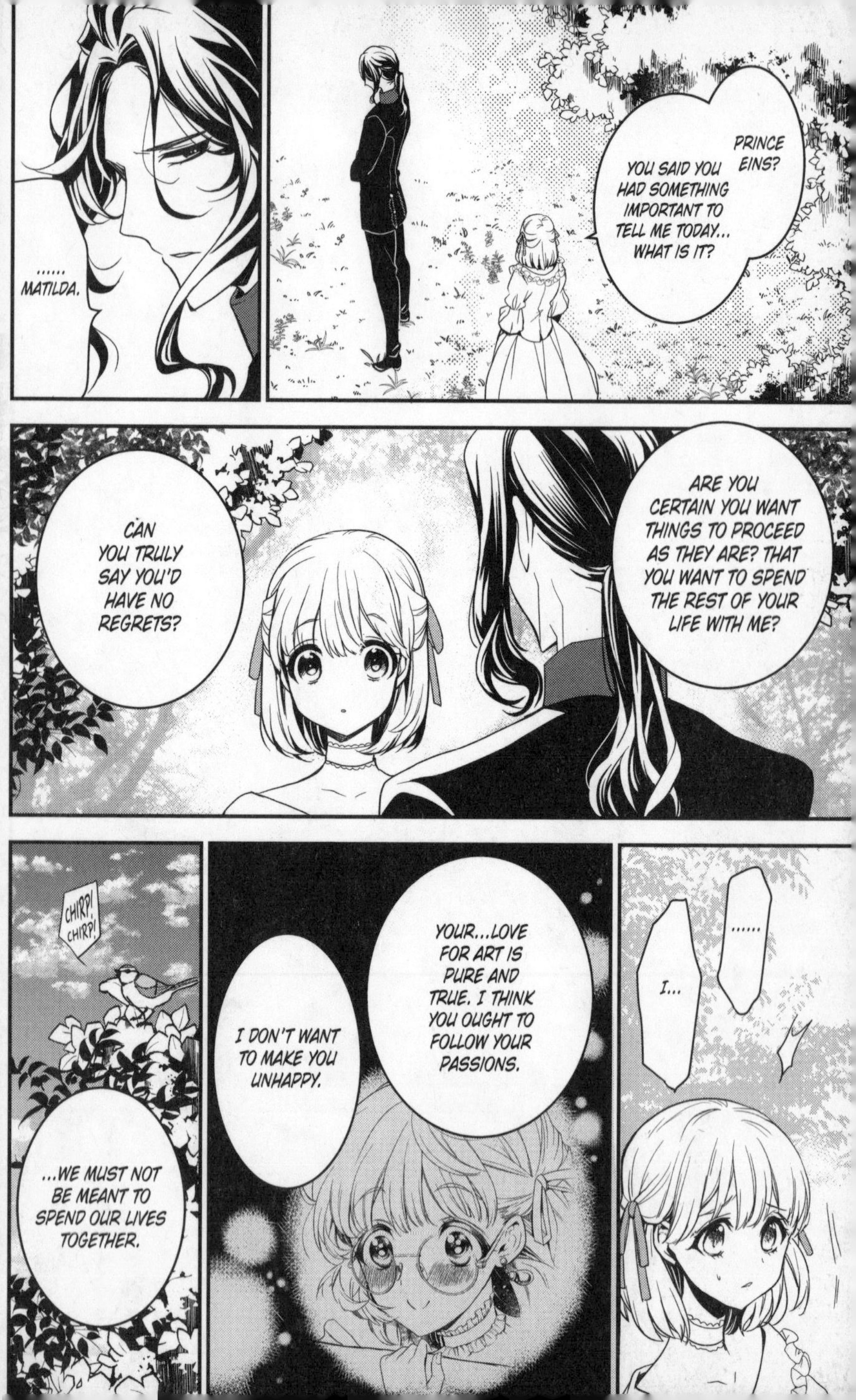
PRINCE EINS? YOU SAID YOU HAD SOMETHING IMPORTANT TO TELL ME TODAY... WHAT IS IT?
...... MATILDA.
ARE YOU CERTAIN YOU WANT THINGS TO PROCEED AS THEY ARE? THAT YOU WANT TO SPEND THE REST OF YOUR LIFE WITH ME?
CAN YOU TRULY SAY YOU'D HAVE NO REGRETS?
......
I...
YOUR...LOVE FOR ART IS PURE AND TRUE. I THINK YOU OUGHT TO FOLLOW YOUR PASSIONS.
I DON'T WANT TO MAKE YOU UNHAPPY.
CHIRP! CHIRP!
...WE MUST NOT BE MEANT TO SPEND OUR LIVES TOGETHER.

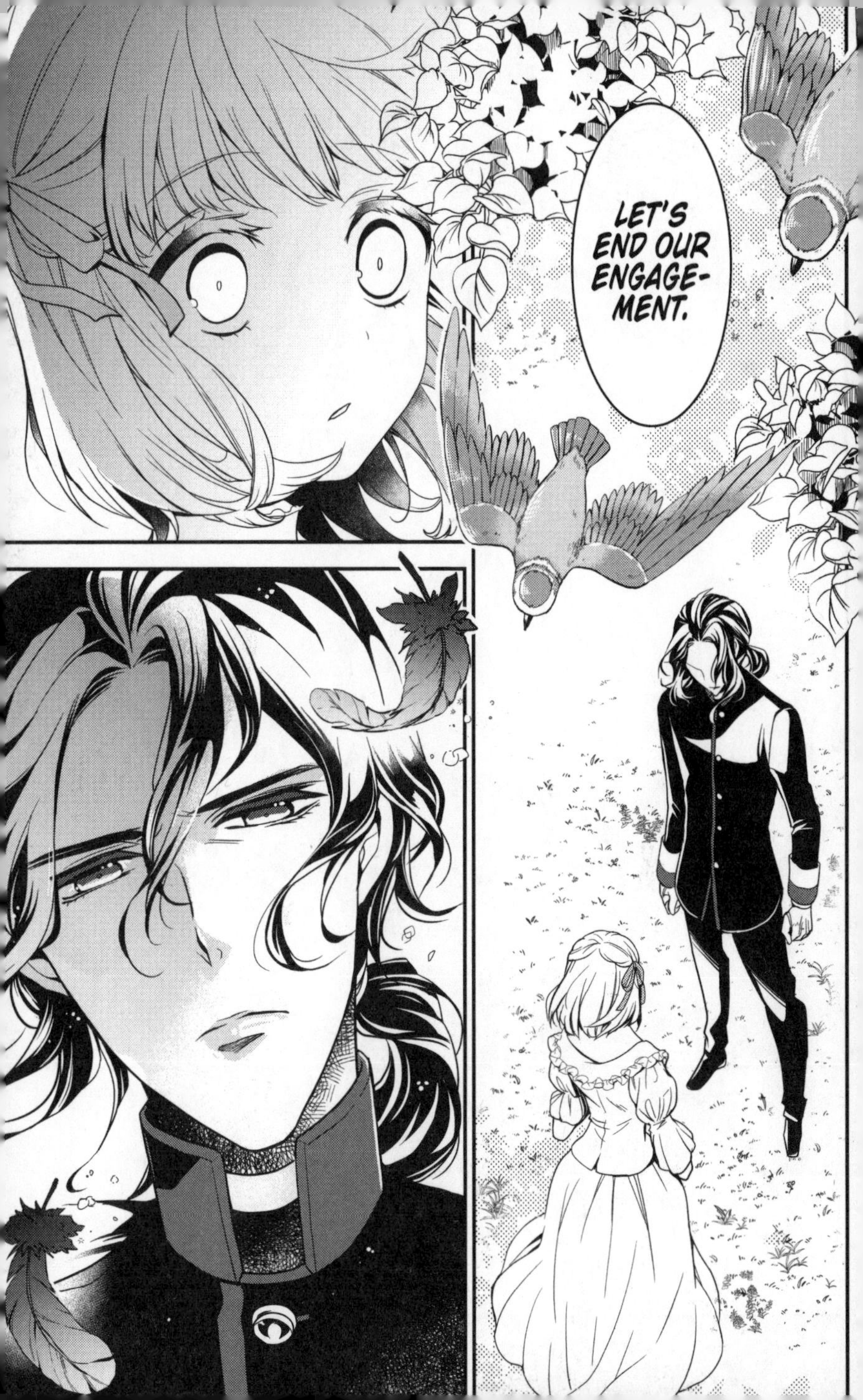
LET'S END OUR ENGAGE-MENT.

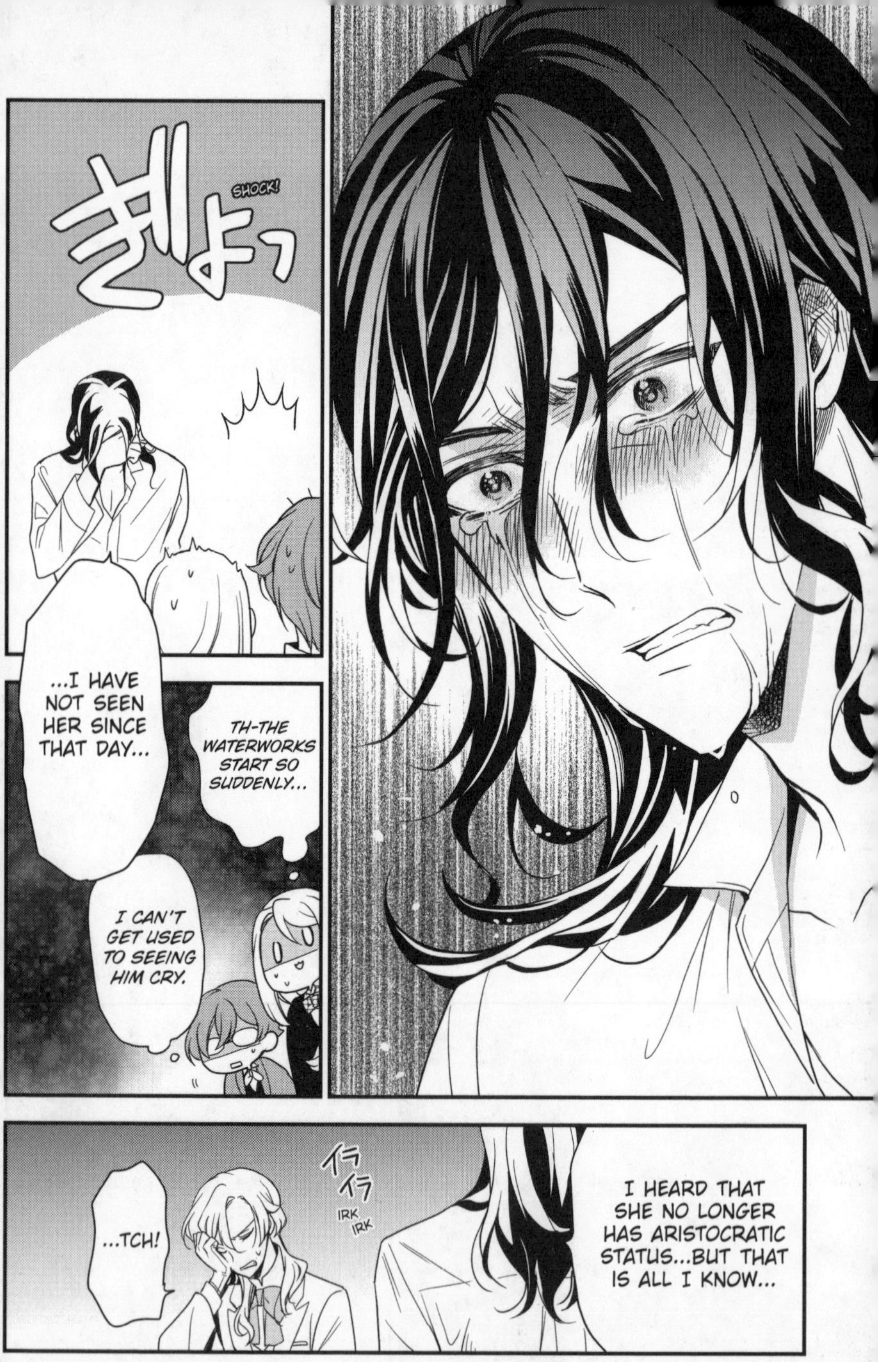
きょっ
SHOCK!
...I HAVE NOT SEEN HER SINCE THAT DAY...
TH-THE WATERWORKS START SO SUDDENLY...
I CAN'T GET USED TO SEEING HIM CRY.
I HEARD THAT SHE NO LONGER HAS ARISTOCRATIC STATUS...BUT THAT IS ALL I KNOW...
イラ イラ
IRK IRK
...TCH!

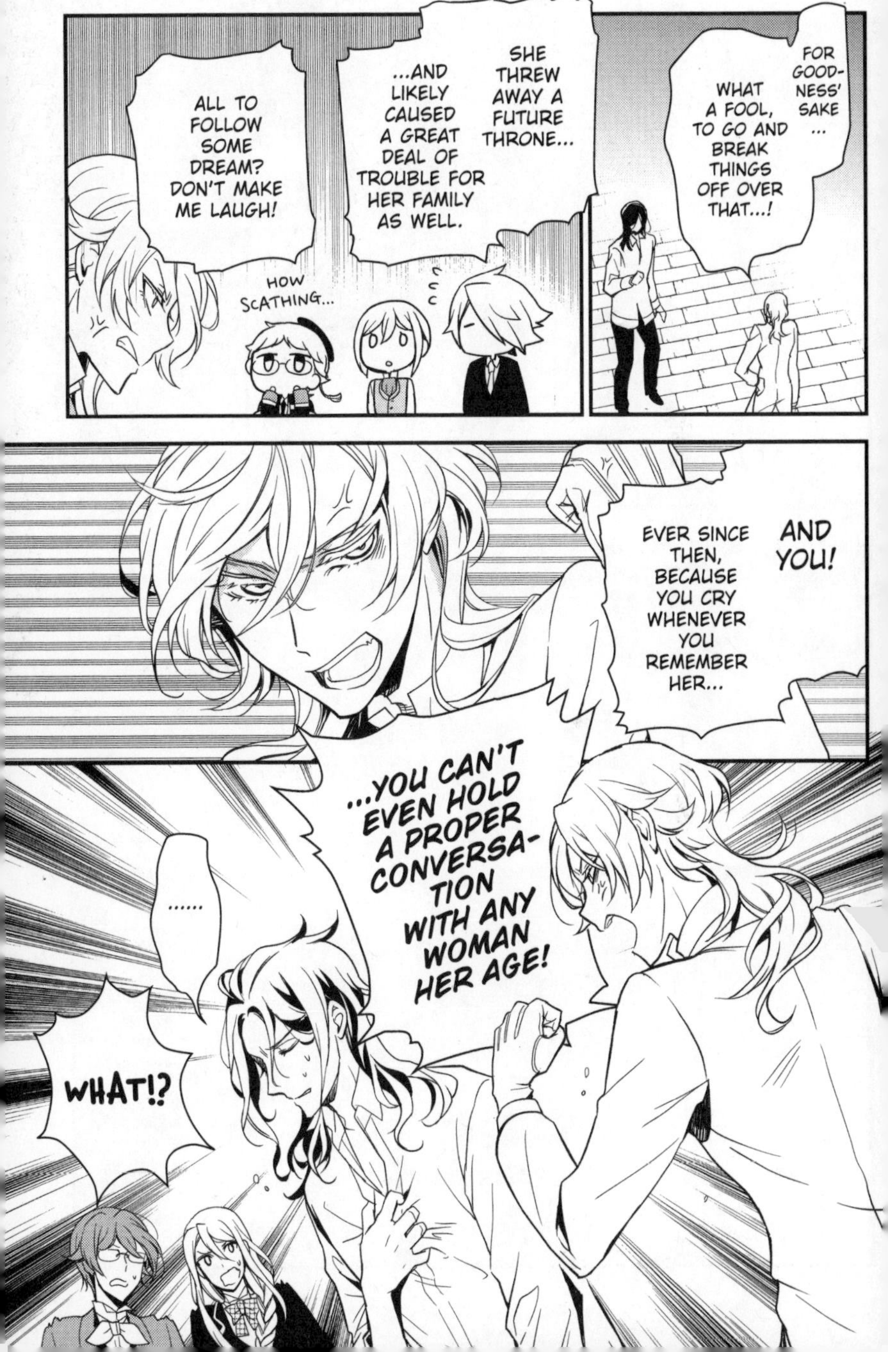
FOR GOODNESS' SAKE...
WHAT A FOOL, TO GO AND BREAK THINGS OFF OVER THAT...!
SHE THREW AWAY A FUTURE THRONE...
...AND LIKELY CAUSED A GREAT DEAL OF TROUBLE FOR HER FAMILY AS WELL.
ALL TO FOLLOW SOME DREAM? DON'T MAKE ME LAUGH!
HOW SCATHING...
AND YOU!
EVER SINCE THEN, BECAUSE YOU CRY WHENEVER YOU REMEMBER HER...
...YOU CAN'T EVEN HOLD A PROPER CONVERSATION WITH ANY WOMAN HER AGE!
......
WHAT!?

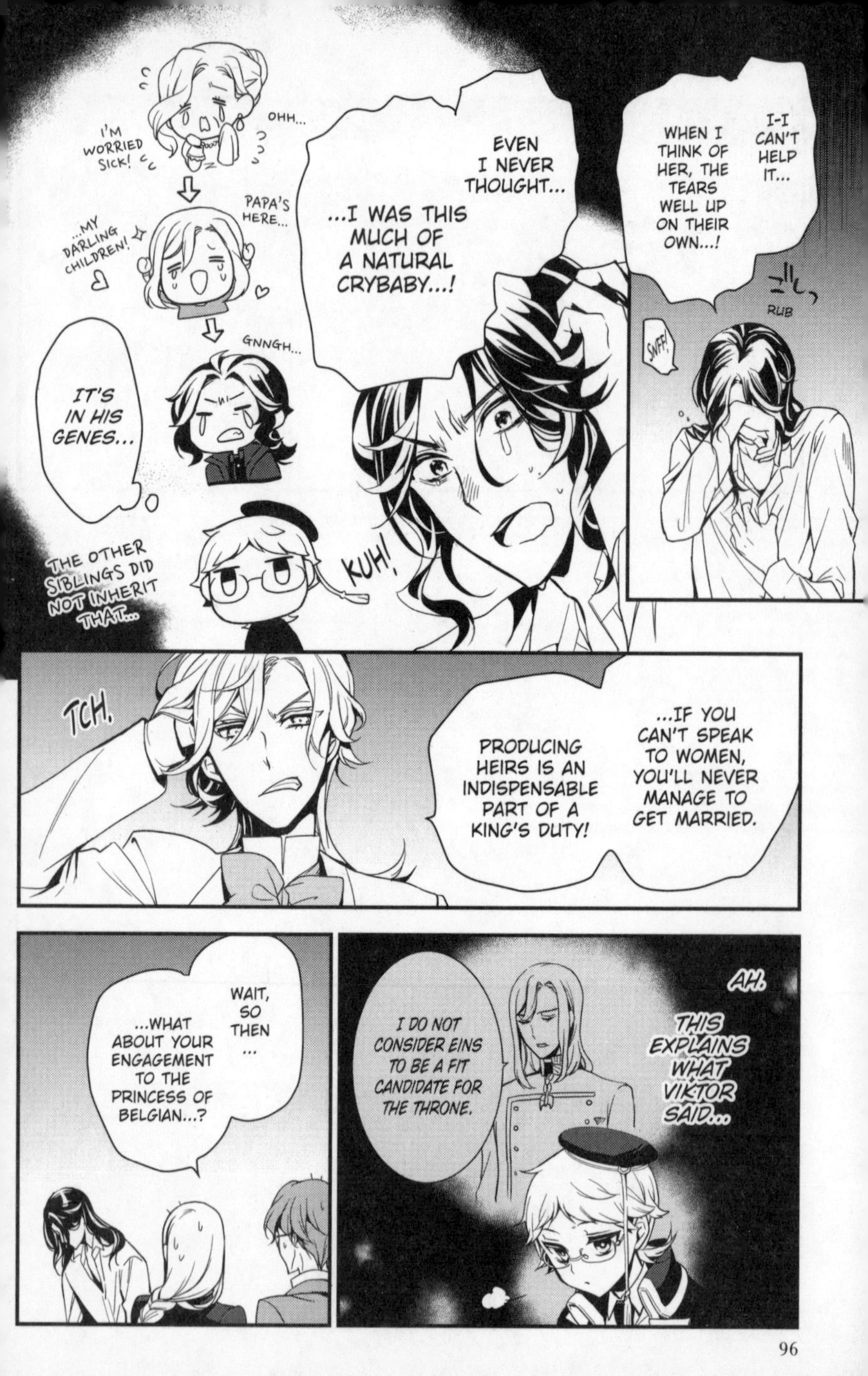
I-I CAN'T HELP IT...
WHEN I THINK OF HER, THE TEARS WELL UP ON THEIR OWN...!
RUB
SNFF!
EVEN I NEVER THOUGHT...
...I WAS THIS MUCH OF A NATURAL CRYBABY...!
KUH!
OHH...
I'M WORRIED SICK!
PAPA'S HERE...
...MY DARLING CHILDREN!
GNNGH...
IT'S IN HIS GENES...
THE OTHER SIBLINGS DID NOT INHERIT THAT...
...IF YOU CAN'T SPEAK TO WOMEN, YOU'LL NEVER MANAGE TO GET MARRIED.
PRODUCING HEIRS IS AN INDISPENSABLE PART OF A KING'S DUTY!
TCH.
AH.
THIS EXPLAINS WHAT VIKTOR SAID...
I DO NOT CONSIDER EINS TO BE A FIT CANDIDATE FOR THE THRONE.
WAIT, SO THEN ...
...WHAT ABOUT YOUR ENGAGEMENT TO THE PRINCESS OF BELGIAN...?

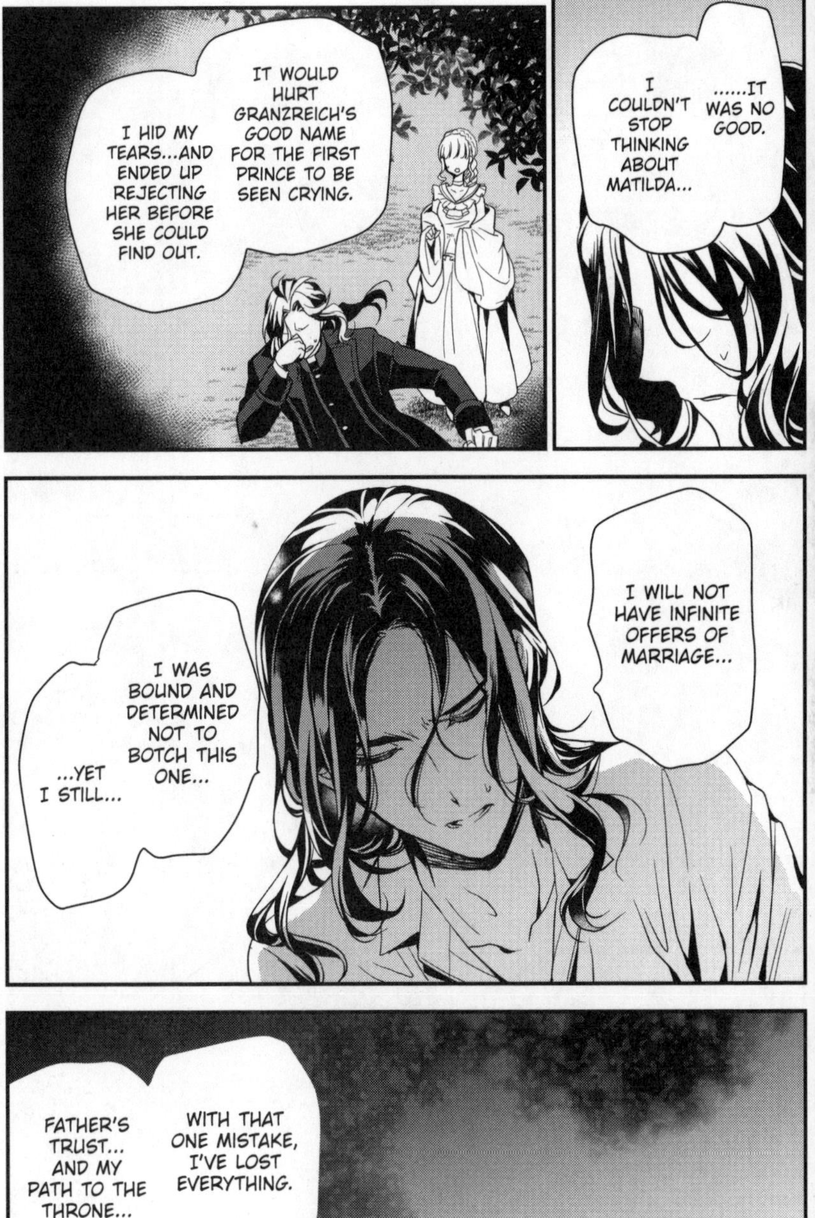
......IT WAS NO GOOD.
I COULDN'T STOP THINKING ABOUT MATILDA...
IT WOULD HURT GRANZREICH'S GOOD NAME FOR THE FIRST PRINCE TO BE SEEN CRYING.
I HID MY TEARS...AND ENDED UP REJECTING HER BEFORE SHE COULD FIND OUT.
I WILL NOT HAVE INFINITE OFFERS OF MARRIAGE...
I WAS BOUND AND DETERMINED NOT TO BOTCH THIS ONE...
...YET I STILL...
WITH THAT ONE MISTAKE, I'VE LOST EVERYTHING.
FATHER'S TRUST... AND MY PATH TO THE THRONE...

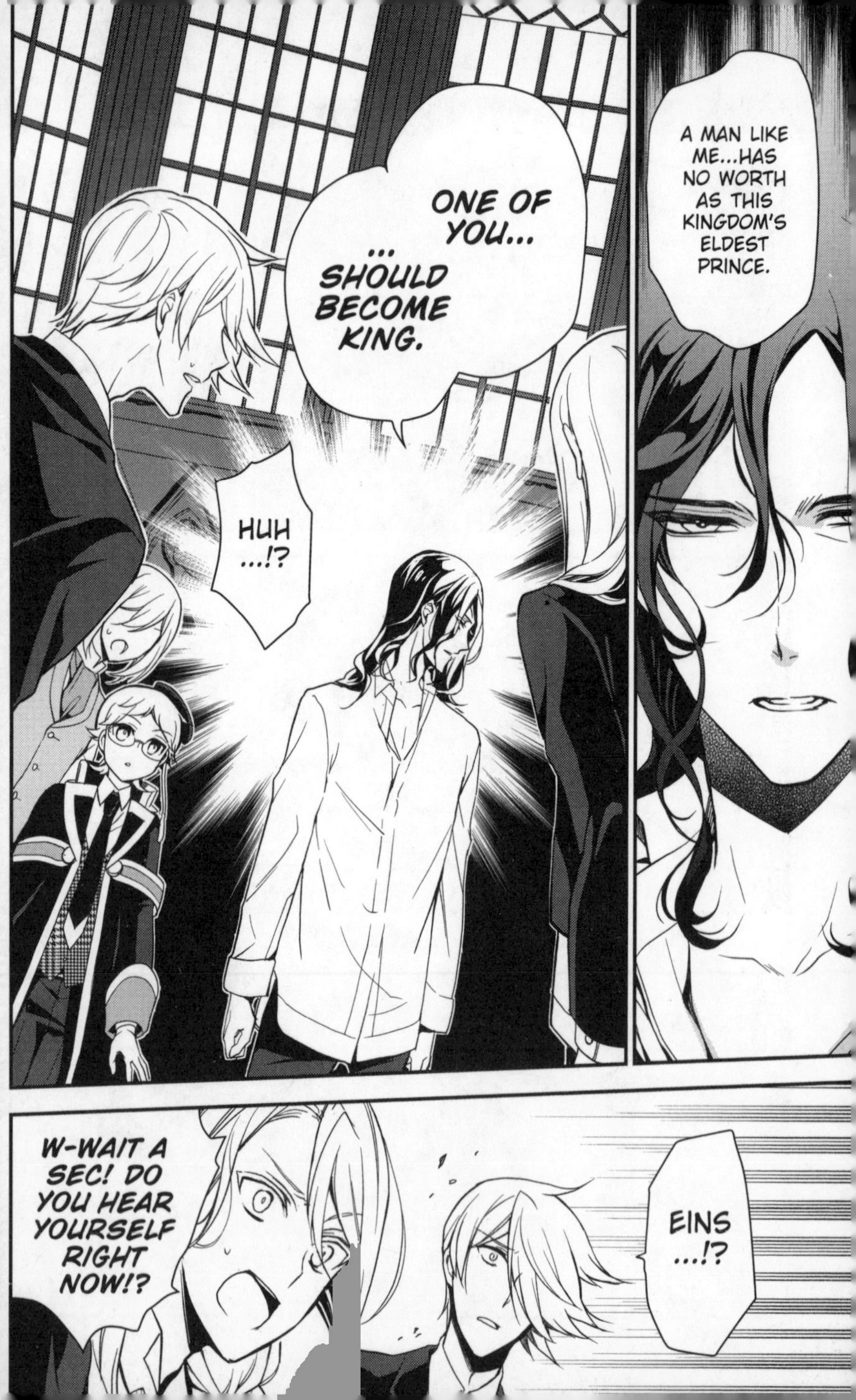
A MAN LIKE ME...HAS NO WORTH AS THIS KINGDOM'S ELDEST PRINCE.
ONE OF YOU...
...SHOULD BECOME KING.
HUH ...!?
EINS ...!?
W-WAIT A SEC! DO YOU HEAR YOURSELF RIGHT NOW!?

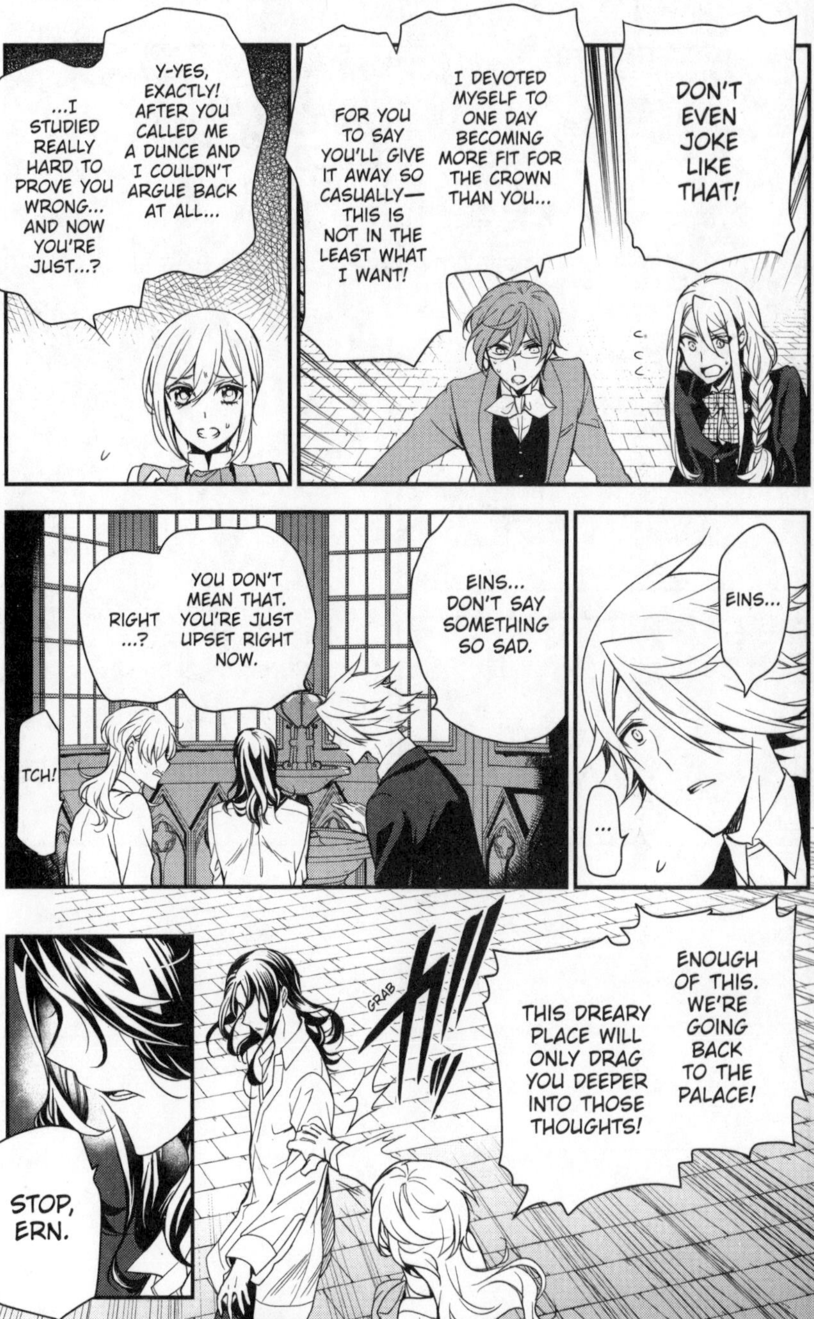
DON'T EVEN JOKE LIKE THAT!
I DEVOTED MYSELF TO ONE DAY BECOMING MORE FIT FOR THE CROWN THAN YOU...
FOR YOU TO SAY YOU'LL GIVE IT AWAY SO CASUALLY—THIS IS NOT IN THE LEAST WHAT I WANT!
Y-YES, EXACTLY! AFTER YOU CALLED ME A DUNCE AND I COULDN'T ARGUE BACK AT ALL...
...I STUDIED REALLY HARD TO PROVE YOU WRONG... AND NOW YOU'RE JUST...?
EINS...
...
EINS... DON'T SAY SOMETHING SO SAD.
YOU DON'T MEAN THAT. YOU'RE JUST UPSET RIGHT NOW.
RIGHT ...?
TCH!
ENOUGH OF THIS. WE'RE GOING BACK TO THE PALACE!
THIS DREARY PLACE WILL ONLY DRAG YOU DEEPER INTO THOSE THOUGHTS!
GRAB
STOP, ERN.

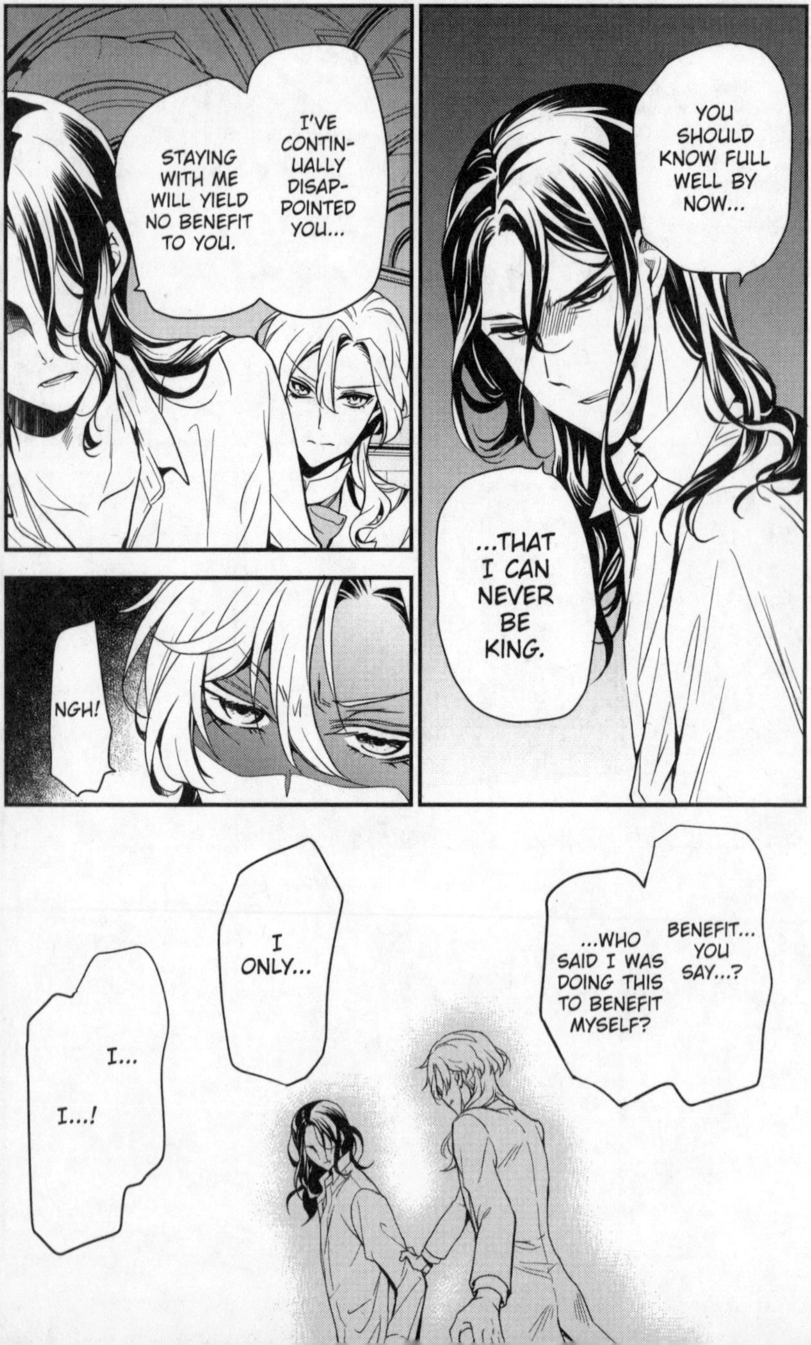
YOU SHOULD KNOW FULL WELL BY NOW...
...THAT I CAN NEVER BE KING.
I'VE CONTIN-UALLY DISAP-POINTED YOU...
STAYING WITH ME WILL YIELD NO BENEFIT TO YOU.
NGH!
BENEFIT... YOU SAY...?
...WHO SAID I WAS DOING THIS TO BENEFIT MYSELF?
I ONLY...
I...
I...!

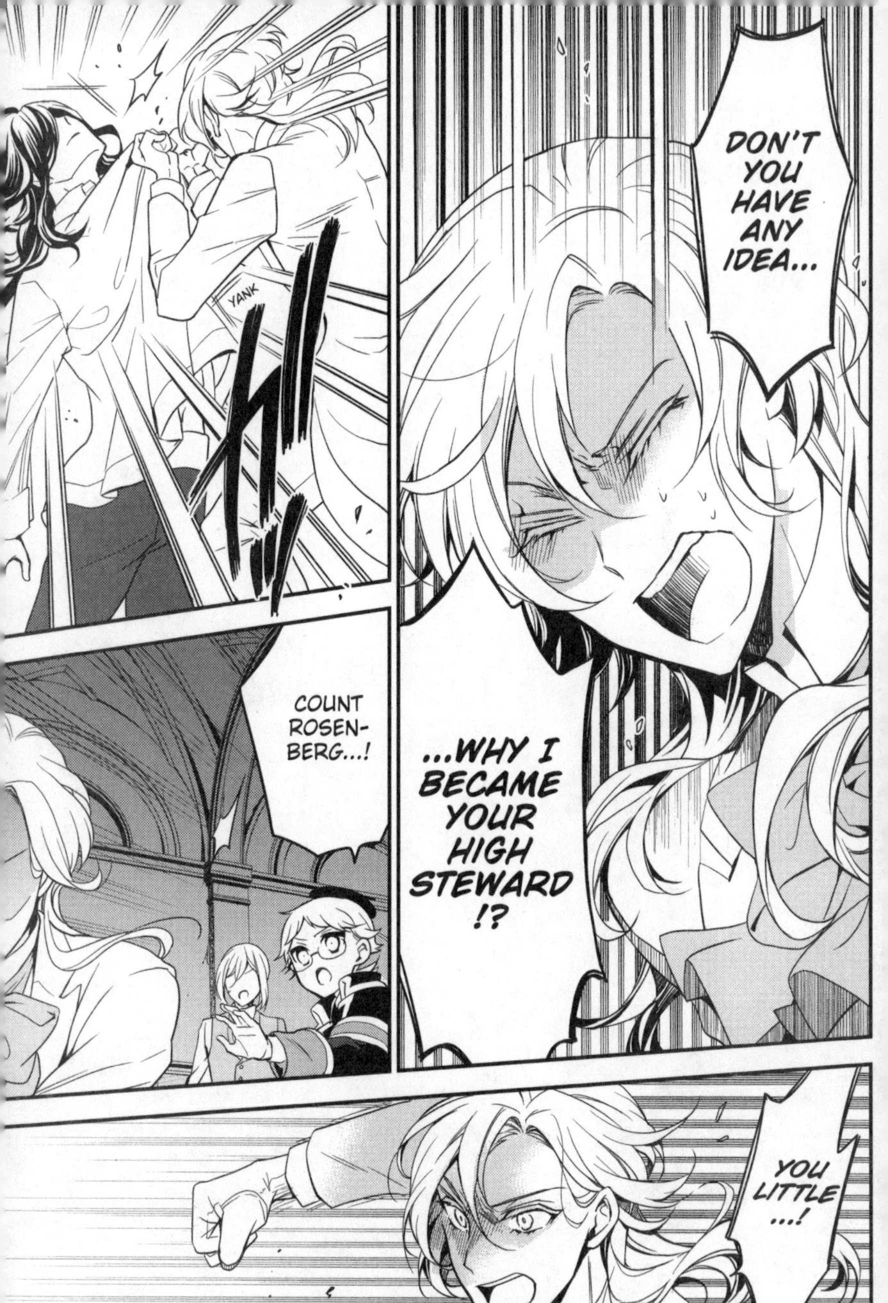
DON'T YOU HAVE ANY IDEA...
...WHY I BECAME YOUR HIGH STEWARD!?
YANK
COUNT ROSEN-BERG...!
YOU LITTLE...!

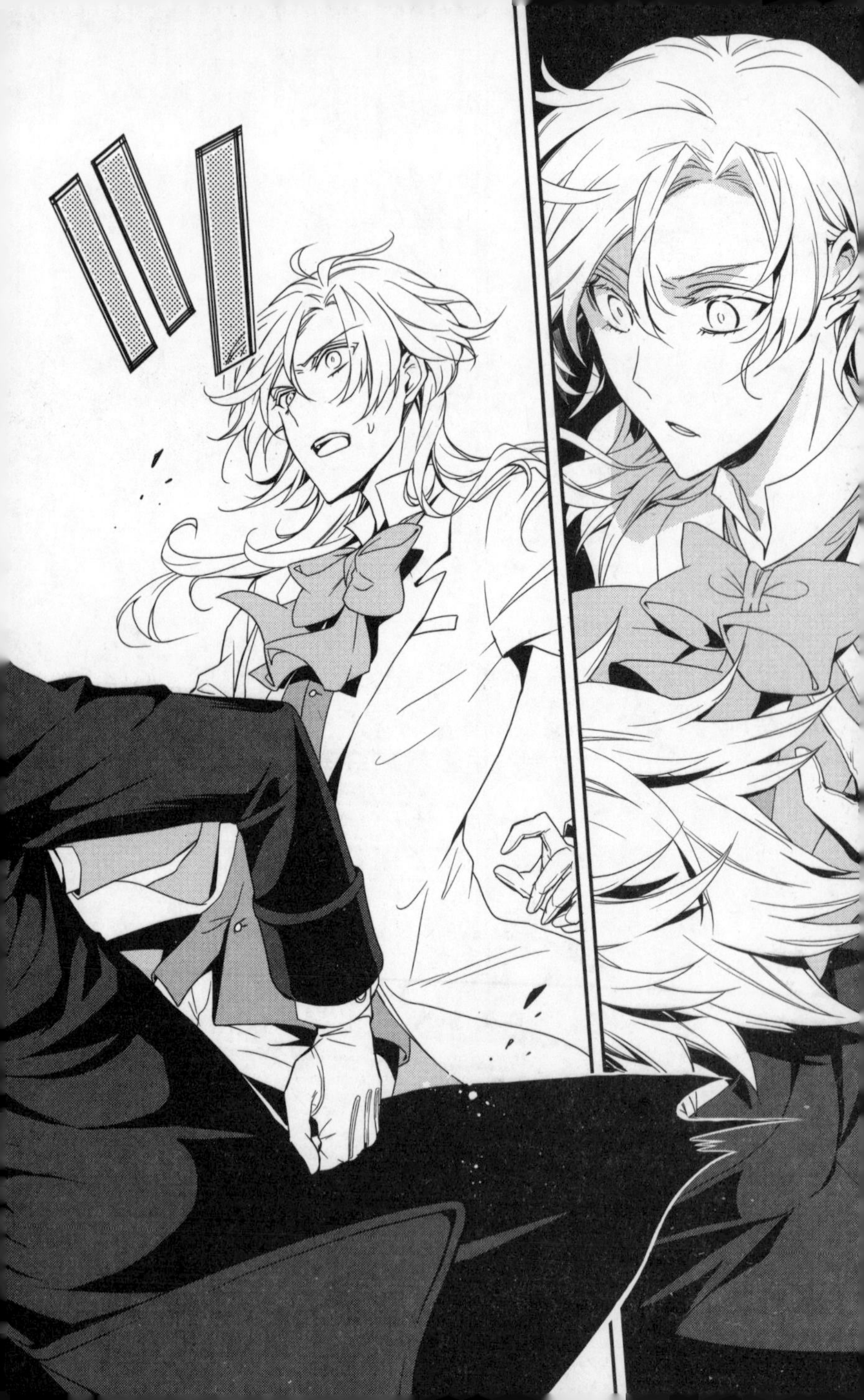

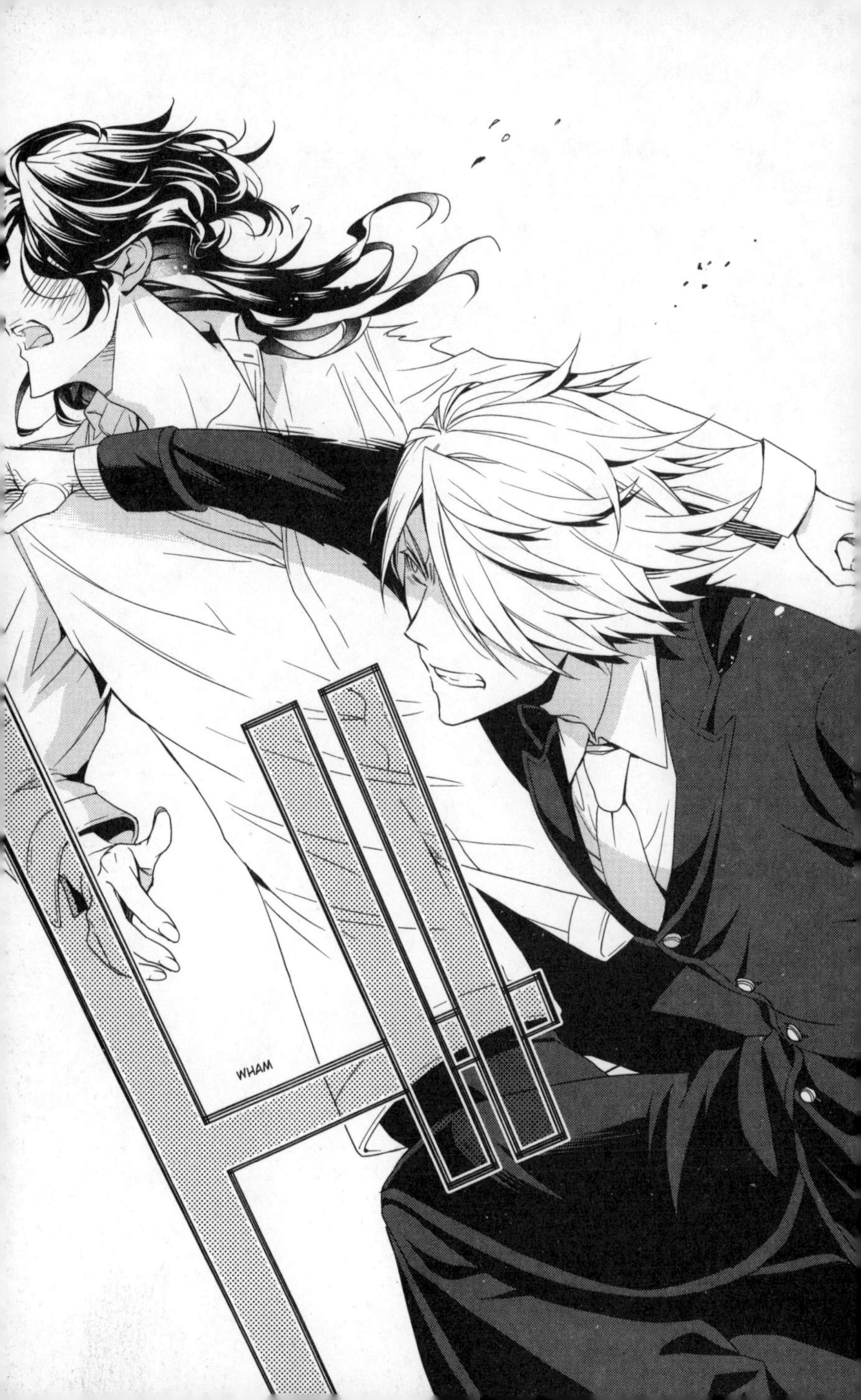
WHAM

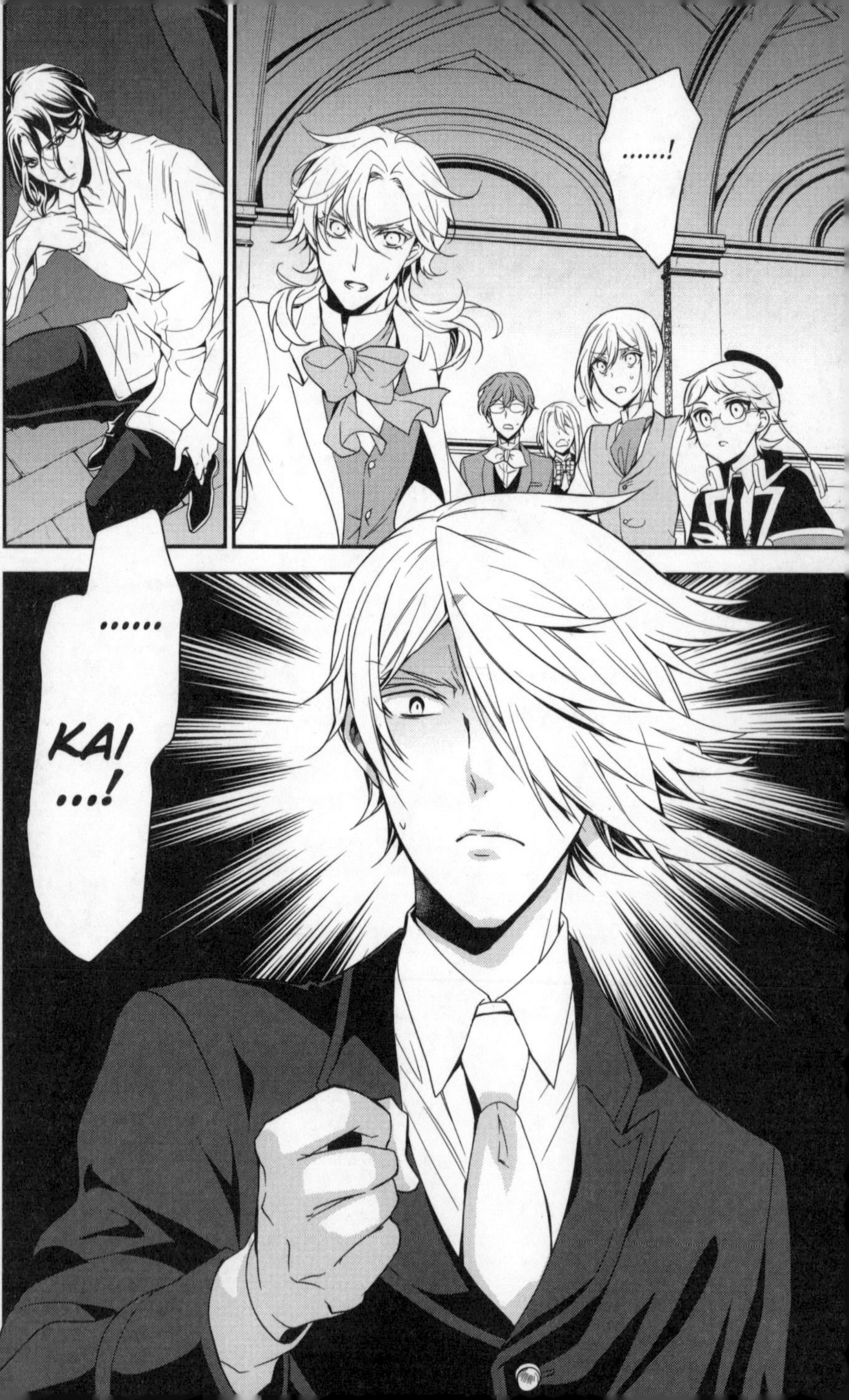
......!
......
KAI
...!

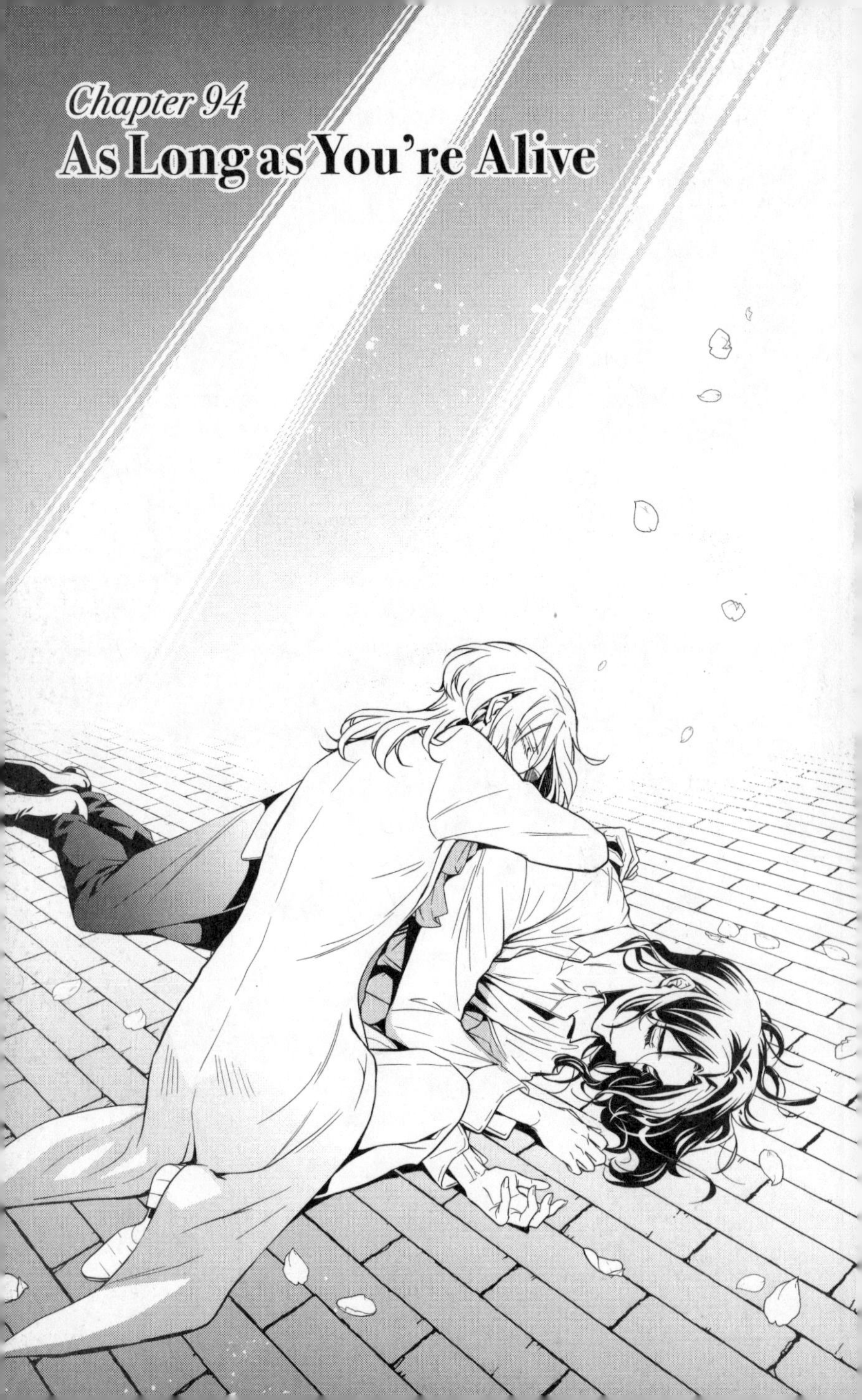
Chapter 94
As Long as You're Alive

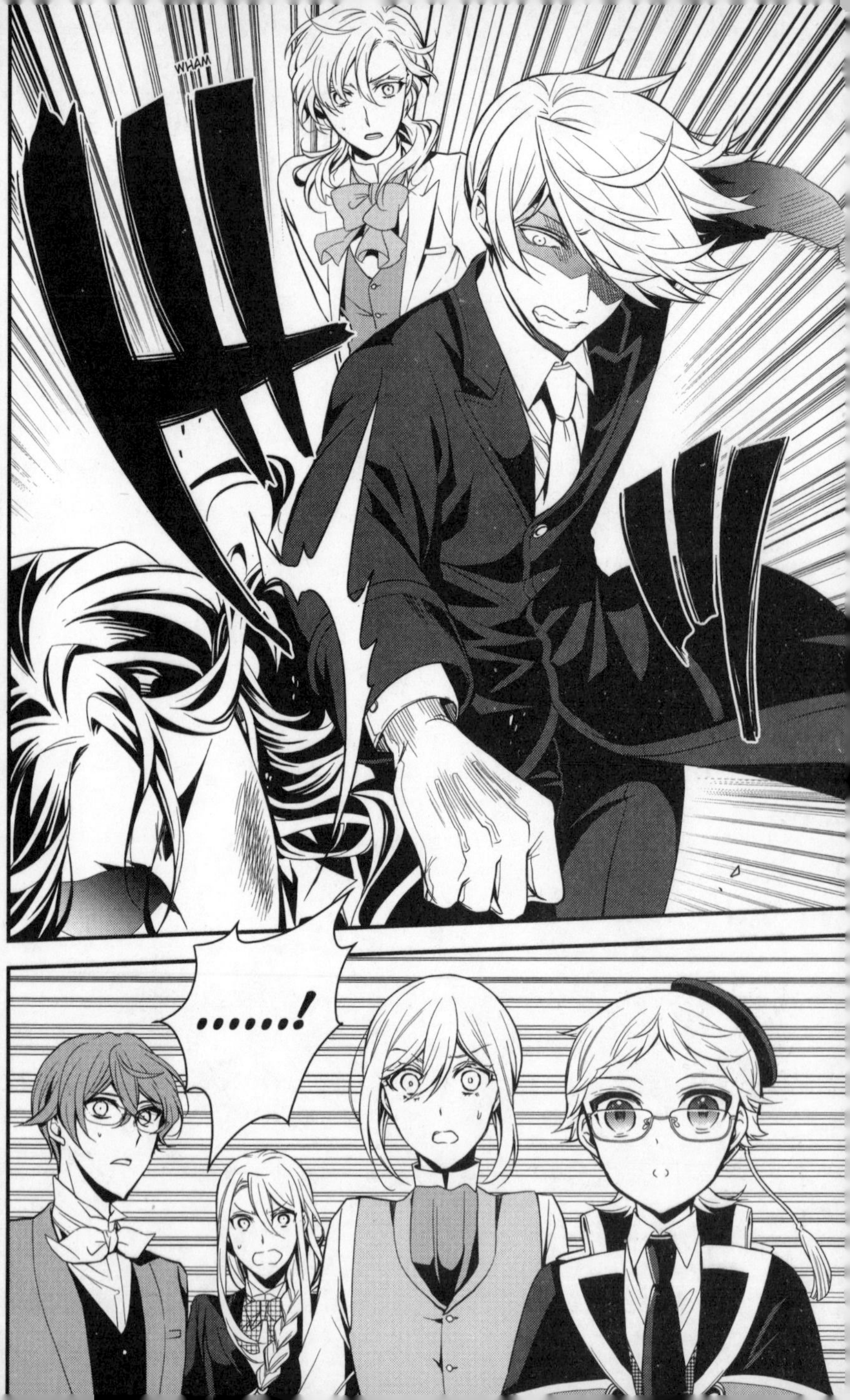
WHAM
......!

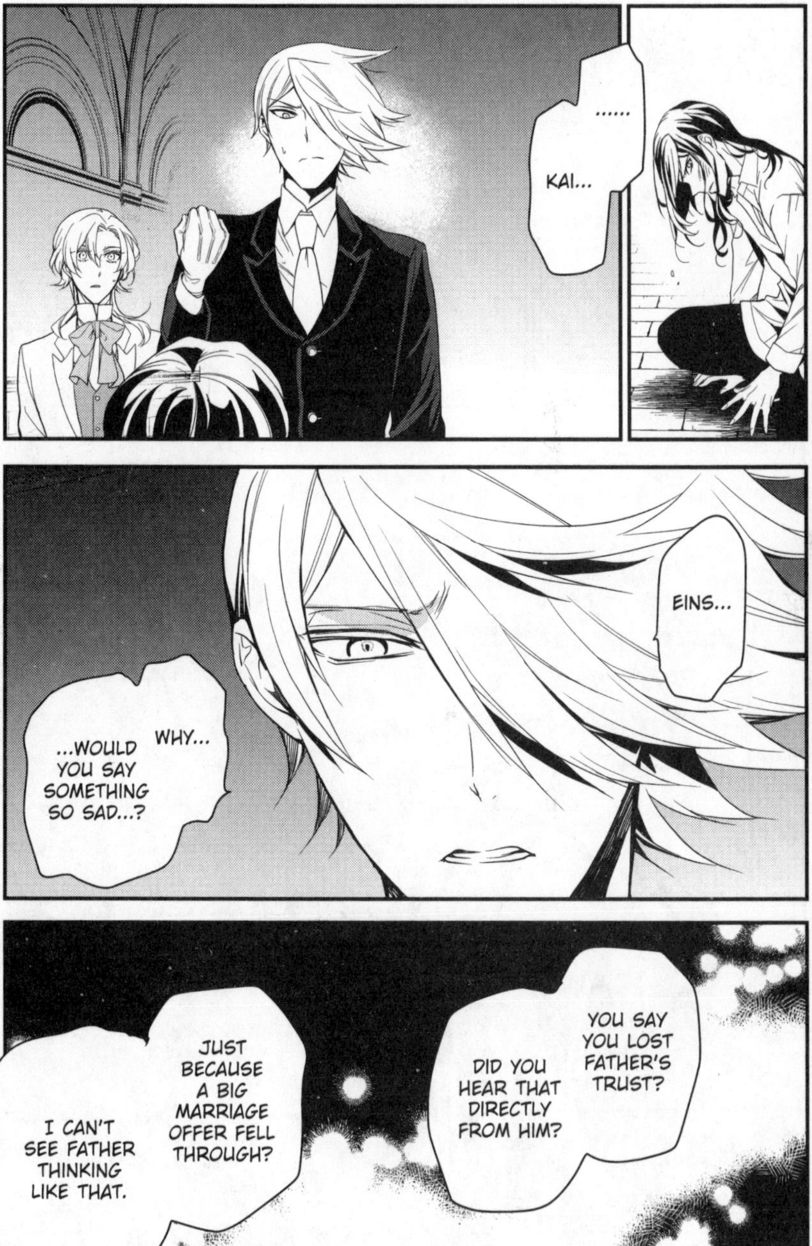
......
KAI...
EINS...
WHY...
...WOULD YOU SAY SOMETHING SO SAD...?
YOU SAY YOU LOST FATHER'S TRUST?
DID YOU HEAR THAT DIRECTLY FROM HIM?
JUST BECAUSE A BIG MARRIAGE OFFER FELL THROUGH?
I CAN'T SEE FATHER THINKING LIKE THAT.

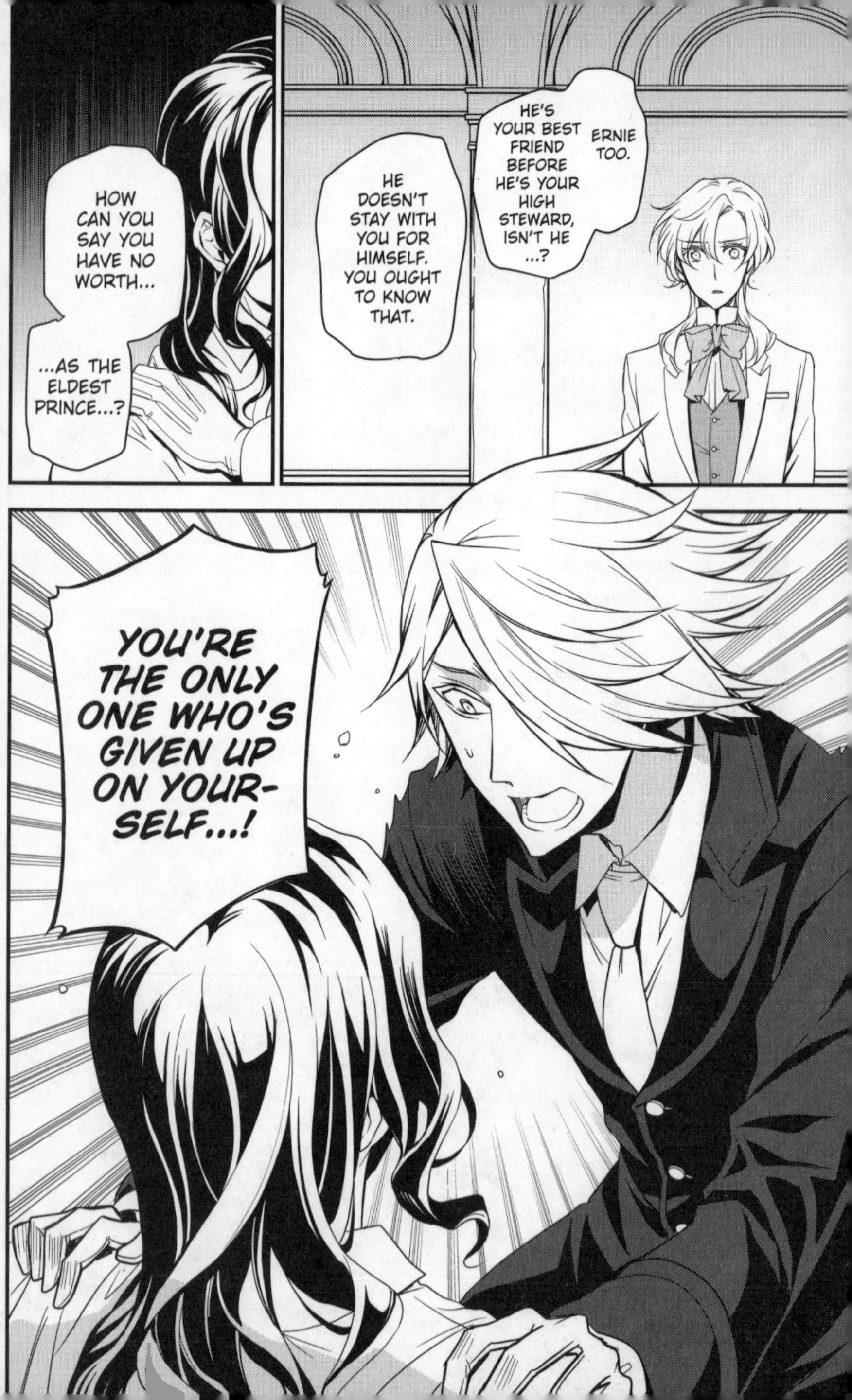
ERNIE TOO.
HE'S YOUR BEST FRIEND BEFORE HE'S YOUR HIGH STEWARD, ISN'T HE ...?
HE DOESN'T STAY WITH YOU FOR HIMSELF. YOU OUGHT TO KNOW THAT.
HOW CAN YOU SAY YOU HAVE NO WORTH...
...AS THE ELDEST PRINCE...?
YOU'RE THE ONLY ONE WHO'S GIVEN UP ON YOUR-SELF...!

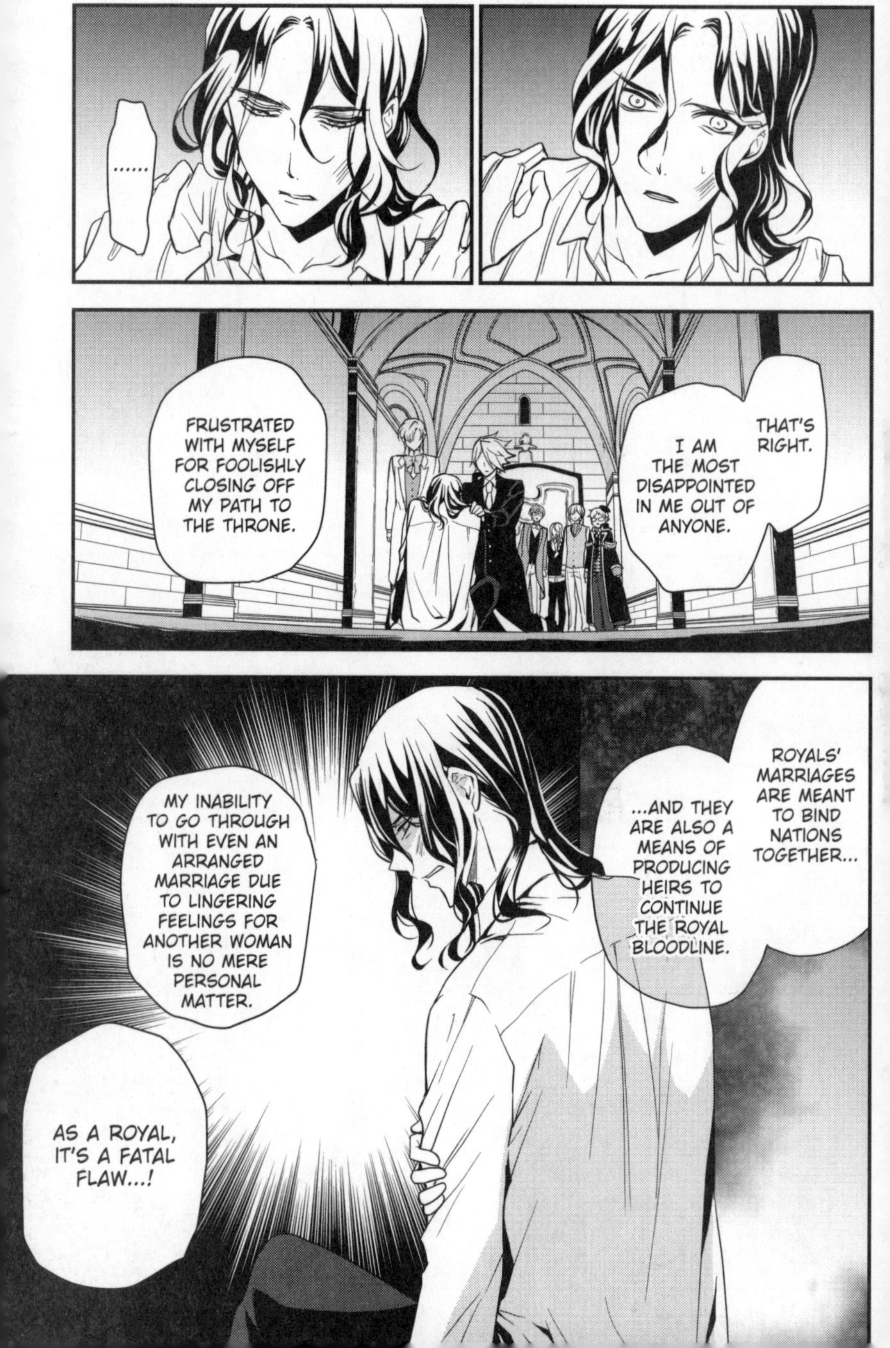
......
THAT'S RIGHT.
I AM THE MOST DISAPPOINTED IN ME OUT OF ANYONE.
FRUSTRATED WITH MYSELF FOR FOOLISHLY CLOSING OFF MY PATH TO THE THRONE.
ROYALS' MARRIAGES ARE MEANT TO BIND NATIONS TOGETHER...
...AND THEY ARE ALSO A MEANS OF PRODUCING HEIRS TO CONTINUE THE ROYAL BLOODLINE.
MY INABILITY TO GO THROUGH WITH EVEN AN ARRANGED MARRIAGE DUE TO LINGERING FEELINGS FOR ANOTHER WOMAN IS NO MERE PERSONAL MATTER.
AS A ROYAL, IT'S A FATAL FLAW...!

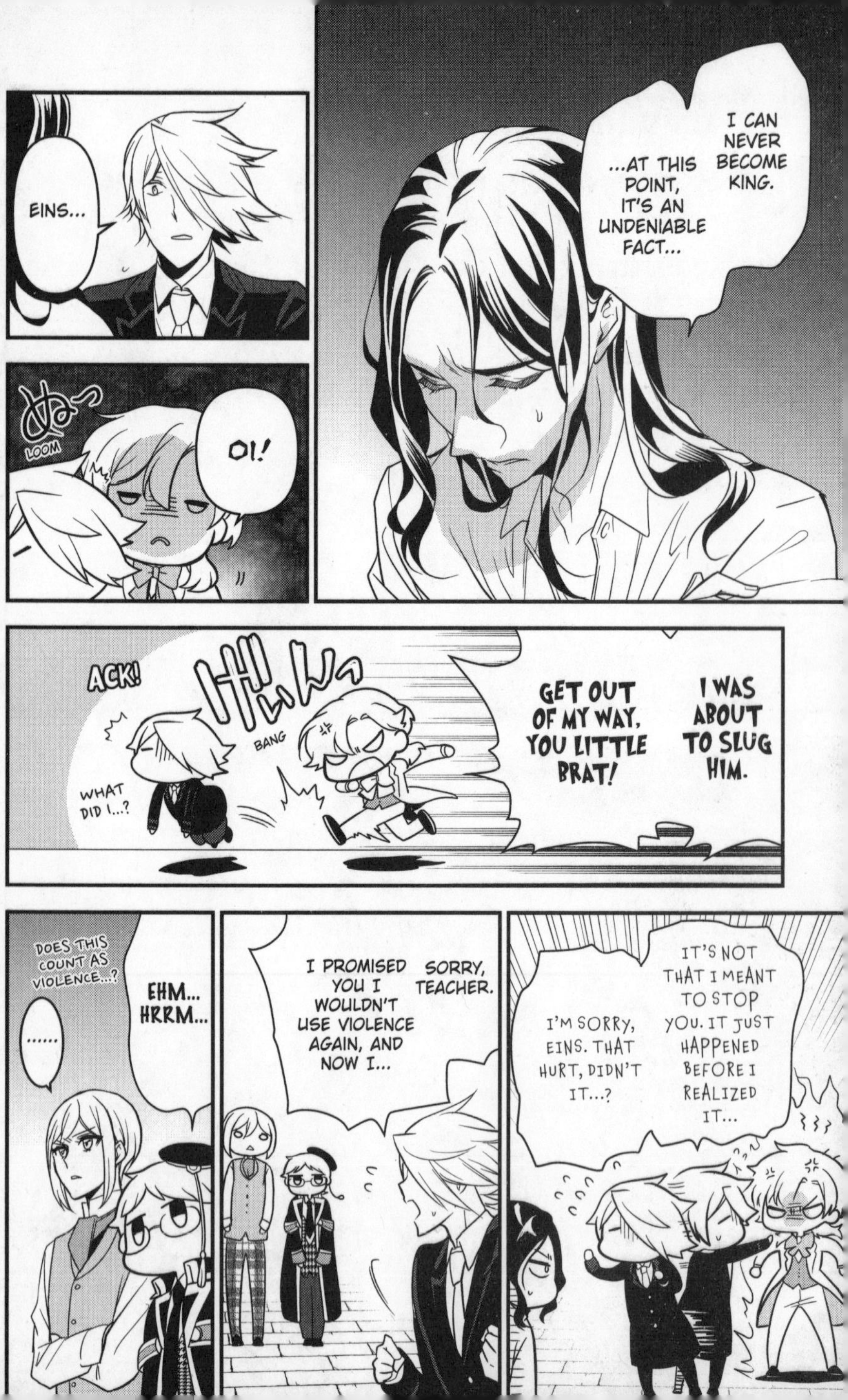
I CAN NEVER BECOME KING.
...AT THIS POINT, IT'S AN UNDENIABLE FACT...
EINS...
ぬっ
LOOM
OI!
I WAS ABOUT TO SLUG HIM.
GET OUT OF MY WAY, YOU LITTLE BRAT!
けいんっ
BANG
ACK!
WHAT DID I...?
IT'S NOT THAT I MEANT TO STOP YOU. IT JUST HAPPENED BEFORE I REALIZED IT...
I'M SORRY, EINS. THAT HURT, DIDN'T IT...?
SORRY, TEACHER.
I PROMISED YOU I WOULDN'T USE VIOLENCE AGAIN, AND NOW I...
EHM... HRRM...
DOES THIS COUNT AS VIOLENCE...?
......

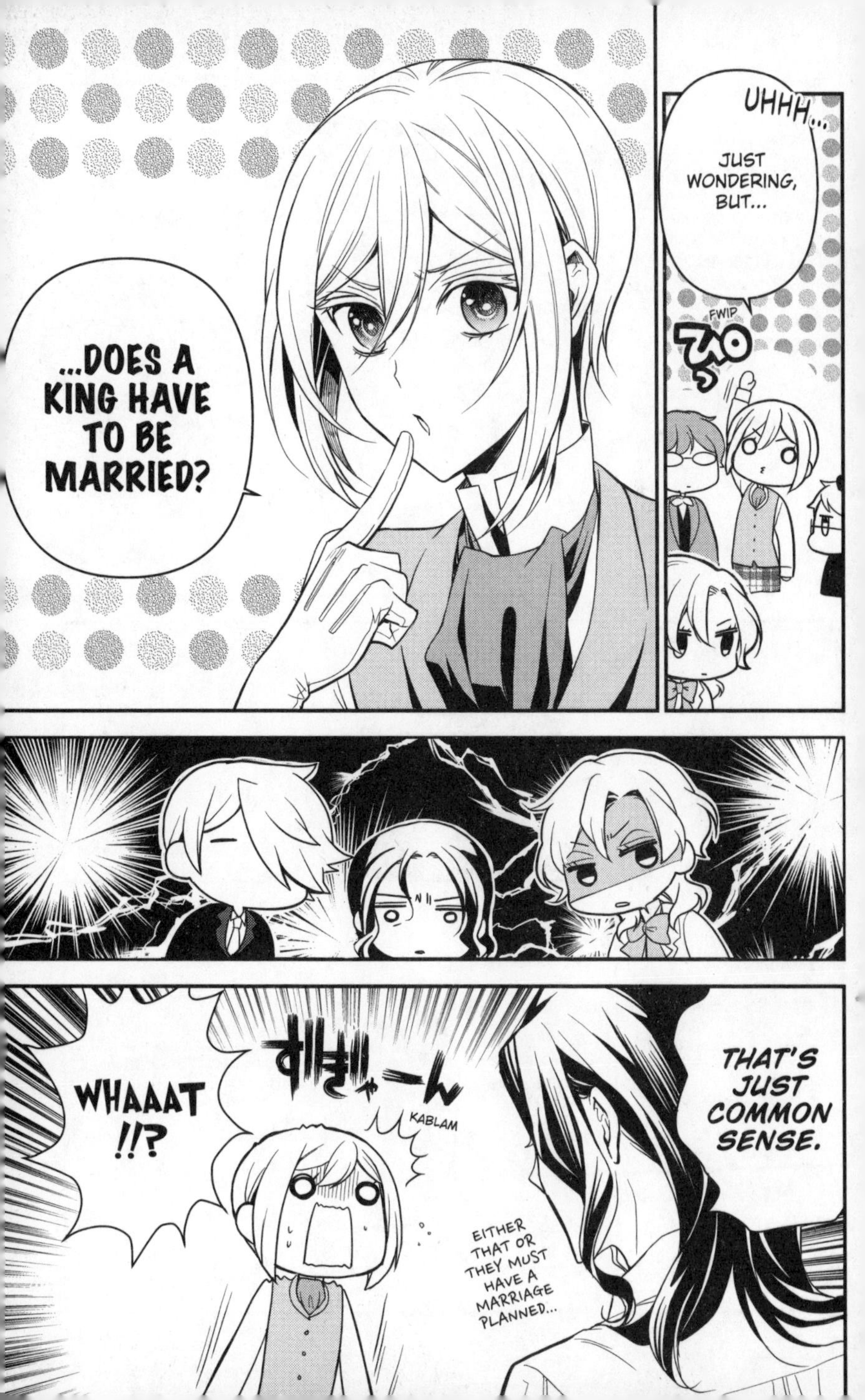
UHHH...
JUST WONDERING, BUT...
FWIP
...DOES A KING HAVE TO BE MARRIED?
THAT'S JUST COMMON SENSE.
EITHER THAT OR THEY MUST HAVE A MARRIAGE PLANNED...
KABLAM
WHAAAT!!?

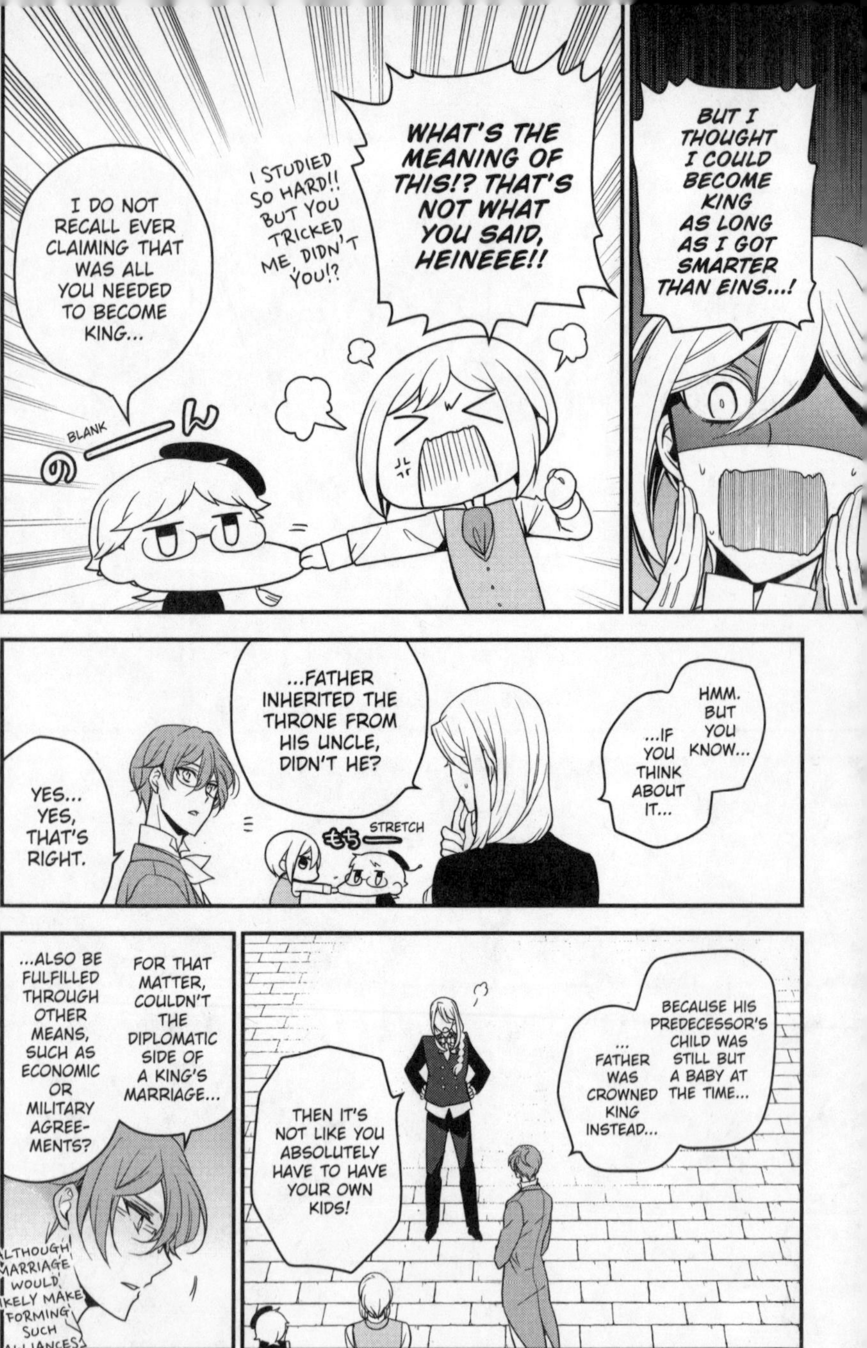
BUT I THOUGHT I COULD BECOME KING AS LONG AS I GOT SMARTER THAN EINS...!
WHAT'S THE MEANING OF THIS!? THAT'S NOT WHAT YOU SAID, HEINEEE!!
I STUDIED SO HARD!! BUT YOU TRICKED ME, DIDN'T YOU!?
I DO NOT RECALL EVER CLAIMING THAT WAS ALL YOU NEEDED TO BECOME KING...
BLANK
HMM. BUT YOU KNOW...
...IF YOU THINK ABOUT IT...
...FATHER INHERITED THE THRONE FROM HIS UNCLE, DIDN'T HE?
STRETCH
YES... YES, THAT'S RIGHT.
BECAUSE HIS PREDECESSOR'S CHILD WAS STILL BUT A BABY AT THE TIME...
...FATHER WAS CROWNED KING INSTEAD...
THEN IT'S NOT LIKE YOU ABSOLUTELY HAVE TO HAVE YOUR OWN KIDS!
FOR THAT MATTER, COULDN'T THE DIPLOMATIC SIDE OF A KING'S MARRIAGE...
...ALSO BE FULFILLED THROUGH OTHER MEANS, SUCH AS ECONOMIC OR MILITARY AGREE-MENTS?
ALTHOUGH MARRIAGE WOULD LIKELY MAKE FORMING SUCH ALLIANCES EASIER...

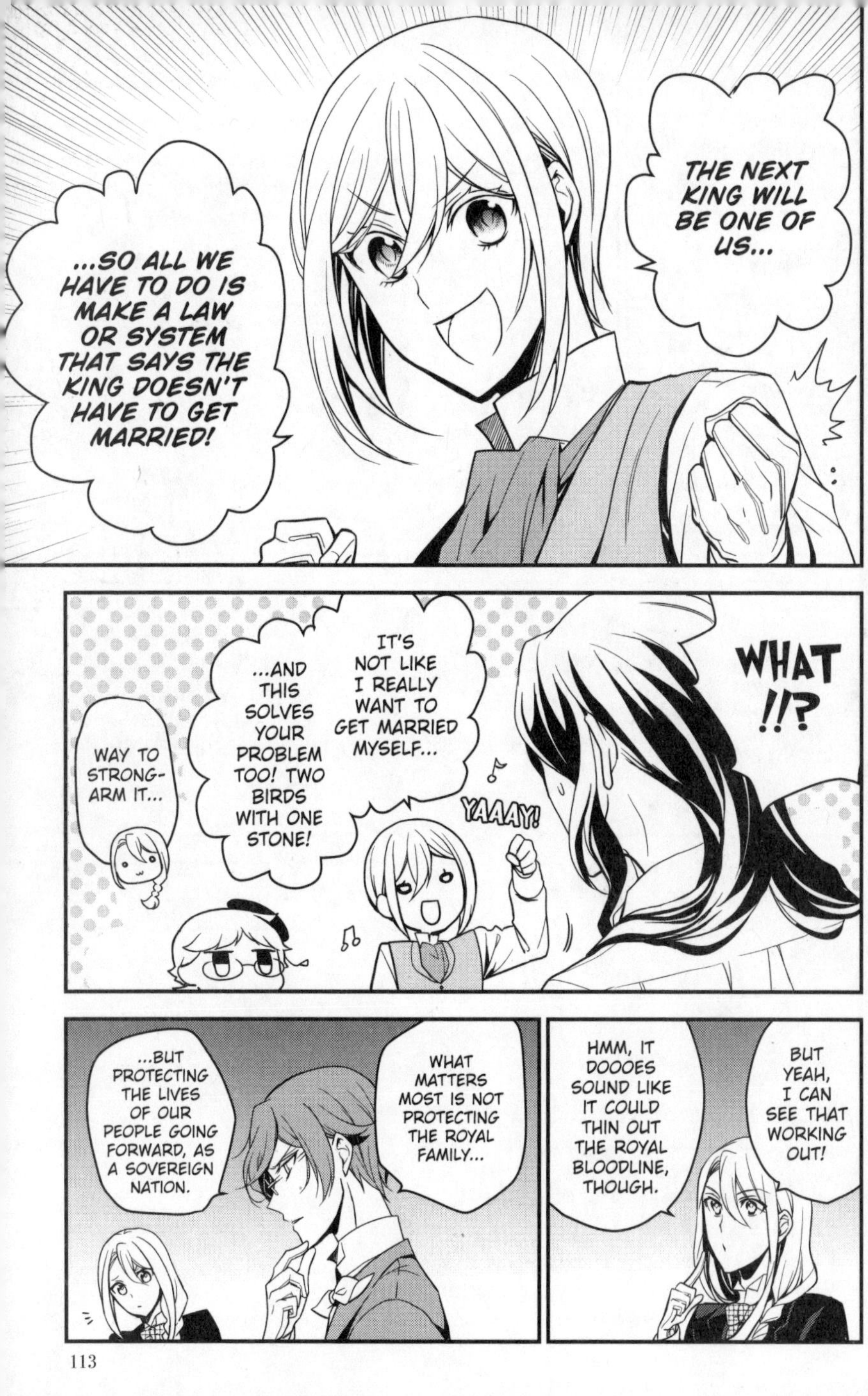
THE NEXT KING WILL BE ONE OF US...
...SO ALL WE HAVE TO DO IS MAKE A LAW OR SYSTEM THAT SAYS THE KING DOESN'T HAVE TO GET MARRIED!
WHAT!!?
IT'S NOT LIKE I REALLY WANT TO GET MARRIED MYSELF...
YAAAY!
...AND THIS SOLVES YOUR PROBLEM TOO! TWO BIRDS WITH ONE STONE!
WAY TO STRONG-ARM IT...
BUT YEAH, I CAN SEE THAT WORKING OUT!
HMM, IT DOOOES SOUND LIKE IT COULD THIN OUT THE ROYAL BLOODLINE, THOUGH.
WHAT MATTERS MOST IS NOT PROTECTING THE ROYAL FAMILY...
...BUT PROTECTING THE LIVES OF OUR PEOPLE GOING FORWARD, AS A SOVEREIGN NATION.

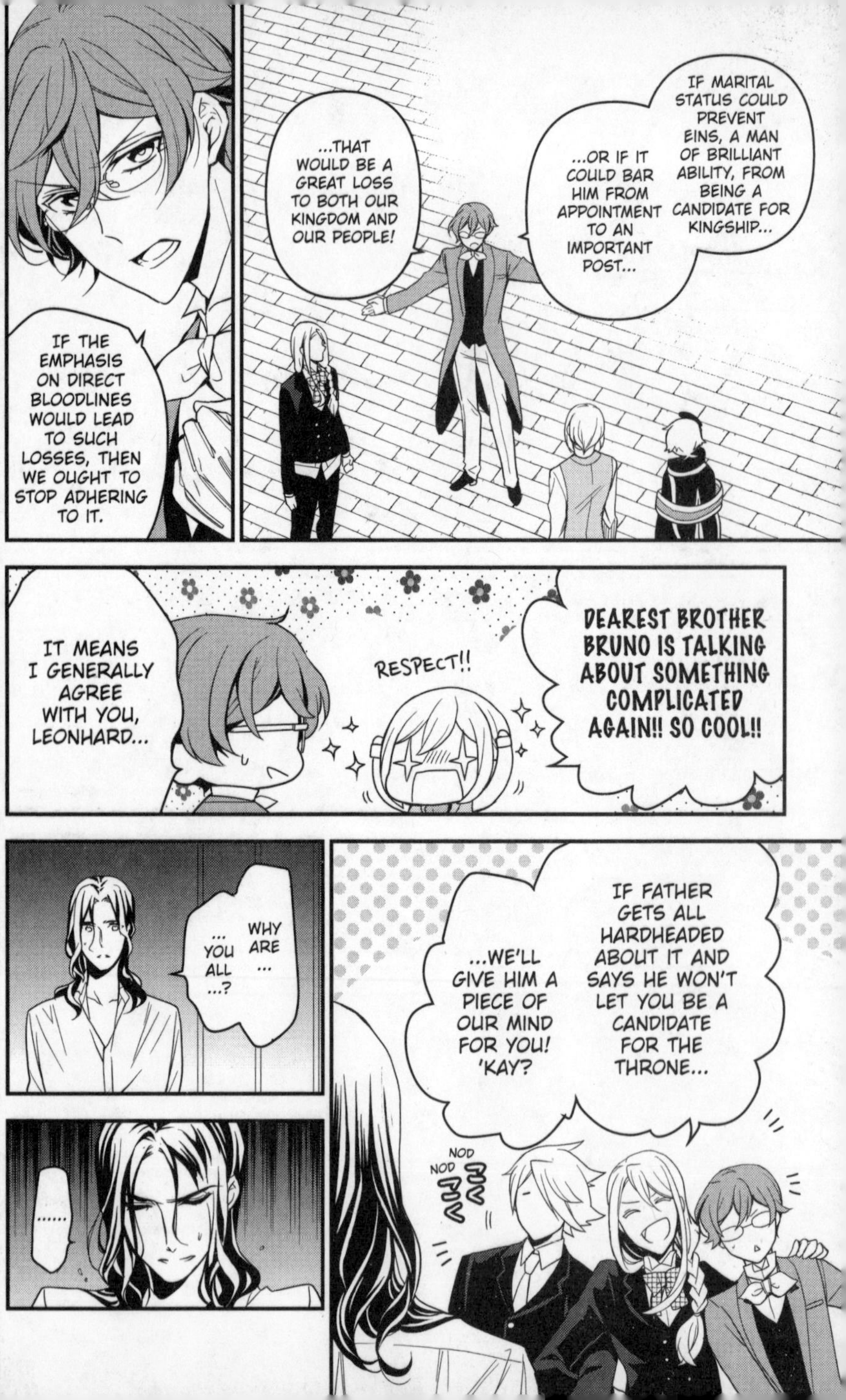
IF MARITAL STATUS COULD PREVENT EINS, A MAN OF BRILLIANT ABILITY, FROM BEING A CANDIDATE FOR KINGSHIP...
...OR IF IT COULD BAR HIM FROM APPOINTMENT TO AN IMPORTANT POST...
...THAT WOULD BE A GREAT LOSS TO BOTH OUR KINGDOM AND OUR PEOPLE!
IF THE EMPHASIS ON DIRECT BLOODLINES WOULD LEAD TO SUCH LOSSES, THEN WE OUGHT TO STOP ADHERING TO IT.
DEAREST BROTHER BRUNO IS TALKING ABOUT SOMETHING COMPLICATED AGAIN!! SO COOL!!
RESPECT!!
IT MEANS I GENERALLY AGREE WITH YOU, LEONHARD...
IF FATHER GETS ALL HARDHEADED ABOUT IT AND SAYS HE WON'T LET YOU BE A CANDIDATE FOR THE THRONE...
...WE'LL GIVE HIM A PIECE OF OUR MIND FOR YOU! 'KAY?
NOD NOD
WHY ARE ... YOU ALL ...?
......

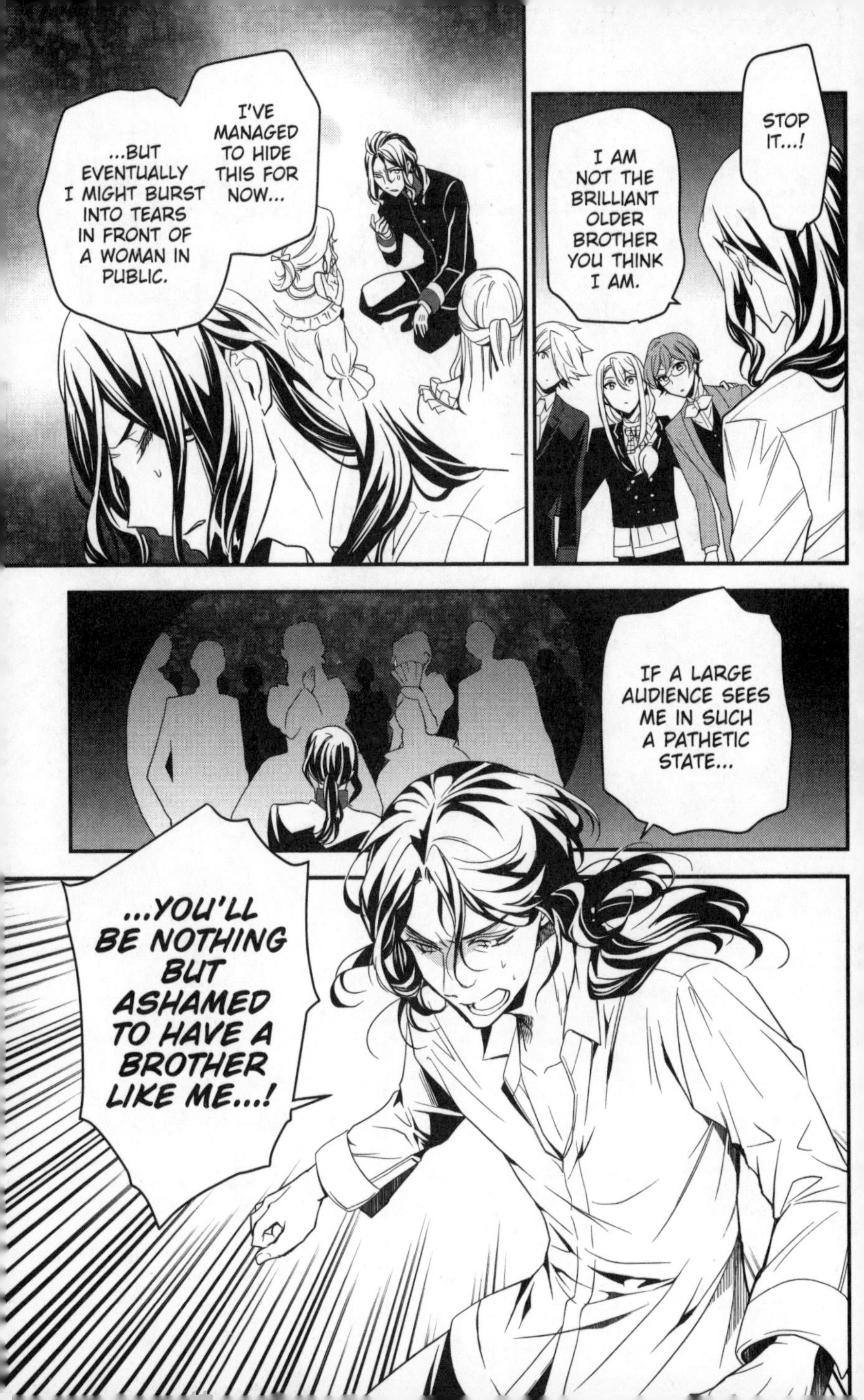
STOP IT...!
I AM NOT THE BRILLIANT OLDER BROTHER YOU THINK I AM.
I'VE MANAGED TO HIDE THIS FOR NOW...
...BUT EVENTUALLY I MIGHT BURST INTO TEARS IN FRONT OF A WOMAN IN PUBLIC.
IF A LARGE AUDIENCE SEES ME IN SUCH A PATHETIC STATE...
...YOU'LL BE NOTHING BUT ASHAMED TO HAVE A BROTHER LIKE ME...!

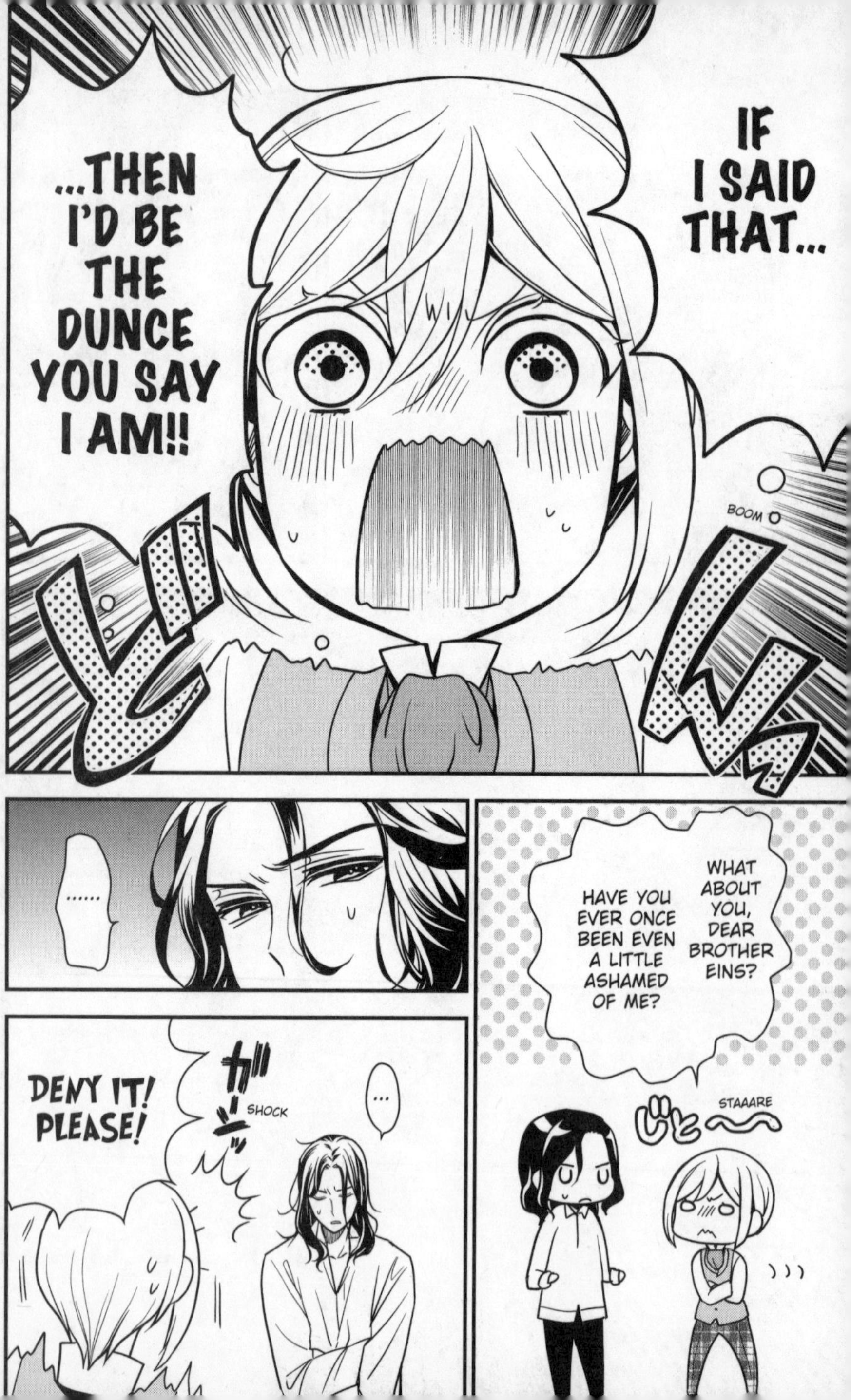
IF I SAID THAT...
...THEN I'D BE THE DUNCE YOU SAY I AM!!
BOOM
WHAT ABOUT YOU, DEAR BROTHER EINS?
HAVE YOU EVER ONCE BEEN EVEN A LITTLE ASHAMED OF ME?
STAAARE
......
...
SHOCK
DENY IT! PLEASE!

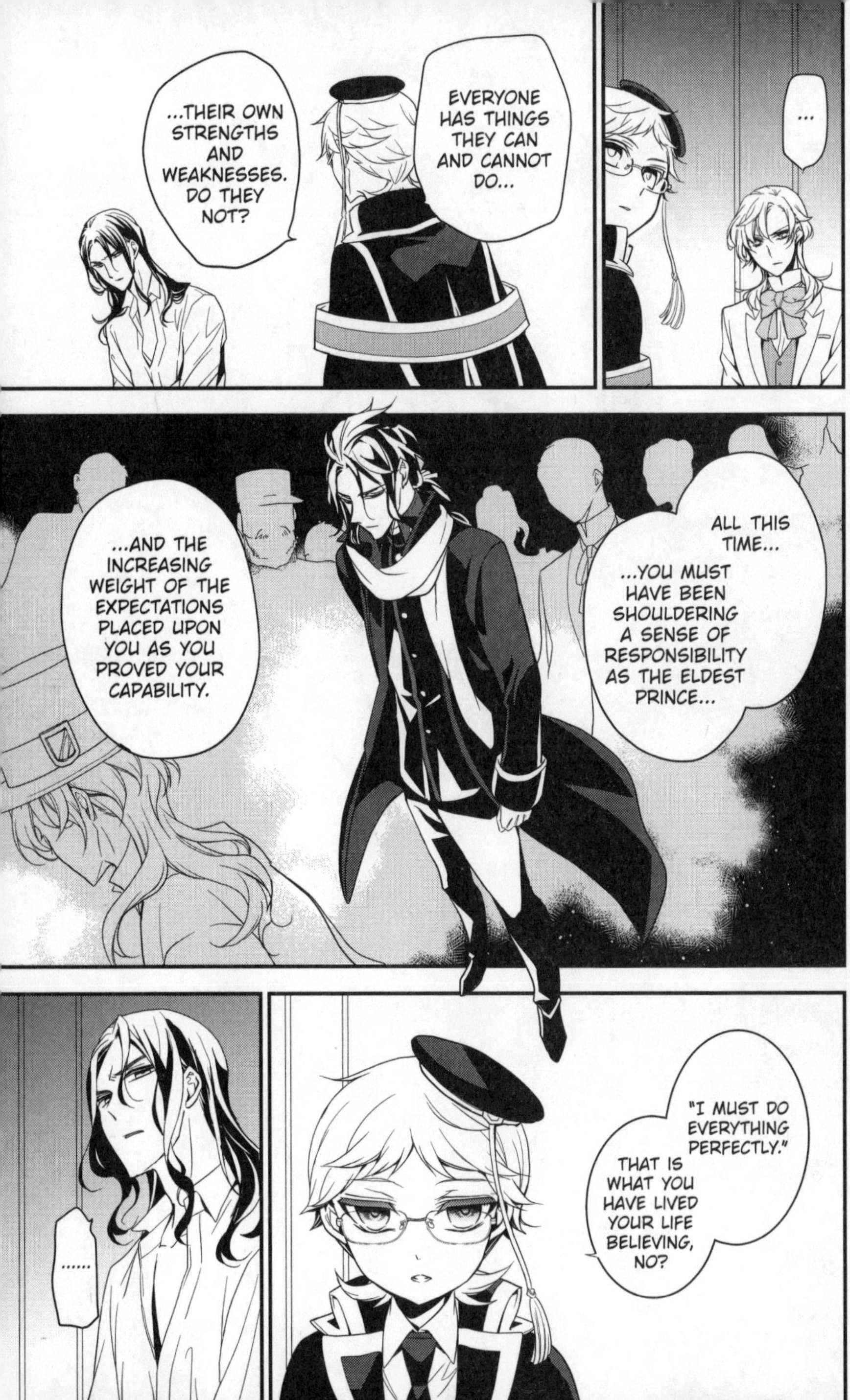
...
EVERYONE HAS THINGS THEY CAN AND CANNOT DO...
...THEIR OWN STRENGTHS AND WEAKNESSES. DO THEY NOT?
ALL THIS TIME...
...YOU MUST HAVE BEEN SHOULDERING A SENSE OF RESPONSIBILITY AS THE ELDEST PRINCE...
...AND THE INCREASING WEIGHT OF THE EXPECTATIONS PLACED UPON YOU AS YOU PROVED YOUR CAPABILITY.
"I MUST DO EVERYTHING PERFECTLY."
THAT IS WHAT YOU HAVE LIVED YOUR LIFE BELIEVING, NO?
......

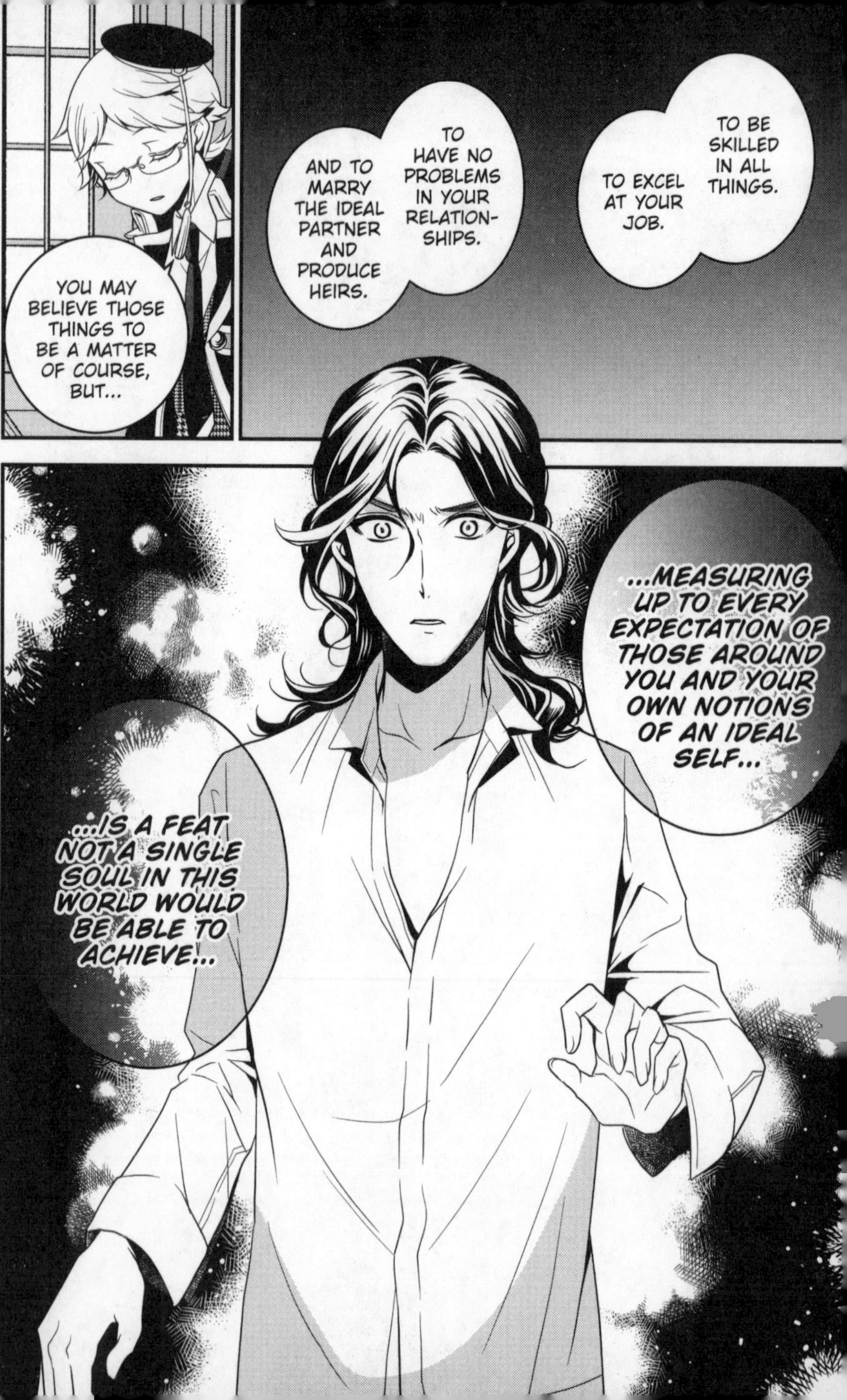
TO BE SKILLED IN ALL THINGS.
TO EXCEL AT YOUR JOB.
TO HAVE NO PROBLEMS IN YOUR RELATION-SHIPS.
AND TO MARRY THE IDEAL PARTNER AND PRODUCE HEIRS.
YOU MAY BELIEVE THOSE THINGS TO BE A MATTER OF COURSE, BUT...
...MEASURING UP TO EVERY EXPECTATION OF THOSE AROUND YOU AND YOUR OWN NOTIONS OF AN IDEAL SELF...
...IS A FEAT NOT A SINGLE SOUL IN THIS WORLD WOULD BE ABLE TO ACHIEVE...

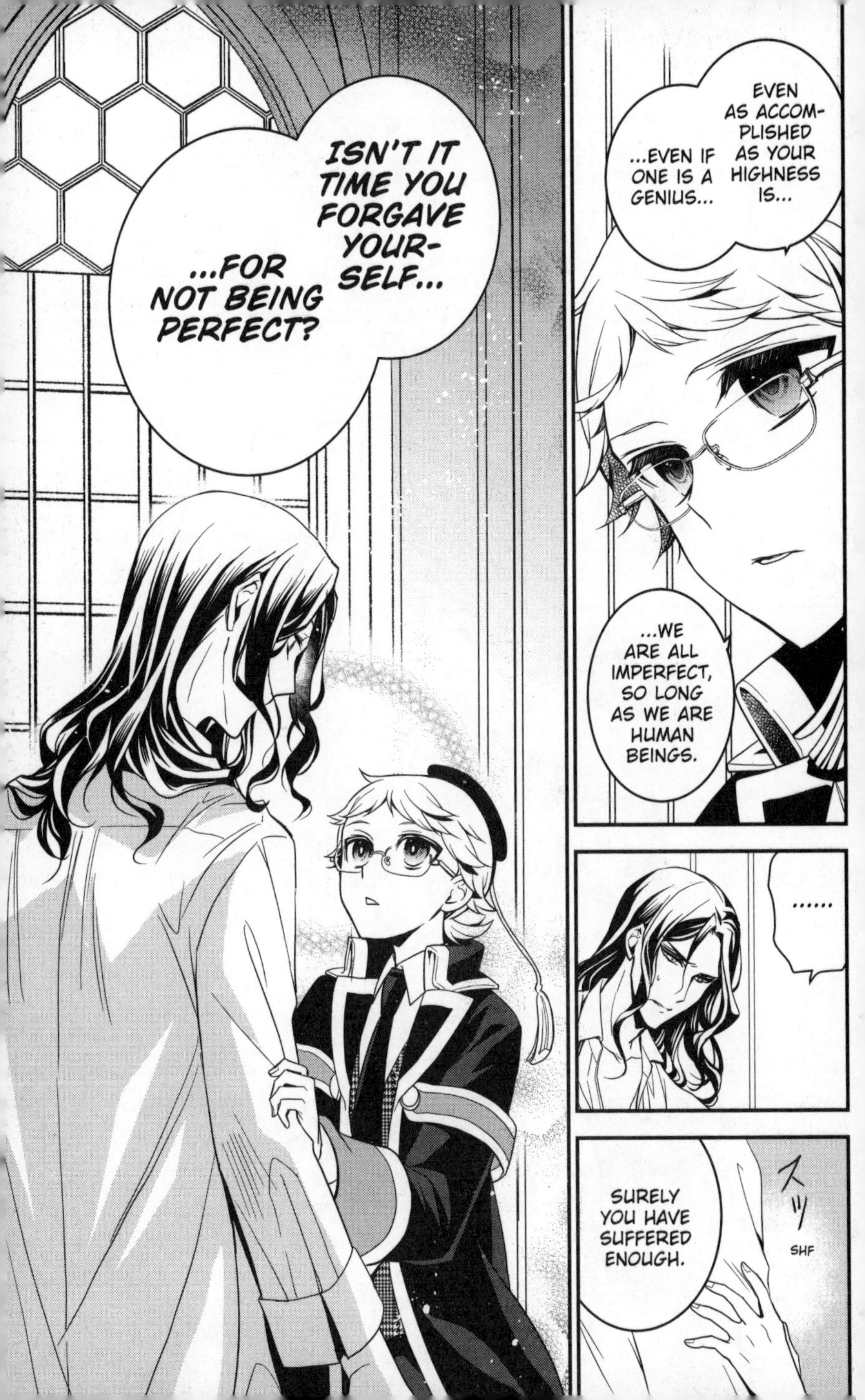
EVEN AS ACCOMPLISHED AS YOUR HIGHNESS IS...
...EVEN IF ONE IS A GENIUS...
...WE ARE ALL IMPERFECT, SO LONG AS WE ARE HUMAN BEINGS.
......
スッ
SHF
SURELY YOU HAVE SUFFERED ENOUGH.
ISN'T IT TIME YOU FORGAVE YOURSELF...
...FOR NOT BEING PERFECT?

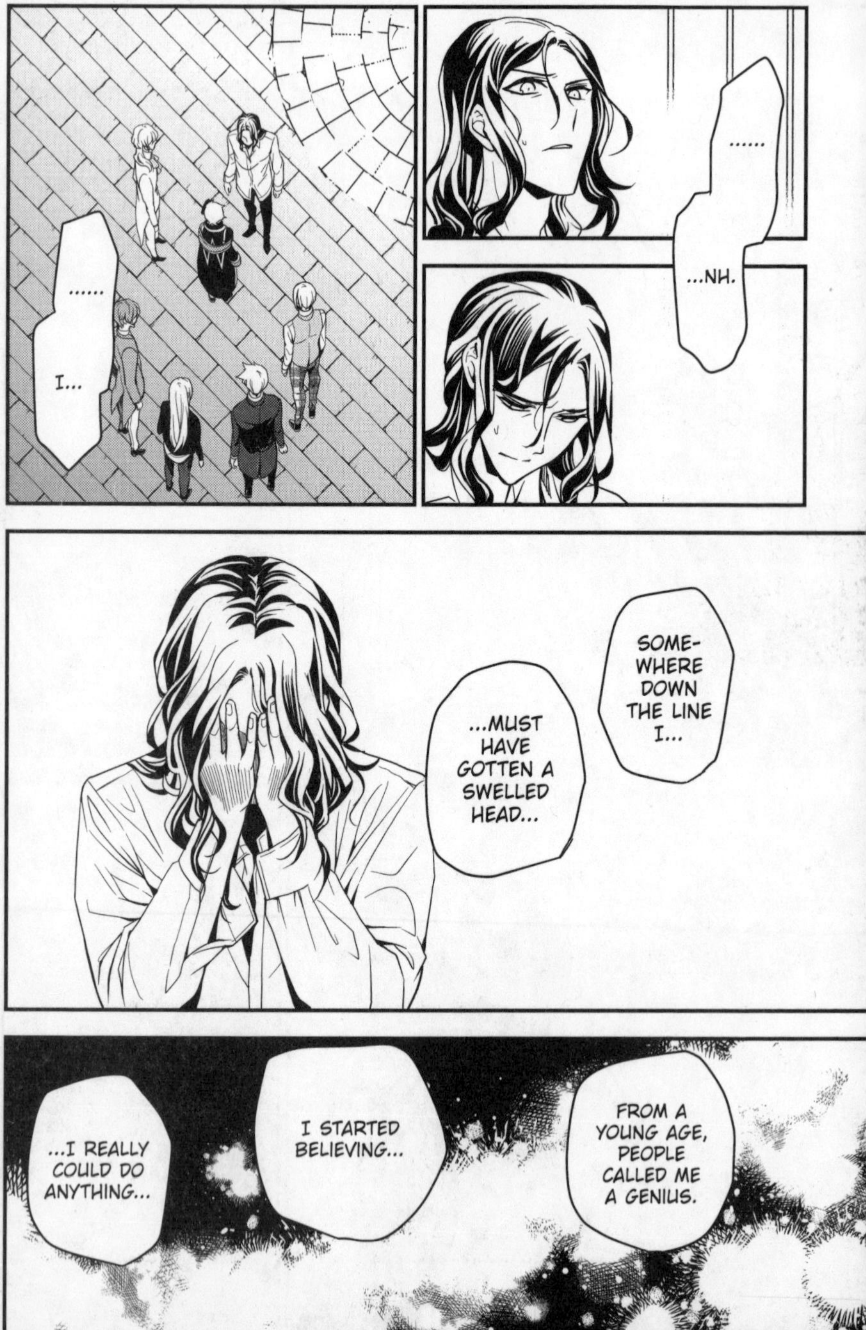
......
...NH.
......
I...
SOME-WHERE DOWN THE LINE I...
...MUST HAVE GOTTEN A SWELLED HEAD...
FROM A YOUNG AGE, PEOPLE CALLED ME A GENIUS.
I STARTED BELIEVING...
...I REALLY COULD DO ANYTHING...

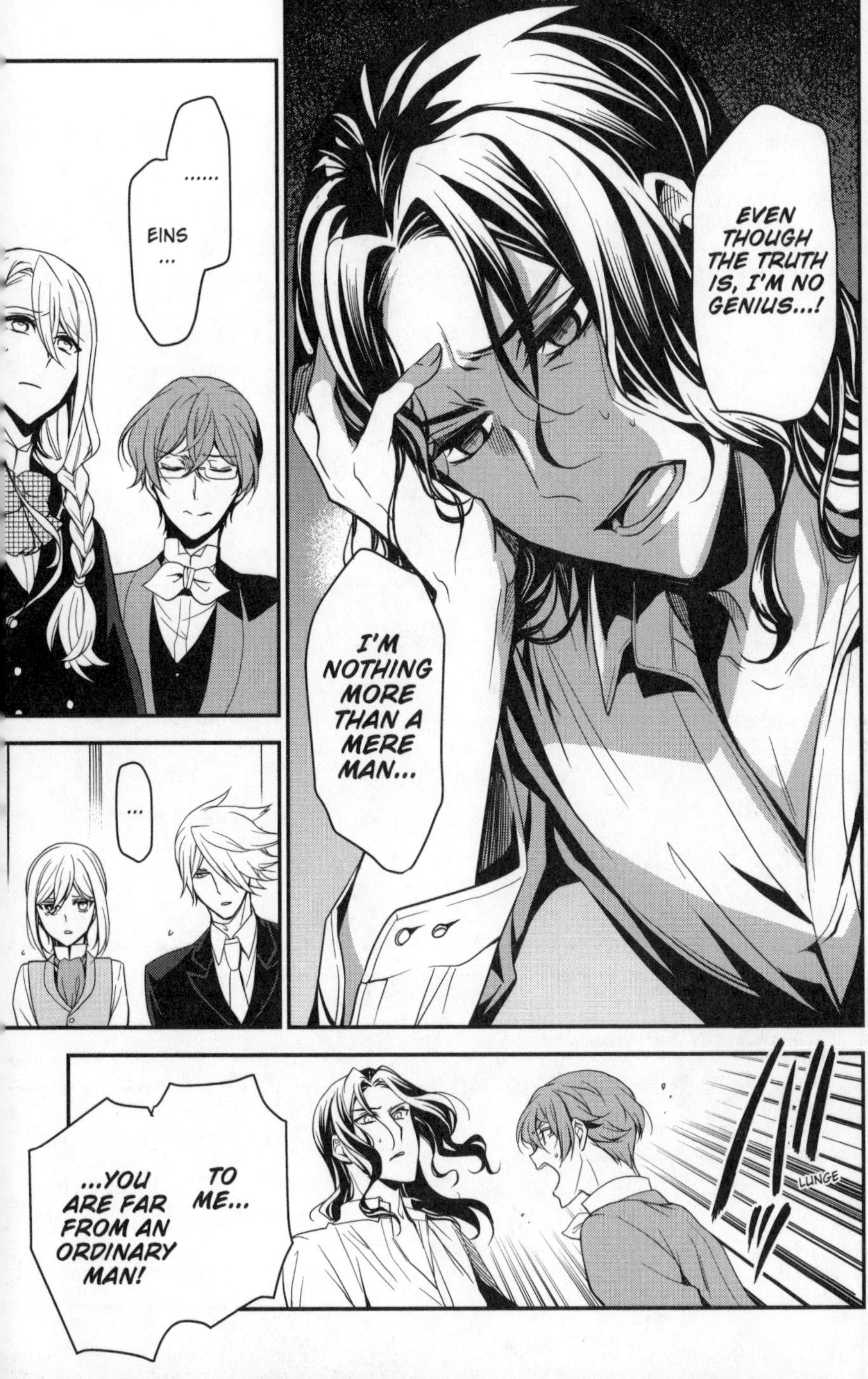
EVEN THOUGH THE TRUTH IS, I'M NO GENIUS...!
I'M NOTHING MORE THAN A MERE MAN...
......
EINS ...
...
LUNGE
TO ME...
...YOU ARE FAR FROM AN ORDINARY MAN!

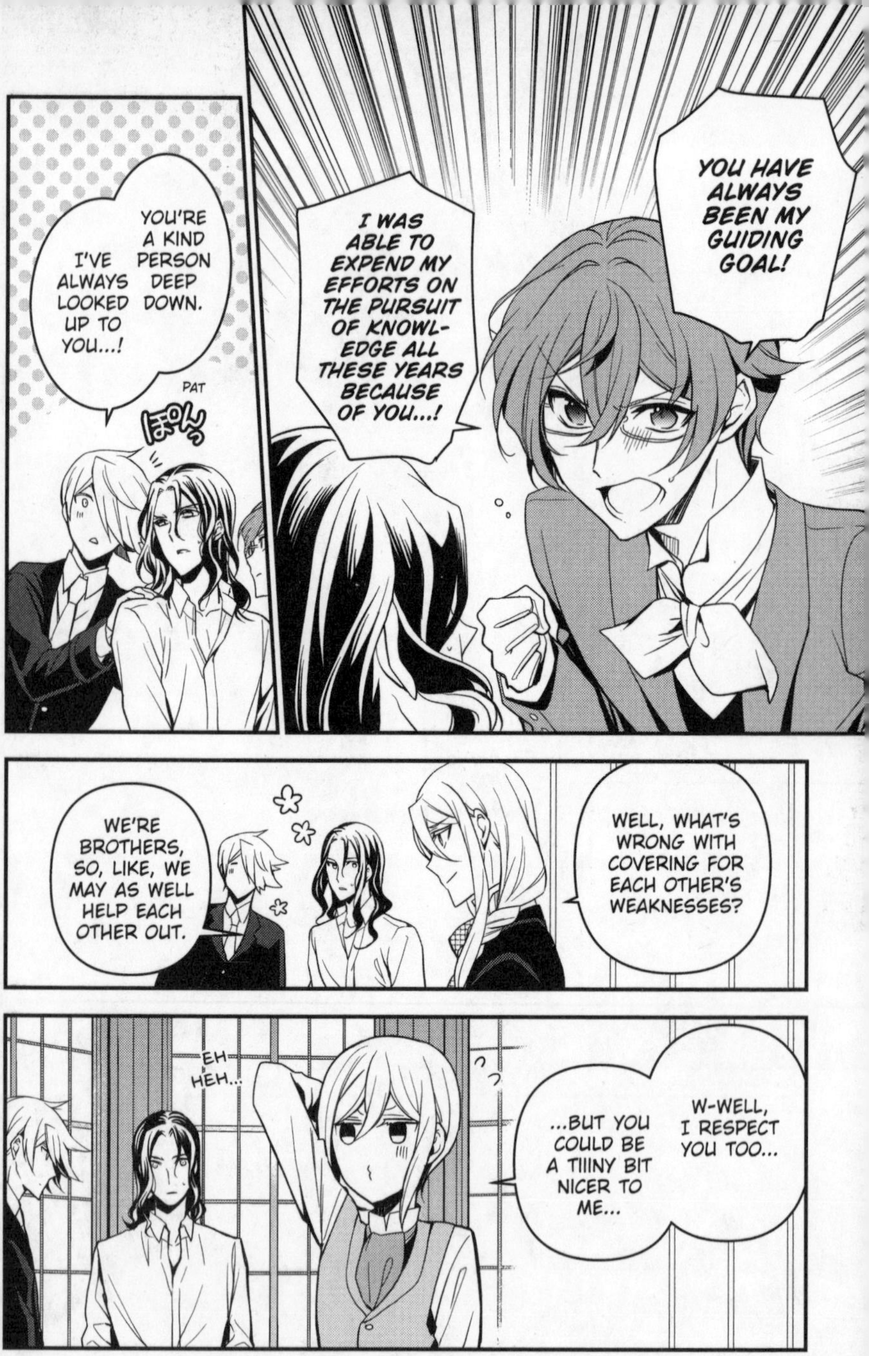
YOU HAVE ALWAYS BEEN MY GUIDING GOAL!
I WAS ABLE TO EXPEND MY EFFORTS ON THE PURSUIT OF KNOWL-EDGE ALL THESE YEARS BECAUSE OF YOU...!
YOU'RE A KIND PERSON DEEP DOWN.
I'VE ALWAYS LOOKED UP TO YOU...!
PAT
ぽんっ
WELL, WHAT'S WRONG WITH COVERING FOR EACH OTHER'S WEAKNESSES?
WE'RE BROTHERS, SO, LIKE, WE MAY AS WELL HELP EACH OTHER OUT.
W-WELL, I RESPECT YOU TOO...
...BUT YOU COULD BE A TIIINY BIT NICER TO ME...
EH HEH...

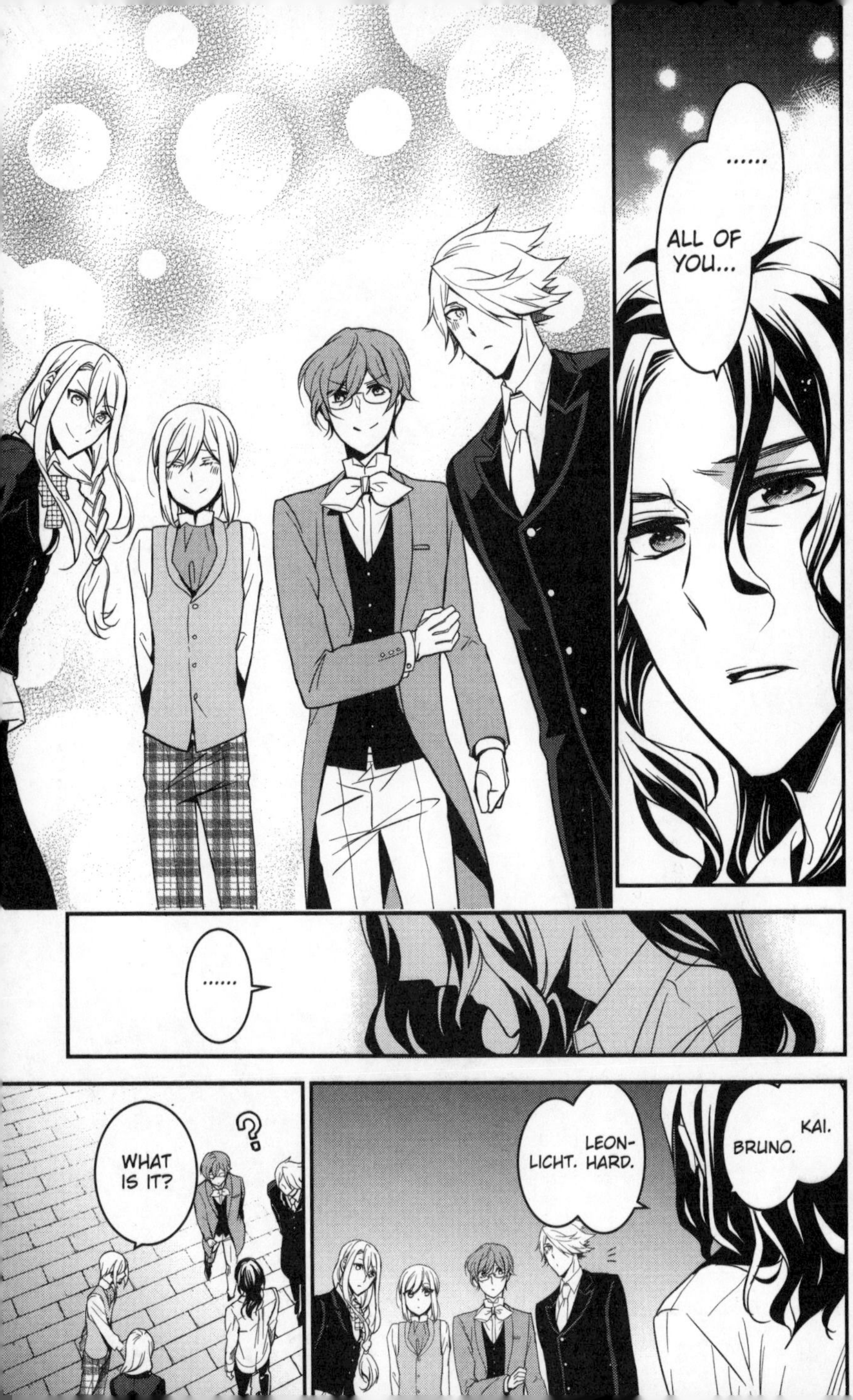
...... ALL OF YOU...
......
KAI. BRUNO.
LEONHARD. LICHT.
?
WHAT IS IT?

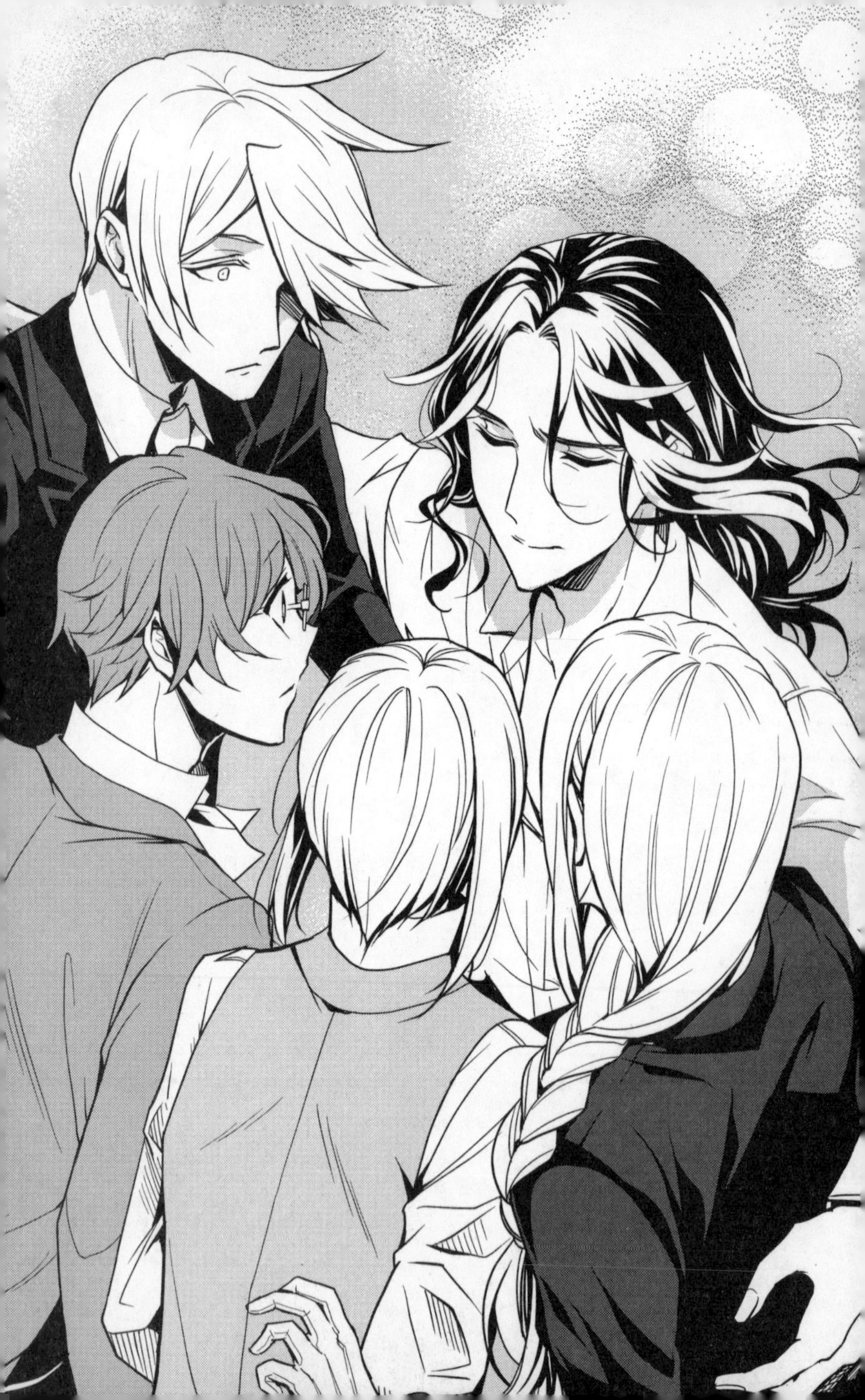

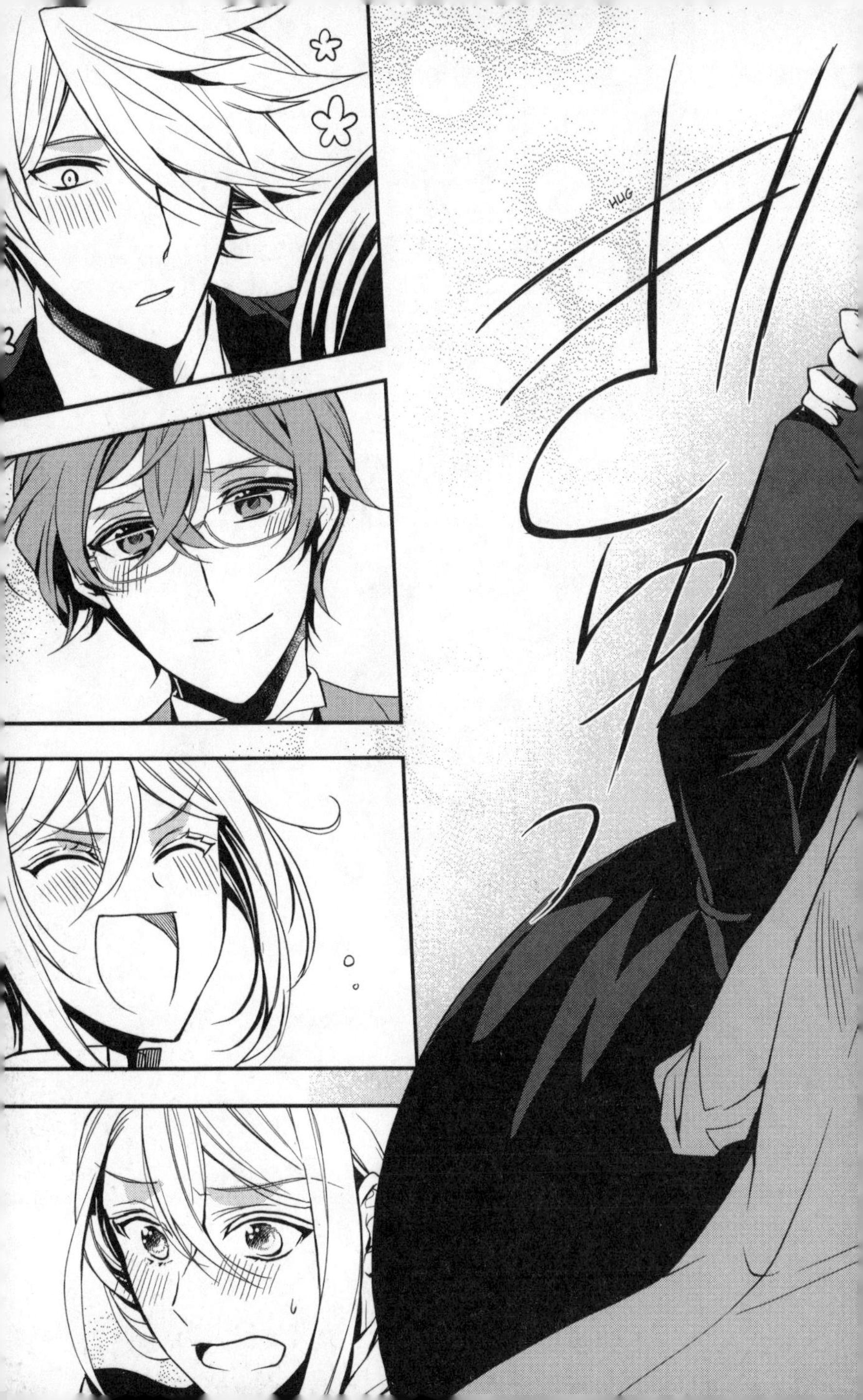
HUG

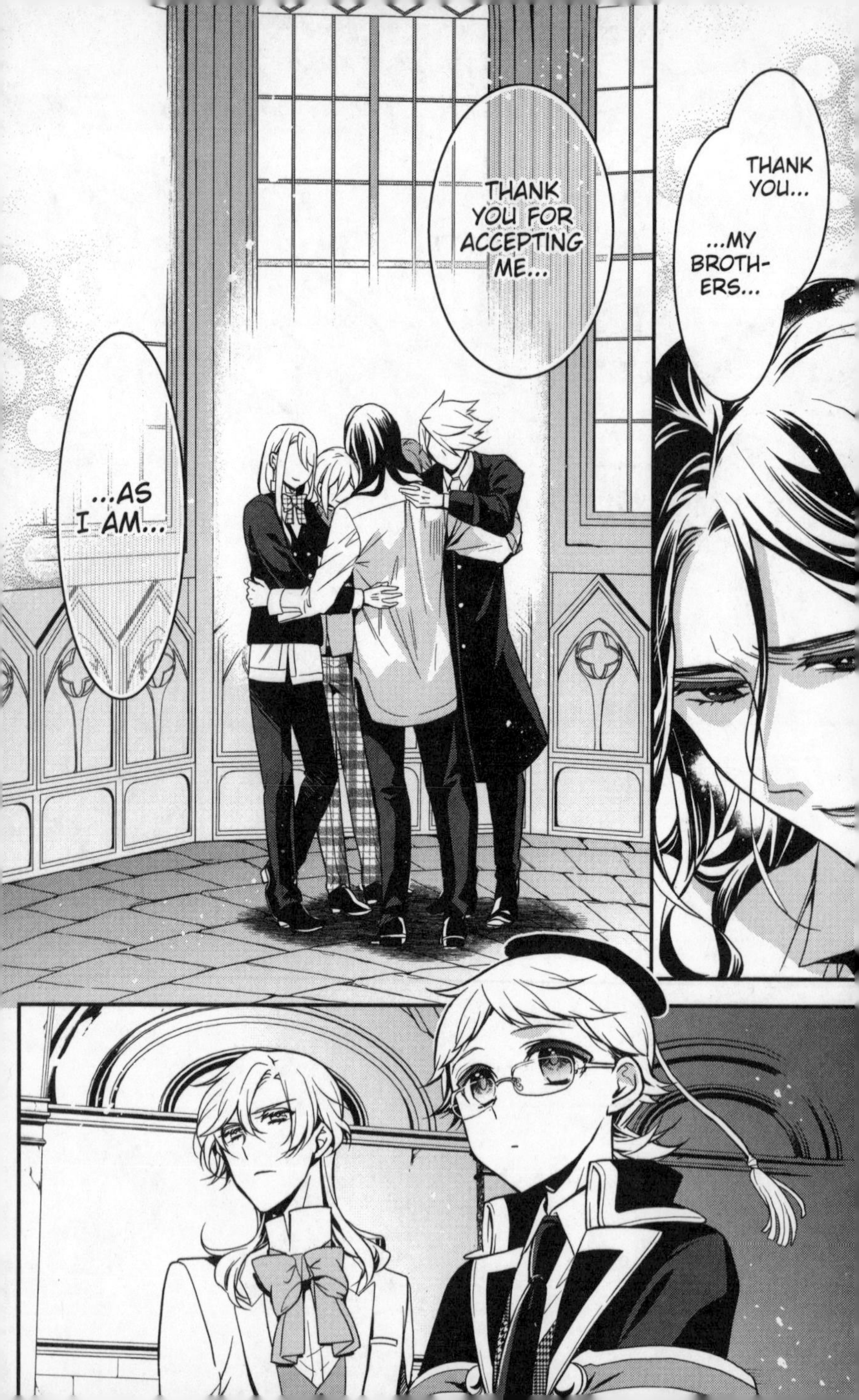
THANK YOU...
...MY BROTH-ERS...
THANK YOU FOR ACCEPTING ME...
...AS I AM...

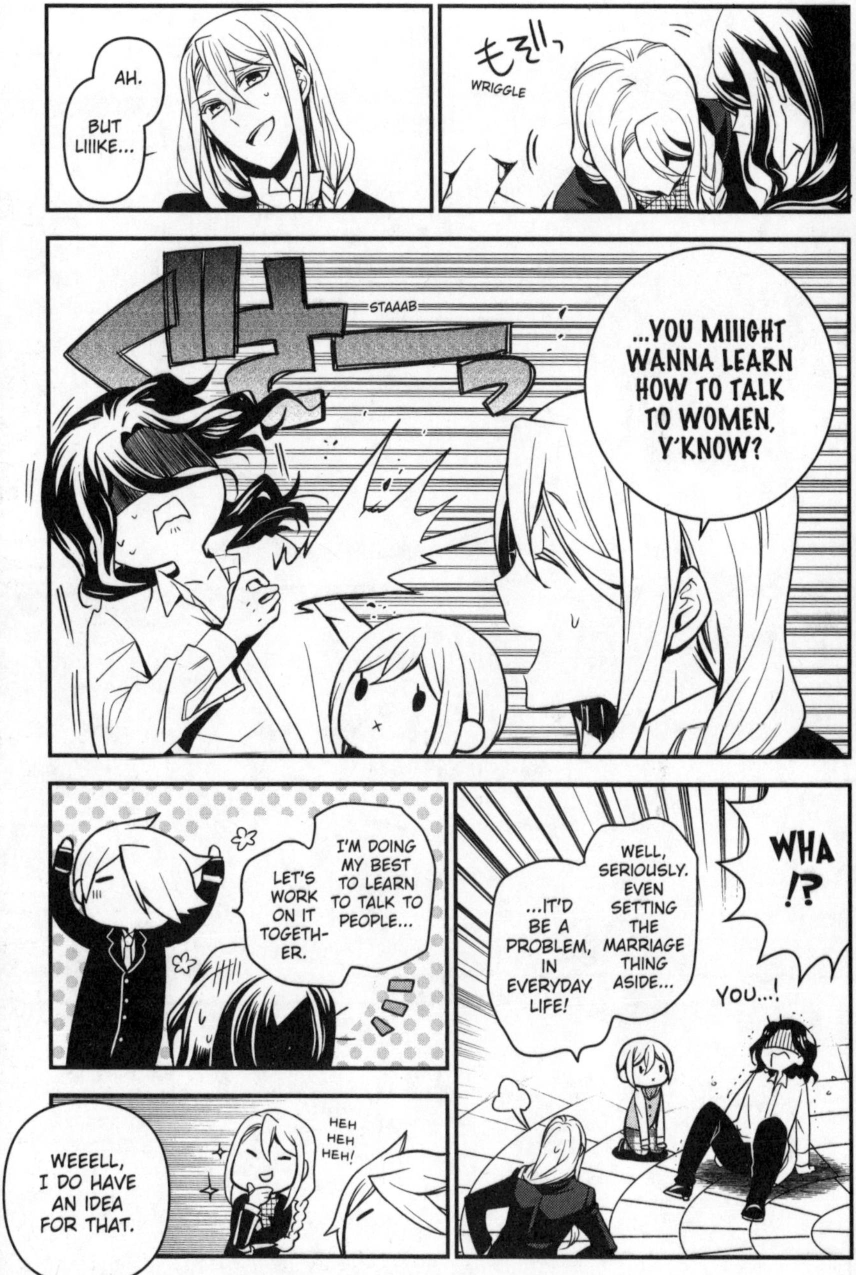
WRIGGLE
AH. BUT LIIIKE...
...YOU MIIIGHT WANNA LEARN HOW TO TALK TO WOMEN, Y'KNOW?
STAAAB
WHA!?
YOU...!
WELL, SERIOUSLY. EVEN SETTING THE MARRIAGE THING ASIDE...
...IT'D BE A PROBLEM, IN EVERYDAY LIFE!
I'M DOING MY BEST TO LEARN TO TALK TO PEOPLE...
LET'S WORK ON IT TOGETHER.
HEH HEH HEH!
WEEELL, I DO HAVE AN IDEA FOR THAT.

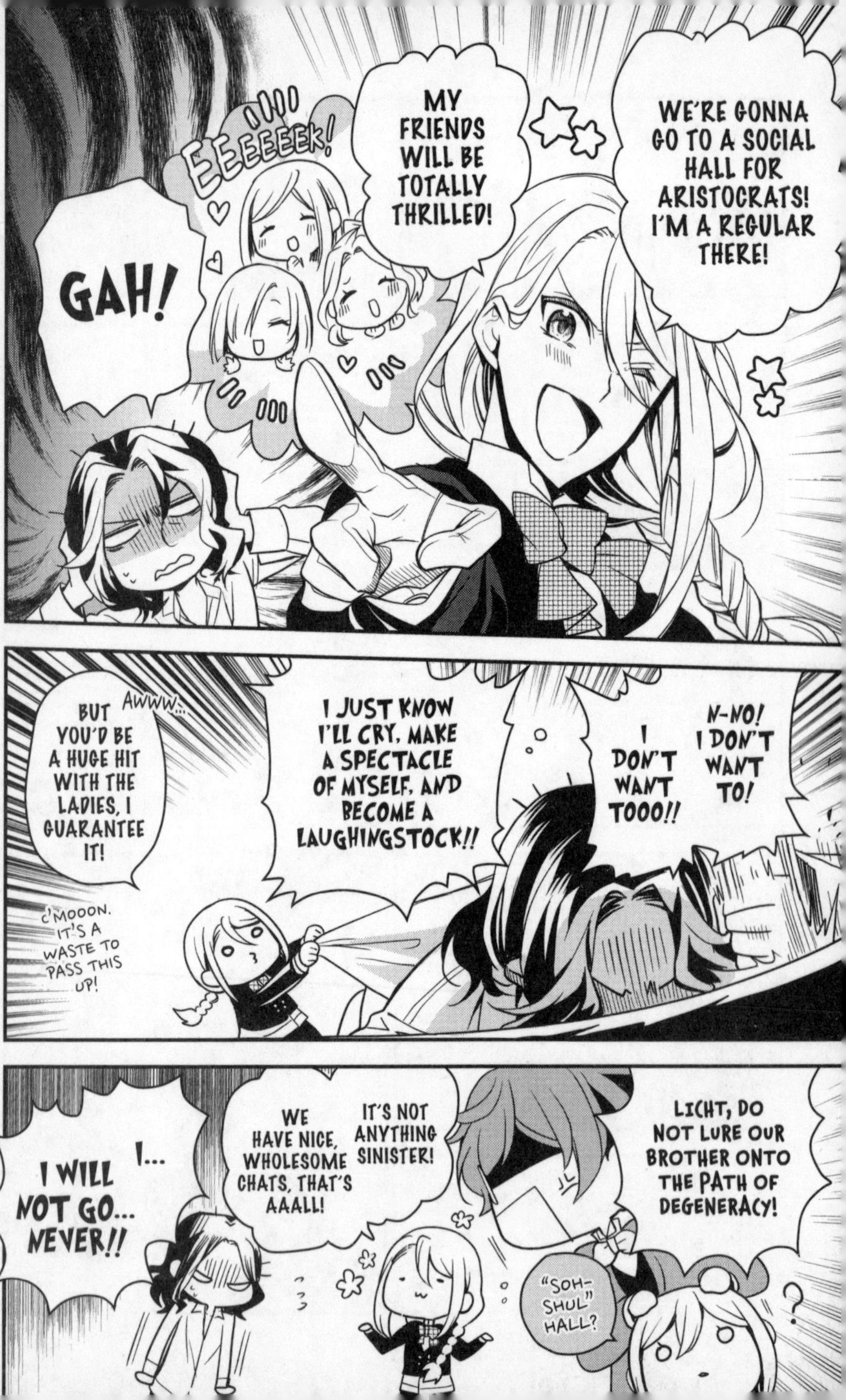
WE'RE GONNA GO TO A SOCIAL HALL FOR ARISTOCRATS! I'M A REGULAR THERE!
MY FRIENDS WILL BE TOTALLY THRILLED!
EEEEEEK!
GAH!
N-NO! I DON'T WANT TO!
I DON'T WANT TOOO!!
I JUST KNOW I'LL CRY, MAKE A SPECTACLE OF MYSELF, AND BECOME A LAUGHINGSTOCK!!
AWWW...
BUT YOU'D BE A HUGE HIT WITH THE LADIES, I GUARANTEE IT!
C'MOOON. IT'S A WASTE TO PASS THIS UP!
LICHT, DO NOT LURE OUR BROTHER ONTO THE PATH OF DEGENERACY!
IT'S NOT ANYTHING SINISTER!
WE HAVE NICE, WHOLESOME CHATS, THAT'S AAALL!
I...
I WILL NOT GO... NEVER!!
"SOH-SHUL" HALL?

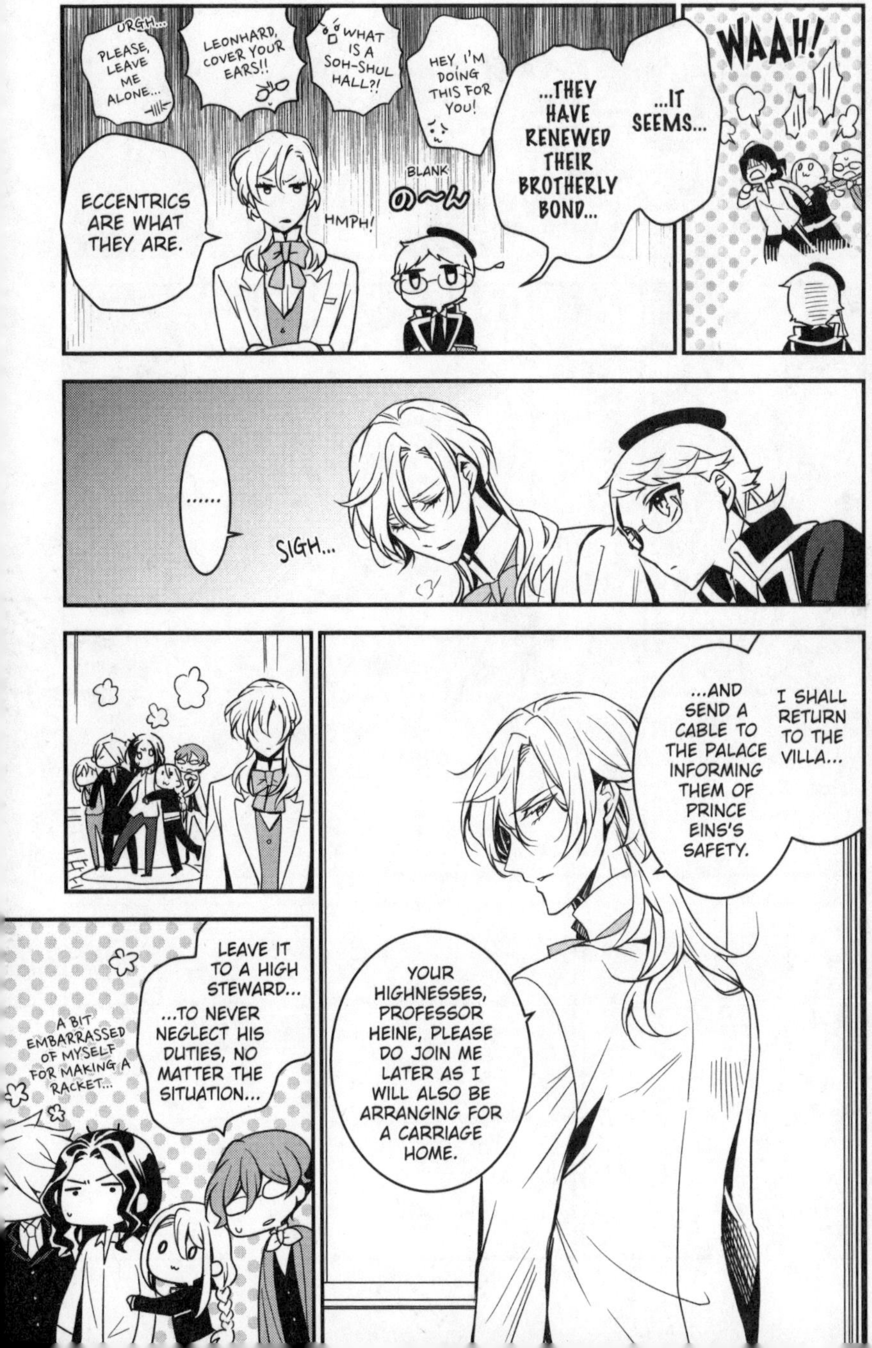
WAAH!
...IT SEEMS...
...THEY HAVE RENEWED THEIR BROTHERLY BOND...
HEY, I'M DOING THIS FOR YOU!
WHAT IS A SOH-SHUL HALL?!
LEONHARD, COVER YOUR EARS!!
URGH...
PLEASE, LEAVE ME ALONE...
BLANK
HMPH!
ECCENTRICS ARE WHAT THEY ARE.
......
SIGH...
I SHALL RETURN TO THE VILLA...
...AND SEND A CABLE TO THE PALACE INFORMING THEM OF PRINCE EINS'S SAFETY.
YOUR HIGHNESSES, PROFESSOR HEINE, PLEASE DO JOIN ME LATER AS I WILL ALSO BE ARRANGING FOR A CARRIAGE HOME.
LEAVE IT TO A HIGH STEWARD...
...TO NEVER NEGLECT HIS DUTIES, NO MATTER THE SITUATION...
A BIT EMBARRASSED OF MYSELF FOR MAKING A RACKET...

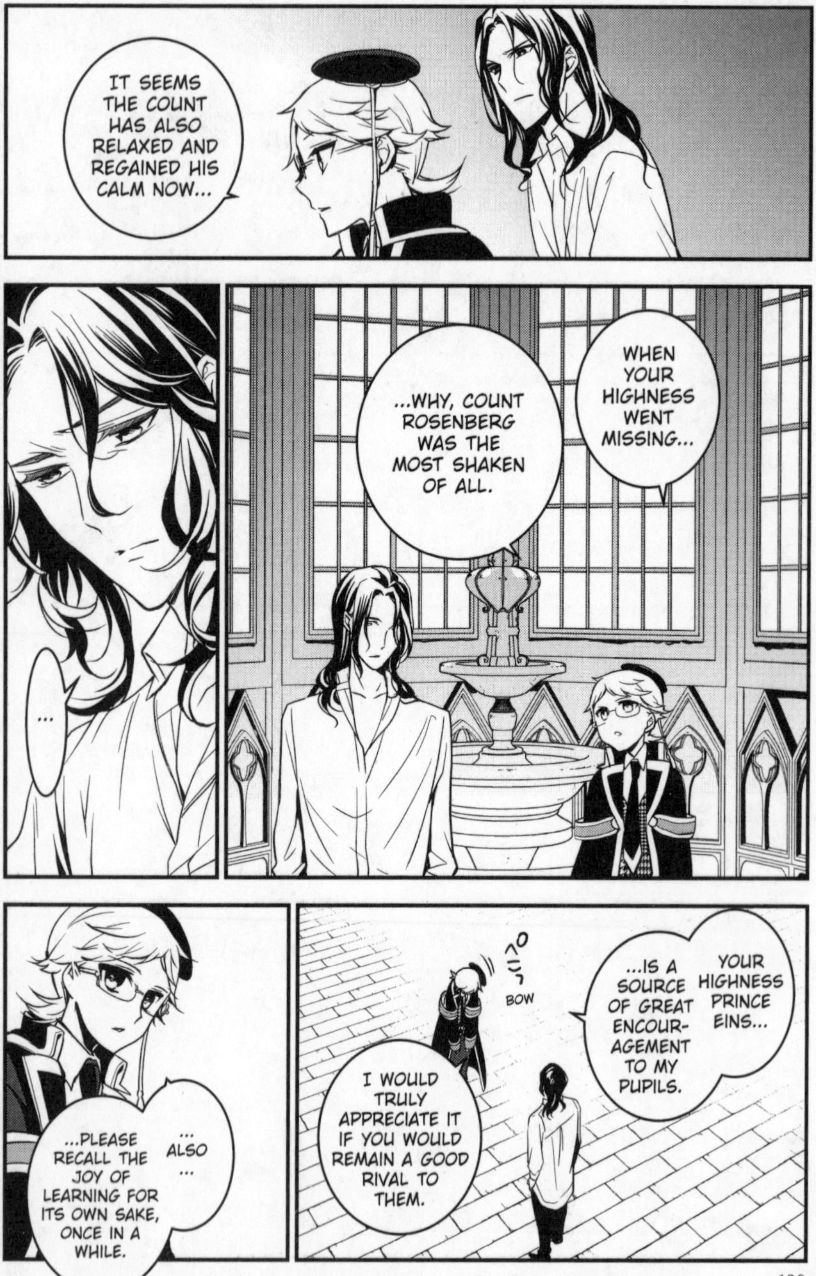
IT SEEMS THE COUNT HAS ALSO RELAXED AND REGAINED HIS CALM NOW...
WHEN YOUR HIGHNESS WENT MISSING...
...WHY, COUNT ROSENBERG WAS THE MOST SHAKEN OF ALL.
...
YOUR HIGHNESS PRINCE EINS...
...IS A SOURCE OF GREAT ENCOURAGEMENT TO MY PUPILS.
BOW
I WOULD TRULY APPRECIATE IT IF YOU WOULD REMAIN A GOOD RIVAL TO THEM.
...ALSO...
...PLEASE RECALL THE JOY OF LEARNING FOR ITS OWN SAKE, ONCE IN A WHILE.

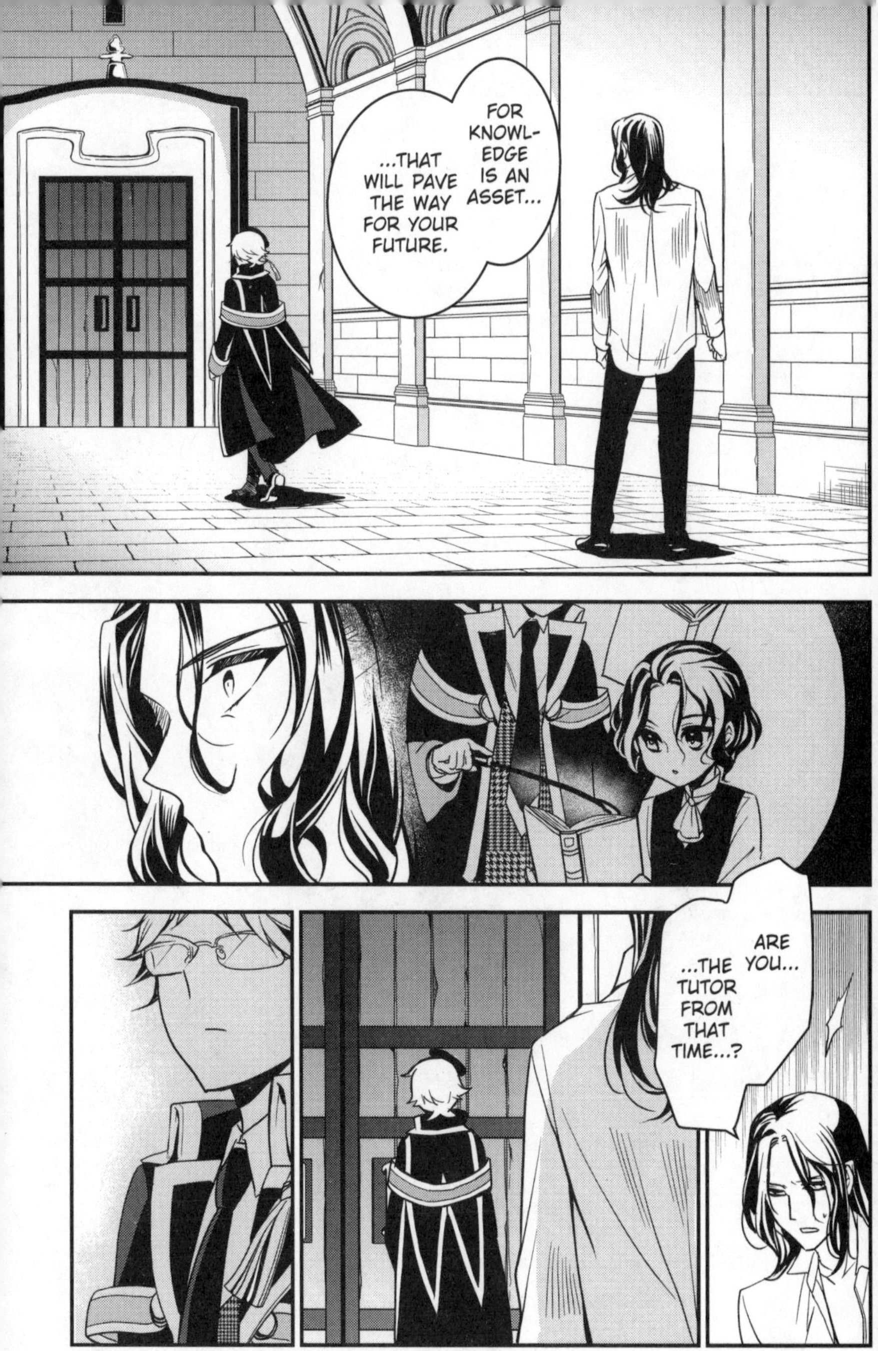
FOR KNOWLEDGE IS AN ASSET...
...THAT WILL PAVE THE WAY FOR YOUR FUTURE.
ARE YOU...
...THE TUTOR FROM THAT TIME...?

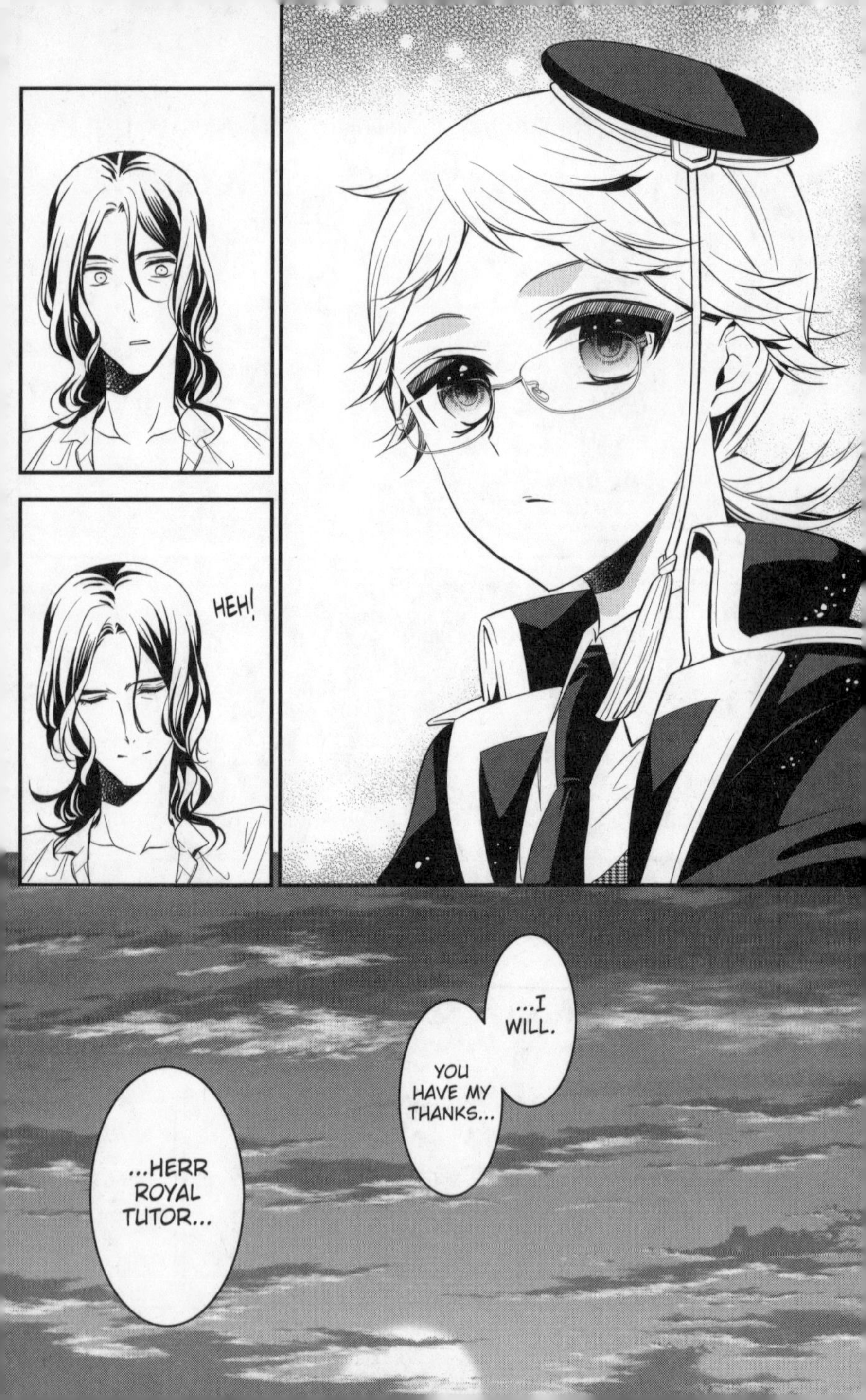
HEH!
...I WILL.
YOU HAVE MY THANKS...
...HERR ROYAL TUTOR...

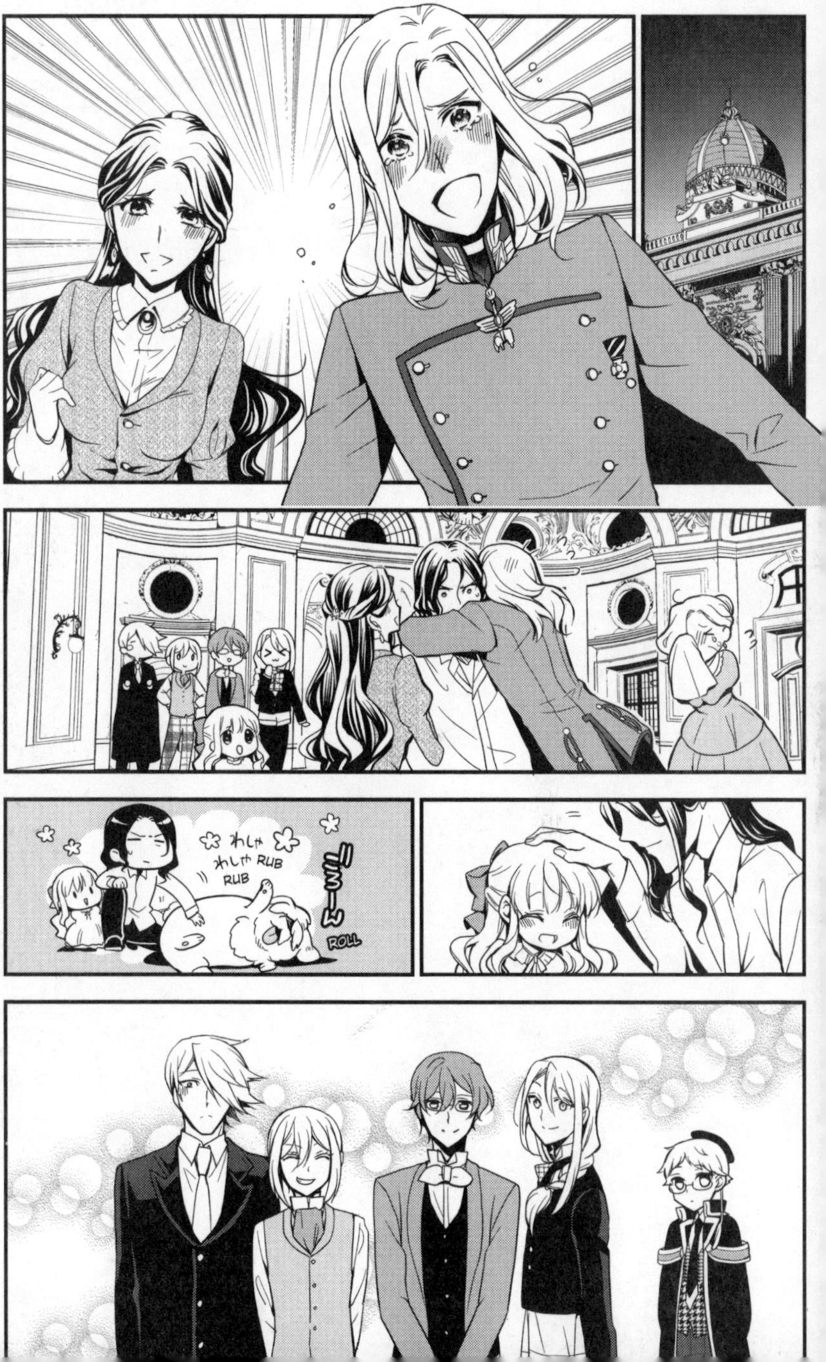
わしゃ
わしゃ RUB
RUB
ROLL

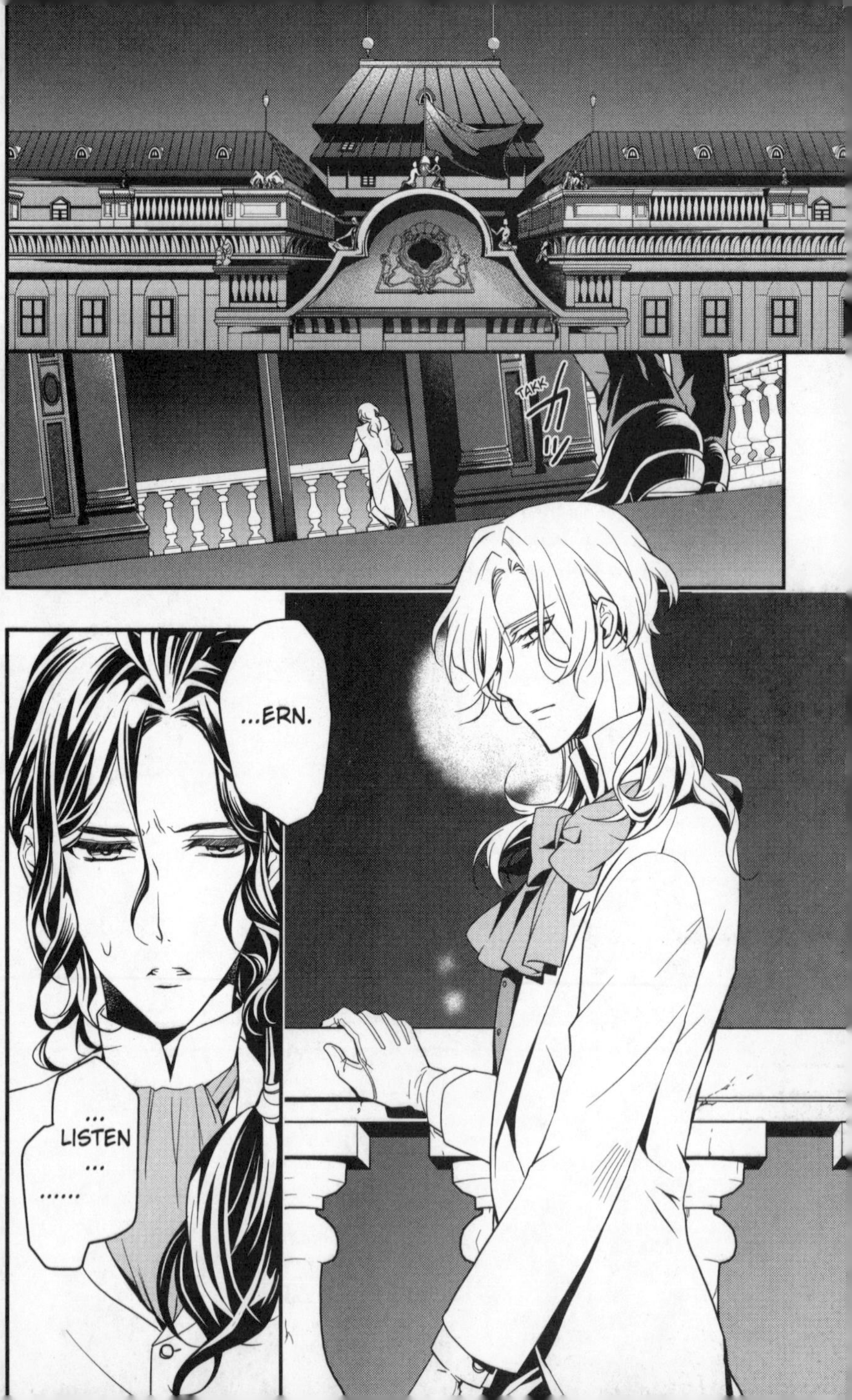
TAKK
...ERN.
...
LISTEN
...
......

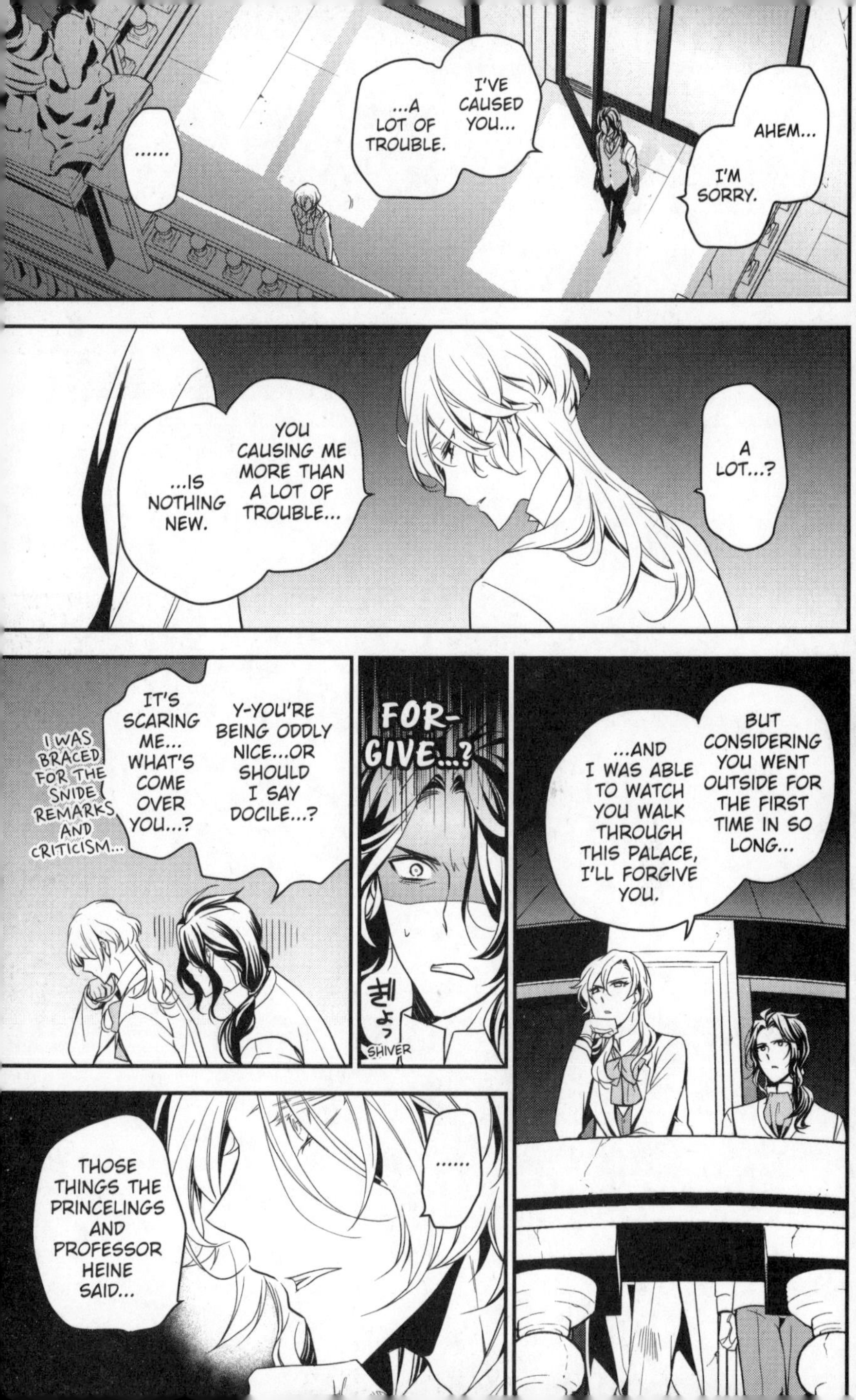
AHEM... I'M SORRY.
I'VE CAUSED YOU... ...A LOT OF TROUBLE.
......
A LOT...?
YOU CAUSING ME MORE THAN A LOT OF TROUBLE... ...IS NOTHING NEW.
BUT CONSIDERING YOU WENT OUTSIDE FOR THE FIRST TIME IN SO LONG...
...AND I WAS ABLE TO WATCH YOU WALK THROUGH THIS PALACE, I'LL FORGIVE YOU.
FOR-GIVE...?
きょっ
SHIVER
Y-YOU'RE BEING ODDLY NICE...OR SHOULD I SAY DOCILE...?
IT'S SCARING ME... WHAT'S COME OVER YOU...?
I WAS BRACED FOR THE SNIDE REMARKS AND CRITICISM...
......
THOSE THINGS THE PRINCELINGS AND PROFESSOR HEINE SAID...

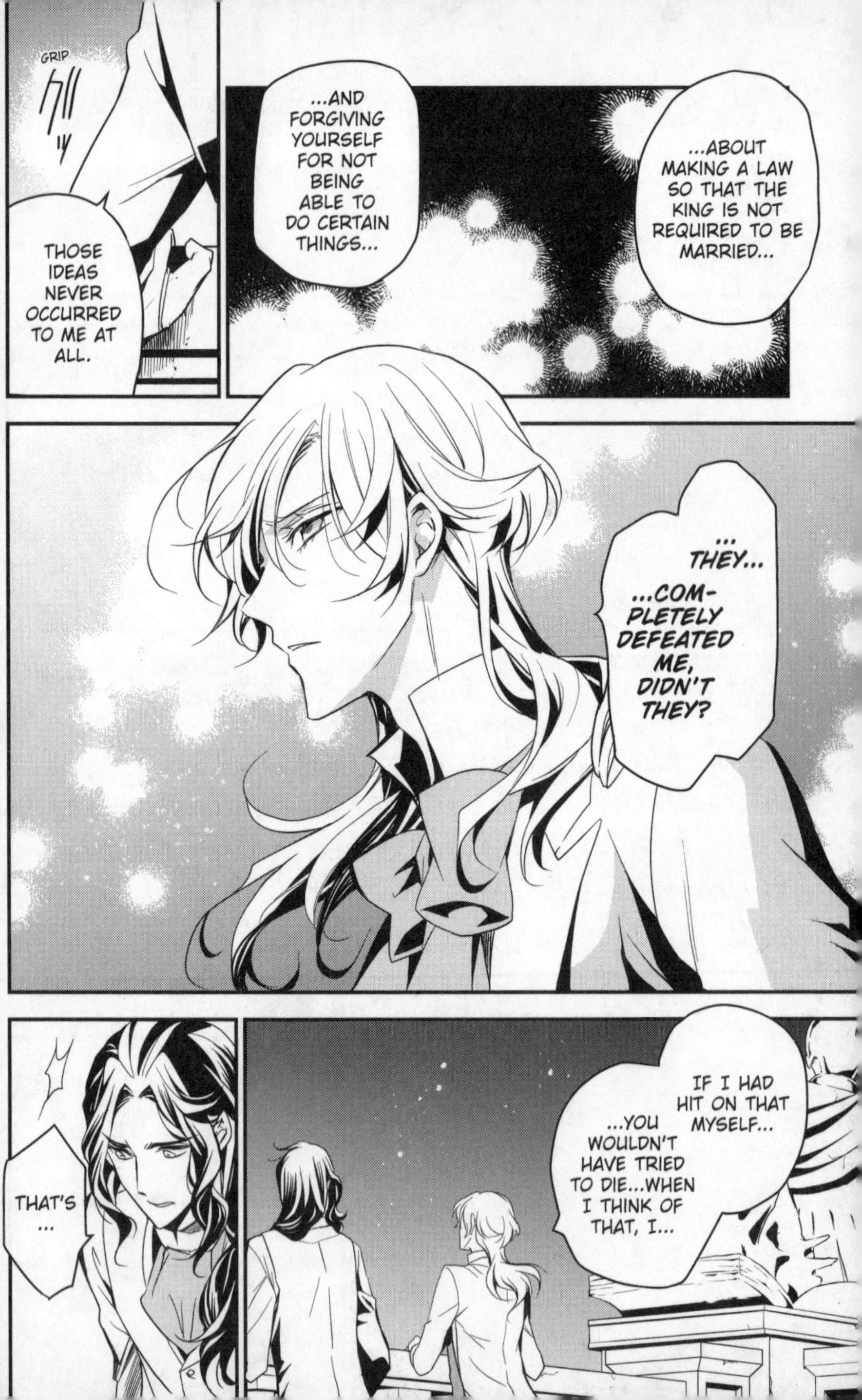
...ABOUT MAKING A LAW SO THAT THE KING IS NOT REQUIRED TO BE MARRIED...
...AND FORGIVING YOURSELF FOR NOT BEING ABLE TO DO CERTAIN THINGS...
GRIP
THOSE IDEAS NEVER OCCURRED TO ME AT ALL.
... THEY... ...COMPLETELY DEFEATED ME, DIDN'T THEY?
IF I HAD HIT ON THAT MYSELF...
...YOU WOULDN'T HAVE TRIED TO DIE...WHEN I THINK OF THAT, I...
THAT'S ...

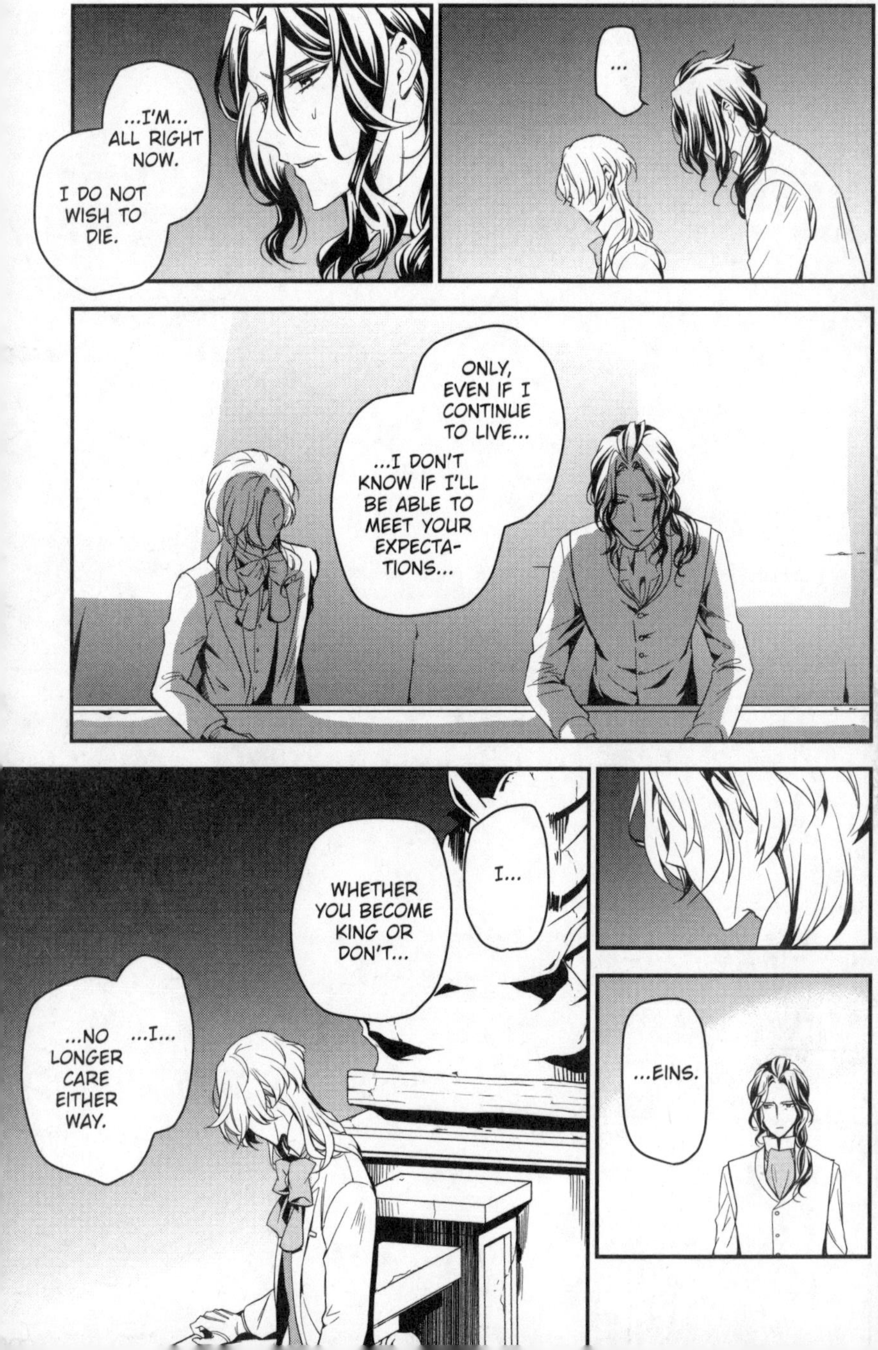
...
...I'M... ALL RIGHT NOW.
I DO NOT WISH TO DIE.
ONLY, EVEN IF I CONTINUE TO LIVE...
...I DON'T KNOW IF I'LL BE ABLE TO MEET YOUR EXPECTATIONS...
...EINS.
I...
WHETHER YOU BECOME KING OR DON'T...
...I...
...NO LONGER CARE EITHER WAY.

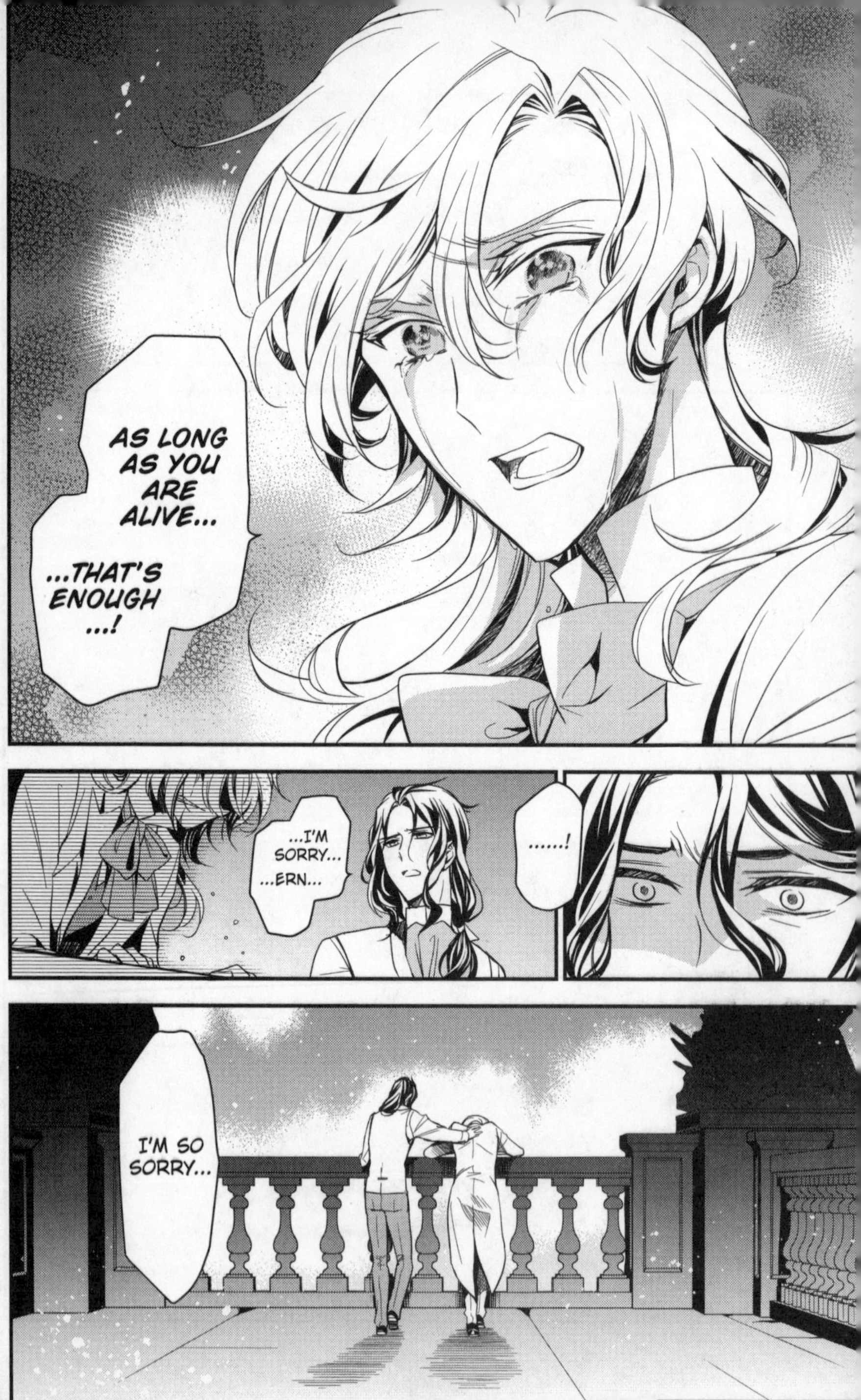

AS LONG AS YOU ARE ALIVE...
...THAT'S ENOUGH ...!
......!
...I'M SORRY... ...ERN...
I'M SO SORRY...

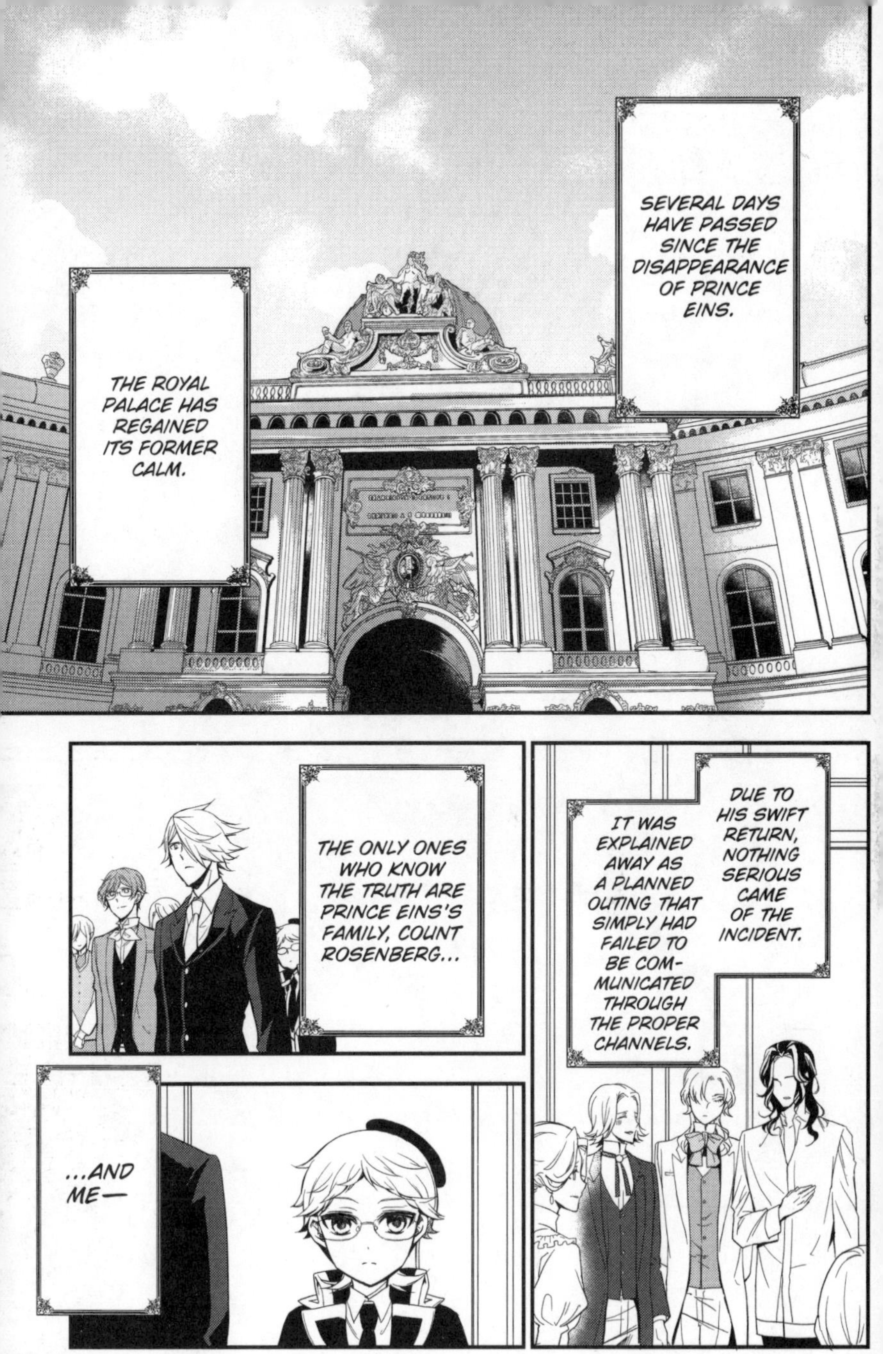
SEVERAL DAYS HAVE PASSED SINCE THE DISAPPEARANCE OF PRINCE EINS.
THE ROYAL PALACE HAS REGAINED ITS FORMER CALM.
DUE TO HIS SWIFT RETURN, NOTHING SERIOUS CAME OF THE INCIDENT.
IT WAS EXPLAINED AWAY AS A PLANNED OUTING THAT SIMPLY HAD FAILED TO BE COM-MUNICATED THROUGH THE PROPER CHANNELS.
THE ONLY ONES WHO KNOW THE TRUTH ARE PRINCE EINS'S FAMILY, COUNT ROSENBERG...
...AND ME—

Chapter 95 Five Princes!

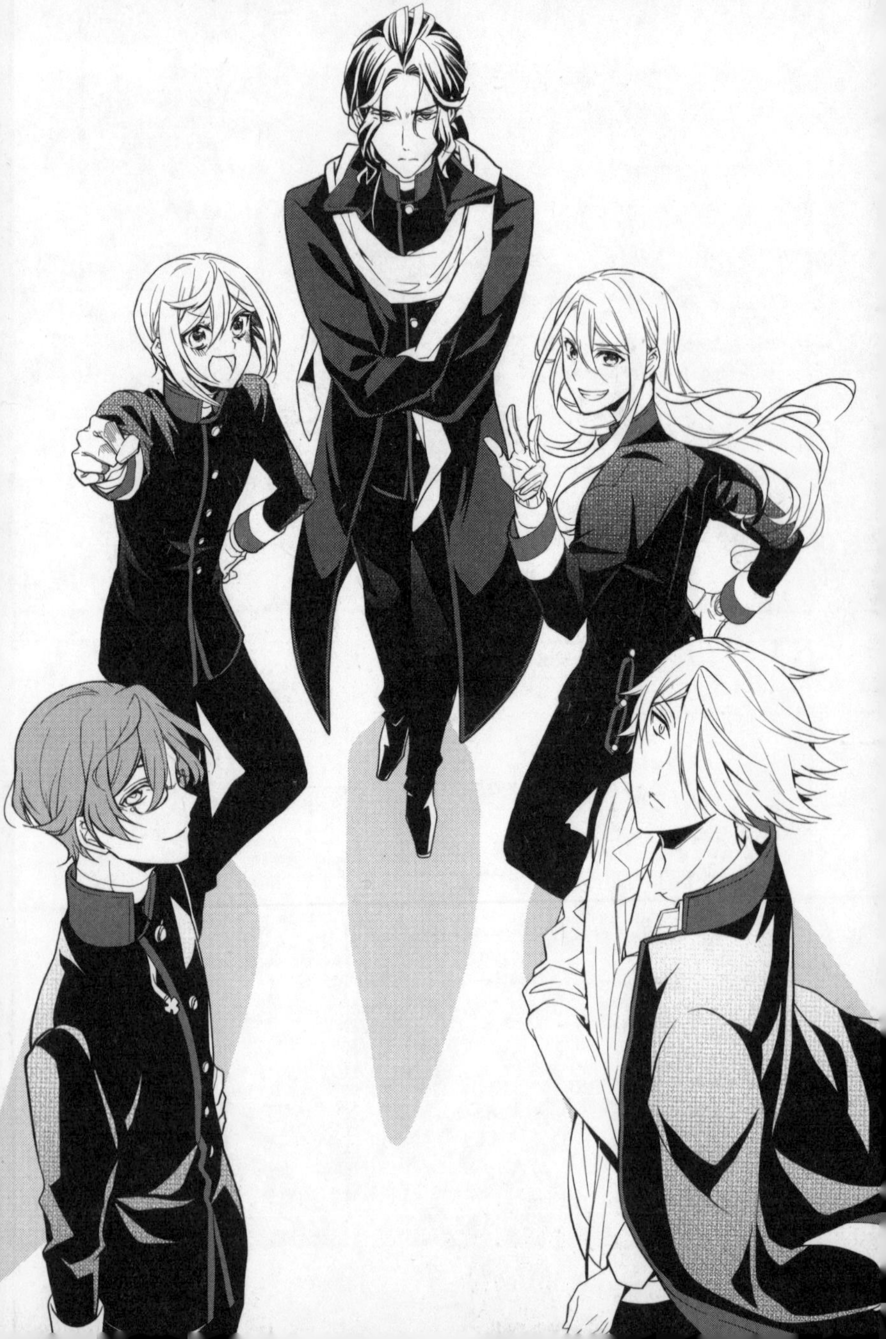

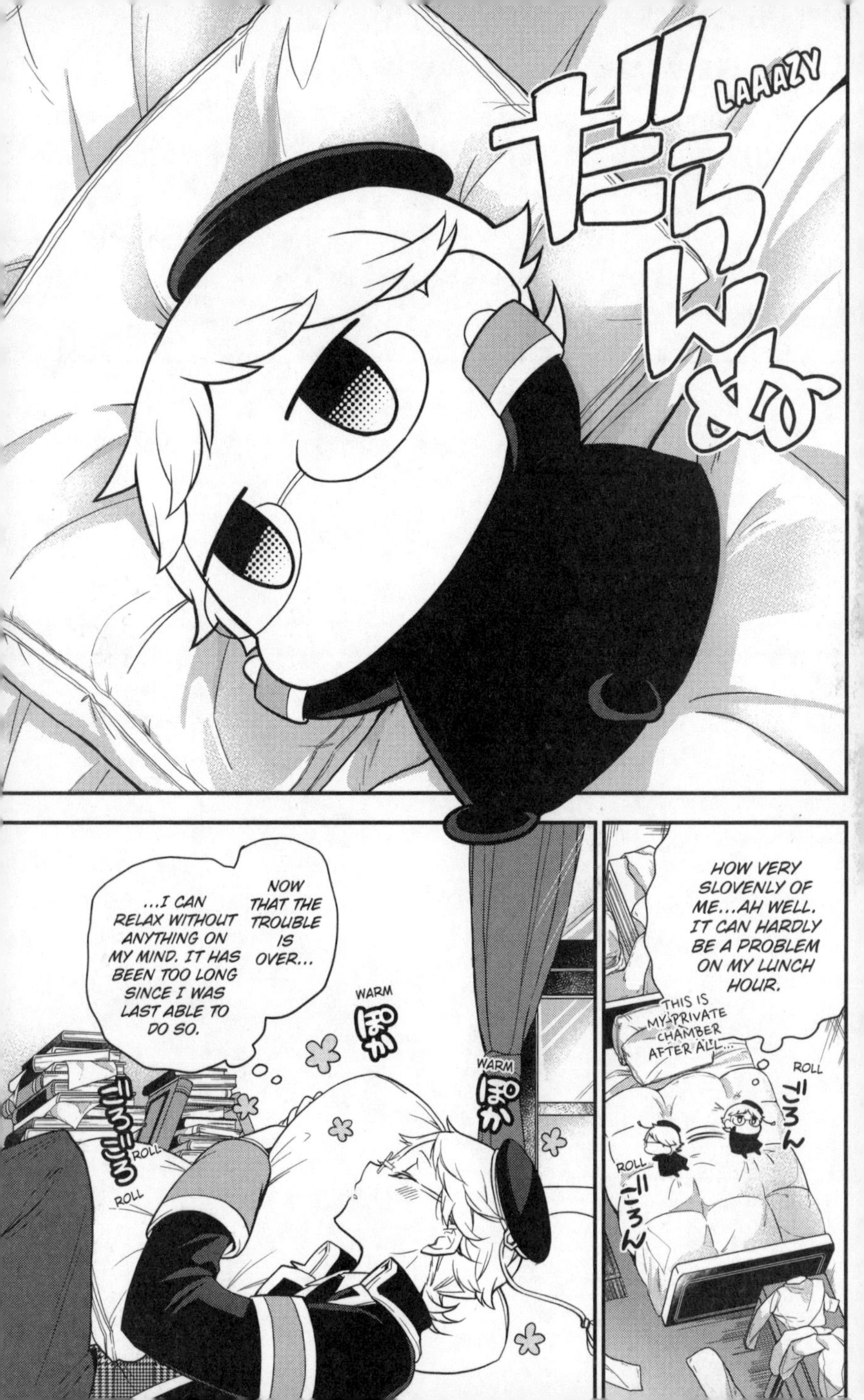
LAAAZY
HOW VERY SLOVENLY OF ME...AH WELL. IT CAN HARDLY BE A PROBLEM ON MY LUNCH HOUR.
THIS IS MY PRIVATE CHAMBER AFTER ALL...
ROLL
ごろん
ROLL
ごろん
NOW THAT THE TROUBLE IS OVER...
...I CAN RELAX WITHOUT ANYTHING ON MY MIND. IT HAS BEEN TOO LONG SINCE I WAS LAST ABLE TO DO SO.
WARM
ぽか
WARM
ぽか
ごろごろ
ROLL
ROLL

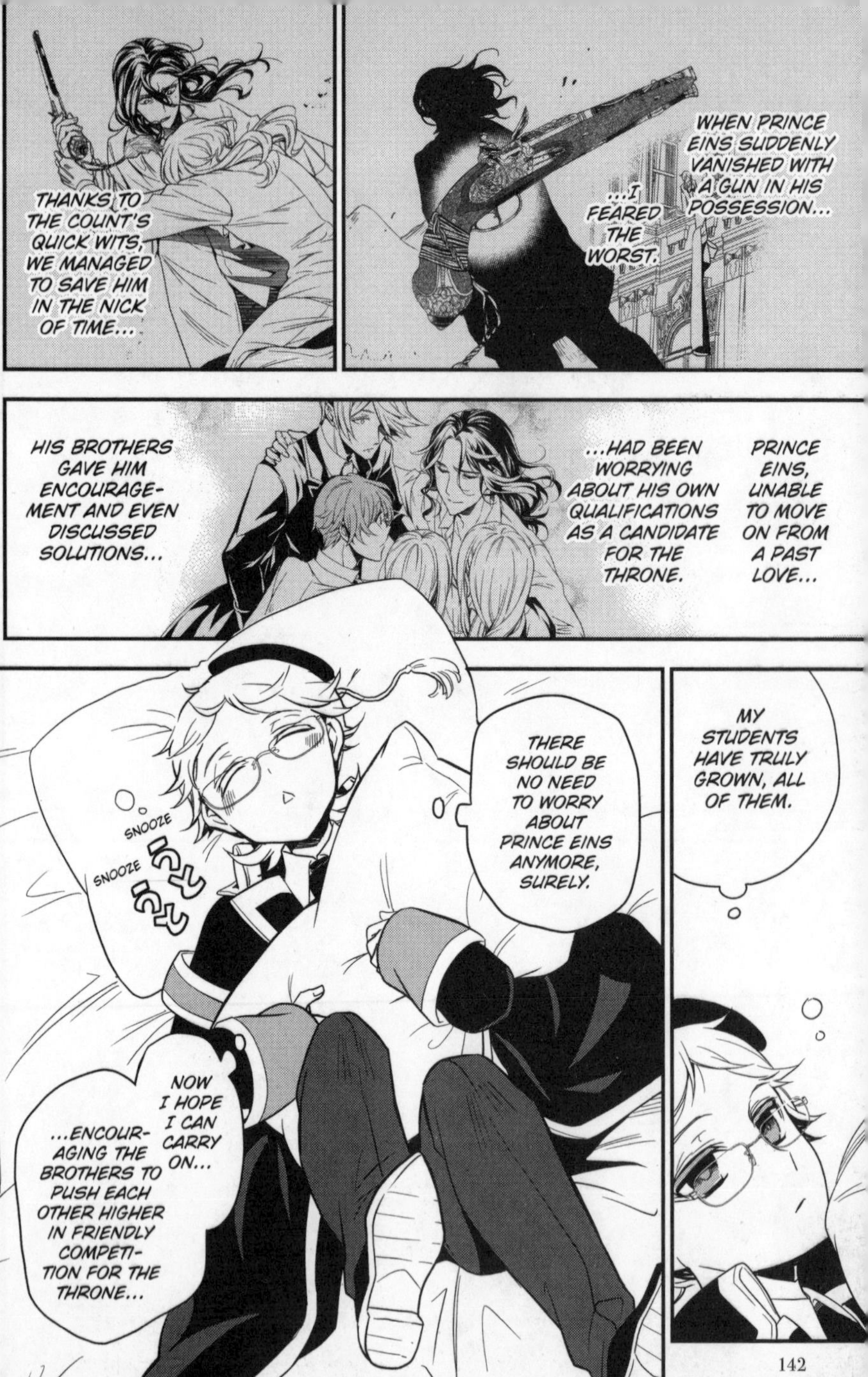
WHEN PRINCE EINS SUDDENLY VANISHED WITH A GUN IN HIS POSSESSION...
...I FEARED THE WORST.
THANKS TO THE COUNT'S QUICK WITS, WE MANAGED TO SAVE HIM IN THE NICK OF TIME...
PRINCE EINS, UNABLE TO MOVE ON FROM A PAST LOVE...
...HAD BEEN WORRYING ABOUT HIS OWN QUALIFICATIONS AS A CANDIDATE FOR THE THRONE.
HIS BROTHERS GAVE HIM ENCOURAGE-MENT AND EVEN DISCUSSED SOLUTIONS...
MY STUDENTS HAVE TRULY GROWN, ALL OF THEM.
THERE SHOULD BE NO NEED TO WORRY ABOUT PRINCE EINS ANYMORE, SURELY.
SNOOZE
SNOOZE
NOW I HOPE I CAN CARRY ON...
...ENCOUR-AGING THE BROTHERS TO PUSH EACH OTHER HIGHER IN FRIENDLY COMPETI-TION FOR THE THRONE...

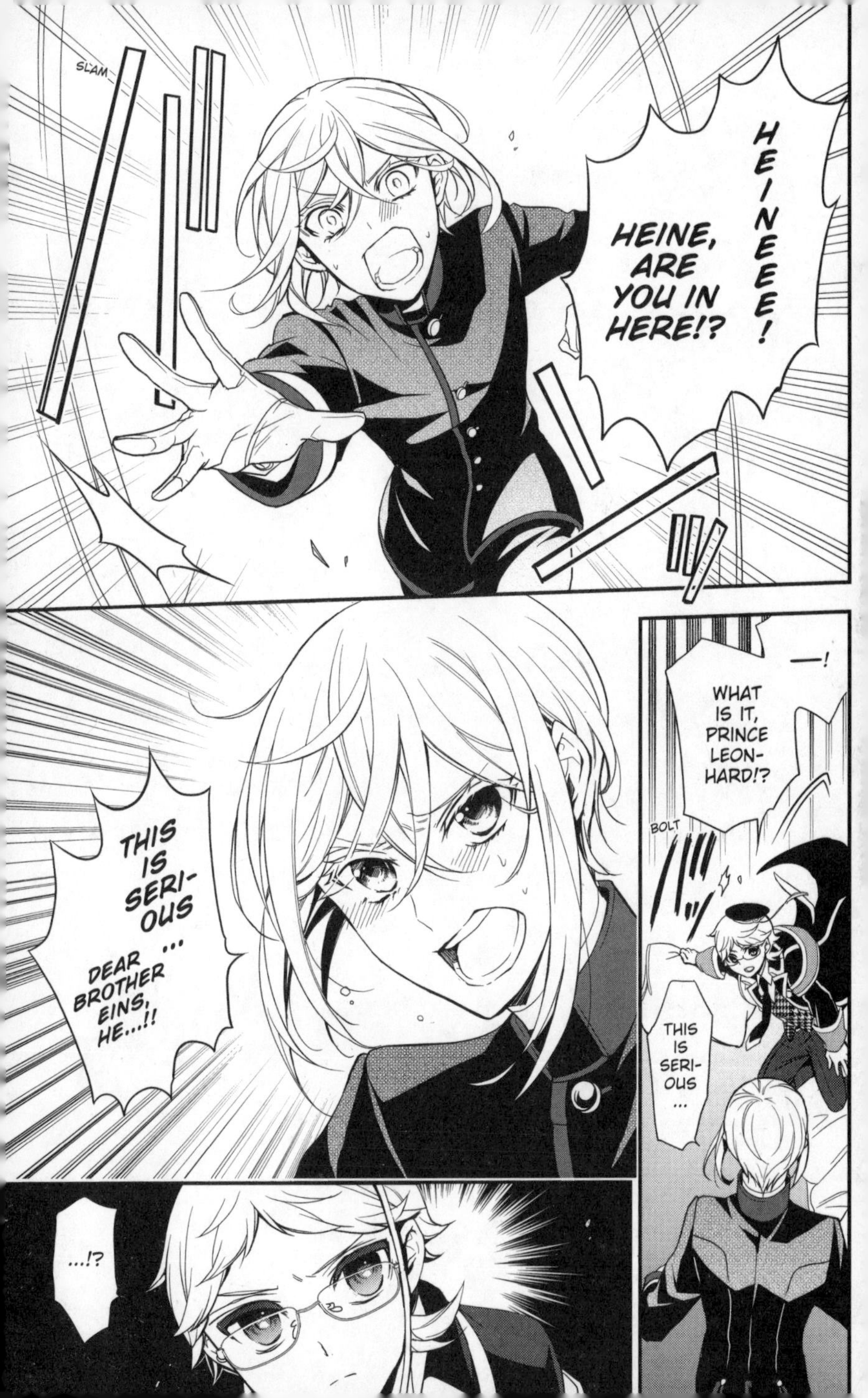

SLAM
HEINEEEE!
HEINE, ARE YOU IN HERE!?
—!
WHAT IS IT, PRINCE LEON-HARD!?
BOLT
THIS IS SERI-OUS...
THIS IS SERI-OUS... DEAR BROTHER EINS, HE...!!
...!?

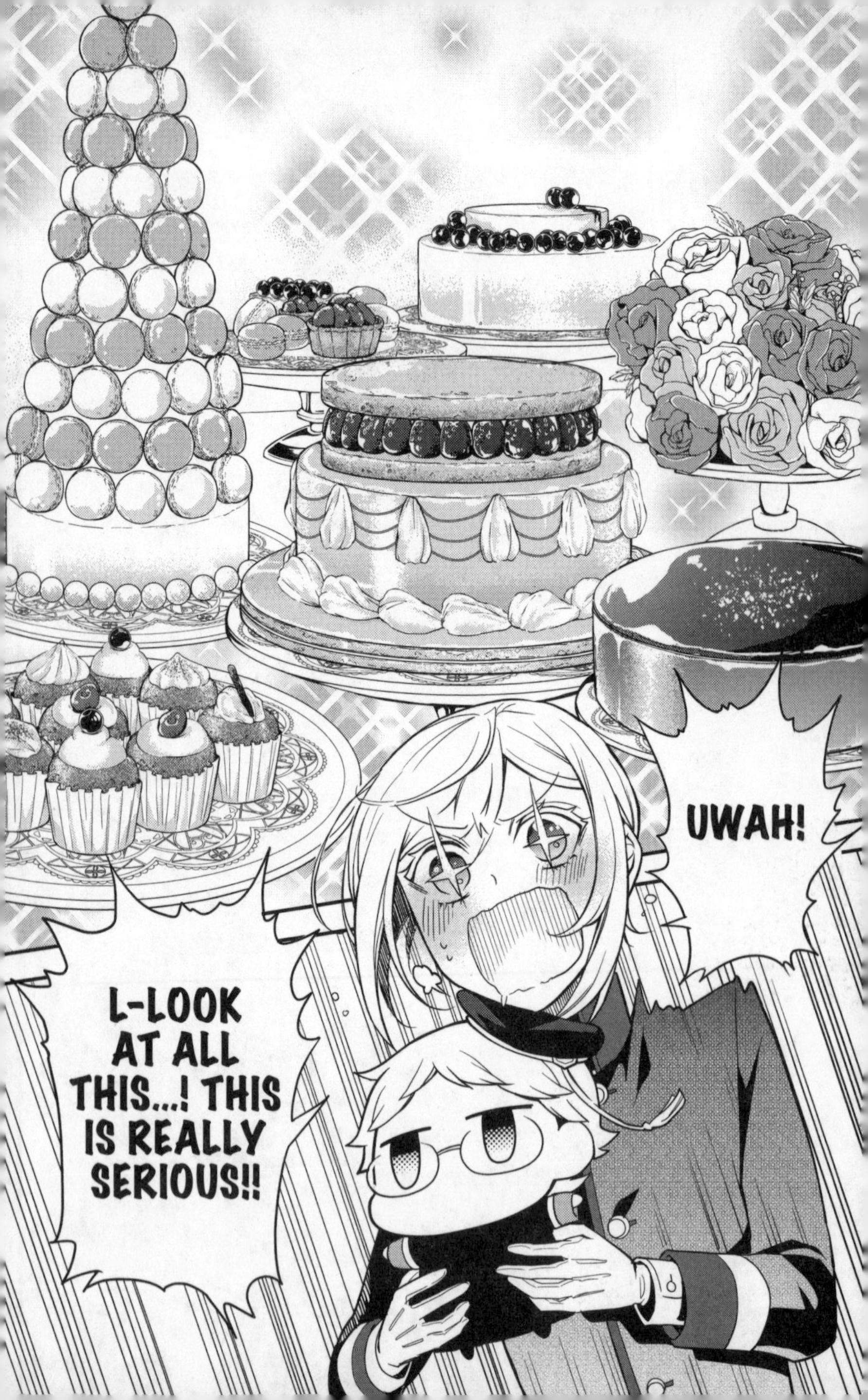
UWAH!
L-LOOK AT ALL THIS...! THIS IS REALLY SERIOUS!!

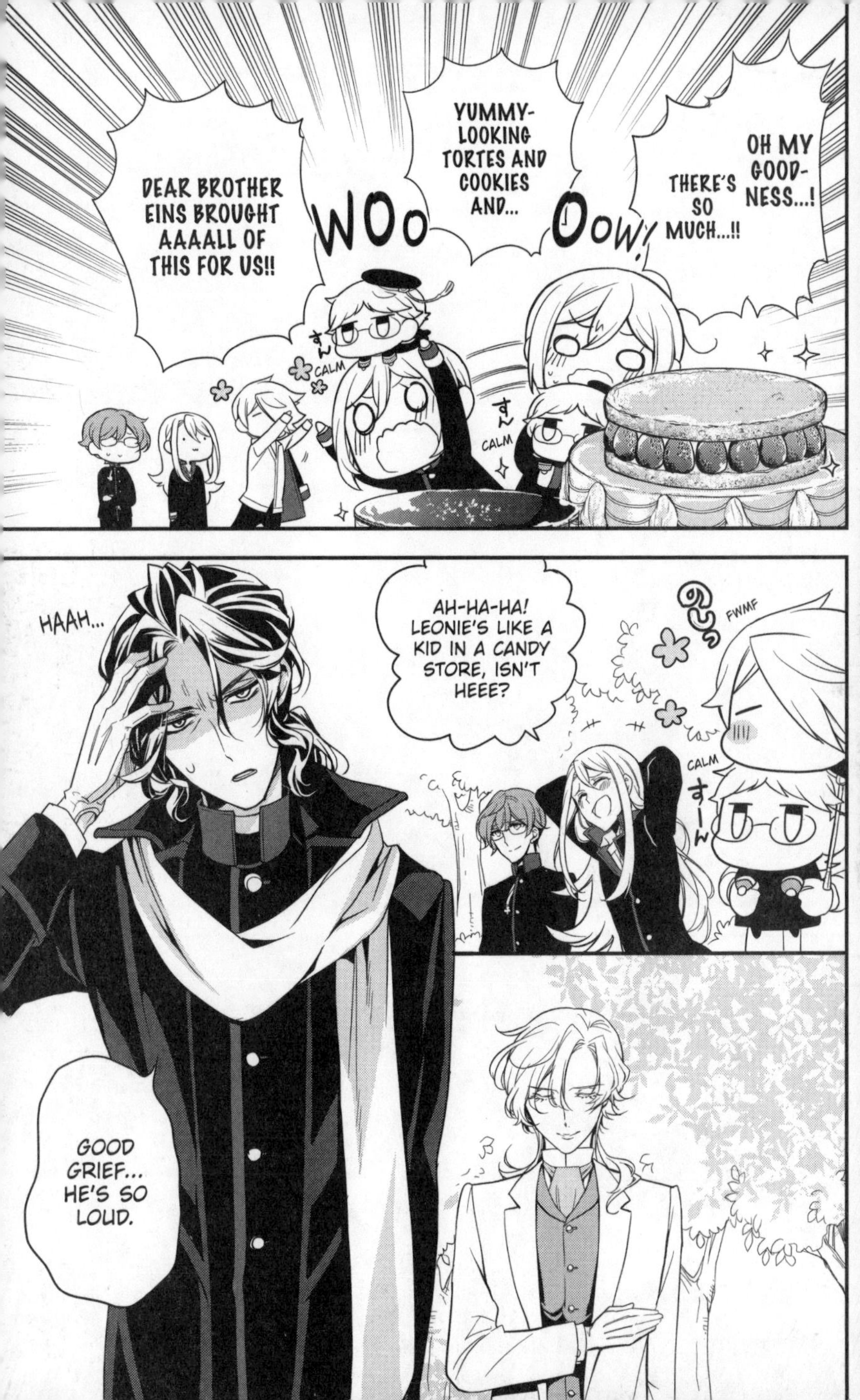
OH MY GOOD-NESS...!
THERE'S SO MUCH...!!
YUMMY-LOOKING TORTES AND COOKIES AND...
WOoOOW!
DEAR BROTHER EINS BROUGHT AAAALL OF THIS FOR US!!
すん
CALM
すん
CALM
のしっ
FWMF
AH-HA-HA! LEONIE'S LIKE A KID IN A CANDY STORE, ISN'T HEEE?
CALM
すーん
HAAH...
GOOD GRIEF... HE'S SO LOUD.

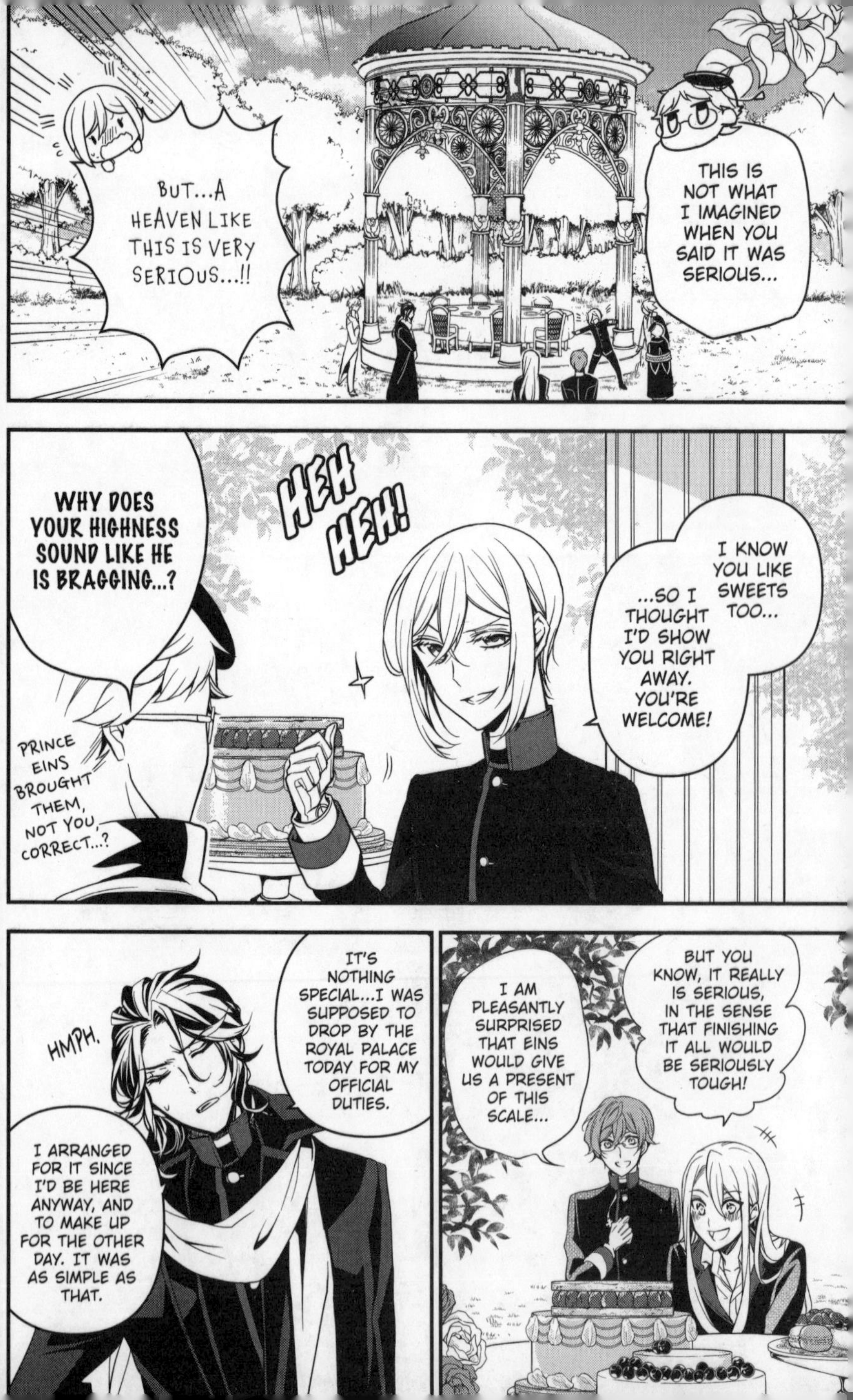
THIS IS NOT WHAT I IMAGINED WHEN YOU SAID IT WAS SERIOUS...
BUT...A HEAVEN LIKE THIS IS VERY SERIOUS...!!
I KNOW YOU LIKE SWEETS TOO...
...SO I THOUGHT I'D SHOW YOU RIGHT AWAY. YOU'RE WELCOME!
HEH HEH!
WHY DOES YOUR HIGHNESS SOUND LIKE HE IS BRAGGING...?
PRINCE EINS BROUGHT THEM, NOT YOU, CORRECT...?
BUT YOU KNOW, IT REALLY IS SERIOUS, IN THE SENSE THAT FINISHING IT ALL WOULD BE SERIOUSLY TOUGH!
I AM PLEASANTLY SURPRISED THAT EINS WOULD GIVE US A PRESENT OF THIS SCALE...
IT'S NOTHING SPECIAL...I WAS SUPPOSED TO DROP BY THE ROYAL PALACE TODAY FOR MY OFFICIAL DUTIES.
HMPH.
I ARRANGED FOR IT SINCE I'D BE HERE ANYWAY, AND TO MAKE UP FOR THE OTHER DAY. IT WAS AS SIMPLE AS THAT.

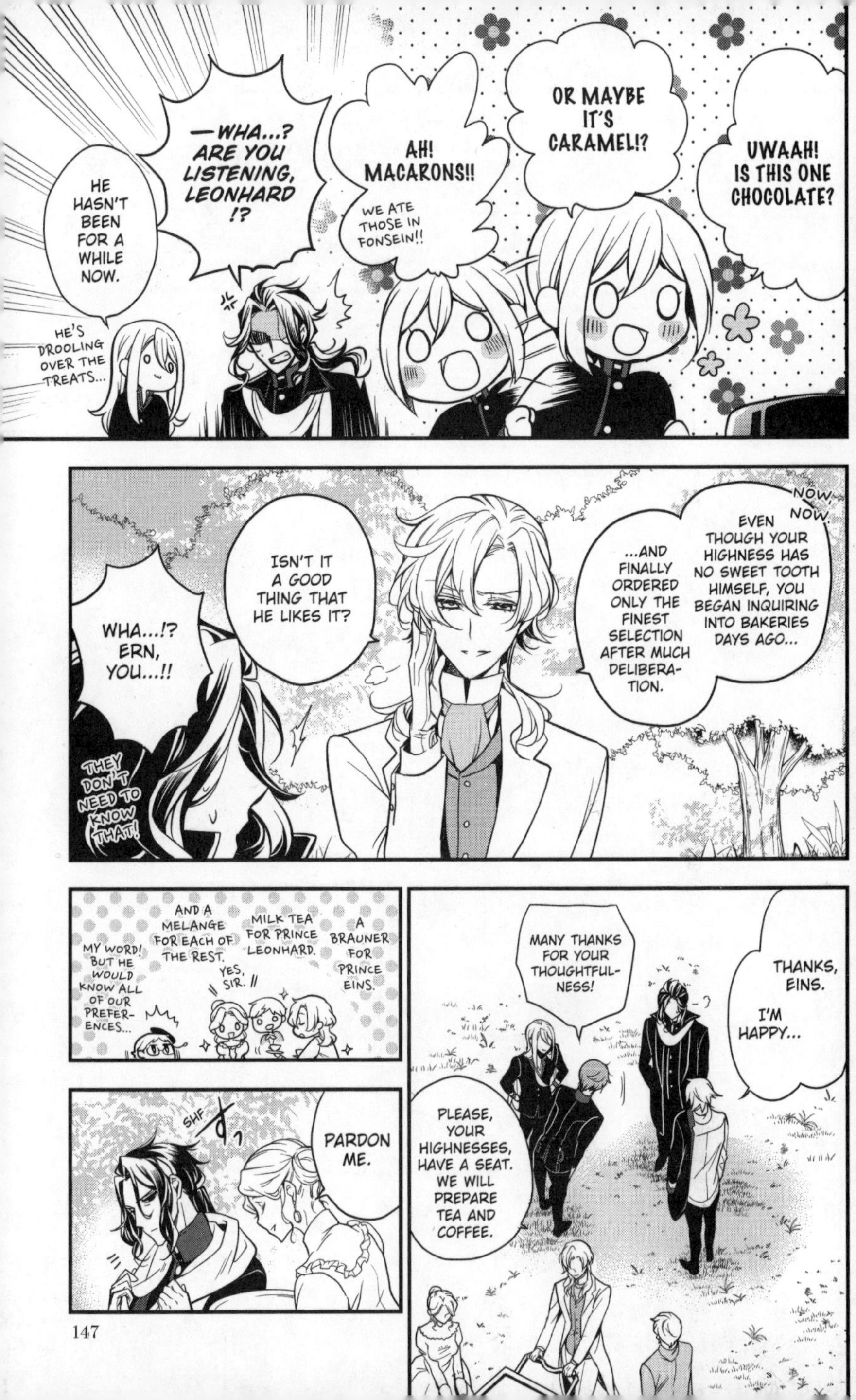
UWAAH! IS THIS ONE CHOCOLATE?
OR MAYBE IT'S CARAMEL!?
AH! MACARONS!!
WE ATE THOSE IN FONSEIN!!
—WHA...? ARE YOU LISTENING, LEONHARD!?
HE HASN'T BEEN FOR A WHILE NOW.
HE'S DROOLING OVER THE TREATS...
NOW, NOW.
EVEN THOUGH YOUR HIGHNESS HAS NO SWEET TOOTH HIMSELF, YOU BEGAN INQUIRING INTO BAKERIES DAYS AGO...
...AND FINALLY ORDERED ONLY THE FINEST SELECTION AFTER MUCH DELIBERA-TION.
ISN'T IT A GOOD THING THAT HE LIKES IT?
WHA...!? ERN, YOU...!!
THEY DON'T NEED TO KNOW THAT!
THANKS, EINS.
I'M HAPPY...
MANY THANKS FOR YOUR THOUGHTFUL-NESS!
PLEASE, YOUR HIGHNESSES, HAVE A SEAT. WE WILL PREPARE TEA AND COFFEE.
A BRAUNER FOR PRINCE EINS.
MILK TEA FOR PRINCE LEONHARD.
AND A MELANGE FOR EACH OF THE REST.
YES, SIR.
MY WORD! BUT HE WOULD KNOW ALL OF OUR PREFER-ENCES...
PARDON ME.
SHF

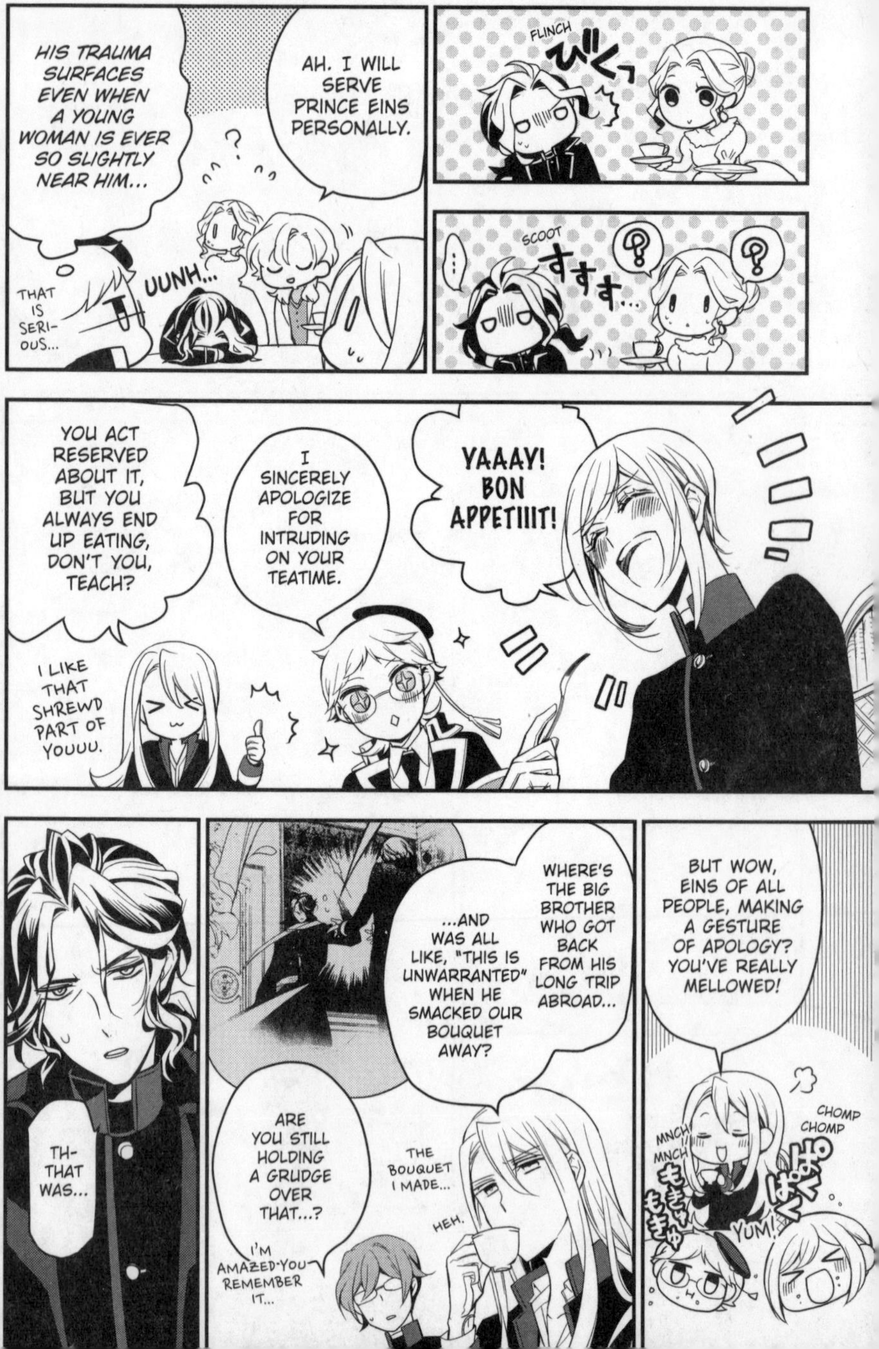
FLINCH
びくっ
SCOOT
すすす...
...
?
?
AH. I WILL SERVE PRINCE EINS PERSONALLY.
?
HIS TRAUMA SURFACES EVEN WHEN A YOUNG WOMAN IS EVER SO SLIGHTLY NEAR HIM...
UUNH...
THAT IS SERI-OUS...
YAAAY! BON APPETIIIIT!
I SINCERELY APOLOGIZE FOR INTRUDING ON YOUR TEATIME.
YOU ACT RESERVED ABOUT IT, BUT YOU ALWAYS END UP EATING, DON'T YOU, TEACH?
I LIKE THAT SHREWD PART OF YOUUU.
BUT WOW, EINS OF ALL PEOPLE, MAKING A GESTURE OF APOLOGY? YOU'VE REALLY MELLOWED!
CHOMP CHOMP
ぱくぱく
MNCH MNCH
もきゅもきゅ
YUM!
WHERE'S THE BIG BROTHER WHO GOT BACK FROM HIS LONG TRIP ABROAD...
...AND WAS ALL LIKE, "THIS IS UNWARRANTED" WHEN HE SMACKED OUR BOUQUET AWAY?
THE BOUQUET I MADE...
HEH.
ARE YOU STILL HOLDING A GRUDGE OVER THAT...?
I'M AMAZED YOU REMEMBER IT...
TH-THAT WAS...

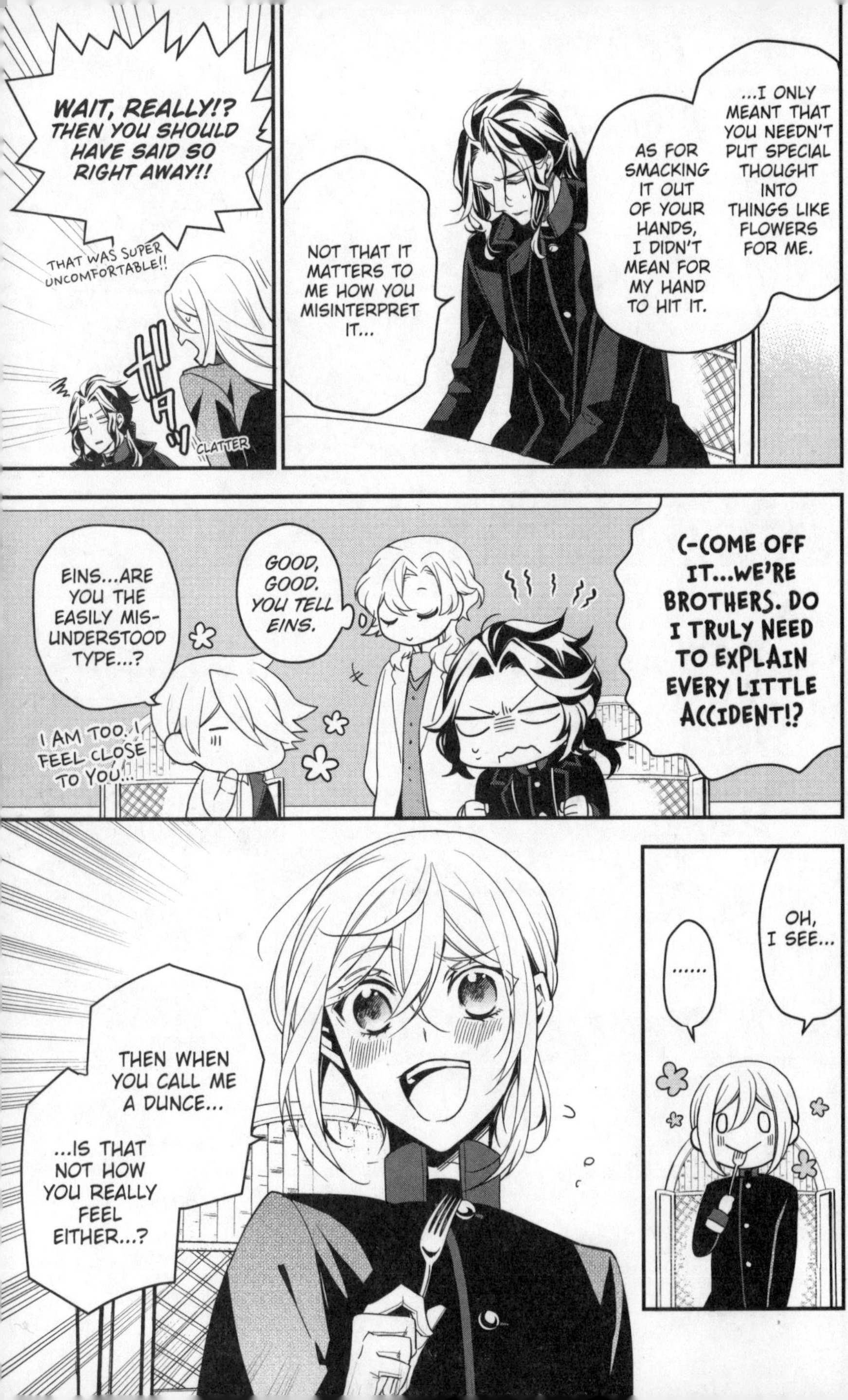

...I ONLY MEANT THAT YOU NEEDN'T PUT SPECIAL THOUGHT INTO THINGS LIKE FLOWERS FOR ME.
AS FOR SMACKING IT OUT OF YOUR HANDS, I DIDN'T MEAN FOR MY HAND TO HIT IT.
NOT THAT IT MATTERS TO ME HOW YOU MISINTERPRET IT...
WAIT, REALLY!? THEN YOU SHOULD HAVE SAID SO RIGHT AWAY!!
THAT WAS SUPER UNCOMFORTABLE!!
CLATTER
(-COME OFF IT...WE'RE BROTHERS. DO I TRULY NEED TO EXPLAIN EVERY LITTLE ACCIDENT!?
GOOD, GOOD. YOU TELL EINS.
EINS...ARE YOU THE EASILY MIS-UNDERSTOOD TYPE...?
I AM TOO. I FEEL CLOSE TO YOU...
OH, I SEE...
......
THEN WHEN YOU CALL ME A DUNCE...
...IS THAT NOT HOW YOU REALLY FEEL EITHER...?

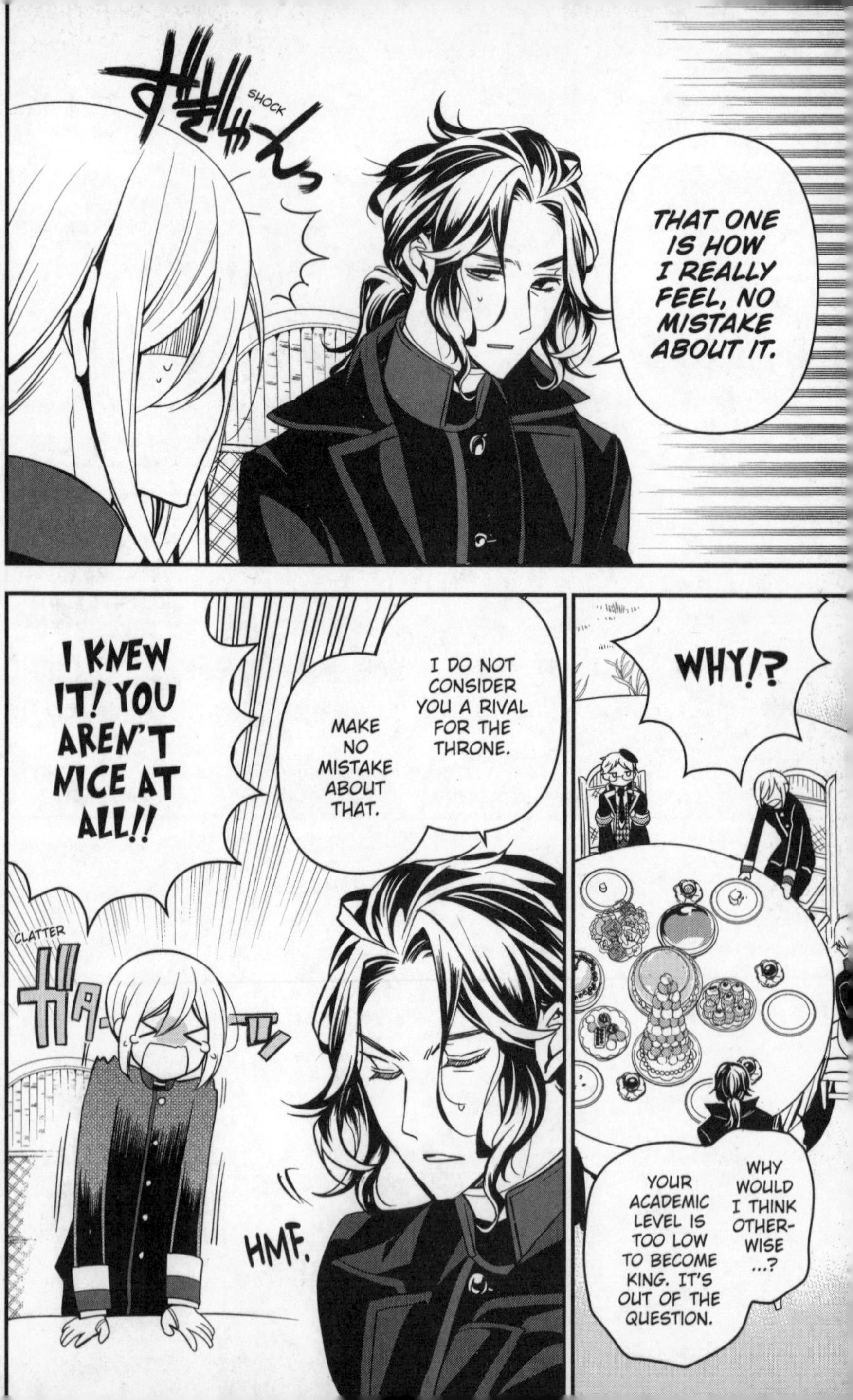
THAT ONE IS HOW I REALLY FEEL, NO MISTAKE ABOUT IT.
SHOCK
WHY!?
WHY WOULD I THINK OTHERWISE ...?
YOUR ACADEMIC LEVEL IS TOO LOW TO BECOME KING. IT'S OUT OF THE QUESTION.
I DO NOT CONSIDER YOU A RIVAL FOR THE THRONE.
MAKE NO MISTAKE ABOUT THAT.
I KNEW IT! YOU AREN'T NICE AT ALL!!
CLATTER
HMF.

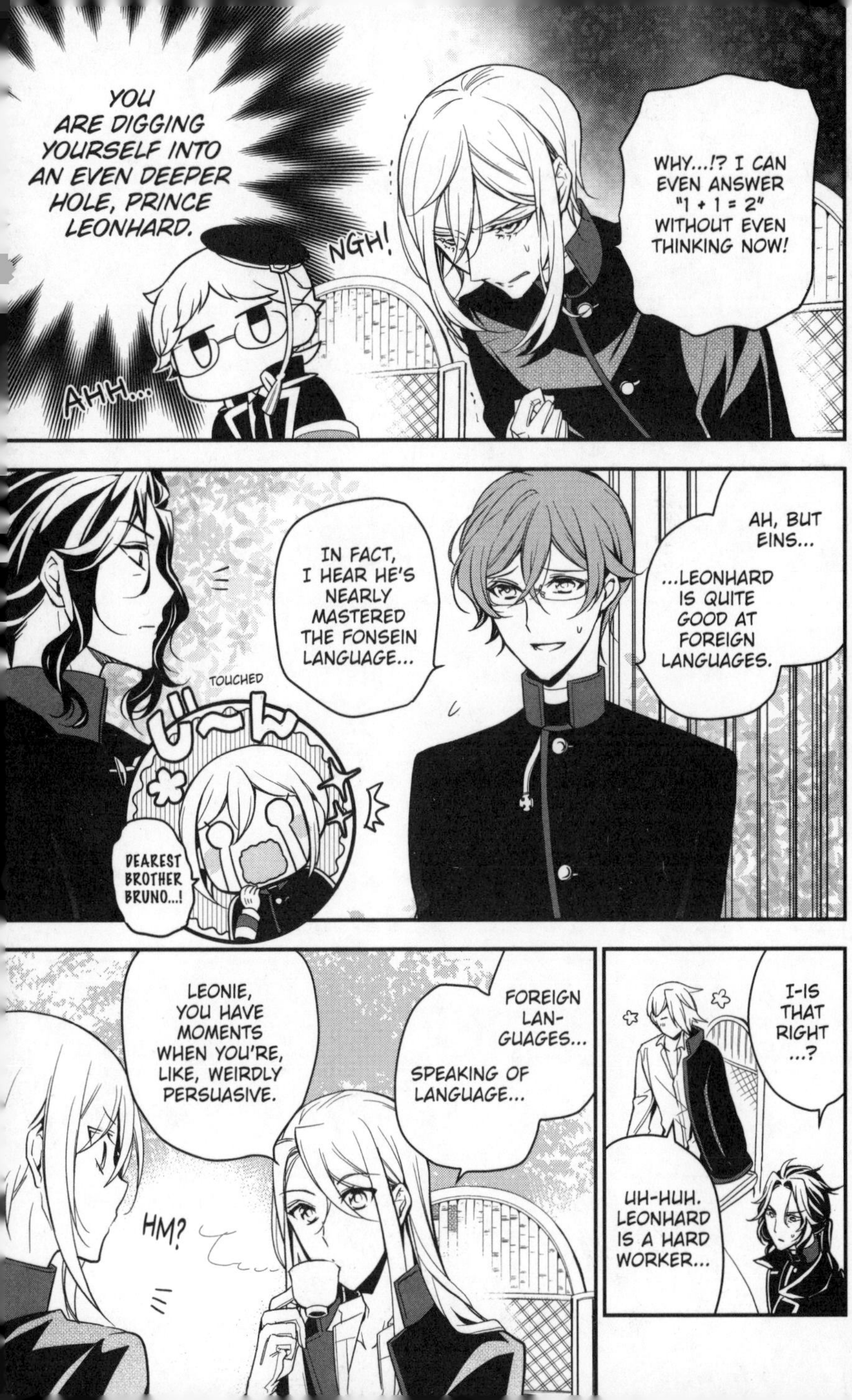
WHY...!? I CAN EVEN ANSWER "1 + 1 = 2" WITHOUT EVEN THINKING NOW!
NGH!
YOU ARE DIGGING YOURSELF INTO AN EVEN DEEPER HOLE, PRINCE LEONHARD.
AHH...
AH, BUT EINS...
...LEONHARD IS QUITE GOOD AT FOREIGN LANGUAGES.
IN FACT, I HEAR HE'S NEARLY MASTERED THE FONSEIN LANGUAGE...
TOUCHED
じ~ん
DEAREST BROTHER BRUNO...!
I-IS THAT RIGHT ...?
UH-HUH. LEONHARD IS A HARD WORKER...
FOREIGN LAN-GUAGES...
SPEAKING OF LANGUAGE...
LEONIE, YOU HAVE MOMENTS WHEN YOU'RE, LIKE, WEIRDLY PERSUASIVE.
HM?

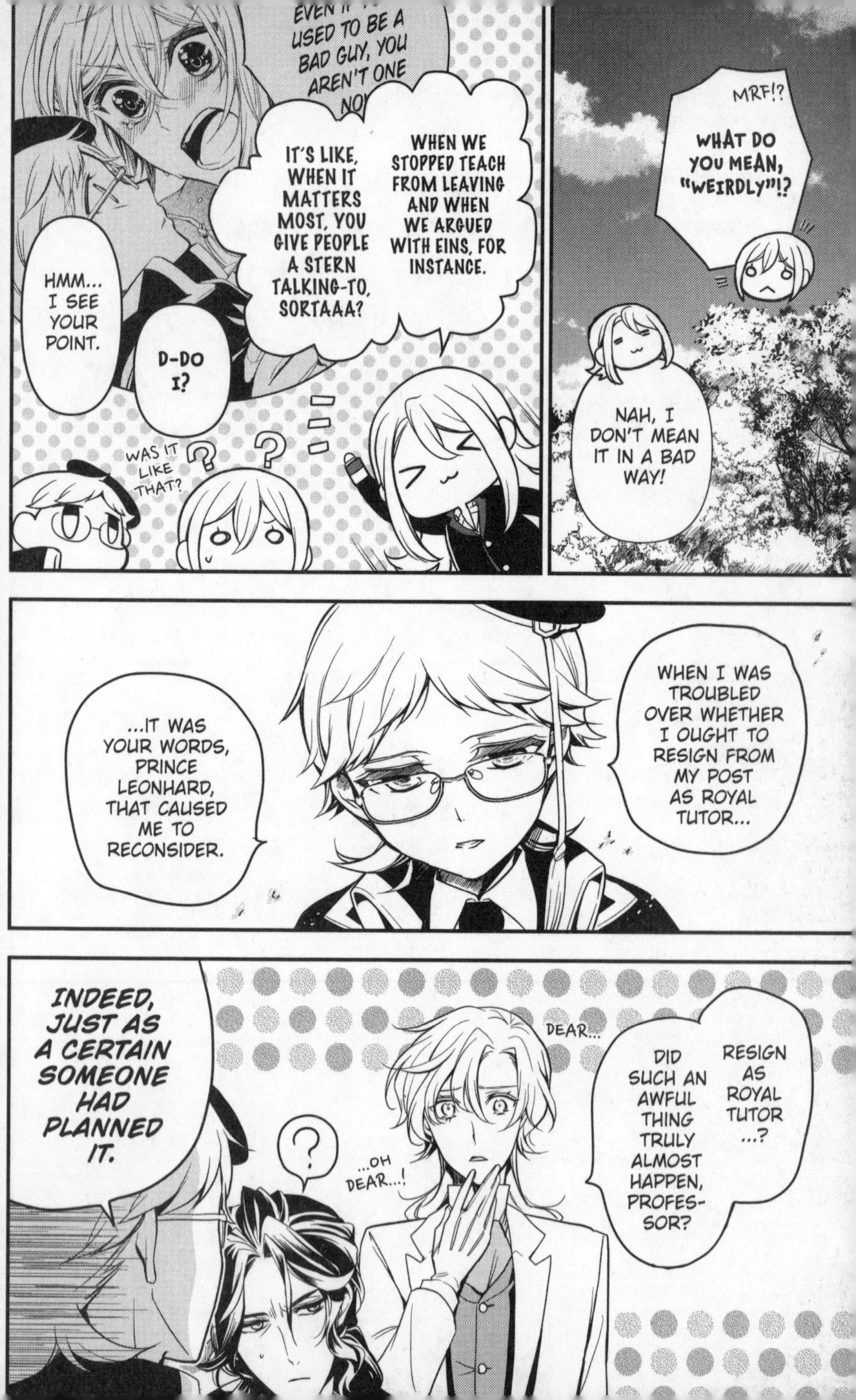
MRF!?
WHAT DO YOU MEAN, "WEIRDLY"!?
NAH, I DON'T MEAN IT IN A BAD WAY!
USED TO BE A BAD GUY, YOU AREN'T ONE
WHEN WE STOPPED TEACH FROM LEAVING AND WHEN WE ARGUED WITH EINS, FOR INSTANCE.
IT'S LIKE, WHEN IT MATTERS MOST, YOU GIVE PEOPLE A STERN TALKING-TO, SORTAAA?
HMM... I SEE YOUR POINT.
D-DO I?
WAS IT LIKE THAT?
WHEN I WAS TROUBLED OVER WHETHER I OUGHT TO RESIGN FROM MY POST AS ROYAL TUTOR...
...IT WAS YOUR WORDS, PRINCE LEONHARD, THAT CAUSED ME TO RECONSIDER.
DEAR...
RESIGN AS ROYAL TUTOR...?
DID SUCH AN AWFUL THING TRULY ALMOST HAPPEN, PROFESSOR?
...OH DEAR...!
INDEED, JUST AS A CERTAIN SOMEONE HAD PLANNED IT.

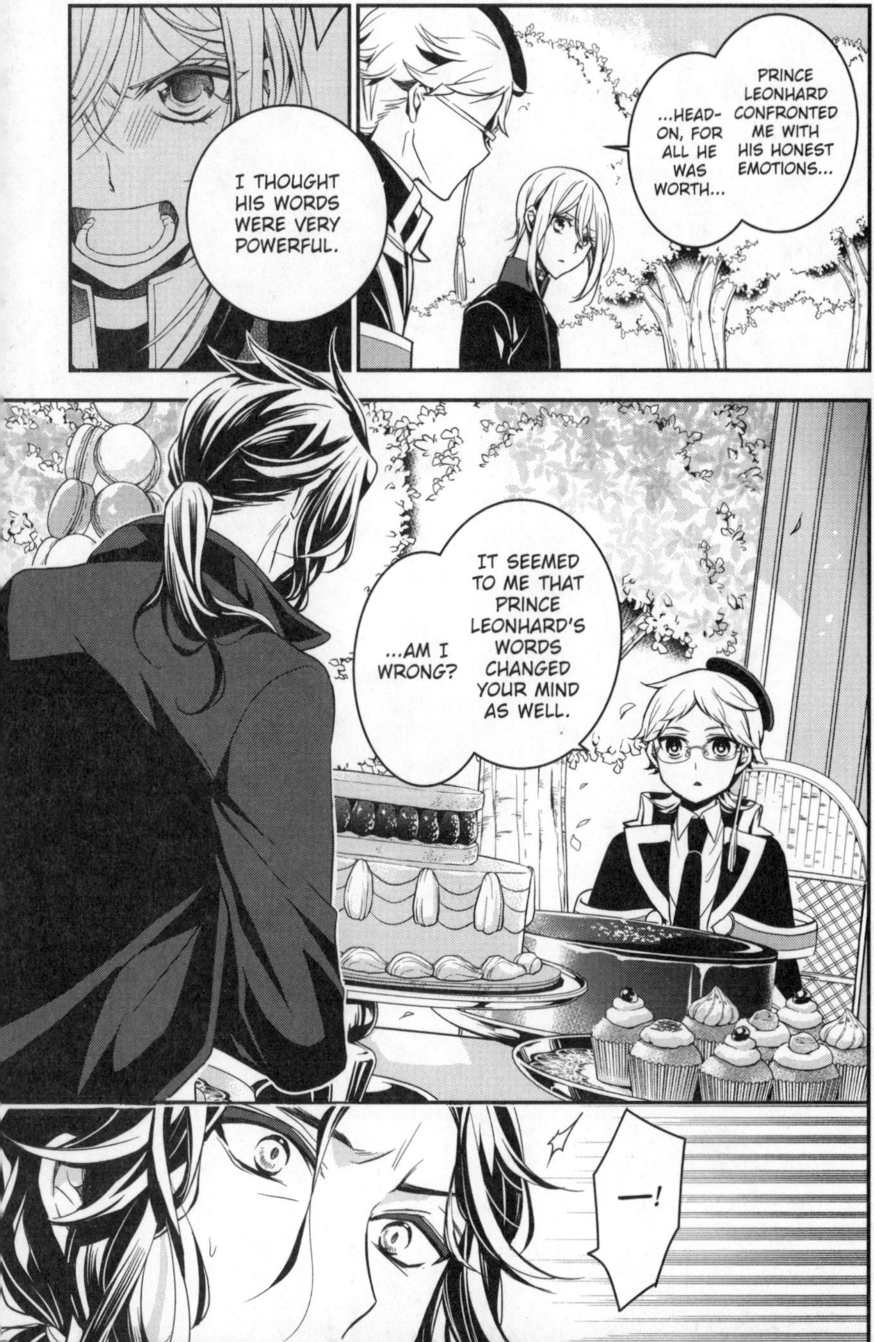
PRINCE LEONHARD CONFRONTED ME WITH HIS HONEST EMOTIONS...
...HEAD-ON, FOR ALL HE WAS WORTH...
I THOUGHT HIS WORDS WERE VERY POWERFUL.
IT SEEMED TO ME THAT PRINCE LEONHARD'S WORDS CHANGED YOUR MIND AS WELL.
...AM I WRONG?
—!

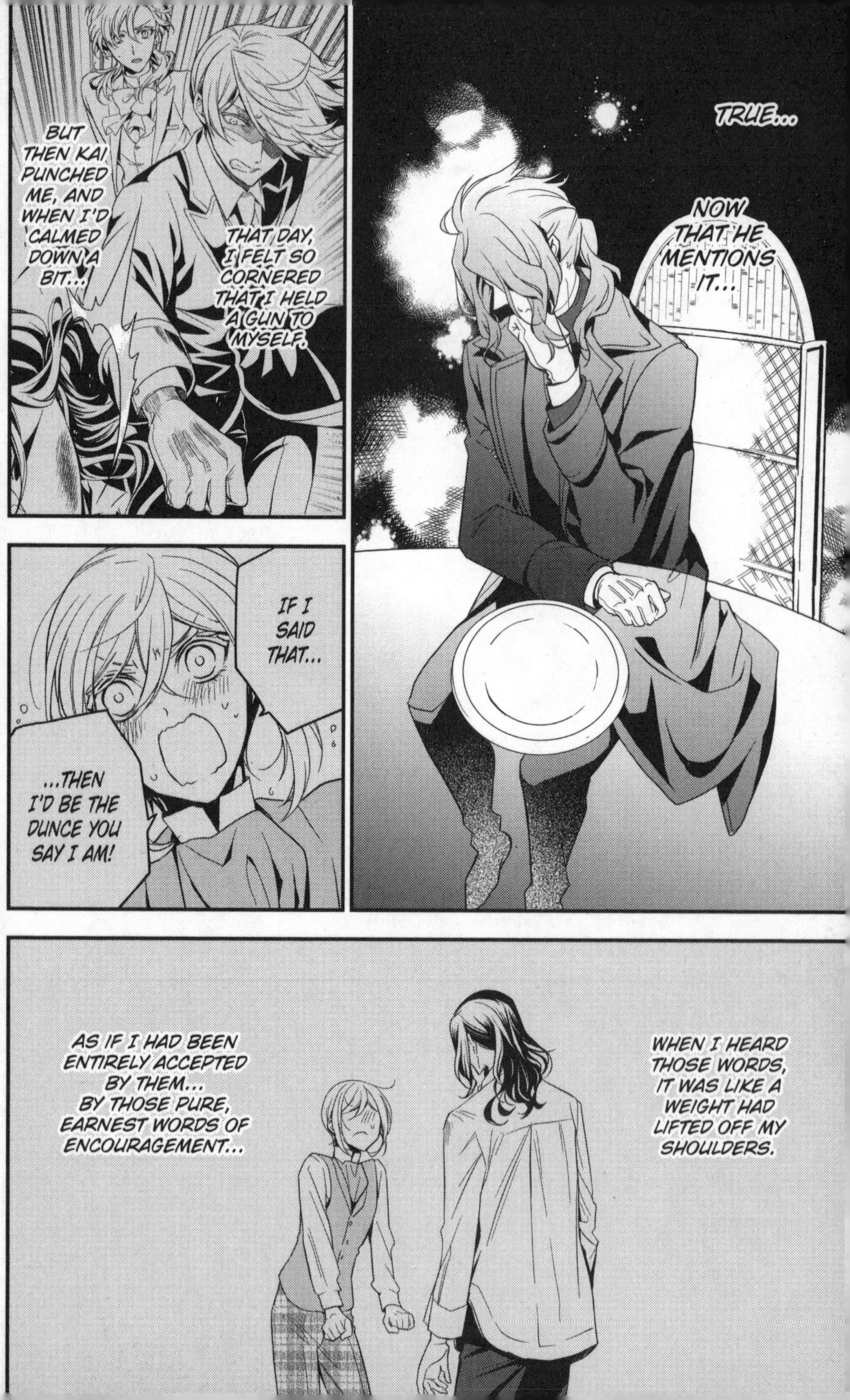
TRUE...
NOW THAT HE MENTIONS IT...
THAT DAY, I FELT SO CORNERED THAT I HELD A GUN TO MYSELF.
BUT THEN KAI PUNCHED ME, AND WHEN I'D CALMED DOWN A BIT...
IF I SAID THAT...
...THEN I'D BE THE DUNCE YOU SAY I AM!
WHEN I HEARD THOSE WORDS, IT WAS LIKE A WEIGHT HAD LIFTED OFF MY SHOULDERS.
AS IF I HAD BEEN ENTIRELY ACCEPTED BY THEM... BY THOSE PURE, EARNEST WORDS OF ENCOURAGEMENT...

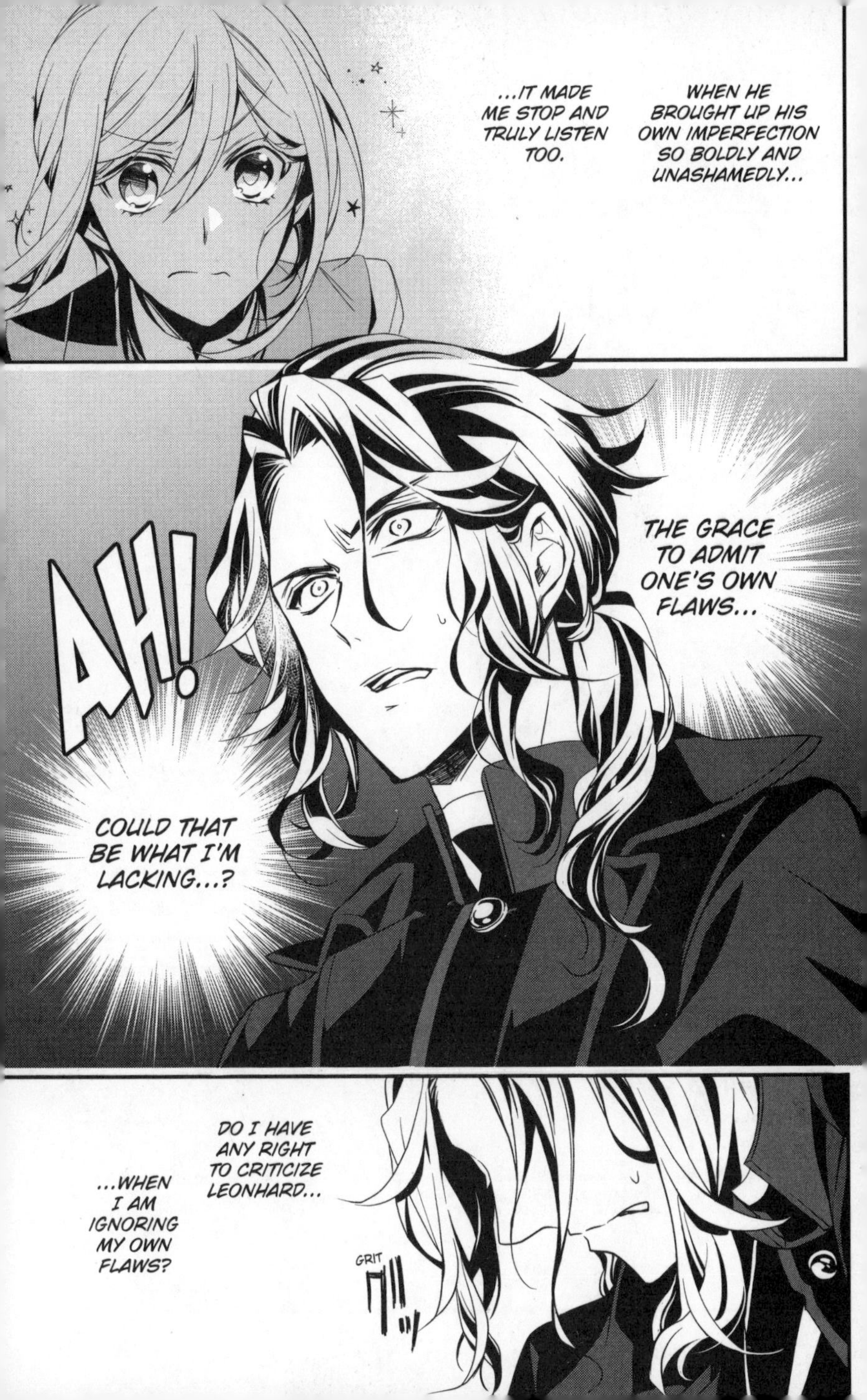
WHEN HE BROUGHT UP HIS OWN IMPERFECTION SO BOLDLY AND UNASHAMEDLY...
...IT MADE ME STOP AND TRULY LISTEN TOO.
THE GRACE TO ADMIT ONE'S OWN FLAWS...
AH!
COULD THAT BE WHAT I'M LACKING...?
DO I HAVE ANY RIGHT TO CRITICIZE LEONHARD...
...WHEN I AM IGNORING MY OWN FLAWS?
GRIT

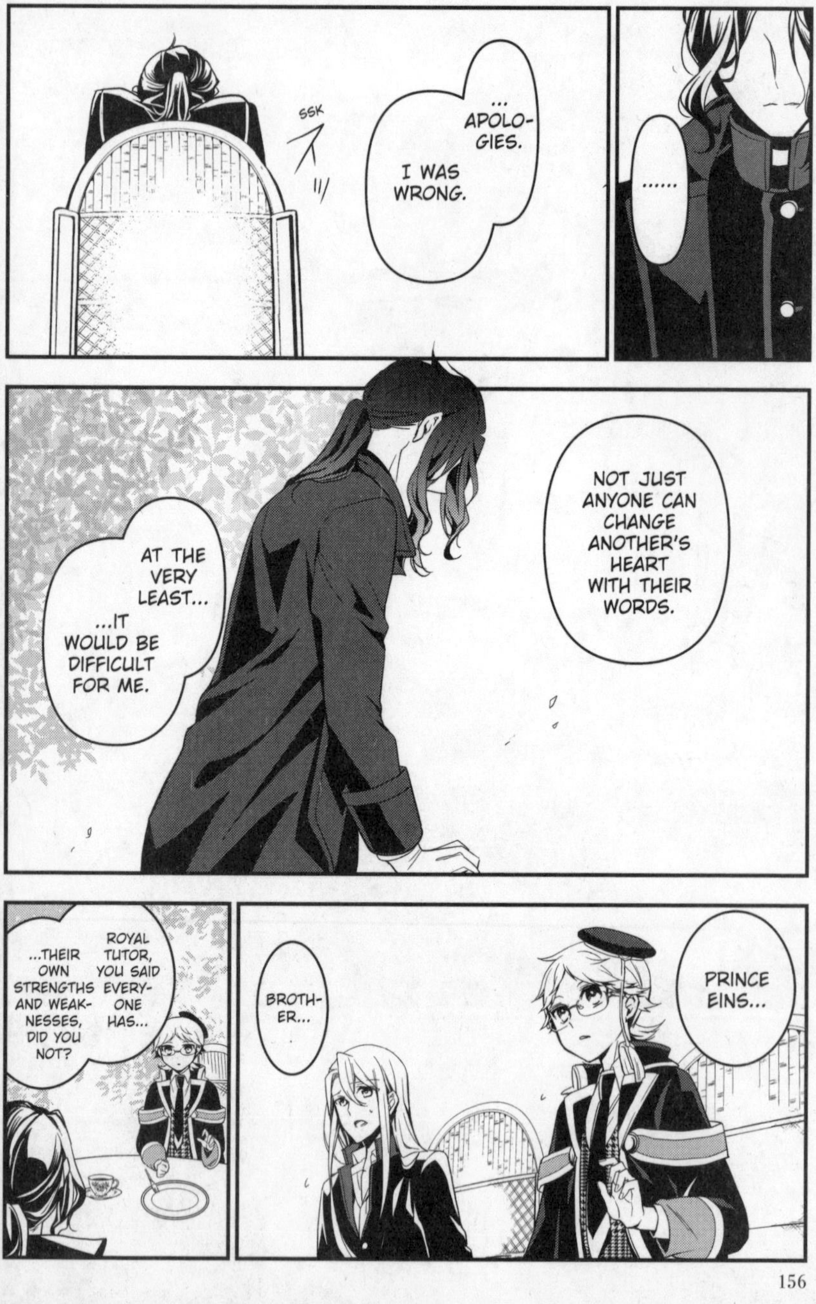
......
... APOLOGIES.
I WAS WRONG.
SSK
NOT JUST ANYONE CAN CHANGE ANOTHER'S HEART WITH THEIR WORDS.
AT THE VERY LEAST...
...IT WOULD BE DIFFICULT FOR ME.
PRINCE EINS...
BROTHER...
ROYAL TUTOR, YOU SAID EVERYONE HAS...
...THEIR OWN STRENGTHS AND WEAKNESSES, DID YOU NOT?

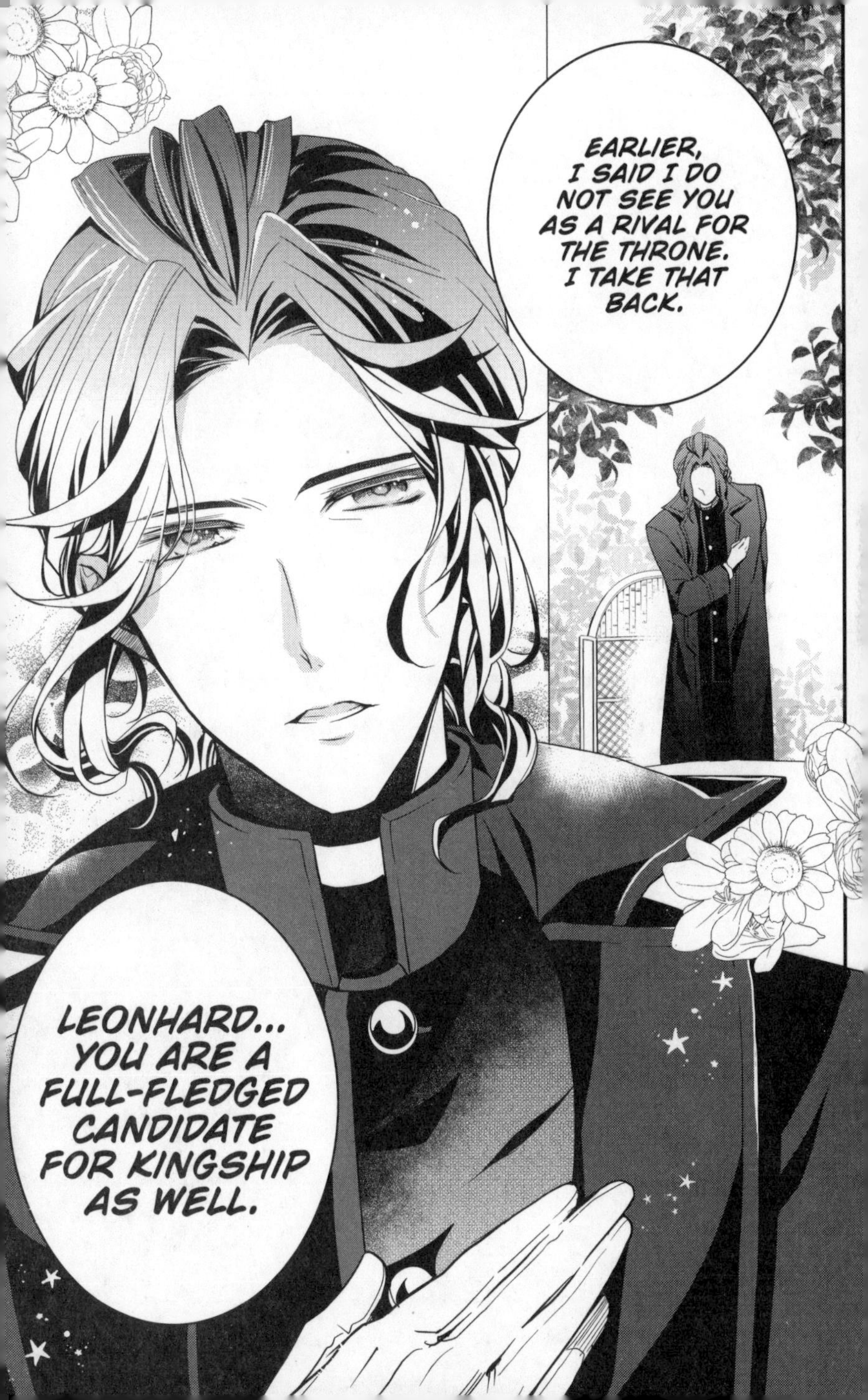
EARLIER, I SAID I DO NOT SEE YOU AS A RIVAL FOR THE THRONE. I TAKE THAT BACK.
LEONHARD... YOU ARE A FULL-FLEDGED CANDIDATE FOR KINGSHIP AS WELL.

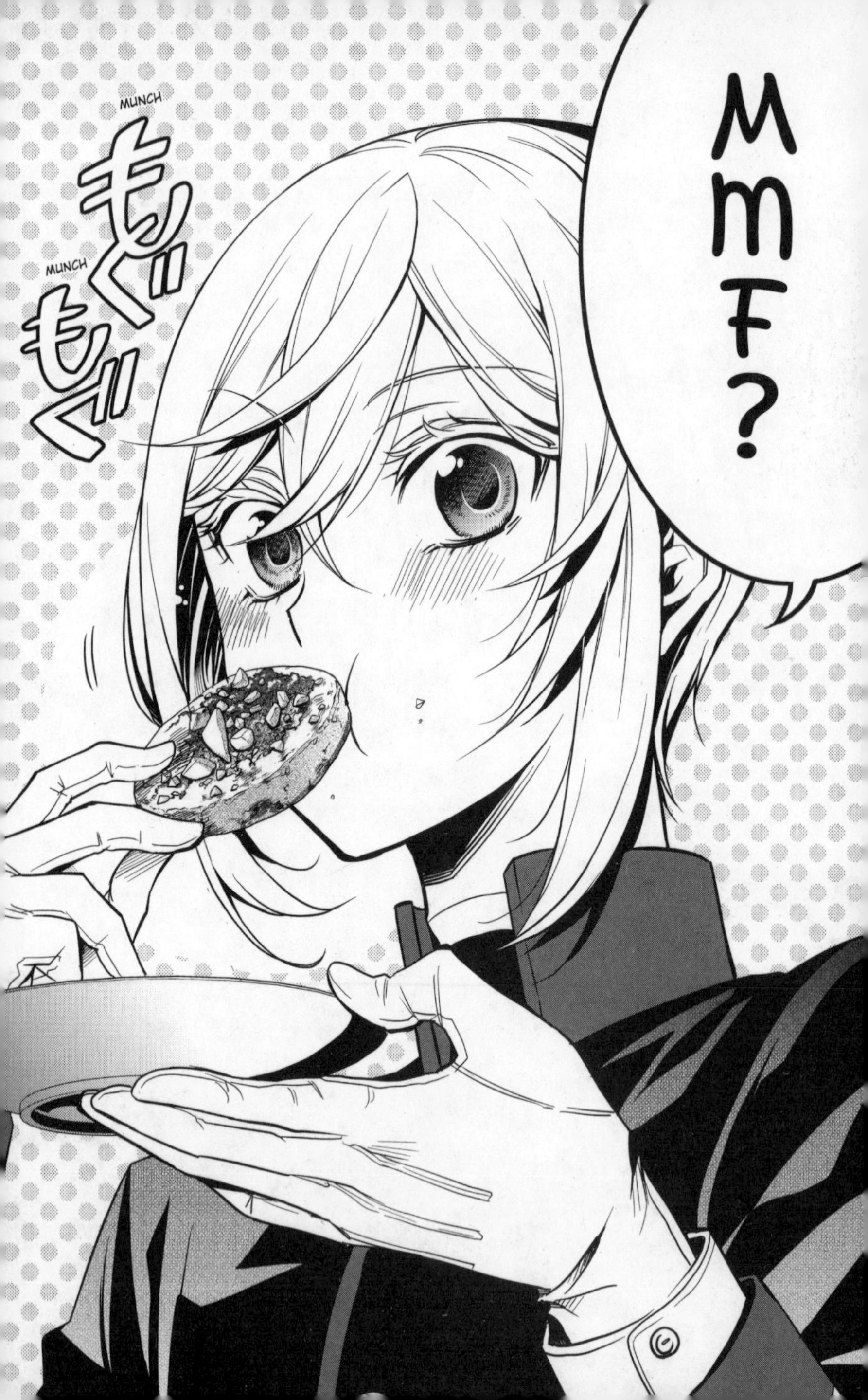
MMF?
もぐもぐ
MUNCH
MUNCH

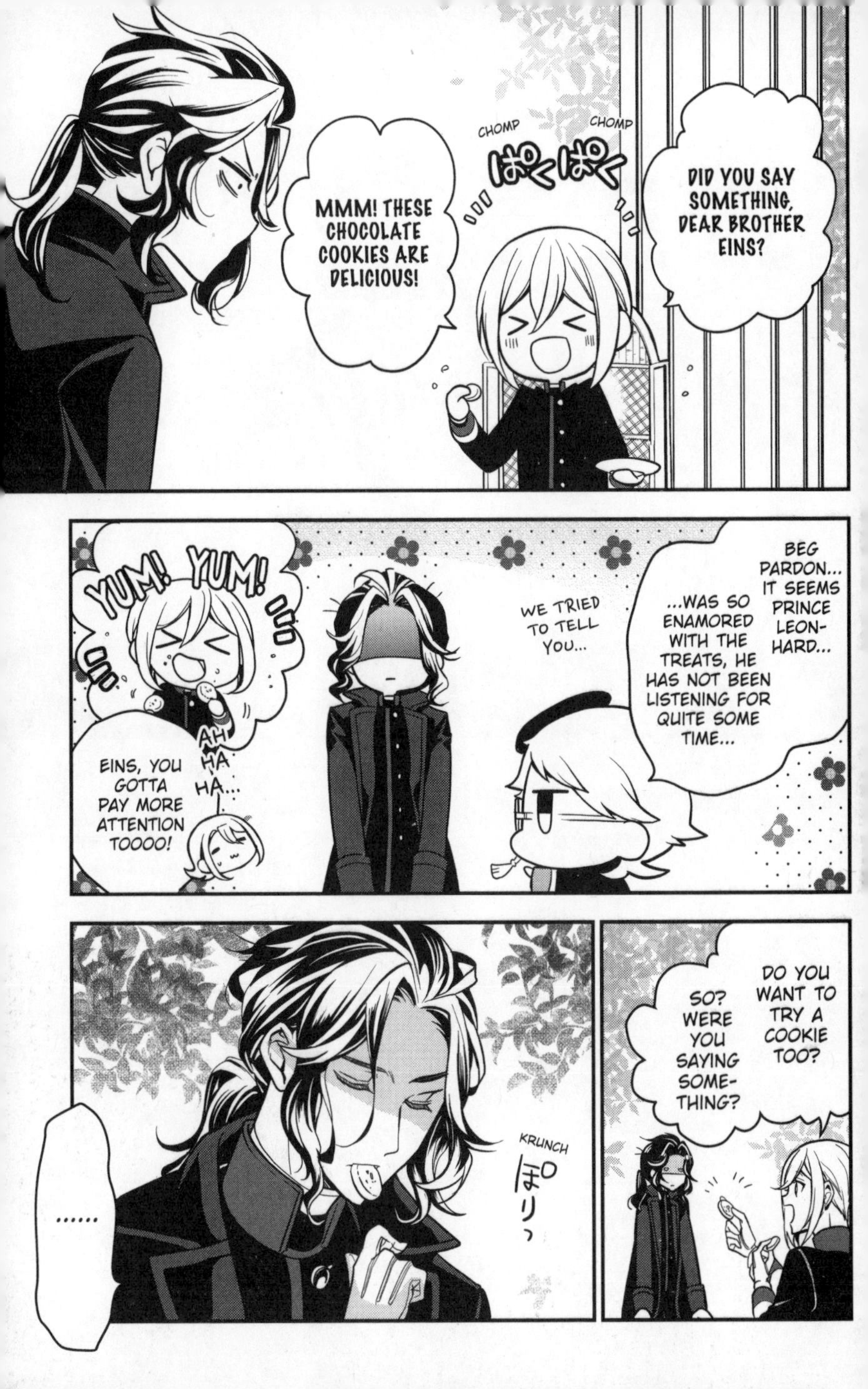

DID YOU SAY SOMETHING, DEAR BROTHER EINS?
CHOMP CHOMP
ぱくぱく
MMM! THESE CHOCOLATE COOKIES ARE DELICIOUS!
BEG PARDON... IT SEEMS PRINCE LEONHARD...
...WAS SO ENAMORED WITH THE TREATS, HE HAS NOT BEEN LISTENING FOR QUITE SOME TIME...
WE TRIED TO TELL YOU...
YUM! YUM!
AH HA HA...
EINS, YOU GOTTA PAY MORE ATTENTION TOOOO!
DO YOU WANT TO TRY A COOKIE TOO?
SO? WERE YOU SAYING SOME-THING?
KRUNCH
ぽりっ
......

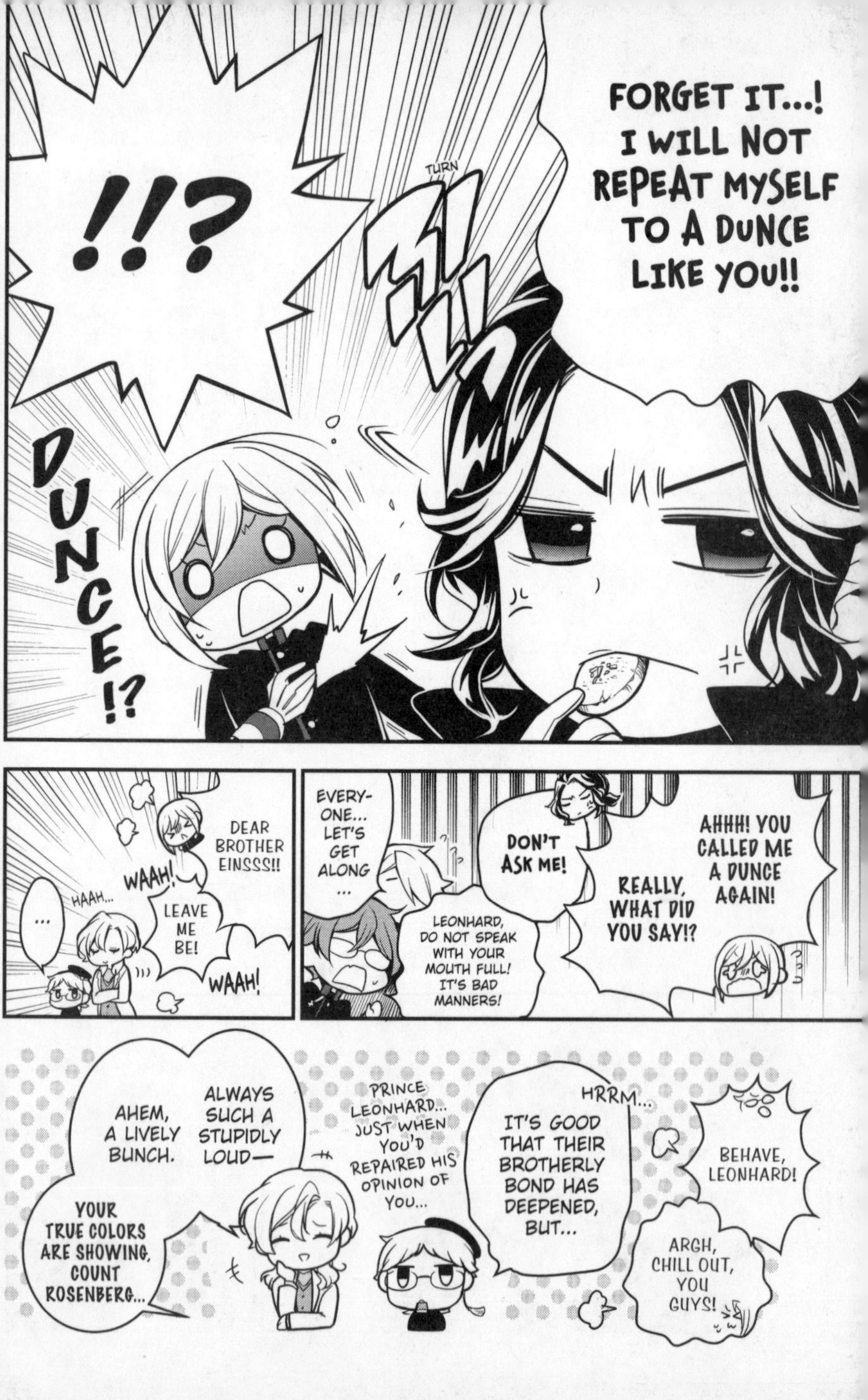
FORGET IT...! I WILL NOT REPEAT MYSELF TO A DUNCE LIKE YOU!!
TURN
!!?
DUNCE!?
AHHH! YOU CALLED ME A DUNCE AGAIN!
REALLY, WHAT DID YOU SAY!?
DON'T ASK ME!
LEONHARD, DO NOT SPEAK WITH YOUR MOUTH FULL! IT'S BAD MANNERS!
EVERY-ONE... LET'S GET ALONG ...
DEAR BROTHER EINSSS!!
WAAH!
LEAVE ME BE!
WAAH!
HAAH...
...
BEHAVE, LEONHARD!
ARGH, CHILL OUT, YOU GUYS!
HRRM...
IT'S GOOD THAT THEIR BROTHERLY BOND HAS DEEPENED, BUT...
PRINCE LEONHARD... JUST WHEN YOU'D REPAIRED HIS OPINION OF YOU...
ALWAYS SUCH A STUPIDLY LOUD—
AHEM, A LIVELY BUNCH.
YOUR TRUE COLORS ARE SHOWING, COUNT ROSENBERG...

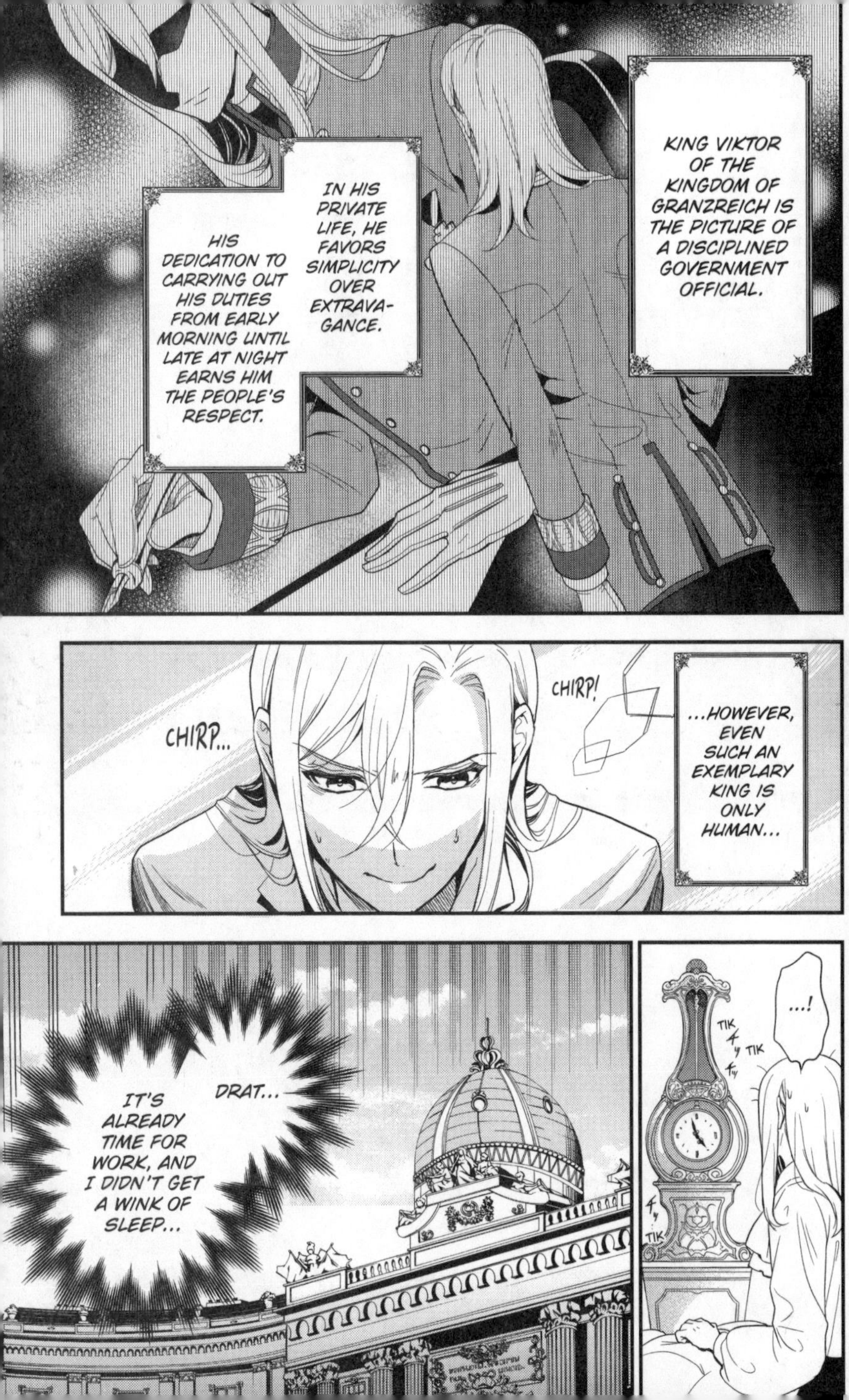
KING VIKTOR OF THE KINGDOM OF GRANZREICH IS THE PICTURE OF A DISCIPLINED GOVERNMENT OFFICIAL.
IN HIS PRIVATE LIFE, HE FAVORS SIMPLICITY OVER EXTRAVA-GANCE.
HIS DEDICATION TO CARRYING OUT HIS DUTIES FROM EARLY MORNING UNTIL LATE AT NIGHT EARNS HIM THE PEOPLE'S RESPECT.
...HOWEVER, EVEN SUCH AN EXEMPLARY KING IS ONLY HUMAN...
CHIRP!
CHIRP...
...!
TIK
TIK
TIK
DRAT...
IT'S ALREADY TIME FOR WORK, AND I DIDN'T GET A WINK OF SLEEP...

Chapter 96
A Day in the Life of His Majesty the King

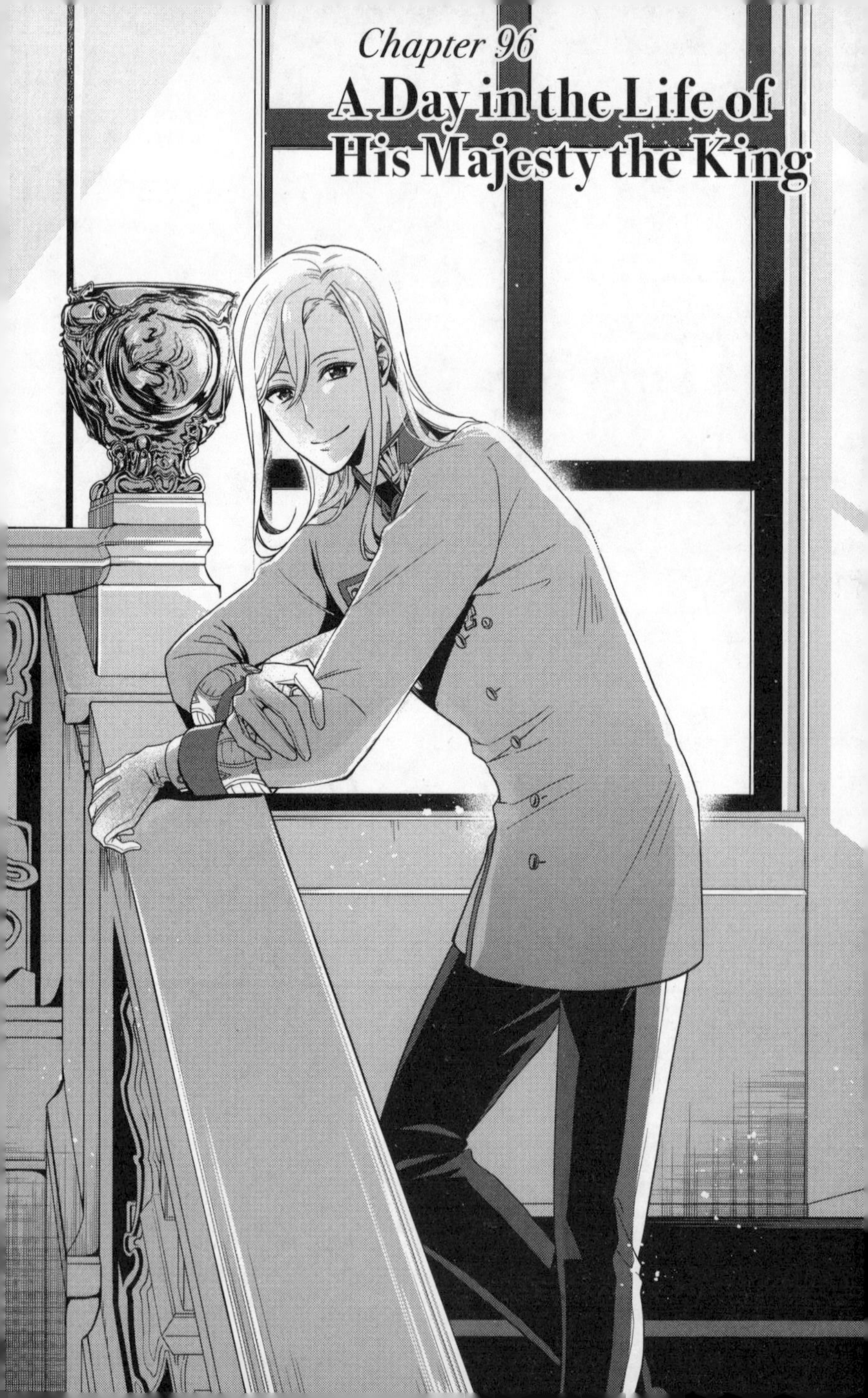

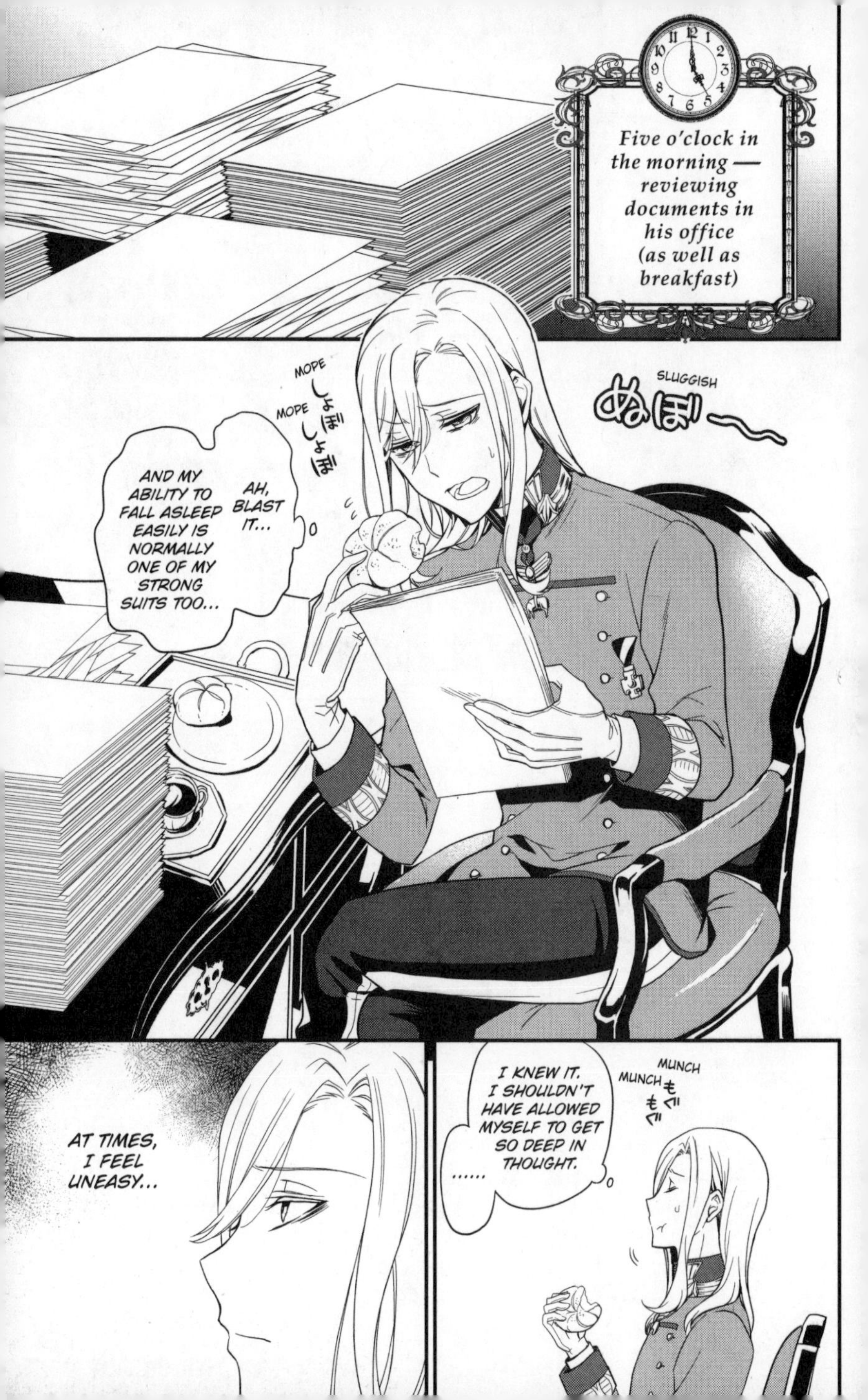
Five o'clock in the morning — reviewing documents in his office (as well as breakfast)
SLUGGISH
ぬぼー
MOPE
しょぼ
MOPE
しょぼ
AH, BLAST IT...
AND MY ABILITY TO FALL ASLEEP EASILY IS NORMALLY ONE OF MY STRONG SUITS TOO...
MUNCH
もぐ
MUNCH
もぐ
I KNEW IT. I SHOULDN'T HAVE ALLOWED MYSELF TO GET SO DEEP IN THOUGHT.
......
AT TIMES, I FEEL UNEASY...

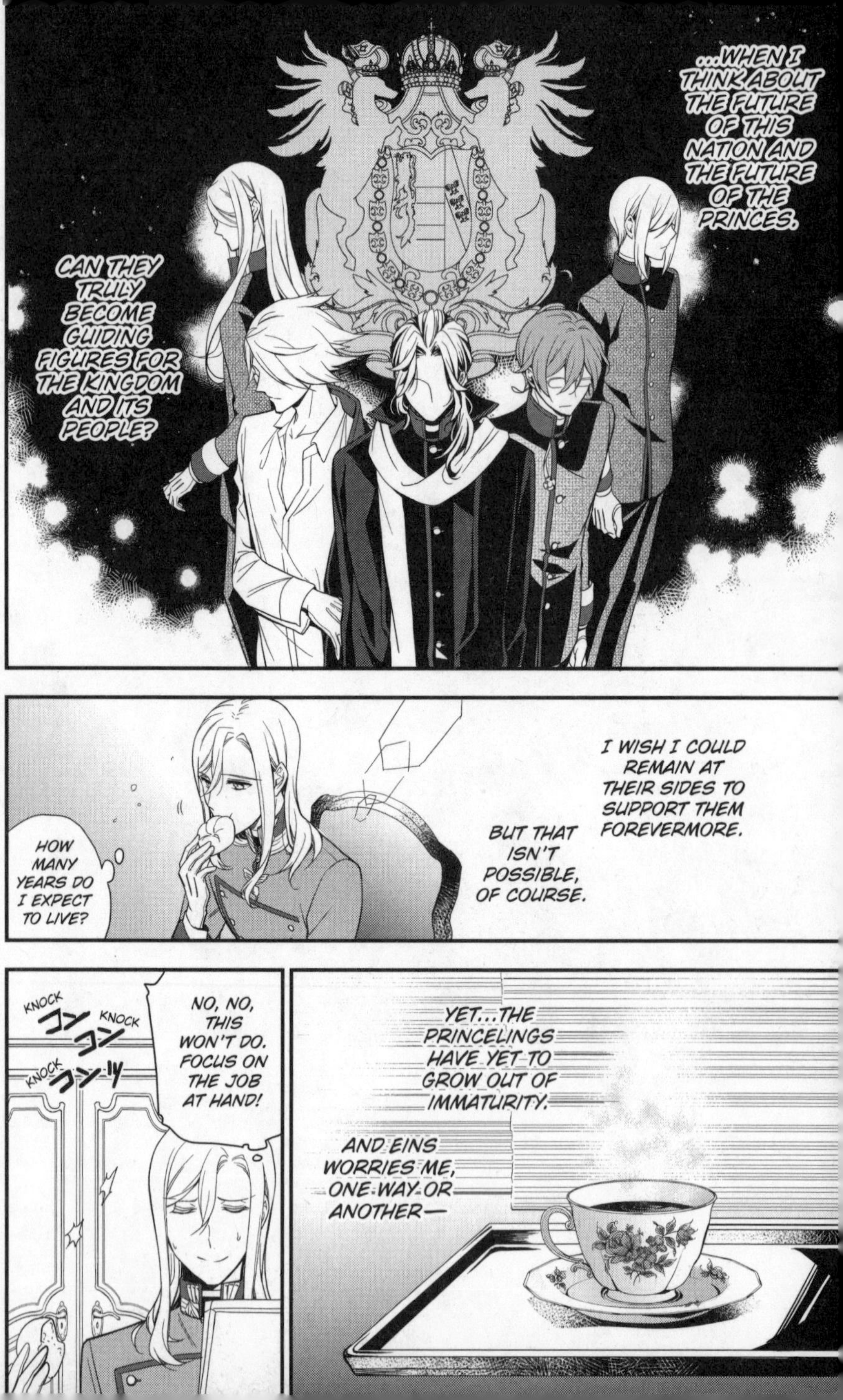
...WHEN I THINK ABOUT THE FUTURE OF THIS NATION AND THE FUTURE OF THE PRINCES.
CAN THEY TRULY BECOME GUIDING FIGURES FOR THE KINGDOM AND ITS PEOPLE?
I WISH I COULD REMAIN AT THEIR SIDES TO SUPPORT THEM FOREVERMORE.
BUT THAT ISN'T POSSIBLE, OF COURSE.
HOW MANY YEARS DO I EXPECT TO LIVE?
YET...THE PRINCELINGS HAVE YET TO GROW OUT OF IMMATURITY.
AND EINS WORRIES ME, ONE WAY OR ANOTHER—
NO, NO, THIS WON'T DO. FOCUS ON THE JOB AT HAND!
KNOCK コン
KNOCK コン
KNOCK コンッ

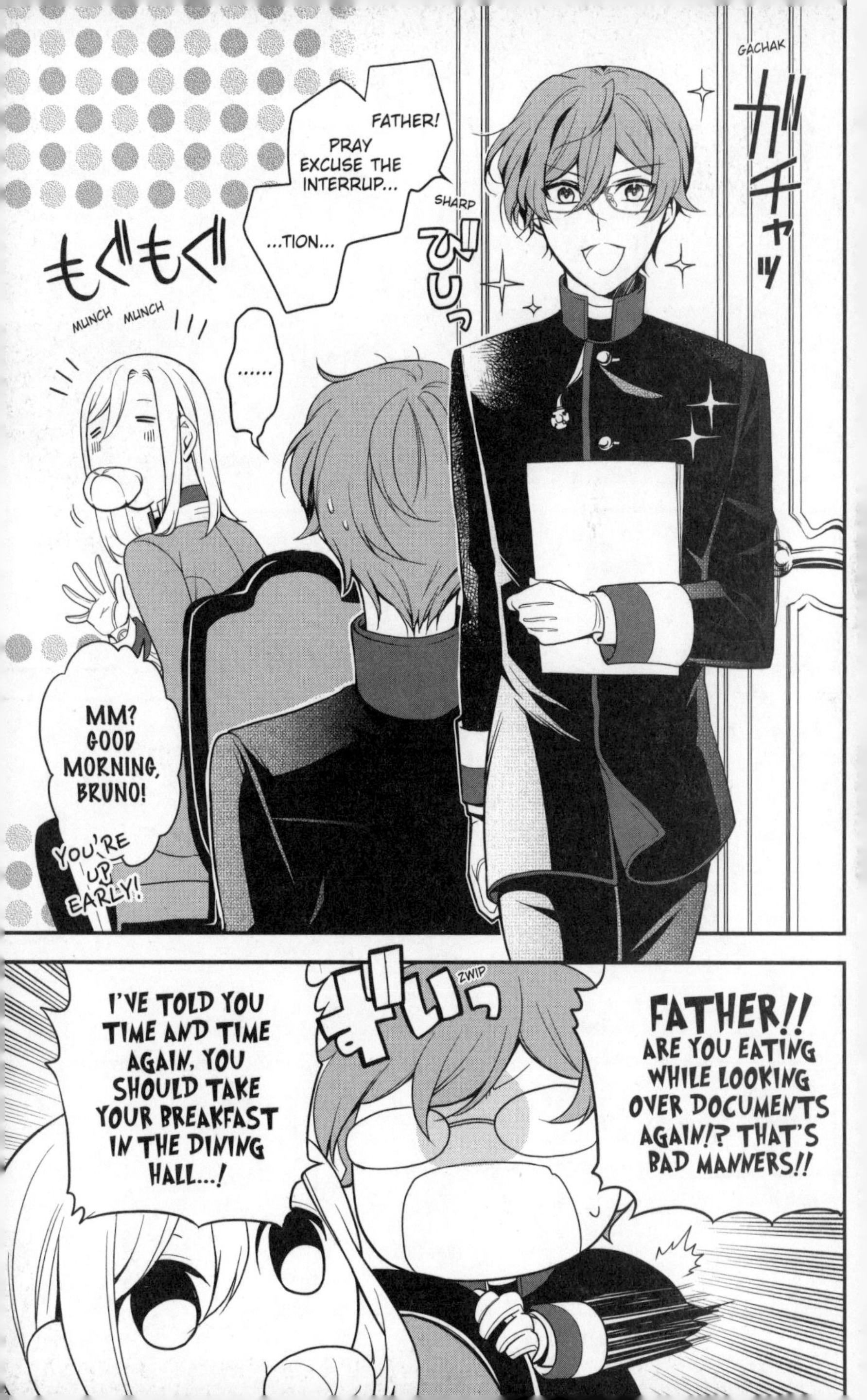
GACHAK
ガチャッ
FATHER!
PRAY EXCUSE THE INTERRUP...
...TION...
SHARP
もぐもぐ
MUNCH MUNCH
......
MM? GOOD MORNING, BRUNO!
YOU'RE UP EARLY!
FATHER!! ARE YOU EATING WHILE LOOKING OVER DOCUMENTS AGAIN!? THAT'S BAD MANNERS!!
ZWIP
I'VE TOLD YOU TIME AND TIME AGAIN, YOU SHOULD TAKE YOUR BREAKFAST IN THE DINING HALL...!

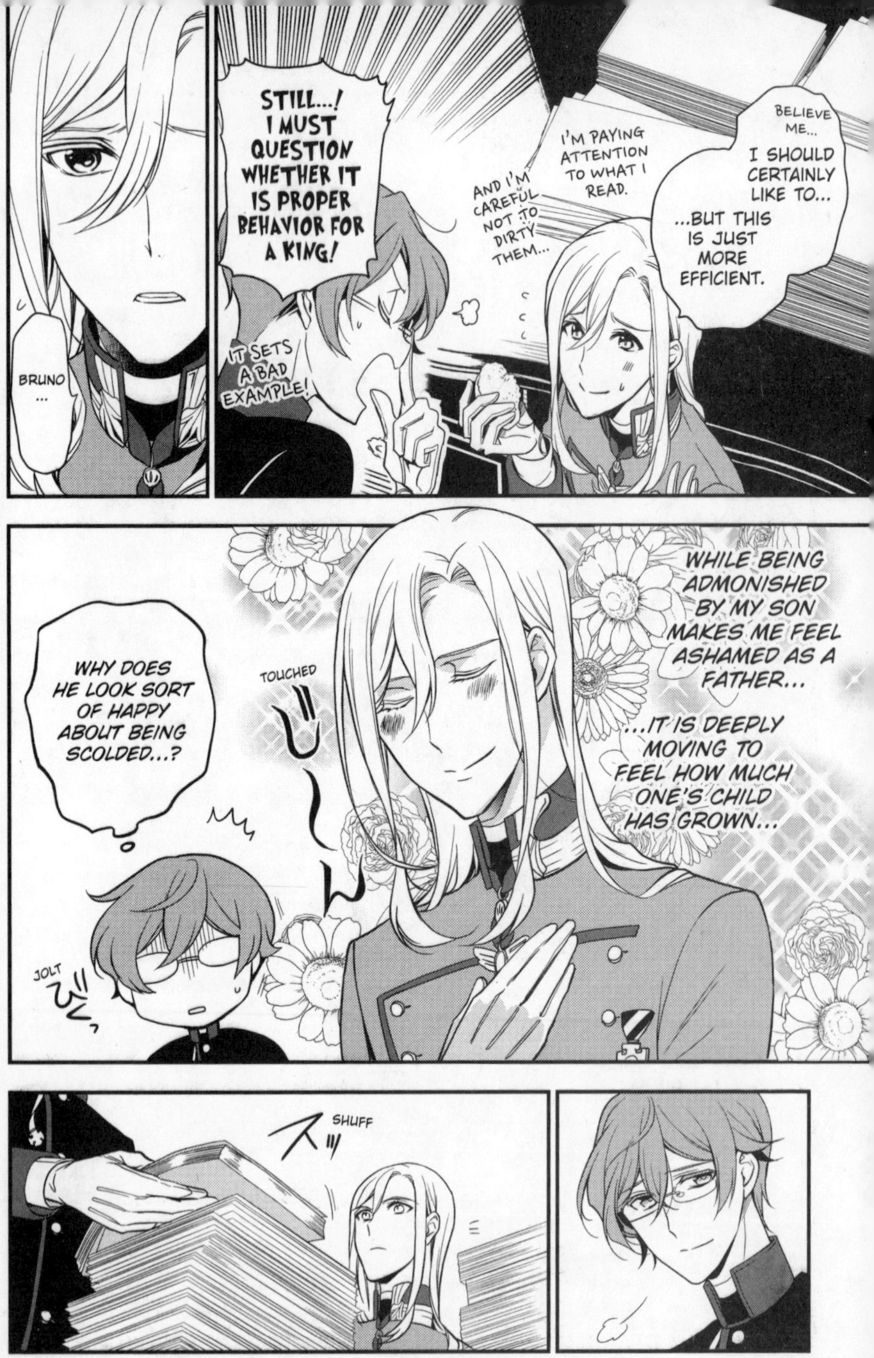
BELIEVE ME... I SHOULD CERTAINLY LIKE TO...
...BUT THIS IS JUST MORE EFFICIENT.
I'M PAYING ATTENTION TO WHAT I READ.
AND I'M CAREFUL NOT TO DIRTY THEM...
STILL...! I MUST QUESTION WHETHER IT IS PROPER BEHAVIOR FOR A KING!
IT SETS A BAD EXAMPLE!
BRUNO ...
WHILE BEING ADMONISHED BY MY SON MAKES ME FEEL ASHAMED AS A FATHER...
...IT IS DEEPLY MOVING TO FEEL HOW MUCH ONE'S CHILD HAS GROWN...
TOUCHED
WHY DOES HE LOOK SORT OF HAPPY ABOUT BEING SCOLDED...?
JOLT
SHUFF

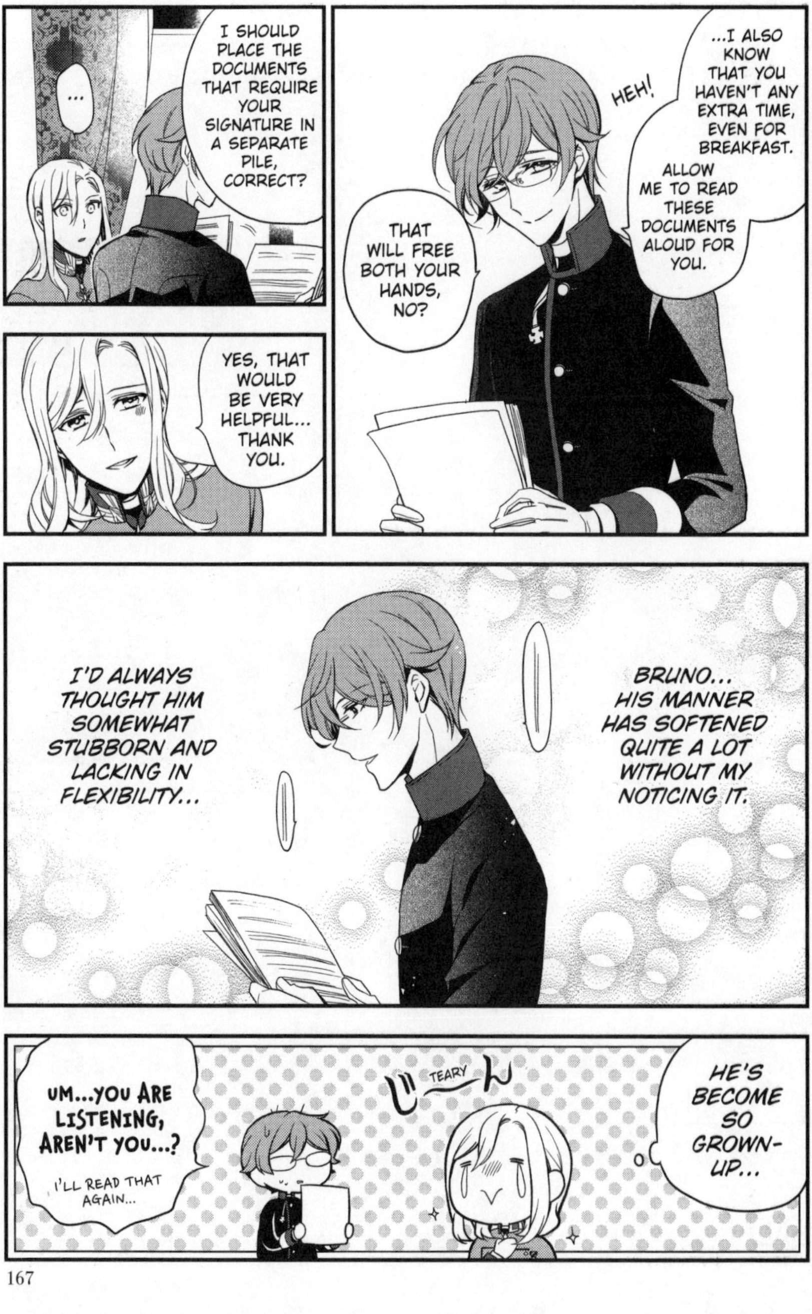
...I ALSO KNOW THAT YOU HAVEN'T ANY EXTRA TIME, EVEN FOR BREAKFAST.
HEH!
ALLOW ME TO READ THESE DOCUMENTS ALOUD FOR YOU.
THAT WILL FREE BOTH YOUR HANDS, NO?
I SHOULD PLACE THE DOCUMENTS THAT REQUIRE YOUR SIGNATURE IN A SEPARATE PILE, CORRECT?
...
YES, THAT WOULD BE VERY HELPFUL... THANK YOU.
BRUNO... HIS MANNER HAS SOFTENED QUITE A LOT WITHOUT MY NOTICING IT.
I'D ALWAYS THOUGHT HIM SOMEWHAT STUBBORN AND LACKING IN FLEXIBILITY...
HE'S BECOME SO GROWN-UP...
じ～ん
TEARY
UM...YOU ARE LISTENING, AREN'T YOU...?
I'LL READ THAT AGAIN...

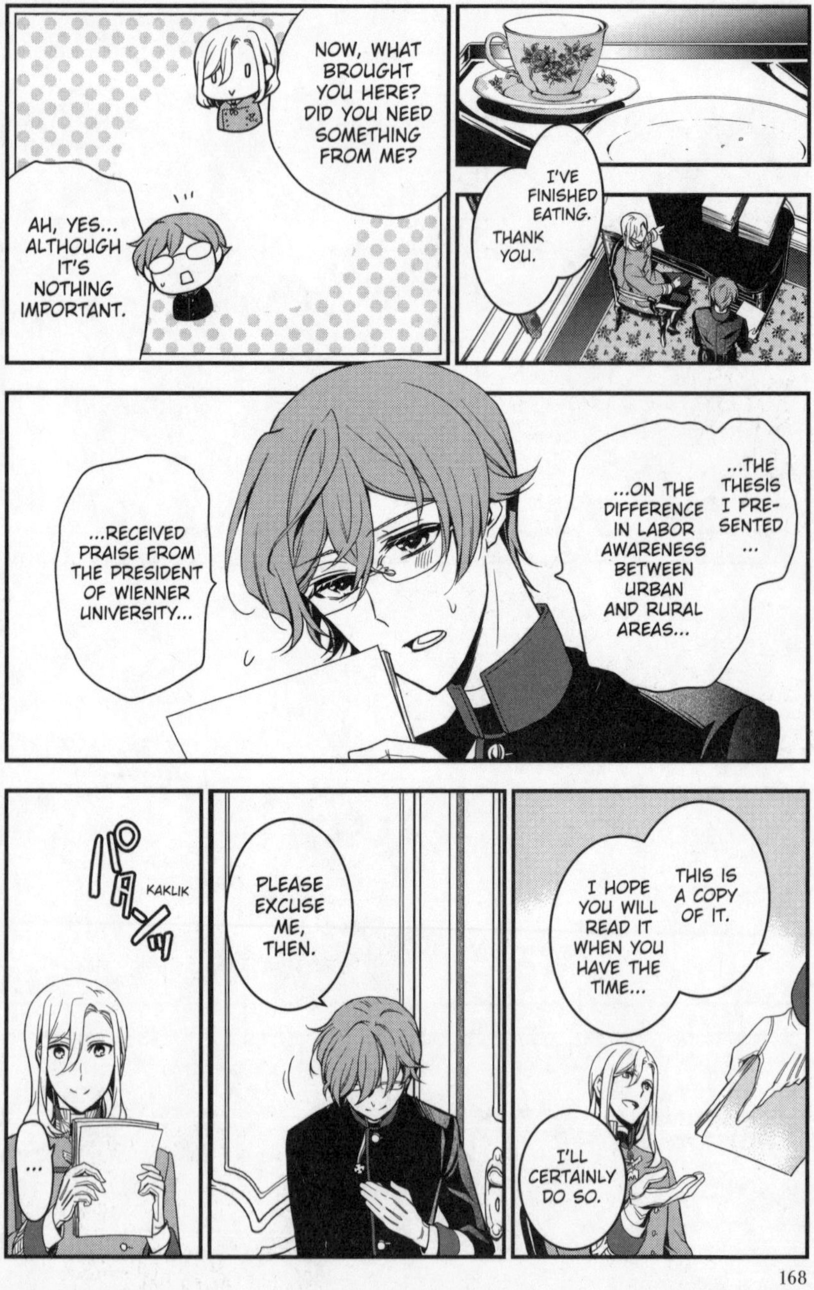
I'VE FINISHED EATING.
THANK YOU.
NOW, WHAT BROUGHT YOU HERE? DID YOU NEED SOMETHING FROM ME?
AH, YES... ALTHOUGH IT'S NOTHING IMPORTANT.
...THE THESIS I PRESENTED ...
...ON THE DIFFERENCE IN LABOR AWARENESS BETWEEN URBAN AND RURAL AREAS...
...RECEIVED PRAISE FROM THE PRESIDENT OF WIENNER UNIVERSITY...
THIS IS A COPY OF IT.
I HOPE YOU WILL READ IT WHEN YOU HAVE THE TIME...
I'LL CERTAINLY DO SO.
PLEASE EXCUSE ME, THEN.
パターン
KAKLIK
...

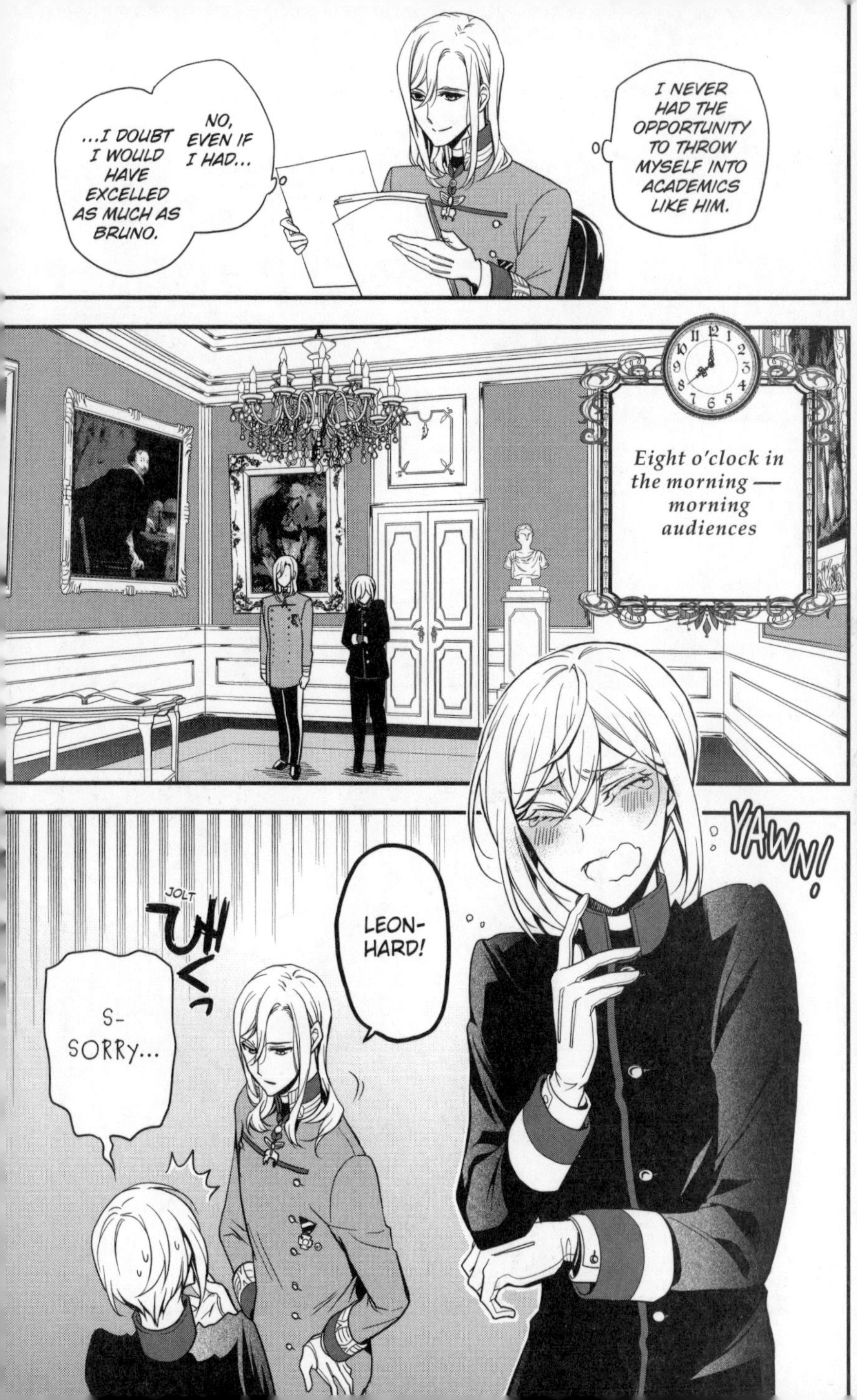
I NEVER HAD THE OPPORTUNITY TO THROW MYSELF INTO ACADEMICS LIKE HIM.
NO, EVEN IF I HAD...
...I DOUBT I WOULD HAVE EXCELLED AS MUCH AS BRUNO.
Eight o'clock in the morning — morning audiences
YAWN!
LEON-HARD!
JOLT
S-SORRY...

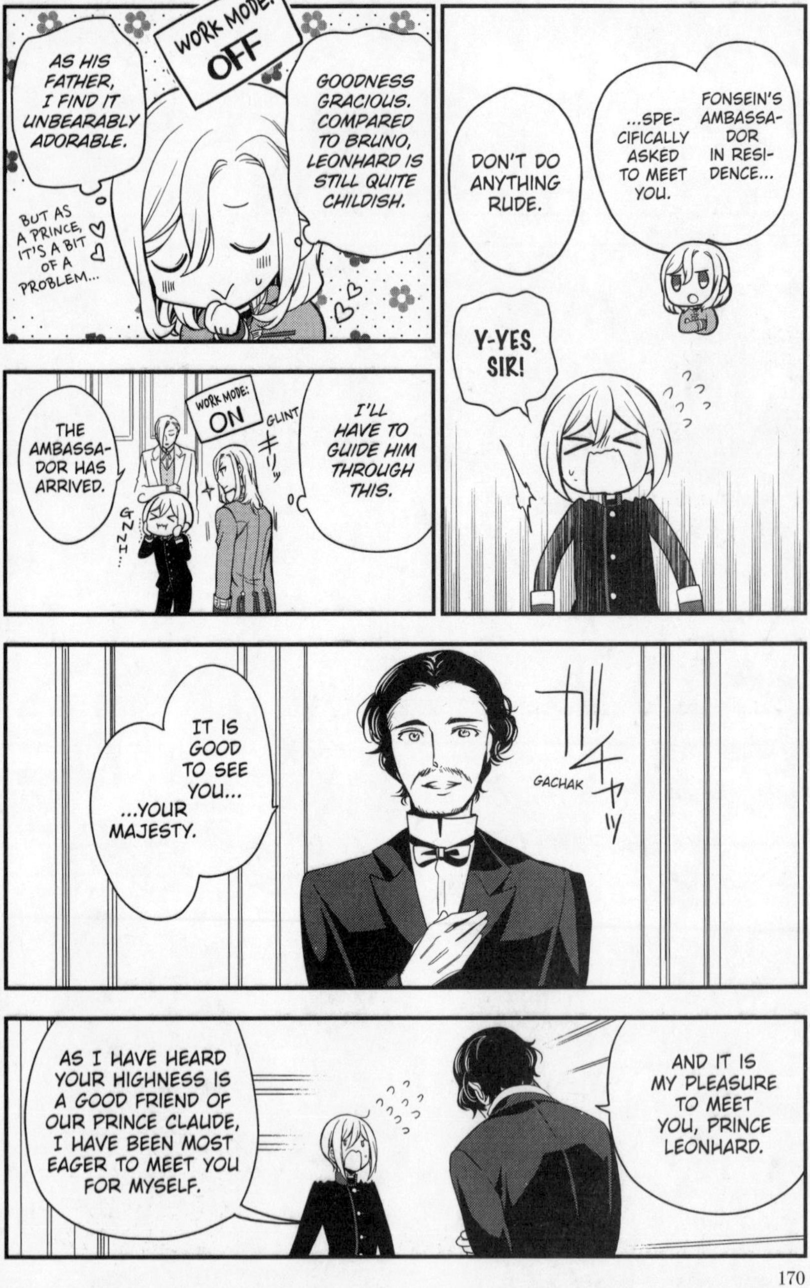
FONSEIN'S AMBASSADOR IN RESIDENCE...
...SPECIFICALLY ASKED TO MEET YOU.
DON'T DO ANYTHING RUDE.
Y-YES, SIR!
GOODNESS GRACIOUS. COMPARED TO BRUNO, LEONHARD IS STILL QUITE CHILDISH.
WORK MODE: OFF
AS HIS FATHER, I FIND IT UNBEARABLY ADORABLE.
BUT AS A PRINCE, IT'S A BIT OF A PROBLEM...
I'LL HAVE TO GUIDE HIM THROUGH THIS.
ギリッ
GLINT
WORK MODE: ON
THE AMBASSADOR HAS ARRIVED.
GNNH...
ガチャッ
GACHAK
IT IS GOOD TO SEE YOU...
...YOUR MAJESTY.
AND IT IS MY PLEASURE TO MEET YOU, PRINCE LEONHARD.
AS I HAVE HEARD YOUR HIGHNESS IS A GOOD FRIEND OF OUR PRINCE CLAUDE, I HAVE BEEN MOST EAGER TO MEET YOU FOR MYSELF.

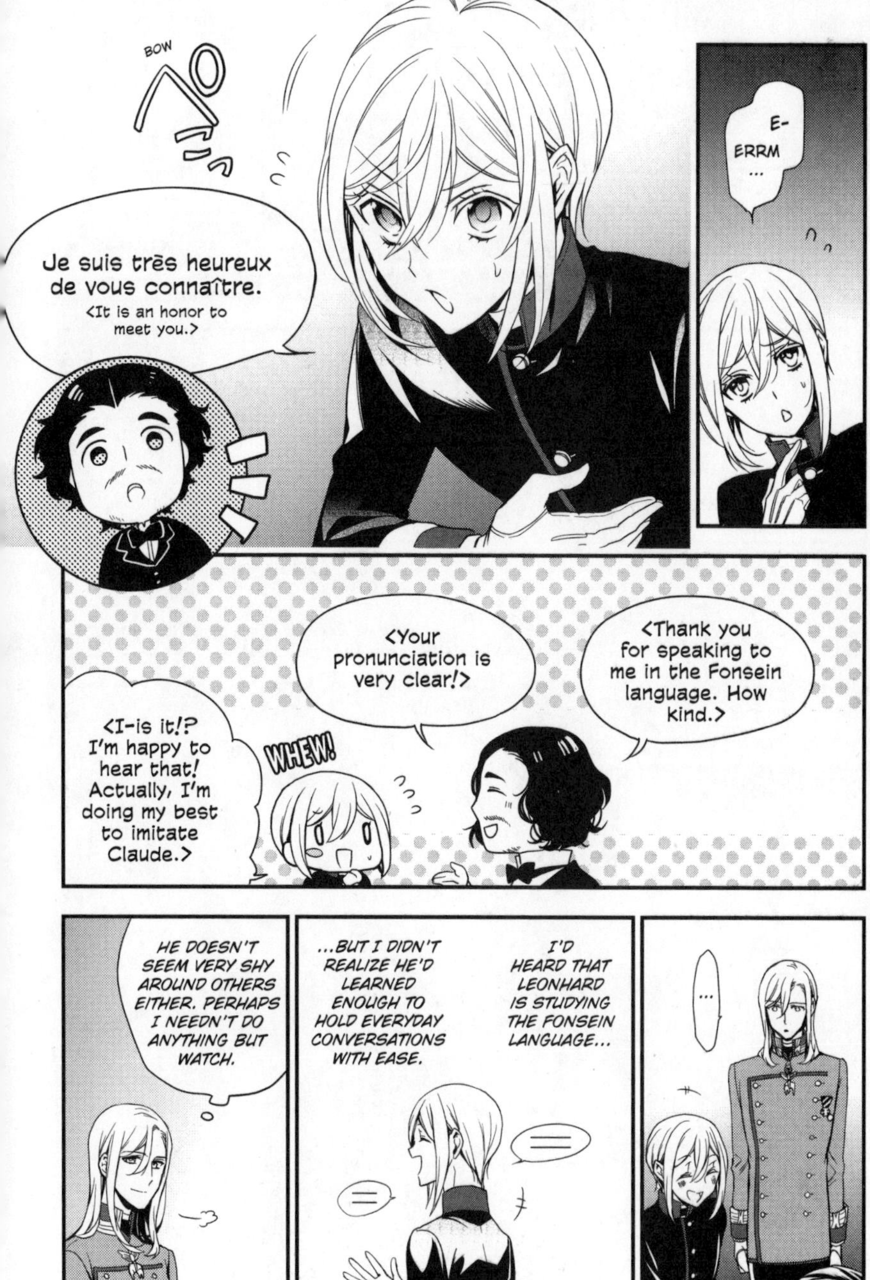

E-ERRM...
BOW
Je suis très heureux de vous connaître.
<It is an honor to meet you.>
<Thank you for speaking to me in the Fonsein language. How kind.>
<Your pronunciation is very clear!>
WHEW!
<I-is it!? I'm happy to hear that! Actually, I'm doing my best to imitate Claude.>
...
I'D HEARD THAT LEONHARD IS STUDYING THE FONSEIN LANGUAGE...
...BUT I DIDN'T REALIZE HE'D LEARNED ENOUGH TO HOLD EVERYDAY CONVERSATIONS WITH EASE.
HE DOESN'T SEEM VERY SHY AROUND OTHERS EITHER. PERHAPS I NEEDN'T DO ANYTHING BUT WATCH.

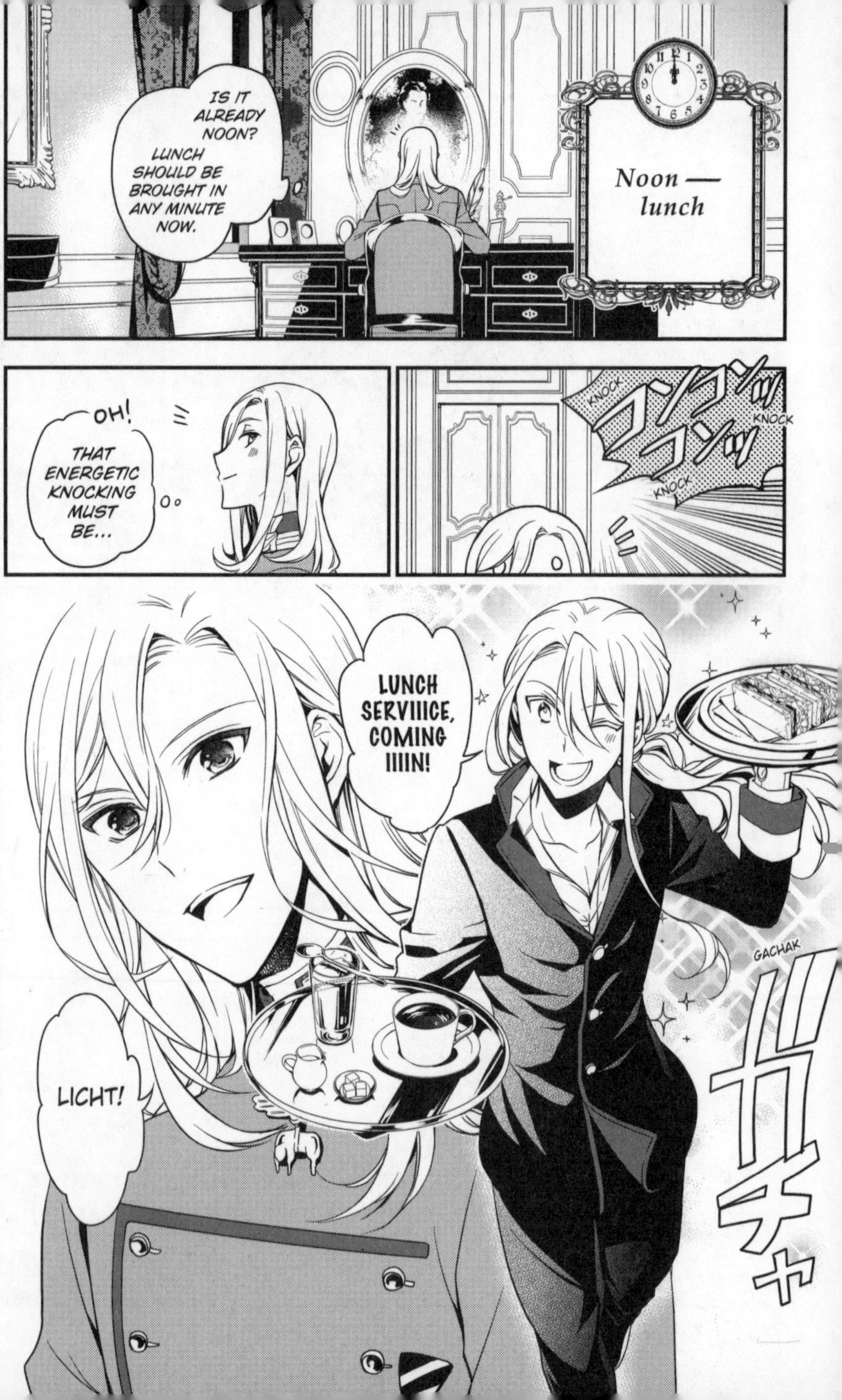
Noon — lunch
IS IT ALREADY NOON? LUNCH SHOULD BE BROUGHT IN ANY MINUTE NOW.
KNOCK KNOCK KNOCK
OH! THAT ENERGETIC KNOCKING MUST BE...
GACHAK
LUNCH SERVIIICE, COMING IIIIN!
LICHT!

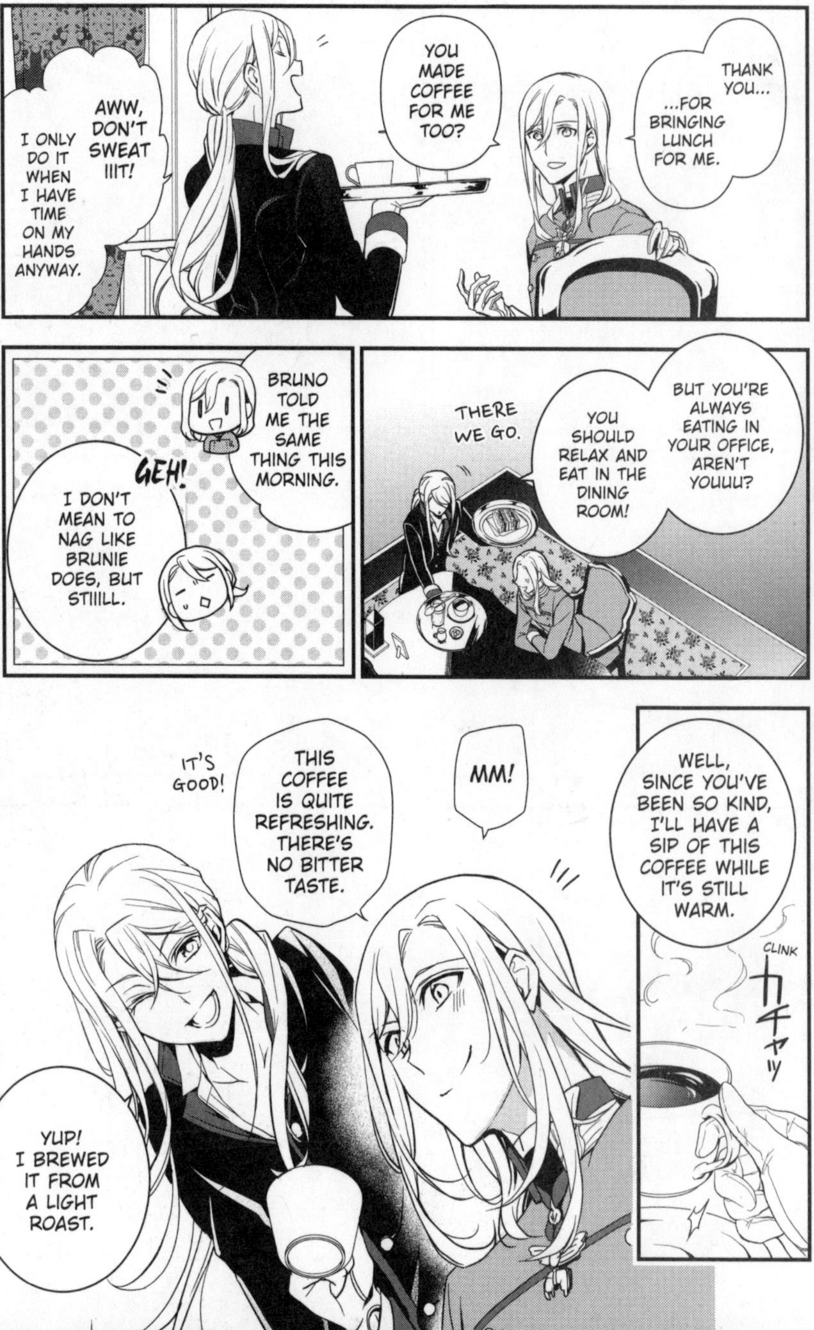
THANK YOU...
...FOR BRINGING LUNCH FOR ME.
YOU MADE COFFEE FOR ME TOO?
AWW, DON'T SWEAT IIIT!
I ONLY DO IT WHEN I HAVE TIME ON MY HANDS ANYWAY.
BUT YOU'RE ALWAYS EATING IN YOUR OFFICE, AREN'T YOUUU?
YOU SHOULD RELAX AND EAT IN THE DINING ROOM!
THERE WE GO.
BRUNO TOLD ME THE SAME THING THIS MORNING.
GEH!
I DON'T MEAN TO NAG LIKE BRUNIE DOES, BUT STIIILL.
WELL, SINCE YOU'VE BEEN SO KIND, I'LL HAVE A SIP OF THIS COFFEE WHILE IT'S STILL WARM.
CLINK
カチャッ
MM!
THIS COFFEE IS QUITE REFRESHING. THERE'S NO BITTER TASTE.
IT'S GOOD!
YUP! I BREWED IT FROM A LIGHT ROAST.

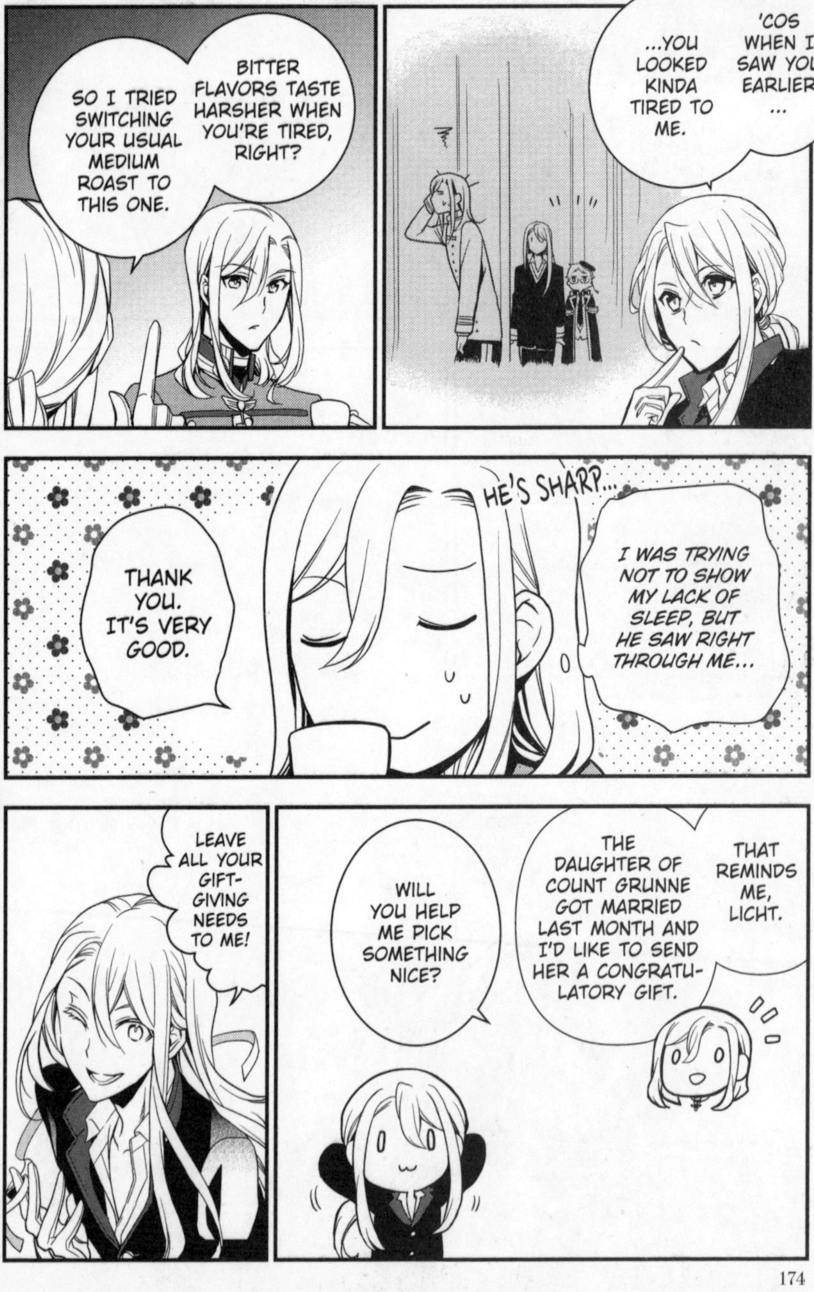
'COS WHEN I SAW YOU EARLIER...
...YOU LOOKED KINDA TIRED TO ME.
BITTER FLAVORS TASTE HARSHER WHEN YOU'RE TIRED, RIGHT?
SO I TRIED SWITCHING YOUR USUAL MEDIUM ROAST TO THIS ONE.
HE'S SHARP...
I WAS TRYING NOT TO SHOW MY LACK OF SLEEP, BUT HE SAW RIGHT THROUGH ME...
THANK YOU. IT'S VERY GOOD.
THAT REMINDS ME, LICHT.
THE DAUGHTER OF COUNT GRUNNE GOT MARRIED LAST MONTH AND I'D LIKE TO SEND HER A CONGRATULATORY GIFT.
WILL YOU HELP ME PICK SOMETHING NICE?
LEAVE ALL YOUR GIFT-GIVING NEEDS TO ME!

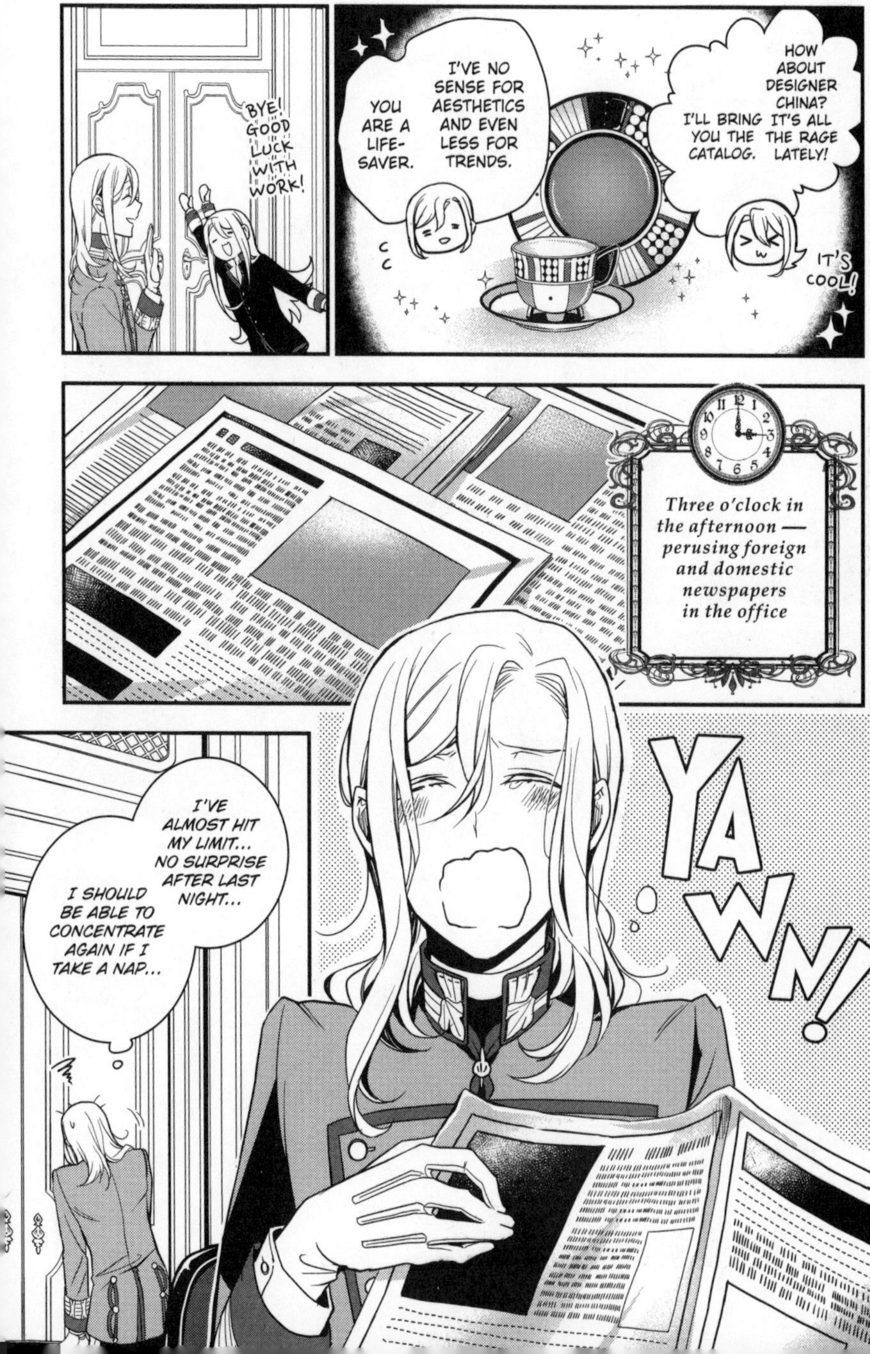
HOW ABOUT DESIGNER CHINA? IT'S ALL THE RAGE LATELY! I'LL BRING YOU THE CATALOG.
IT'S COOL!
I'VE NO SENSE FOR AESTHETICS AND EVEN LESS FOR TRENDS. YOU ARE A LIFE-SAVER.
BYE! GOOD LUCK WITH WORK!
Three o'clock in the afternoon — perusing foreign and domestic newspapers in the office
YAWN!
I'VE ALMOST HIT MY LIMIT... NO SURPRISE AFTER LAST NIGHT... I SHOULD BE ABLE TO CONCENTRATE AGAIN IF I TAKE A NAP...

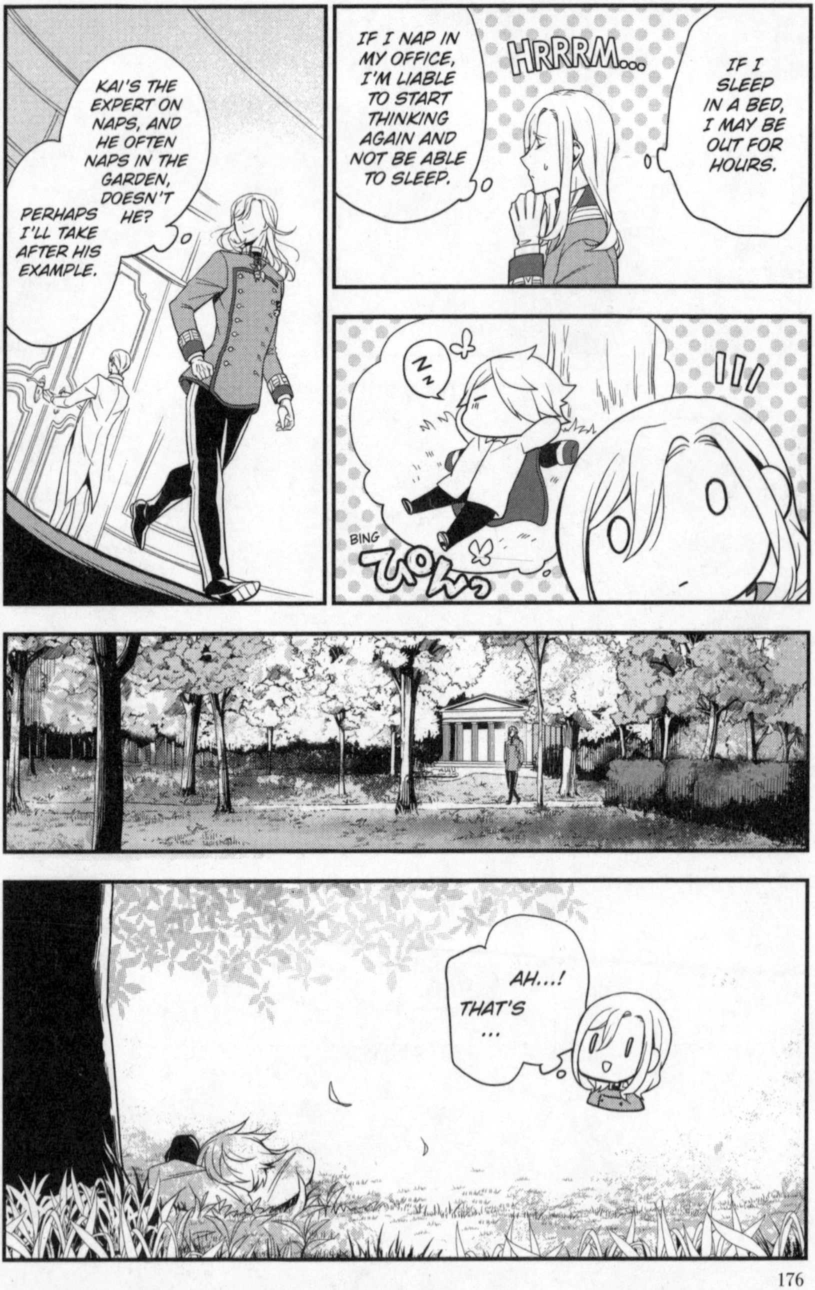
IF I SLEEP IN A BED, I MAY BE OUT FOR HOURS.
HRRRM...
IF I NAP IN MY OFFICE, I'M LIABLE TO START THINKING AGAIN AND NOT BE ABLE TO SLEEP.
Z z
BING
ぴょんっ
KAI'S THE EXPERT ON NAPS, AND HE OFTEN NAPS IN THE GARDEN, DOESN'T HE?
PERHAPS I'LL TAKE AFTER HIS EXAMPLE.
AH...! THAT'S ...

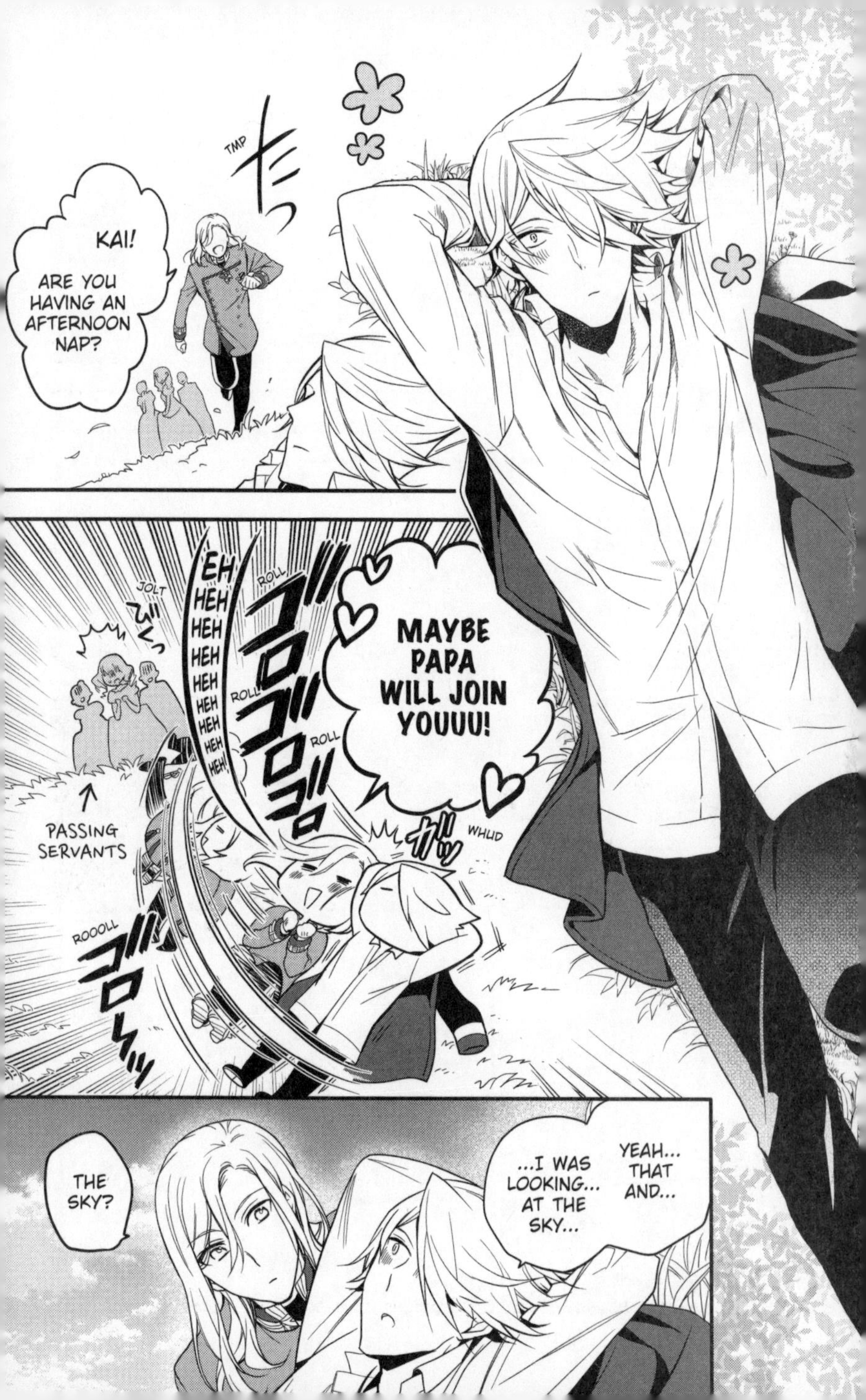

TMP
KAI!
ARE YOU HAVING AN AFTERNOON NAP?
MAYBE PAPA WILL JOIN YOUUU!
WHUD
ROLL
ROLL
ROLL
EH HEH HEH HEH HEH HEH HEH HEH HEH HEH!
JOLT
PASSING SERVANTS
ROOOLL
YEAH... THAT AND...
...I WAS LOOKING... AT THE SKY...
THE SKY?

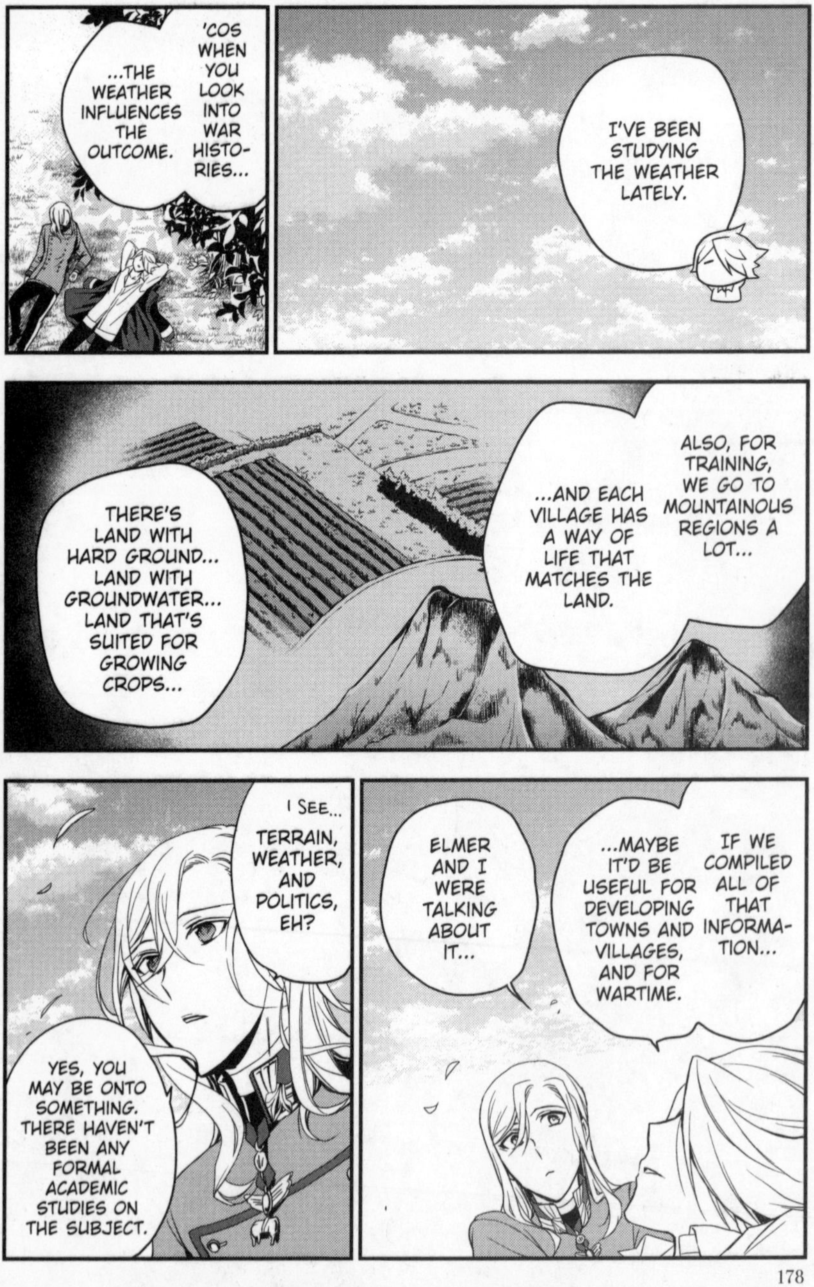
I'VE BEEN STUDYING THE WEATHER LATELY.
'COS WHEN YOU LOOK INTO WAR HISTORIES...
...THE WEATHER INFLUENCES THE OUTCOME.
ALSO, FOR TRAINING, WE GO TO MOUNTAINOUS REGIONS A LOT...
...AND EACH VILLAGE HAS A WAY OF LIFE THAT MATCHES THE LAND.
THERE'S LAND WITH HARD GROUND... LAND WITH GROUNDWATER... LAND THAT'S SUITED FOR GROWING CROPS...
IF WE COMPILED ALL OF THAT INFORMATION...
...MAYBE IT'D BE USEFUL FOR DEVELOPING TOWNS AND VILLAGES, AND FOR WARTIME.
ELMER AND I WERE TALKING ABOUT IT...
I SEE...
TERRAIN, WEATHER, AND POLITICS, EH?
YES, YOU MAY BE ONTO SOMETHING. THERE HAVEN'T BEEN ANY FORMAL ACADEMIC STUDIES ON THE SUBJECT.

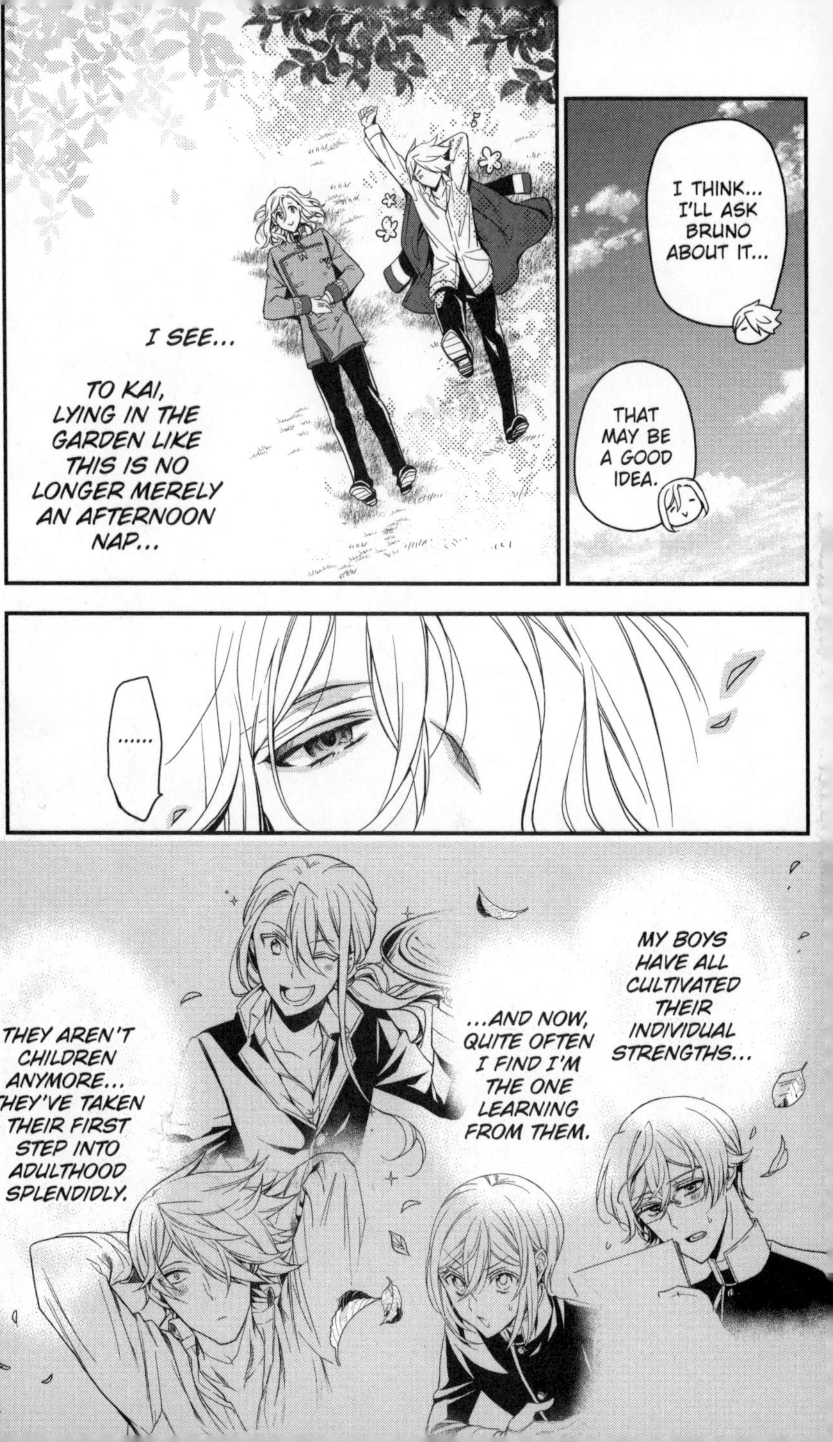
I THINK... I'LL ASK BRUNO ABOUT IT...
THAT MAY BE A GOOD IDEA.
I SEE...
TO KAI, LYING IN THE GARDEN LIKE THIS IS NO LONGER MERELY AN AFTERNOON NAP...
......
MY BOYS HAVE ALL CULTIVATED THEIR INDIVIDUAL STRENGTHS...
...AND NOW, QUITE OFTEN I FIND I'M THE ONE LEARNING FROM THEM.
THEY AREN'T CHILDREN ANYMORE... THEY'VE TAKEN THEIR FIRST STEP INTO ADULTHOOD SPLENDIDLY.

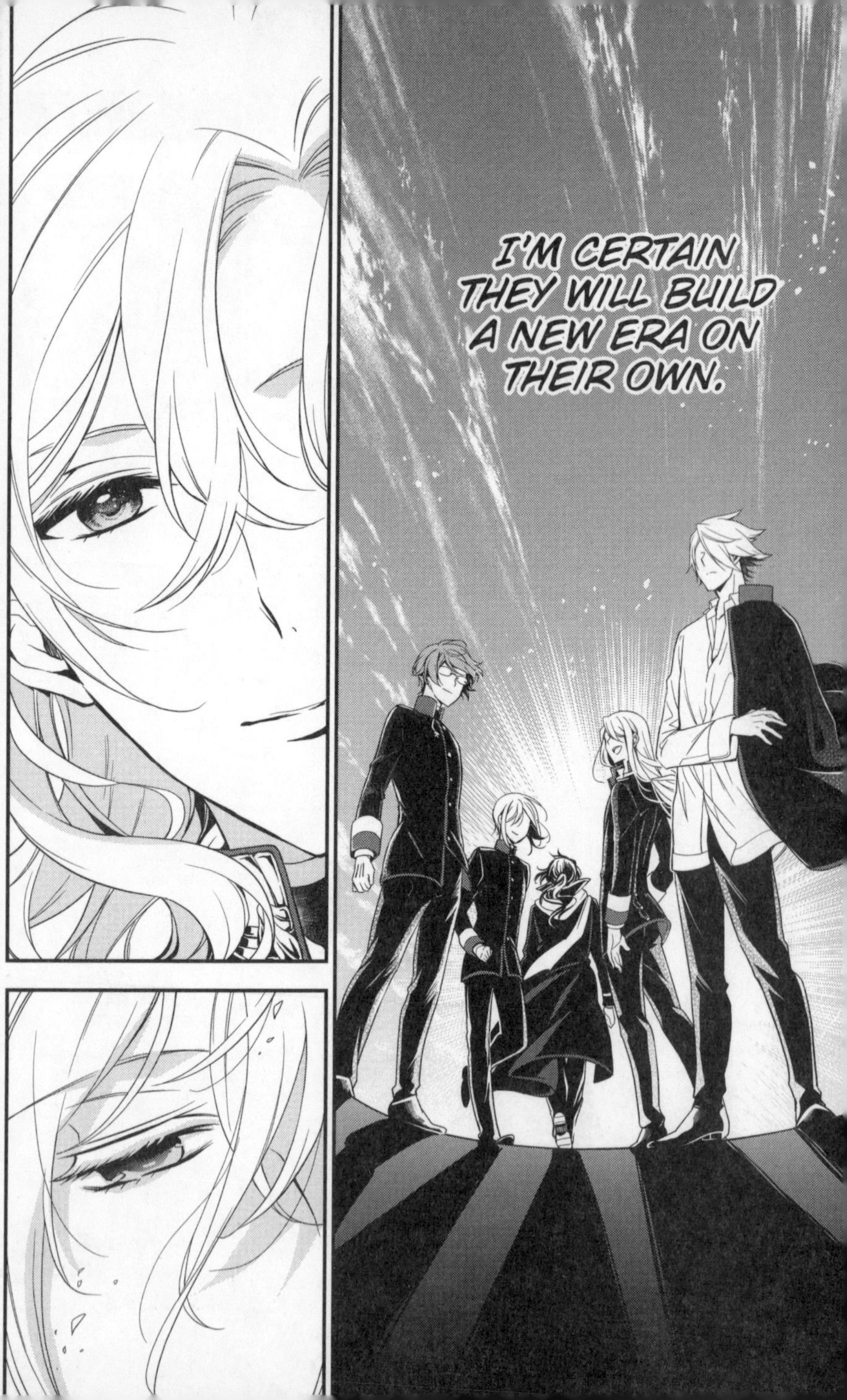
I'M CERTAIN THEY WILL BUILD A NEW ERA ON THEIR OWN.

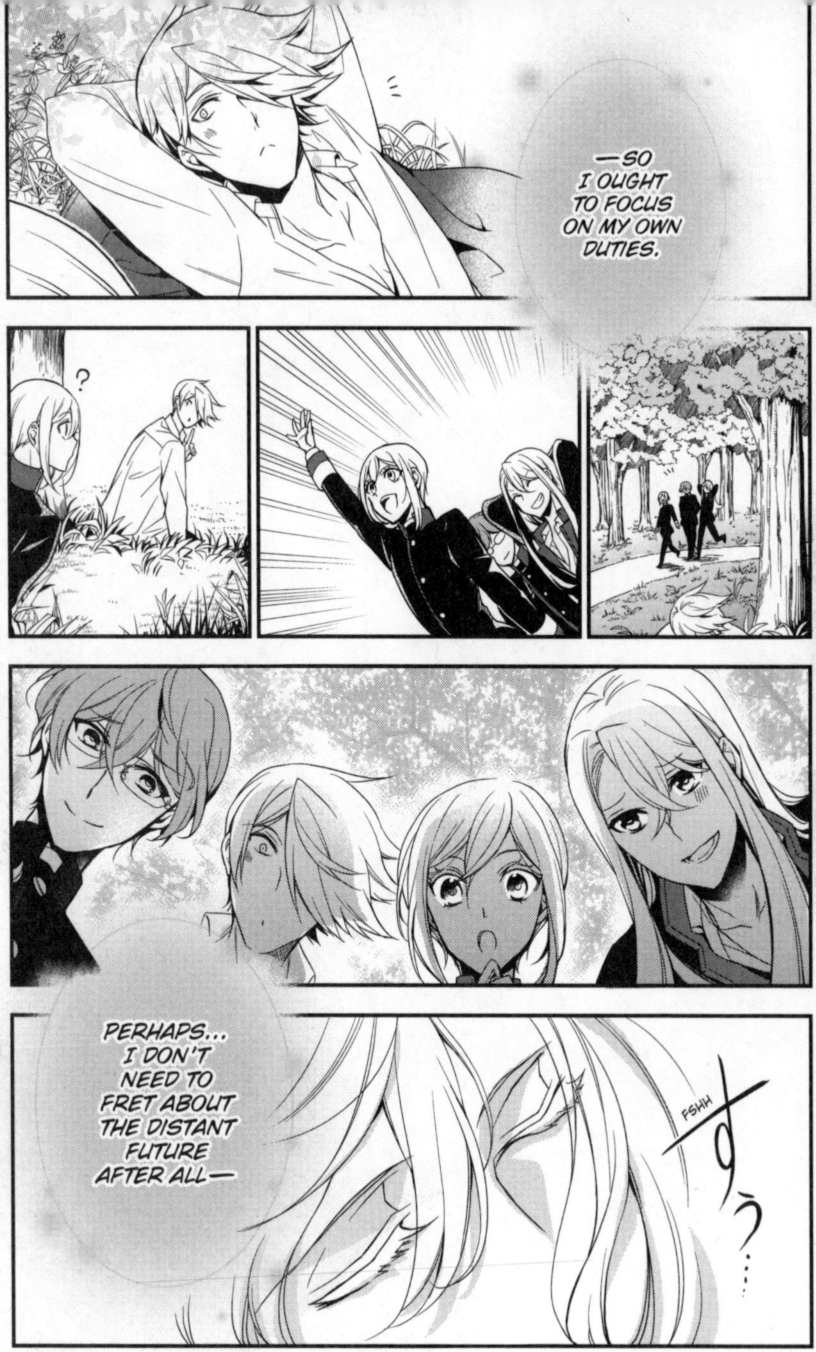
—SO I OUGHT TO FOCUS ON MY OWN DUTIES.
PERHAPS... I DON'T NEED TO FRET ABOUT THE DISTANT FUTURE AFTER ALL—
FSHH

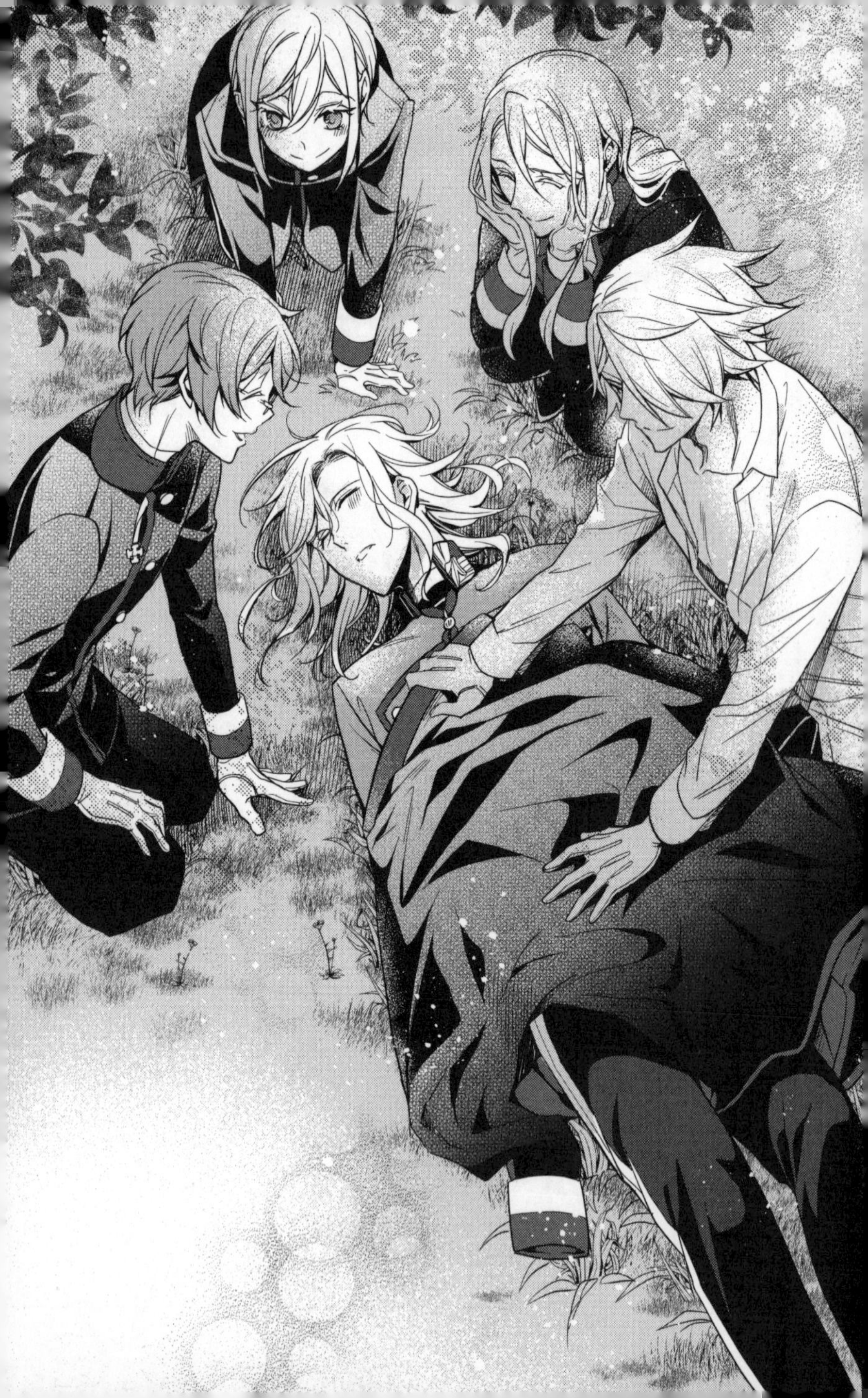

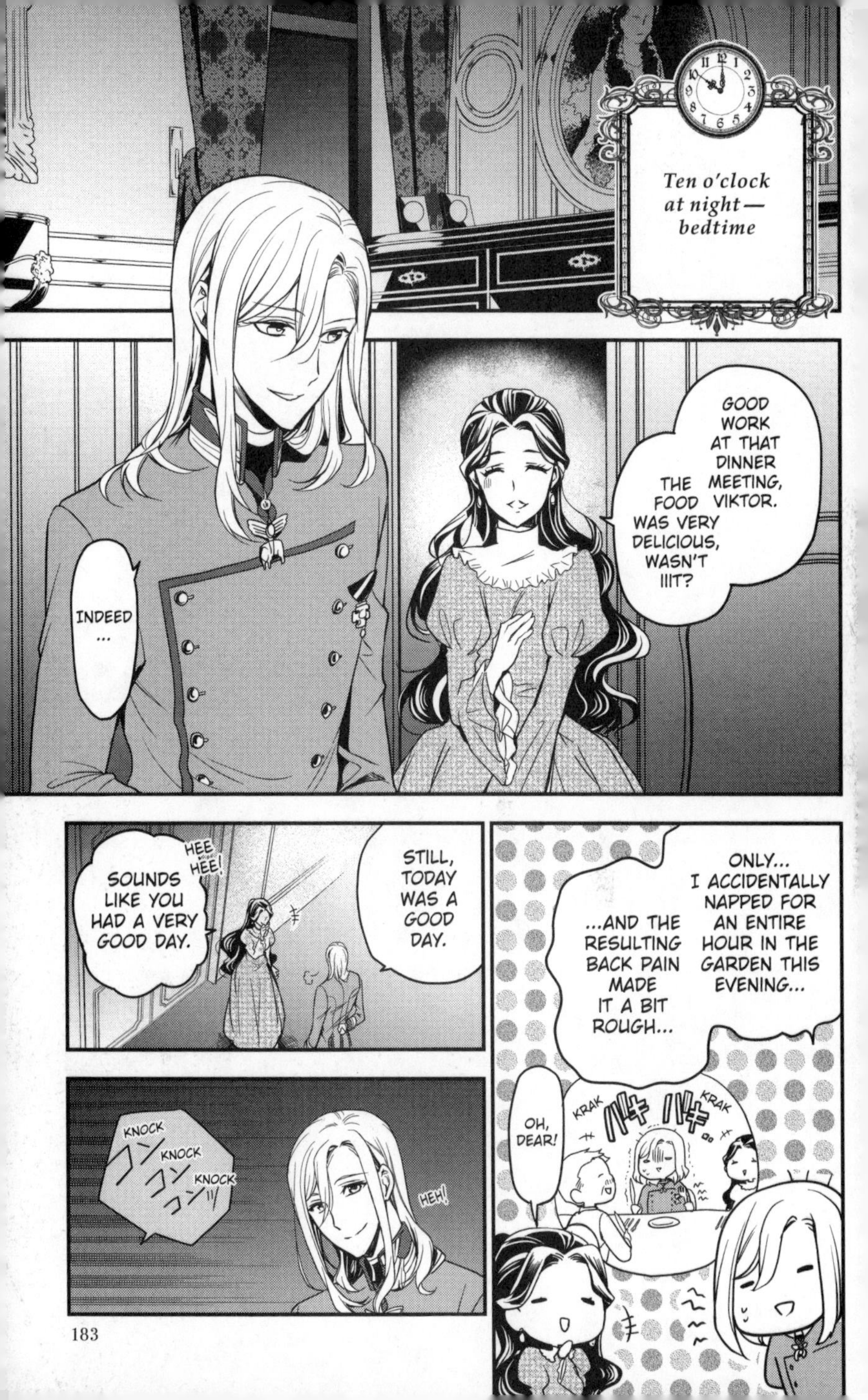
Ten o'clock at night—bedtime
GOOD WORK AT THAT DINNER MEETING, VIKTOR. THE FOOD WAS VERY DELICIOUS, WASN'T IIIT?
INDEED...
ONLY... I ACCIDENTALLY NAPPED FOR AN ENTIRE HOUR IN THE GARDEN THIS EVENING...
...AND THE RESULTING BACK PAIN MADE IT A BIT ROUGH...
KRAK
KRAK
OH, DEAR!
STILL, TODAY WAS A GOOD DAY.
SOUNDS LIKE YOU HAD A VERY GOOD DAY.
HEE HEE!
HEH!
KNOCK
KNOCK
KNOCK

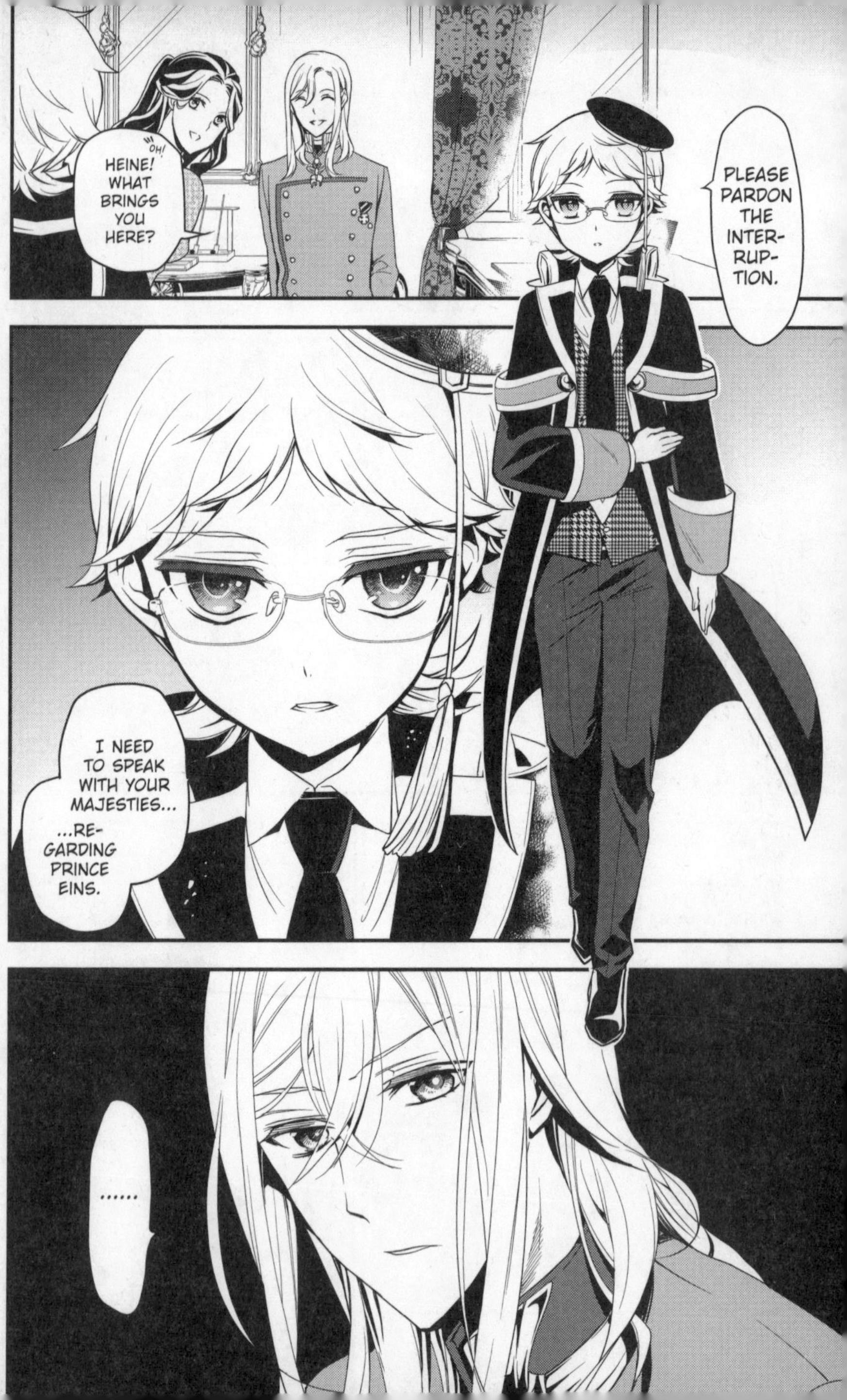
PLEASE PARDON THE INTER-RUP-TION.
OH!
HEINE! WHAT BRINGS YOU HERE?
I NEED TO SPEAK WITH YOUR MAJESTIES...
...RE-GARDING PRINCE EINS.
......

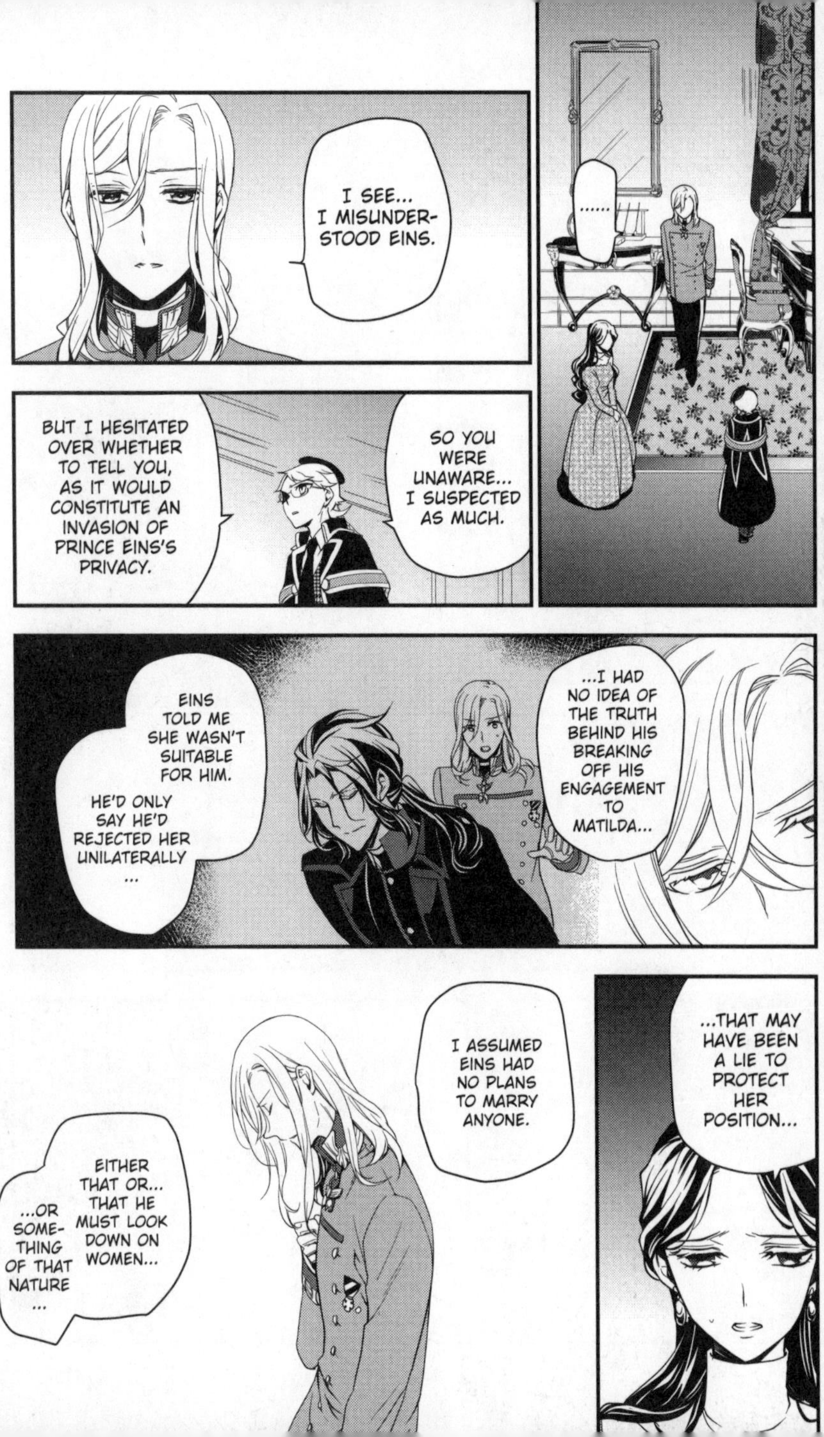
......
I SEE... I MISUNDER-STOOD EINS.
SO YOU WERE UNAWARE... I SUSPECTED AS MUCH.
BUT I HESITATED OVER WHETHER TO TELL YOU, AS IT WOULD CONSTITUTE AN INVASION OF PRINCE EINS'S PRIVACY.
...I HAD NO IDEA OF THE TRUTH BEHIND HIS BREAKING OFF HIS ENGAGEMENT TO MATILDA...
EINS TOLD ME SHE WASN'T SUITABLE FOR HIM.
HE'D ONLY SAY HE'D REJECTED HER UNILATERALLY...
...THAT MAY HAVE BEEN A LIE TO PROTECT HER POSITION...
I ASSUMED EINS HAD NO PLANS TO MARRY ANYONE.
EITHER THAT OR... THAT HE MUST LOOK DOWN ON WOMEN...
...OR SOME-THING OF THAT NATURE...

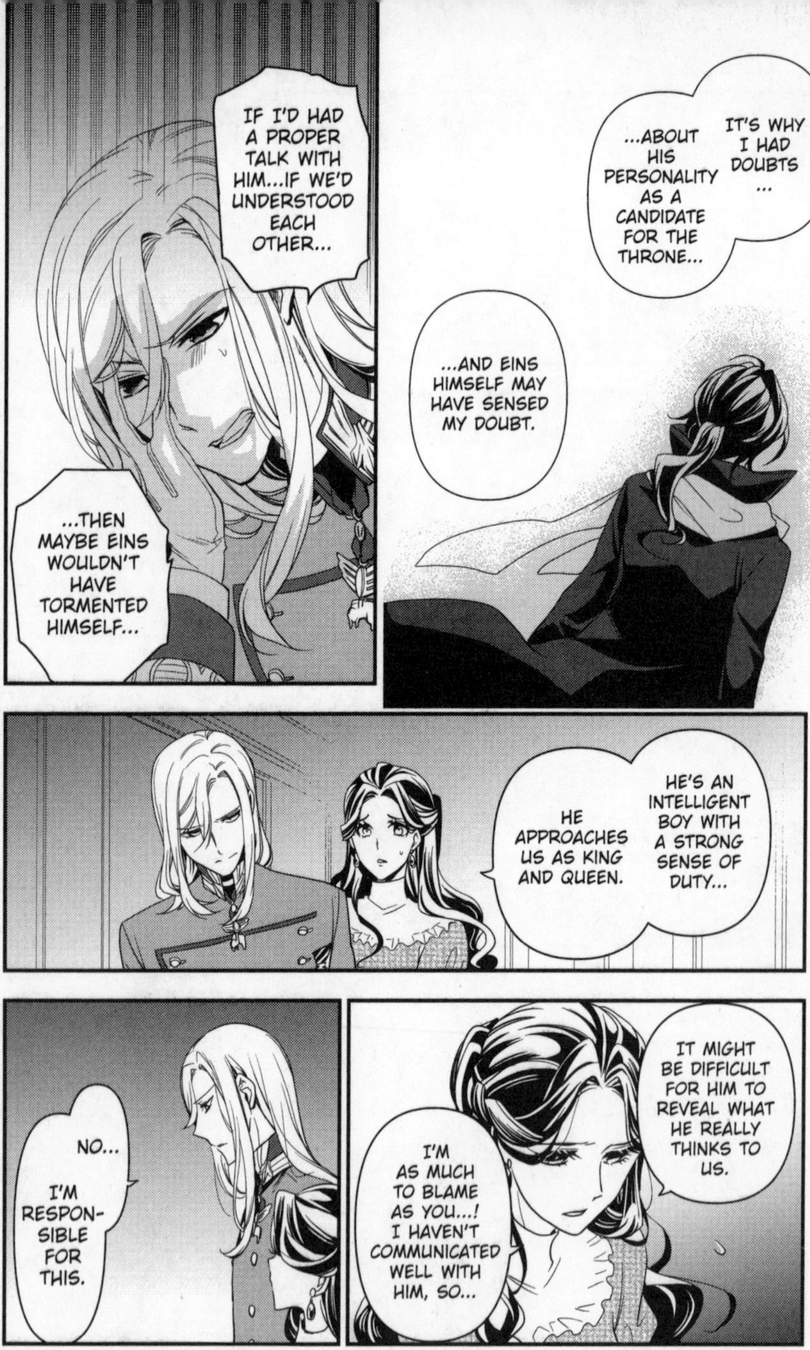
IT'S WHY I HAD DOUBTS...
...ABOUT HIS PERSONALITY AS A CANDIDATE FOR THE THRONE...
...AND EINS HIMSELF MAY HAVE SENSED MY DOUBT.
IF I'D HAD A PROPER TALK WITH HIM...IF WE'D UNDERSTOOD EACH OTHER...
...THEN MAYBE EINS WOULDN'T HAVE TORMENTED HIMSELF...
HE'S AN INTELLIGENT BOY WITH A STRONG SENSE OF DUTY...
HE APPROACHES US AS KING AND QUEEN.
IT MIGHT BE DIFFICULT FOR HIM TO REVEAL WHAT HE REALLY THINKS TO US.
I'M AS MUCH TO BLAME AS YOU...! I HAVEN'T COMMUNICATED WELL WITH HIM, SO...
NO...
I'M RESPON-SIBLE FOR THIS.

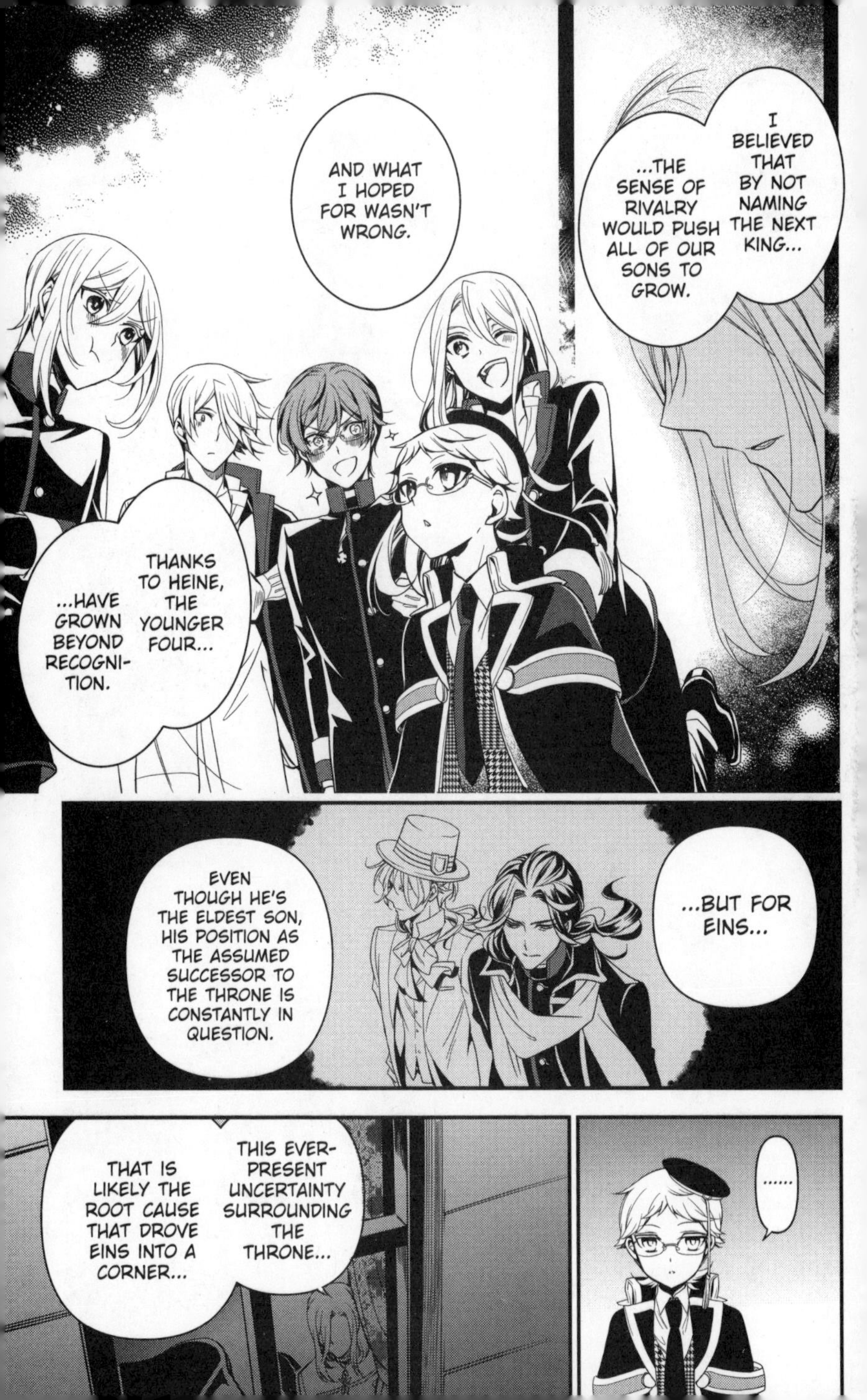
I BELIEVED THAT BY NOT NAMING THE NEXT KING...
...THE SENSE OF RIVALRY WOULD PUSH ALL OF OUR SONS TO GROW.
AND WHAT I HOPED FOR WASN'T WRONG.
THANKS TO HEINE, THE YOUNGER FOUR...
...HAVE GROWN BEYOND RECOGNI-TION.
...BUT FOR EINS...
EVEN THOUGH HE'S THE ELDEST SON, HIS POSITION AS THE ASSUMED SUCCESSOR TO THE THRONE IS CONSTANTLY IN QUESTION.
......
THIS EVER-PRESENT UNCERTAINTY SURROUNDING THE THRONE...
THAT IS LIKELY THE ROOT CAUSE THAT DROVE EINS INTO A CORNER...

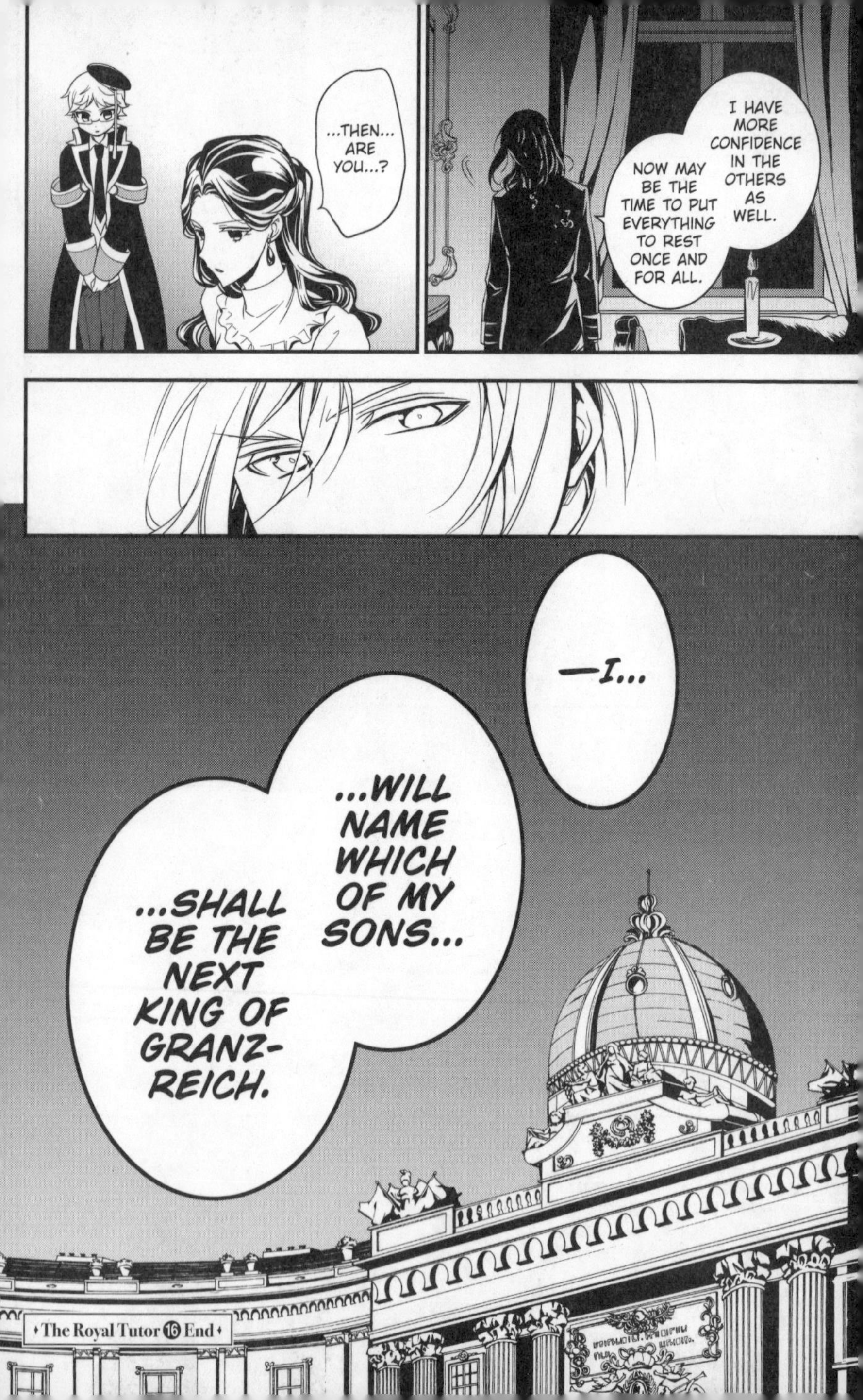
I HAVE MORE CONFIDENCE IN THE OTHERS AS WELL.
NOW MAY BE THE TIME TO PUT EVERYTHING TO REST ONCE AND FOR ALL.
...THEN... ARE YOU...?
—I...
...WILL NAME WHICH OF MY SONS...
...SHALL BE THE NEXT KING OF GRANZ-REICH.
The Royal Tutor 16 End

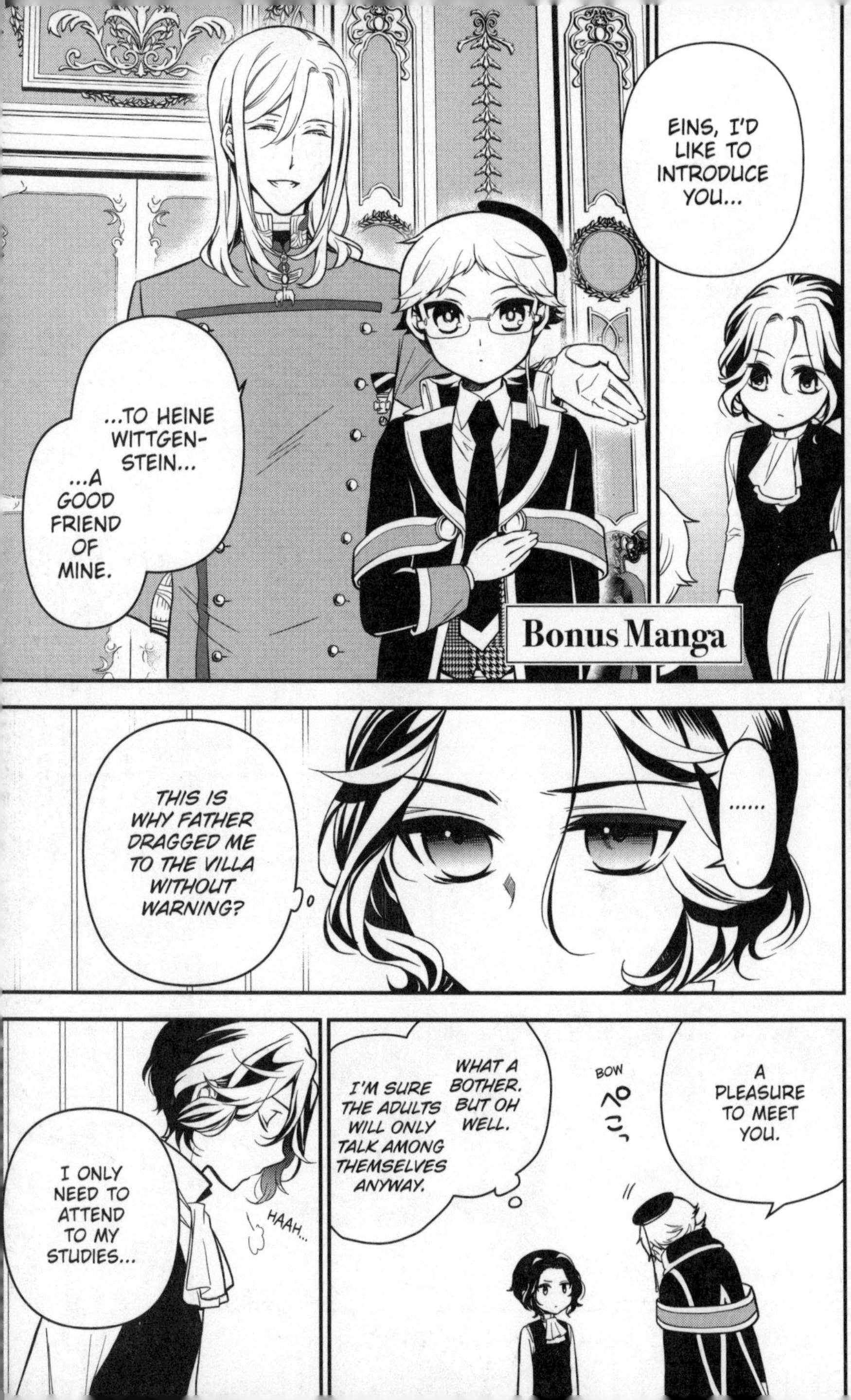
EINS, I'D LIKE TO INTRODUCE YOU...
...TO HEINE WITTGENSTEIN...
...A GOOD FRIEND OF MINE.
Bonus Manga
......
THIS IS WHY FATHER DRAGGED ME TO THE VILLA WITHOUT WARNING?
A PLEASURE TO MEET YOU.
BOW
WHAT A BOTHER. BUT OH WELL.
I'M SURE THE ADULTS WILL ONLY TALK AMONG THEMSELVES ANYWAY.
HAAH...
I ONLY NEED TO ATTEND TO MY STUDIES...

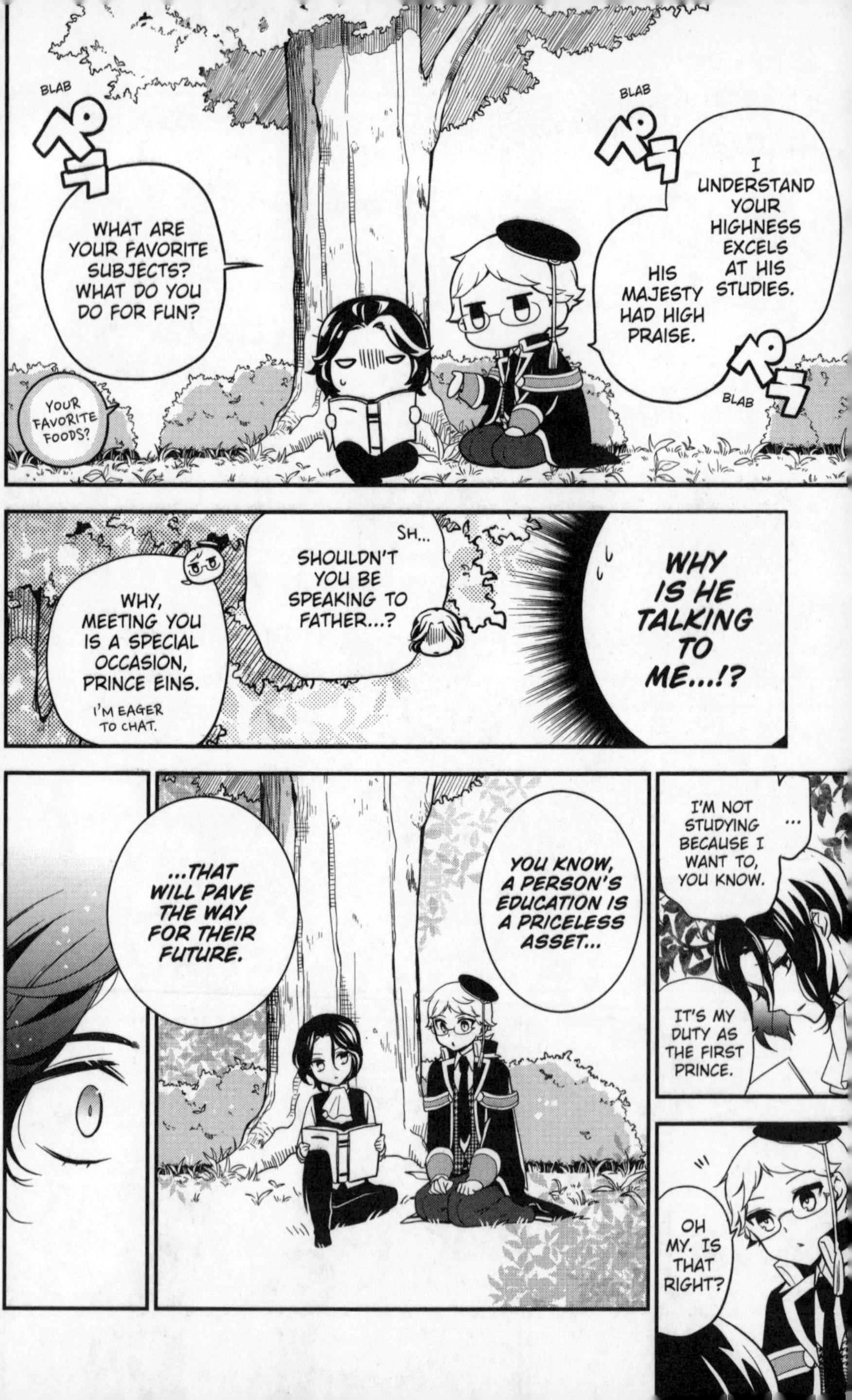
BLAB
I UNDERSTAND YOUR HIGHNESS EXCELS AT HIS STUDIES.
HIS MAJESTY HAD HIGH PRAISE.
BLAB
BLAB
WHAT ARE YOUR FAVORITE SUBJECTS? WHAT DO YOU DO FOR FUN?
YOUR FAVORITE FOODS?
WHY IS HE TALKING TO ME...!?
SH...
SHOULDN'T YOU BE SPEAKING TO FATHER...?
WHY, MEETING YOU IS A SPECIAL OCCASION, PRINCE EINS.
I'M EAGER TO CHAT.
I'M NOT STUDYING BECAUSE I WANT TO, YOU KNOW.
...
IT'S MY DUTY AS THE FIRST PRINCE.
OH MY. IS THAT RIGHT?
YOU KNOW, A PERSON'S EDUCATION IS A PRICELESS ASSET...
...THAT WILL PAVE THE WAY FOR THEIR FUTURE.

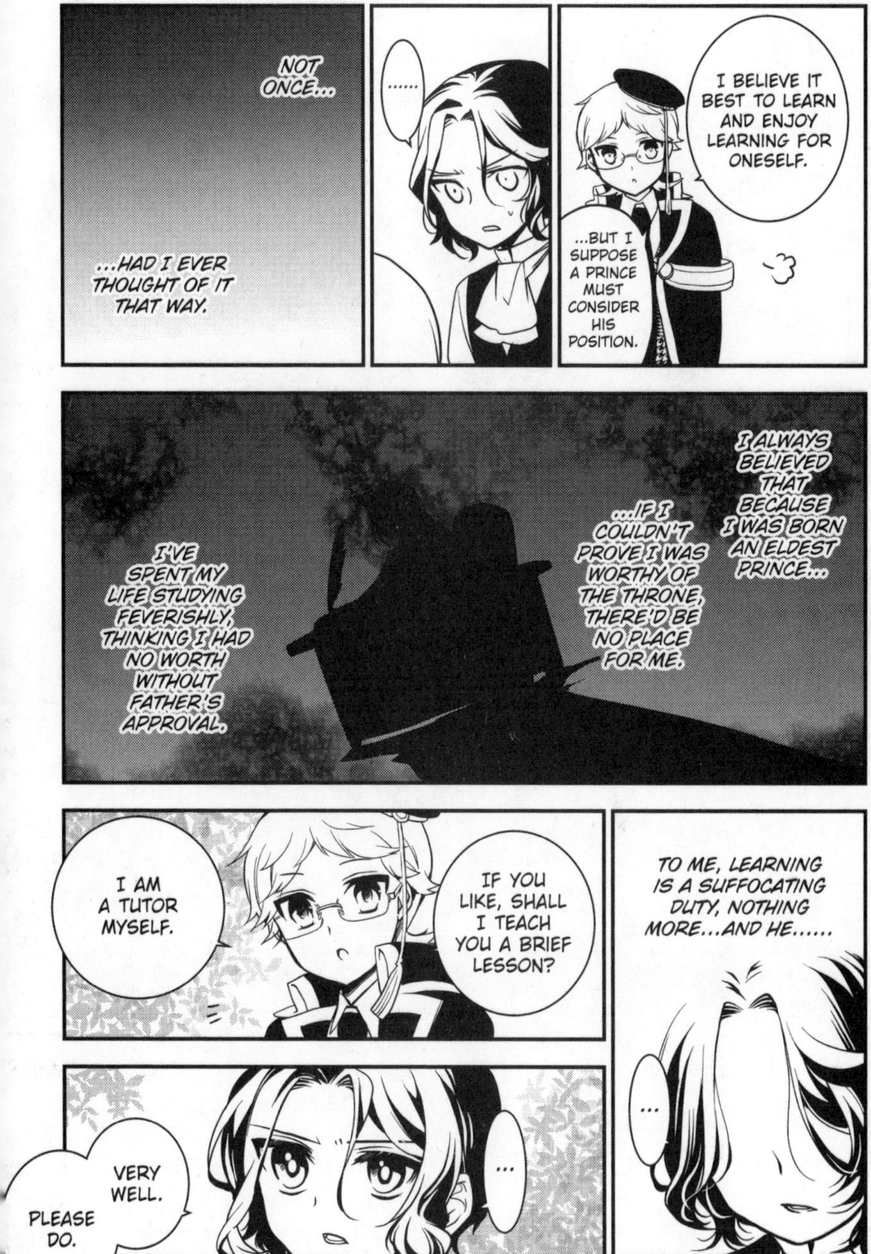
I BELIEVE IT BEST TO LEARN AND ENJOY LEARNING FOR ONESELF.
...BUT I SUPPOSE A PRINCE MUST CONSIDER HIS POSITION.
......
NOT ONCE...
...HAD I EVER THOUGHT OF IT THAT WAY.
I ALWAYS BELIEVED THAT BECAUSE I WAS BORN AN ELDEST PRINCE...
...IF I COULDN'T PROVE I WAS WORTHY OF THE THRONE, THERE'D BE NO PLACE FOR ME.
I'VE SPENT MY LIFE STUDYING FEVERISHLY, THINKING I HAD NO WORTH WITHOUT FATHER'S APPROVAL.
TO ME, LEARNING IS A SUFFOCATING DUTY, NOTHING MORE...AND HE......
...
IF YOU LIKE, SHALL I TEACH YOU A BRIEF LESSON?
I AM A TUTOR MYSELF.
...
VERY WELL.
PLEASE DO.

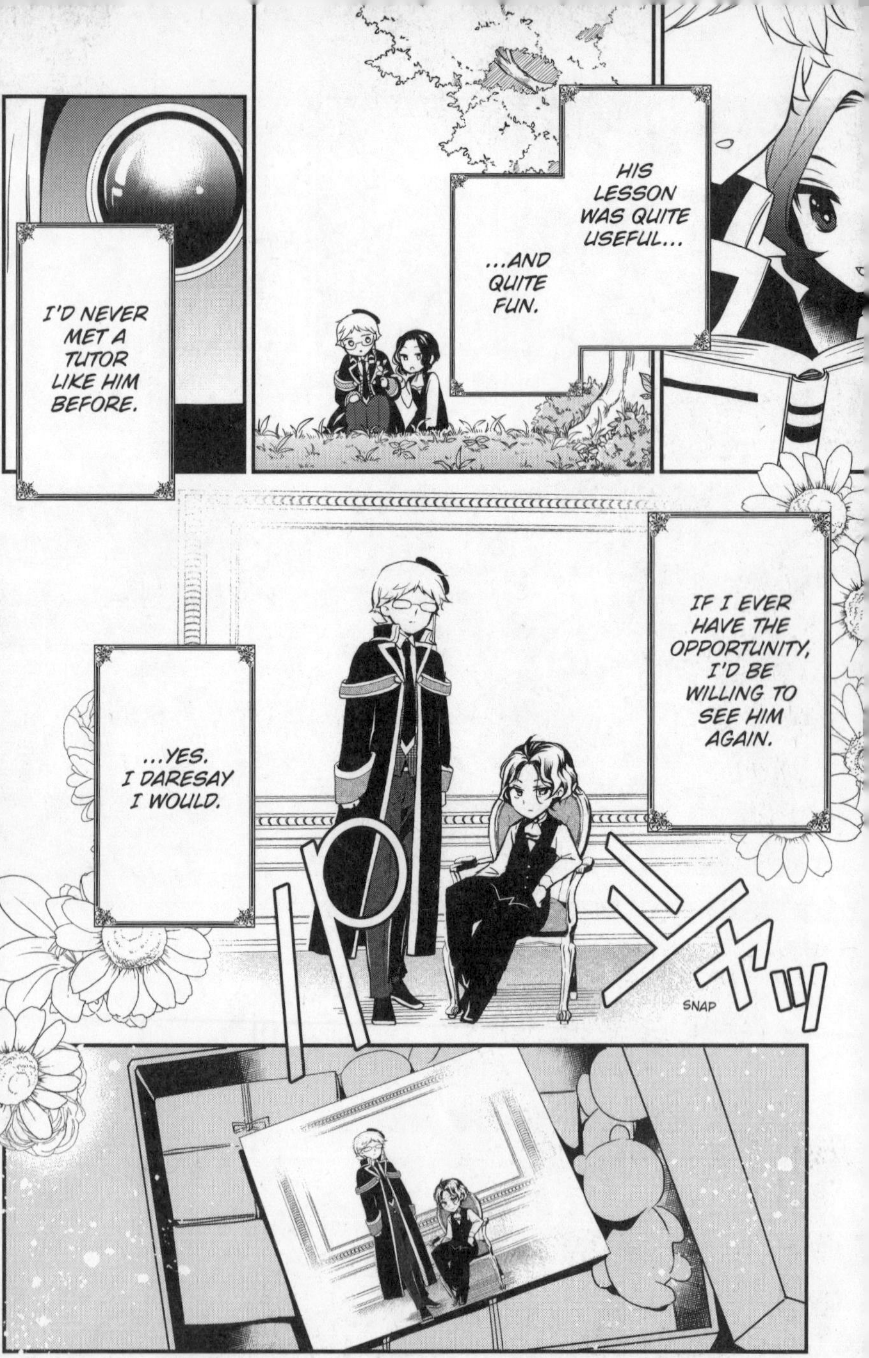
HIS LESSON WAS QUITE USEFUL...
...AND QUITE FUN.
I'D NEVER MET A TUTOR LIKE HIM BEFORE.
IF I EVER HAVE THE OPPORTUNITY, I'D BE WILLING TO SEE HIM AGAIN.
...YES. I DARESAY I WOULD.
パシャッ
SNAP

• SPECIAL THANKS • Tsuchiya-san • K-san • Ao-san My editor, Akiyama-san

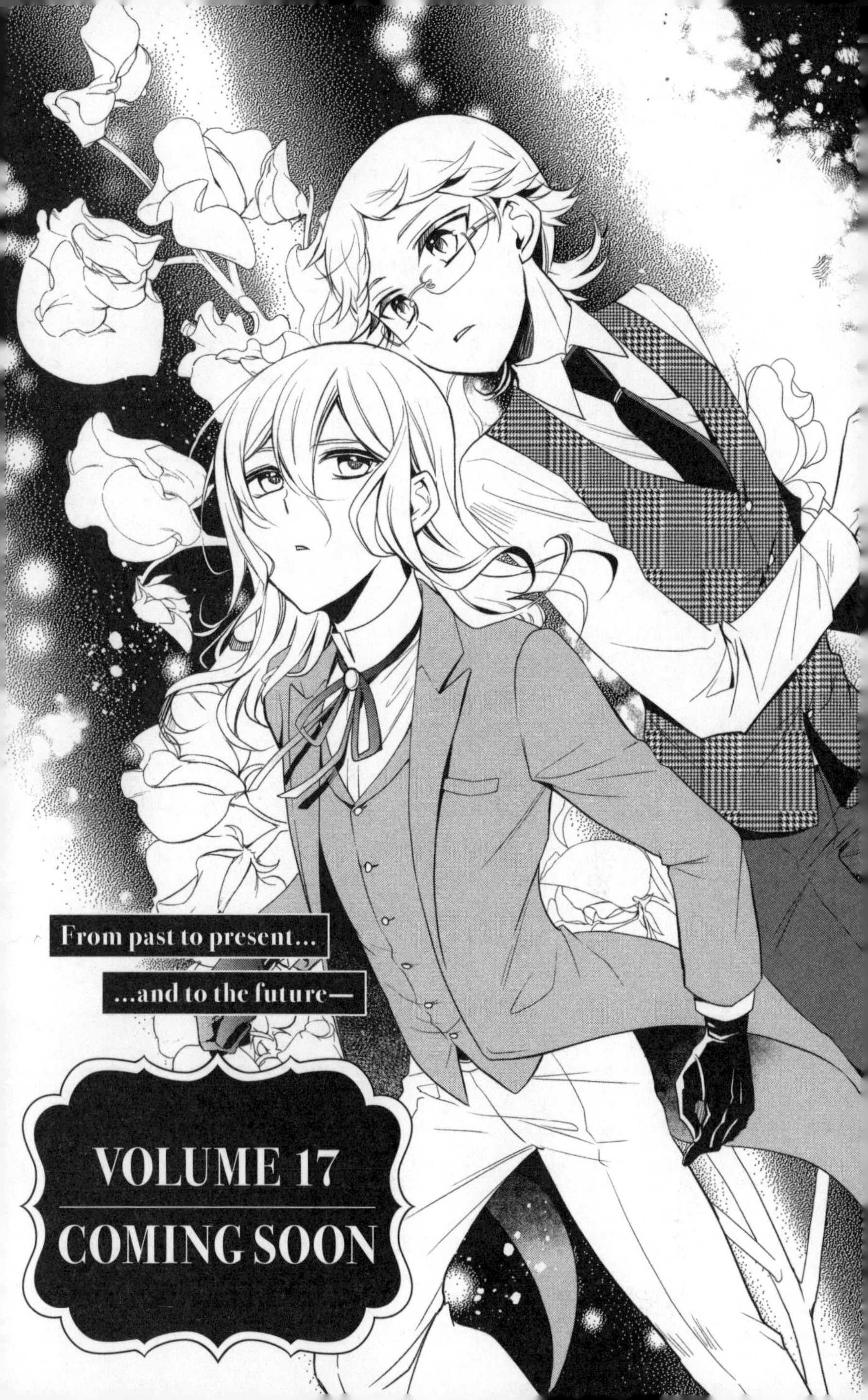
From past to present...
...and to the future—
VOLUME 17
COMING SOON

The Royal Tutor ⓰

Higasa Akai

Translation: Amanda Haley • Lettering: Abigail Blackman

THE ROYAL TUTOR Vol. 16 © 2021 Higasa Akai / SQUARE ENIX CO., LTD. First published in Japan in 2021 by SQUARE ENIX CO., LTD. English translation rights arranged with SQUARE ENIX CO., LTD. and Yen Press, LLC through Tuttle-Mori Agency, Inc., Tokyo.

English translation © 2022 by SQUARE ENIX CO., LTD.

Yen Press
150 West 30th Street, 19th Floor
New York, NY 10001

Visit us at yenpress.com
facebook.com/yenpress
twitter.com/yenpress
yenpress.tumblr.com
instagram.com/yenpress

First Yen Press Print Edition: April 2022
The chapters in this volume were originally published as ebooks by Yen Press.

Yen Press is an imprint of Yen Press, LLC.
The Yen Press name and logo are trademarks of Yen Press, LLC.

The publisher is not responsible for websites (or their content) that are not owned by the publisher.

Library of Congress Control Number: 2017938422

ISBNs: 978-1-9753-4078-0 (paperback)
       978-1-9753-4079-7 (ebook)

10 9 8 7 6 5 4 3 2 1

WOR

Printed in the United States of America